LIBERTY
for
WOMEN

The INDEPENDENT INSTITUTE

THE INDEPENDENT INSTITUTE is a non-profit, non-partisan, scholarly research and educational organization that sponsors comprehensive studies of the political economy of critical social and economic issues.

The politicization of decision-making in society has too often confined public debate to the narrow reconsideration of existing policies. Given the prevailing influence of partisan interests, little social innovation has occurred. In order to understand both the nature of and possible solutions to major public issues, The Independent Institute's program adheres to the highest standards of independent inquiry and is pursued regardless of prevailing political or social biases and conventions. The resulting studies are widely distributed as books and other publications, and are publicly debated through numerous conference and media programs.

In pursuing this uncommon independence, depth, and clarity, The Independent Institute seeks to push at the frontiers of our knowledge, redefine the debate over public issues, and foster new and effective directions for government reform.

THE INDEPENDENT INSTITUTE
100 Swan Way, Oakland, California 94621-1428, U.S.A.
Telephone: 510-632-1366 • Facsimile: 510-568-6040
E-mail: info@independent.org • Website: http://www.independent.org

LIBERTY

for

WOMEN

Freedom and Feminism in the Twenty-first Century

Edited with an Introduction by

Wendy McElroy

IVAN R. DEE

Chicago 2002

Published in Association with The Independent Institute

To Queen Silver, a progressive feminist who taught me that concern
for justice did not belong to any one movement.

LIBERTY FOR WOMEN. Copyright © 2002 by The Independent Institute. All rights reserved, including the right to reproduce this book or portions thereof in any form. For information, address: Ivan R. Dee, Publisher, 1332 North Halsted Street, Chicago, 60622. Manufactured in the United States of America and printed on acid-free paper.

Published in Association with The Independent Institute

Library of Congress Cataloging-in-Publication Data:
Liberty for women : freedom and feminism in the twenty-first century / edited with an introduction by Wendy McElroy.
    p. cm.
Includes bibliographical references and index.
ISBN 1-56663-434-2 (paper : alk. paper) — ISBN 1-56663-435-0 (cloth : alk. paper)
1. Feminism.   2. Women—Social conditions.   I. McElroy, Wendy.

HQ1154 .L5354 2002
305.42—dc21   2001052989

CONTENTS

FOREWORD

If no one article of faith unites all feminists, most do profess allegiance to freedom of choice. Still this consensus is mostly semantic, cloaking divergent opinions about what constitutes choice. Are women free to choose their professions if employment discrimination is not prohibited? Are they free to choose prostitution or surrogate motherhood if society values women primarily for their sexual and reproductive abilities? Are they free to choose their words if they feel "silenced" by pornography?

Libertarian feminists answer "yes" to all or most questions like these. So long as the state imposes no special restrictions on women's basic civil rights and liberties—such as their rights to vote, speak, pray, bear or not bear children, work, or possess property—women must be considered free to choose. They are, after all, capable of self-determination, as nineteenth-century women's rights advocates insisted in the 1848 Declaration of Rights. To suggest that they are constrained from exercising their freedoms, by external or internal pressures, is to deny women their own human agency.

While libertarians focus on legal restrictions, liberals (those fractious, left-of-center feminists) are apt to focus additionally on restrictive social and cultural norms, which an individual woman is deemed helpless to combat. They argue that, like it or not, women constitute a class (however bisected by race, ethnicity, or wealth) because historically they have been treated as a class, by both law and culture. Some believe that women are also bound together biologically, by cognitive and personality traits, manifested in a presumptively feminine "moral voice." But biological essentialism, which also flourishes on the right among social conservatives, is not as powerful a force in contemporary feminism as cultural and political essentialism—the notion that women continue to share subordinate status today because of their shared history.

If the left-of-center feminists (sometimes called gender feminists) are correct in their view that cultural biases against women are stronger than the formal rights extended equally to both sexes, then justice for women depends on collective, not individual action, and on a regulated market-place: Since social engineering was responsible for subordinating women, perhaps only social engineering can free them. In this view, the fight to provide women with professional choices, for example, requires laws pro-hibiting discrimination by private employers, as well as formal guarantees of women's right to work. The ablest, strongest women will find their right to work merely symbolic if sexism prevails and employers refuse to hire them.

Libertarians respond by questioning the presumption that sexism would prevail in the absence of regulation, so long as women were bur-dened by no special legal disabilities. They contend that in a free market the profit motive would encourage employers to hire qualified women; and, they add, those employers inclined to continue discriminating on the basis of sex, even against their own economic interests, should be free to do so. This is, then, both an empirical and a moral argument: While we ought to prohibit the state from favoring any one group of citizens over an-other, it is wrong to deprive private individuals of the right to act on their own biases in private transactions, no matter how distasteful we may find them. In the long run, libertarians argue, a free market will benefit women and men alike.

Since the professional advancement of women has coincided with the passage and enforcement of laws prohibiting discrimination in education and employment and requiring affirmative action favoring women (as well as minority males), the libertarian claim is difficult to confirm empirically. But if there is relatively little evidence of the good that might have come to women from the absence of regulation, there is strong historical evidence of the harm that regulation can cause. The criminalization of commercial sex does not eliminate prostitution but does make it more dangerous for women. The "protective" regulation of female employment, which pre-vailed in the late nineteenth and early twentieth centuries, limited women's hours of work and choice of occupations and helped to maintain a sex-segregated labor market that shunted women into a pink-collar ghetto.

Laws prohibiting sex discrimination are not easily compared to laws "protecting" women from the rigors of the workplace: anti-discrimination laws apply to both sexes equally, while protective laws applied only to women. But some laws that are nominally gender neutral—such as prohi-bitions on sexual harassment or prostitution—were enacted and have most often been invoked in order to protect women from the sexual advances of men in the workplace and sexual exploitation in general. The criminalization of prostitution is also viewed by some critics as an effort to control—and domesticate—female sexuality. There is little public support for legalizing prostitution (which is widely condemned as a vice), but sexual harassment laws have been quite controversial. They are apt to restrict speech as well as behavior and raise hard questions about the public regulation of interpersonal relations.

Libertarian and liberal feminists differ vehemently in their notions of private and public behavior. Put very simply, libertarians want to expand or, at least, not contract the private sphere, keeping it immune from government regulation. Liberals want to expand the public sphere, transforming what were once considered private transactions—such as relations between co-workers, or employer's decisions about hiring and firing—into public matters that ought to be governed by law. The divide over privacy reflects the divide over the libertarian belief in individual action and the liberal penchant for collectivity.

Notions of privacy are continually changing: marital rape was once deemed private (accounting for some feminist hostility toward privacy), and race discrimination in places of public accommodation was a private prerogative, Many libertarians continue to oppose laws prohibiting discrimination by private businesses, including restaurants and hotels. It is the tension between liberal and libertarian notions of privacy that helps define the boundaries between the personal and political.

Late twentieth-century feminism often seemed bent on erasing those boundaries, to the dismay of virtually all libertarians and some liberals. While feminism has never been a monolithic movement, it was dominated in the last two decades by a left-wing critique of American society, mistrust of individual liberty, and the belief that regulation of sexist behavior and language was essential to achieving equality. The crusade against pornography, which aligned some feminists with anti-feminists on the right, exemplified the mistrust of liberty that has marked and marred the contemporary women's movement.

The prevailing feminist analysis of American society as systematically unfair to women inevitably leads some to regard liberty as a male prerogative, even a tool of male oppression. Some feminists regard economic and sexual freedom, as well as freedom of speech, simply as vehicles for men to exploit women. In the nineteenth century, for example, leading women's rights activists opposed the use of contraception in the belief that it facilitated marital rape. Today some feminists oppose the use of new reproductive technologies for fear of turning women into breeders. The rights afforded criminal suspects are also likely to be attacked by feminists whenever men are accused of victimizing women. While the feminist movement has always included women who cared deeply about the rights and freedoms of both sexes, it has also fostered campaigns to liberate women by restraining men.

The divisions between libertarian and liberal feminists are not neat or especially consistent (the ideological divides are more readily summarized). Some women champion free markets but not free speech. Some (like myself) favor free speech but not free markets. Some, from both camps, want to decriminalize prostitution, while others believe in prohibiting it. Differences like these—the complexities of women's liberation—invigorate this important book. Few feminists will agree with every essay in this book; the contributors probably disagree fairly often with each other. But they share a love of liberty that the feminist movement should have the courage to embrace.

WENDY KAMINER

ACKNOWLEDGMENTS

AN ANTHOLOGY IS A COOPERATIVE VENTURE BETWEEN PEOPLE, MANY OF WHOM are not adequately acknowledged in the list of contributors—to whom, of course, primary thanks are due.

First and foremost, I wish to thank Alexander Tabarrok, research director at The Independent Institute, whose input on some essays rose to the level of co-editorship. Parts of the book are entirely to his credit. For example, Faith Gibson's fine essay entitled "The Official Plan to Eliminate the Midwife 1899–1999" was included and adapted to our needs through his efforts alone. I wish to also thank David Theroux, president of The Independent Institute, with whom I worked two decades ago on an earlier anthology, *Freedom, Feminism, and the State*. The present work grew from the seeds of discussion between David and myself about revising that volume, which focused on individualist feminism in the nineteenth century. The project took on a new life and became a celebration of the twenty-first century.

Joan Kennedy Taylor is underrepresented in this book. The founder of the Association for Libertarian Feminists (www.alf.org), her writings on individualist feminism have been key in keeping the tradition alive. The pioneering work of Sharon Presley should be noted. Were this book to be assembled today, rather than yesterday, I would have eagerly sought an essay on human cloning from Linda Rader, who is fast becoming an authority on the subject.

As a collective, though no less sincere thank you, I must acknowledge the input of those who frequent my feminist website www.ifeminists.com for their feedback and suggestions on the topics that should be covered and the best contributors to approach. Those who post on the Bulletin Board and subscribe to the e-newsletter helped me brainstorm my way out of more than one problem.

My delight at being published by Ivan R. Dee only increased as I worked with my editor, Hilary Schaefer. She was prompt, helpful, and—in a few cases—downright brilliant in her suggestions. Ivan R. Dee is simply the most efficient and author-friendly publisher with whom I have worked.

Finally and always, the last word goes to my husband Bradford Rodriguez whose patience in proofreading and just living with an author can never be over-praised. Thank you, love.

LIBERTY
for
WOMEN

FOUNDATIONS

Wendy McElroy

❧

Introduction

INDIVIDUALIST FEMINISM, OR IFEMINISM, IS BASED UPON THE BELIEF THAT ALL human beings have a right to the protection of their persons and property. It consistently applies the principle of "a woman's body, a woman's right" to every issue that confronts women today from reproductive choice to pornography, from economic opportunity to prostitution. In doing so, ifeminism recognizes the rights of men, who share the same political concerns as women based on our common humanity. The primary political characteristic of both women and men is that each of us is an individual with a right to make any peaceful choice whatsoever with her or his own body.

In an ideal society, the legal system would make no distinction based upon secondary characteristics such as sex or race but would protect the rights of each individual equally. Women would neither be oppressed by nor receive any privileges under the law. The police and court systems would treat violence against women as seriously as violence against men. The law would not extend economic privileges to women such as those embodied in affirmative action. This society does not currently exist. As long as the law distinguishes between the sexes, as long as it does not treat human beings as individuals, women need to stand up and demand their full and equal rights. No more, no less.

Historical Background

Ifeminism is currently a subcategory within the broader American feminist movement. This was not always the case. In the 1830s, the abolitionists, a radical anti-slavery movement, declared that each human being was a self-owner. That is, every individual had a moral jurisdiction over his own person that no one could rightfully violate. Abolitionism provided the context from which American feminism originally emerged, both ideologically and in a practical sense.[1] William Lloyd Garrison (1805–1879), around whom abolitionism coalesced, insisted that anti-slavery was a battle for human rights, not male rights. Accordingly it became the first radical movement in which women were encouraged to play prominent roles and trained to speak in public to mixed audiences of both men and women. Angelina Emily Grimké (1805–1879), Sarah Moore Grimké (1792–1873), and Abigail Kelly (1810–1887) became the first women to tour and address the general public. The Quaker background shared by many of the abolitionist women undoubtedly contributed to their success as Quakerism had long promoted female ministries at Friends' meetings.[2]

Not all anti-slavery advocates embraced women's rights and abolitionist women soon felt the brunt of male dismissal. Even the anti-slavery leader Samuel J. May, who had insisted that women be admitted into the American Anti-Slavery Society on the same basis as men, was appalled by the women's public lecturing. Abolitionist women began to ask themselves, "Do not we—as women—own ourselves as well? Or do we fight only for the rights of male slaves?" From such questions, the individualist feminist movement was born.

Before abolitionism women had fought for their own conscience against authority but they had done so as individuals rather than as members of an organized movement. Anne Marbury Hutchinson (1591–1643), for example, led the first organized attack on the Puritan orthodoxy of the Massachusetts Bay Colony, evoking the sexual equality practiced by some European Protestant sects.[3] The extensive correspondence of Abigail Adams (1744–1818), wife of President John Adams, is replete with praise for the competence of her sex and with condemnations of slavery on the grounds that all human beings have equal rights.[4] Mercy Otis Warren (1728–1814), the most prolific woman writer of the American Revolution, viewed history and politics as a struggle between liberty and power.[5] These women and many others enriched the foundation from which individualist feminism eventually sprang in the 1830s.

One of the first ifeminist arrows was Sarah Grimké's essay "Letters on the Equality of the Sexes and the Condition of Woman, Addressed to Mary Parker, President of the Boston Female Anti-Slavery Society" which drew a parallel between the legal status of slaves and of women. In the same year, Angelina Grimké published a series of letters in Garrison's periodical the *Liberator*, which later were printed as a pamphlet entitled "Letters to Catherine Beecher in Reply to an Essay on Slavery and Abolitionism." Two of these letters defended the rights of woman both as a citizen and as a human being.[6] The Grimkés demanded not merely equality under the law but equality under just law that protected self-ownership.

The 1840 World Anti-Slavery Conference held in London, England, constituted a turning point in the attitude of abolitionist women toward their fellow radicals. The Americans had appointed several women as delegates. When the hosting British abolitionists protested, the women's commissions were revoked. Several women, including Elizabeth Cady Stanton (1815–1902), journeyed to the London meeting where they were refused a seat in the convention. Instead they sat apart from the proceedings in a curtained-off area along with Garrison who joined them in protest. The "woman's" gallery soon became a focus of the convention as Lady Byron and other notables trooped up to join the exiles.[7]

Upon their return to the United States, the abolitionist Quaker Lucretia Mott and Stanton began to plan the 1848 Seneca Falls Convention specifically to discuss the promotion of women's rights.

In 1840 another event impacted ifeminist history. Margaret Fuller (1810–1850) began to edit and publish in the *Dial*, a transcendentalist periodical. Transcendentalism—a tradition that grew up around the philosopher Ralph Waldo Emerson—proved to be another important vehicle for individualistic women. The philosophy was rooted in a moral belief in the perfectibility of human beings and a political commitment to natural law and equal rights.[8] Although women such as Elizabeth Palmer Peabody (1804–1894) flourished in this atmosphere, they did not generally join a feminist movement.[9]

Between 1861 and 1865, the Civil War absorbed the energy of abolitionist feminists who deliberately put aside the fight for women's rights in order to further a war they viewed as a battle against slavery. After the war the key issue for feminism became the Constitution; specifically, women wished to be included in the wording of the Fourteenth and Fifteenth Amendments which aimed at securing freedom for blacks. Unfortunately the Fourteenth Amendment introduced the word "male" into the United States Constitution. The Fifteenth Amendment assured that the right to vote could not be abridged because of "race, color, or previous condition of servitude." It made no reference to sex. The abolitionist women felt betrayed by their male counterparts at whose behest they had subordinated their own political interests in favor of blacks.

"Do you believe the African race is composed entirely of males?" Stanton asked her former associates.[10] Susan B. Anthony pleaded, "We [women] have stood with the black man in the Constitution over half a century. . . . Enfranchise him, and we are left outside with lunatics, idiots and criminals."[11]

At this juncture the feminist movement diversified, with the mainstream focusing its efforts almost entirely into a drive for woman's suffrage. Other feminists were suspicious of political solutions to social problems. This was especially true of abolitionist women who had been influenced by Quakerism and the anarchistic philosophy of Garrison. At the 1848 Seneca Falls Convention, where a woman's suffrage resolution had been introduced, it had not been clear whether political or anti-political sentiments would win the day. The suffrage resolution met stiff resistance from Lucretia Mott and passed by a narrow margin, becoming the only resolution not to receive a unanimous vote.[12] By the time the Fourteenth and Fifteenth Amendments were passed, however, woman's suffrage had become the dominant goal of the movement.

Preferring grassroots activism, ifeminists found expression within a variety of reform movements where they often constituted the most radical faction.[13] Their voices found expression through radical periodicals, especially those that espoused free love, free thought, and individualist anarchism. Proponents of free love declared all sexual matters to be the province of the adult individuals involved, not of government. Free lovers advocated marriage reforms that ensured women's equality and free access to birth control information. Advocates of free thought insisted on the separation of church and state, leaving all spiritual matters to the conscience of individuals.[14] Individualist anarchists argued for a voluntary society, which was commonly referred to as "society by contract."[15]

Of these three movements, free love was the most important vehicle of individualist feminism. In his book *The Sex Radicals*, the historian Hal D. Sears observed, "The doctrine of free love was bound to develop as an ethical counterpart of laissez-faire economics; both are anarchism; both were stimulated by the spacious freedom of the new world."[16]

The foremost free love periodical of the nineteenth century was *Lucifer the Light Bearer* which was published and edited by Moses Harman (1830–1910), who was persecuted for decades under the Comstock obscenity laws.[17] Briefly describing one incident from the history of the "Lucifer circle" serves to dramatize the struggle for sexual freedom conducted by the late-nineteenth-century ifeminists.[18]

Harman had a policy of publishing frank letters without editing language. In June 1886 *Lucifer* printed "The Markland Letter" which described an especially brutal instance of forced sex within marriage and called it rape—perhaps the first such discussion in American newsprint. In sending that issue of *Lucifer* through the mails, Harman ran afoul of the 1873 Comstock Act that provided a penalty of up to ten years' imprisonment for anyone who intentionally mailed or received obscene material.

Ominously, the word "obscene" had not been defined by the act but Anthony Comstock, the moving force behind censorship in late-nineteenth-century America, defined obscenity in such a manner as to include the discussion of rape within marriage.

In February 1887 a warrant was served for the arrest of the editors and publishers, who traveled to Topeka where they were released upon the execution of bonds to appear in court in April.[19] After attending the April court, the two remaining defendants executed another bond to reappear the following July. At the July term, they were told the weather was "too hot." Another bond was executed to appear at the October term. Over the next eight years, Harman—the sole remaining defendant—was forced to travel back and forth to Topeka at the whim of the court. Dozens of bonds were required even though one bond alone would have satisfied the law.

Finally, in October, the grand jury indicted the *Lucifer* staff on 270 counts of obscenity, which were eventually quashed because neither the judge nor the district attorney could discern a legally intelligible charge among the counts. Not to be thwarted, the district attorney procured a new set of indictments, totaling 216 counts. The *Lucifer* articles upon which the indictment was based were originally four in number but then reduced to two: the Markland letter and a letter written by Mrs. Celia B. Whitehead, a well-respected mainstream reformer, which argued against the use of birth control devices. The discussion of birth control *per se* was deemed obscene despite the author's perspective.

Harman remained defiant. The June 22, 1888 issue of *Lucifer* reprinted the Markland letter alongside a parallel column reprinting the thirty-eighth chapter of Genesis. Harman's purpose was to demonstrate that the language of the Markland letter was no more offensive than that of the Bible. As a result of widespread protest over the elderly editor's persecution, the district attorney continued the case until 1890, at which point he was no longer in office.

In February 1890 Harman was arrested on fresh charges arising from "the O'Neill letter" written by a New York physician. Dr. O'Neill spoke of witnessing many cases of the derangement or early death of women caused by "rape within marriage." Harman was escorted to Topeka once more and released on bail of one thousand dollars and a bond to appear. He was finally sentenced to five years' imprisonment for the Markland letter but released due to a technical error in the proceedings. Then, in January of 1891, Harman was sentenced to one year imprisonment for the O'Neill letter. In March another writ of error ensued. The legal harassment continued for years until, in June of 1895, new sentencing placed a seventy-five-year-old Harman in the Kansas state prison at Lansing.[20]

The foregoing is merely one of many incidents through which nineteenth-century ifeminists fought to discuss and distribute information on issues such as birth control, sexual hygiene, and rape within marriage.

At the turn of the century, the repression of sexuality within American society remained pervasive. With the assassination of McKinley, political radicalism in almost all forms was suppressed as well, thereby silencing many ifeminists. World War I—with the expanded governmental powers and the political intolerance that it ushered in—dealt a further blow to individualist movements in general.

When ifeminism reemerged, the voices were isolated and altered. A major change in the voice of ifeminism was that twentieth-century advocates generally embraced a different view of economics than their nineteenth-century counterparts. Nineteenth-century individualists generally accepted a labor theory of value. Although they championed the free market as an extension of the right to contract, they opposed capitalism as a distortion of the marketplace. By contrast, twentieth-century individualist feminism abandoned the labor theory of value and tended to incorporate a defense of laissez-faire capitalism.

Because this evolution of economic theory can be viewed as a dividing line between the centuries rather than as a bridge, it is important to appreciate how the two positions arrive at the same political conclusion. As a paradigm of the nineteenth-century individualist feminist position on economics, consider Gertrude B. Kelly. Kelly viewed capitalism as the major cause of poverty and social injustice. This conviction sprang from two other beliefs. First, she accepted a version of the labor theory of value. Second, she believed that capitalism was an alliance between business and government, in which the latter guaranteed legal privileges to the rich. In essence Kelly considered all forms of capitalism to be what contemporary individualism calls "state capitalism." Accordingly she believed that interest, profit, and rent were usuries through which capitalists exploited laborers by usurping the product of their labor.

Although it sounds ironic to modern ears, Kelly—along with other early individualist theorists—considered the free market to be a cure for capitalism. She considered voluntary cooperation, unregulated by anything but the laws of economics and the desires of individuals, to be the solution to this social injustice. For example, in her article "The Unconscious Evolution of Mutual Banking," Kelly suggested a remedy for the state monopoly of money that caused the usury of "interest": her remedy was the establishment of private banks and currencies. She exuded, "the free monetary system with its destruction of interest and profit, looms up before us!

The exchange of product against product is inaugurated! The social revolution accomplishes itself!" [21]

In other words, to sever the alliance between government and business that constituted capitalism, it was necessary to deny government any power over the economic arrangements of individuals, for "all the laws have no other object than to perpetrate injustice, to support at any price the monopolists in their plunder."[22] In her opinion, a free market in which individual contracts—and not government—set prices would eliminate practices such as charging interest.

But what if she were proven wrong? What if interest and other forms of usury continued to exist within the framework of a free market? The answer was clear. Individuals had the absolute right to enter into agreements that were foolish and self-destructive. Any interference into such voluntary contracts constituted the use of force which was the primary evil of which the state was merely a subset. Kelly advocated a society by contract, an economic system free of forceful intervention. Later ifeminists such as Suzanne La Follette would have agreed wholeheartedly.

In 1926 Suzanne La Follette's *Concerning Women* appeared and became the first book-length treatment of individualist feminism. La Follette transmitted individualist feminism into a new century. Her defense of the free market, of laissez-faire capitalism, led her to vigorously oppose state intrusion into women's lives, such as protective labor and minimum wage laws. She championed the liberating force of technology. "It is to the industrial revolution more than anything else, perhaps," La Follette declared, "that women owe such freedom as they now enjoy." Her analysis of the impact on women was far from one-dimensional, however. "[Y]et if proof were wanting of the distance they [women] have still to cover in order to attain, not freedom, but mere equality with men, their position in the industrial world would amply supply it."[23] As a journalist, La Follette worked with her mentor the libertarian Albert Jay Nock on both the *Nation* and the *Freeman*.

Give Me Liberty by Rose Wilder Lane (1886–1968)—one of the most influential women of her day—did not specifically address feminism but Lane emerged from the pages of her books as a strong woman who argued for individualism. She wrote:

> I hold the truth to be self-evident, that all men are endowed by
> the Creator with inalienable liberty, with individual self-control
> and responsibility for thoughts, speech and acts, in every situa-
> tion. The extent to which this natural liberty can be exercised

depends upon the amount of external coercion imposed upon
the individual. No jailer can compel any prisoner to speak or act
against that prisoner's will, but chains can prevent his acting,
and a gag can prevent his speaking.[24]

The booklet charted Lane's progress from socialism to libertarianism as a
result of directly experiencing life under socialist regimes. Published during the Great Depression by the *Saturday Evening Post*, it warned against
the state socialism inherent in Roosevelt's New Deal. A consistent critic of
Roosevelt, Lane withdrew to her farm in Connecticut where she refused to
participate in social security or to earn enough to pay taxes.[25]

Another important voice for emerging ifeminism came from the successful novelist Isabel Paterson with her defense of capitalism in her nonfiction work *The God of the Machine*.

Aside from the individuals who served as vehicles to continue the tradition, two movements also carried on the threads of individualist feminism. The movement known as the School of Living stood for
decentralization, self-sufficiency, and for replacing governmental action
with individual initiative. It drew on the ideas of nineteenth-century individualists Henry George, Josiah Warren, Ezra Heywood, and William B.
Greene. Mildred J. Loomis's *Decentralism; Where It Came From; Where Is
It Going?* has been republished under the title *Alternative Americas*; it sets
out the basics of this tradition.

The second movement was Christian pacifism as expressed through
the periodical the *Catholic Worker*—perhaps the most widely circulated of
all libertarian newspapers. Even the FBI was hard pressed to classify the
Catholic Worker's brand of subversion: it opposed communism and capitalism, while supporting private property and decentralization. Followers
often called themselves anarchists, yet respected the authority of church.
Radical Christian pacifism places the duty to conscience above any possible duty to the state. In her autobiography *The Long Loneliness*, Dorothy
Day (1897–1980)—the founder of the *Catholic Worker*—gives a sense of
the philosophy and history behind this movement.[26]

In the 1950s and 1960s Ayn Rand exploded onto the intellectual scene
with her philosophy of objectivism, which she expressed through both fiction and nonfiction works. Her first published book, a novelette, sets the
tone for the rest of her career. *Anthem* is the futuristic story of a man who
rediscovers individualism in a society of absolute collectivism. Her two
subsequent novels *We the Living* and *The Fountainhead* continue this
theme of rational egoism confronted by collectivization. Rand's most fa-

mous novel *Atlas Shrugged* chronicles the breakdown of society as rational egoists resist collectivization by going "on strike."

The themes dramatized in Rand's fiction became explicit ideas in her nonfiction works. The titles of two other nonfiction works are self-explanatory. *Capitalism: The Unknown Ideal* and *The Virtue of Selfishness: A New Concept of Egoism.*[27]

Rand built an interdisciplinary system that carried the defense of individualism and capitalism to sophisticated heights. Although Rand herself shunned the term "feminism" because she associated it with the theory, policies, and attitude of liberal feminism, her work has ushered in a revival in ifeminism. One indication of the vigor with which Rand has infused ifeminism is the recent and pathbreaking anthology co-edited by Mimi Gladstein and Chris Sciabarra entitled *Feminist Interpretations of Ayn Rand.*[28] Gladstein's paper in this volume continues her iconoclastic analysis by celebrating the choice of housewife as a preparation for academia.

Natural Law

Every tradition has internal disputes on ideology but, as a general statement, individualist feminism is based on natural law theory. Natural law is an attempt to delineate the duties that are universal to every human being. As a logical corollary, it also outlines the rights possessed by everyone—that is, those things that every human being can rightfully demand of others. Rights and duties are mirror images. For example, the right of a woman to her own body implies the duty of all others not to aggress against her.

The word "law" in natural law is not a synonym for legislation. Rather "law" refers to a principle or governing rule, much as one might speak of the law of gravity. The meaning of the word "natural" is more complicated and has occasioned great debate. The interpretation that ifeminism tends to favor argues that human values should be grounded in or based upon fact. This approach is an attempt to answer the question, "given what we know about reality and human nature, is it possible to reason out universal principles of behavior that maximize human well-being?" Thus, the concepts of right and wrong—or rights and duties—are discovered by reasoning from facts.

The philosopher Henry Veatch argues:

> If the goal is human well-being, then which behaviour is naturally right or wrong is evaluated on the basis of whether it contributes or detracts from the prospect of achieving it. Therefore, a natural right involves behaviours that one "ought" or "should"

adopt in order to achieve well-being. This is the sense in which "values" or ethics accompany the doctrine of natural law. This is where "ought" enters the equation.

But, in order to make any useful statement on human nature, such "oughts" must be universalizable. That is, they must apply to all human beings.[29]

Every ought has a corresponding duty. If a woman says she ought to be able to choose, then she must extend the same "ought" to every other human being. Otherwise she is claiming a privilege rather than a right. As a broad and simplistic statement, this is the form of individualism that underlies ifeminism: all human beings have an equal claim to natural rights.

If every human being has an equal claim to self-ownership, why separate out one class of people and deal with their rights separately? Why speak of women's rights rather than individual rights?

The need for ifeminism arises when women receive different treatment under the law because they are women. It arises when women are either oppressed or privileged based upon their sex. It is analogous to the black rights movement that emerged, not because blacks have different rights than whites, but because they have the same rights and these rights had been denied.

In nineteenth-century America, for example, most married women did not have a legal claim to their own wages. Instead the money belonged to their husbands. Because the law artificially created married women as a separate category of "wage-earner," it became necessary for women to address the inequity. They insisted that their individual rights receive equal treatment with men—that the law make no reference at all to sex.

Ifeminism in the Current Ideological Context

Ideologically speaking, individualist and radical or gender feminism are mirror images of each other.

Radical feminism is the ideology that views men and women as separate and politically antagonistic classes. Men oppress women. They do so through the twin evils of the patriarchal state and the free-market system. The goal of radical feminism is not equality with men: it is gender justice (equity) for women as a class. Radical feminism states: all pornography and prostitution is an act of violence against women; the free market inherently oppresses women; and technology is a tool of white-male culture.

Ifeminism claims the opposite ground and considers men and women to be human beings whose commonality far outweighs any secondary characteristics that might divide them. Men and women share the same political interests. Ifeminism states: in the absence of coercion, pornography and prostitution are merely choices; the free market liberates women; and technology can be used for good or evil but tends toward the good because it empowers the individual.

Radical feminists have not been a numerical majority within the late-twentieth-century movement, but their ideology has been the dominant political influence. It has defined issues such as sexual harassment that have, in turn, defined our society. Radical feminists such as Joan Acker take issue with the free market and see free-market economics as an ideology which supports women's oppression. Acker challenges "the theory that wages are set by the unseen hand of the market, or by genderless returns to human capital. These theories are major ideological justifications for the contemporary class structure [of men versus women]."[30]

Radical feminist ideology did not begin as the dominant voice within second-wave feminism, which arose during the 1960s. Two decades before, World War II had drawn a generation of women out of the home and into the workforce, where many of them experienced emotional and financial independence for the first time. In 1946 Congress voted for the first time on the Equal Rights Amendment (ERA): it was defeated. In 1950 and in 1953 Congress voted down the ERA again.

With the economic boom of the fifties, many women seemed to gradually accept the contented affluence of becoming a homemaker and raising children. This *Feminine Mystique*—as Betty Friedan would label it in her pivotal book of the same name—was shattered by social change. A sexual revolution was occasioned by many factors, including the availability of new birth control methods such as the Pill. The Vietnam War made an entire generation question the values of their parents' world and to resist the authority of government. For many, drugs seemed to open doors of consciousness that led them into alternate lifestyles.

Women rode the social chaos of the sixties into an invigorating freedom. By 1965 women activists at a key conference of Students for a Democratic Society raised the idea of women's rights as a separate social issue in an open meeting. They were appalled by the derision they encountered from the male attendees—men beside whom they protested the Vietnam War. In a backlash of anger, the seed of second-wave feminism was sown. In 1966 the National Organization for Women (NOW) was founded. Across the country, "speak-outs" on rape were held and women marched for the right to choose. Yet their demands were not revolutionary: they did not call for the elimination of the existing system. They cried out for reform, for more respect from men, and for more equality within the system.

At the same time, Simone de Beauvoir's work, *The Second Sex* expressed a more radical form of feminism. It claimed that lesbianism was the embodiment of sexual freedom and that the existing institutions of society were to blame for the oppression of women. Radical feminism began to spin out a revolutionary theory that sought a sweeping away of white-male culture or patriarchy as a means to liberate women.

In 1973 feminism won a tremendous victory when the Supreme Court's decision on *Roe v. Wade* ensured legal access to abortion.[31] The movement now focused its attention on a fresh effort to pass the ERA. In March 1978 100,000 demonstrators marched on Washington, D.C., to express their determined support for ratification of a newly proposed ERA. After extensions and delays, in 1984 the measure was finally defeated in Congress.

The defeat of the ERA was a stunning blow to the liberal voices which had dominated the feminist movement. Radical feminists, who had never rushed to embrace the ERA, offered a new solution to a discouraged movement—a new political theory based on gender oppression and viewing men as class enemies.[32] Radical feminism slowly came to dominate the movement.

There is reason to believe that this trend has changed, however. The voices of third- and fourth-wave feminism—the new generations of women with their own contexts and concerns—are heretical. They want to judge issues such as pornography and reproductive technology for themselves, unburdened by the conclusions of their mothers and grandmothers.

Feminism can only benefit from rebellion in the ranks by women who want their own answers. This could be a working definition of healthy feminism itself. Hopefully the younger generation's dissatisfaction with contemporary feminism will not prejudice them against arguments and answers from a more distant past, from the tradition of ifeminism.

The true ideological contest within the movement is between ifeminism and radical feminism. These two schools define the extremes of what constitutes justice and equality for women. In order to appreciate the depth of this schism, let us consider in some detail merely one concept—albeit a key one—upon which the two schools disagree. Consider the concept of "class."

A class is nothing more than an arbitrary grouping of entities that share common characteristics as determined from a certain epistemological point of view. A researcher studying drug addiction, for example, may break society into classes of drug-using and non-drug-using people. Perhaps he will further establish subclasses within drug users based on the particular substance used, the frequency of use, or some other factor salient to the researcher's purposes. Classes can be defined by almost any factor salient to the definer.

Many fields of endeavor use biology as a dividing line. Medical science often separates the sexes in order to apply different medical treatment and techniques. For example, women are examined for breast cancer and men for prostate problems. But medical science does not claim that the basic interests of men and women as human beings conflict or even diverge. The sexes share a basic biology that requires the same approach of nutrition, exercise, and common sense lifestyle choices. In short although the biology of the sexes differ, they share the basic goal of good health which can be roughly defined and pursued in the same manner.

The most familiar form of political class analysis is undoubtedly the Marxist version: that is, an analysis of the relationship to the means of production. Are you a worker or are you a capitalist? For radical feminists, gender is the salient political factor that defines classes into male and female. Catharine MacKinnon explains clearly how feminist class analysis extends to all women, not merely ones who believe themselves to be oppressed. She writes, "Sexuality is to feminism what work is to Marxism. . . . As an example of post-Marxist feminism, I want to consider the often-raised question of whether 'all women' are oppressed by heterosexuality. . . . If you applied such an analysis to the issue of work . . . would you agree, as people say about heterosexuality, that a worker chooses to work?"[33] Thus all women are drawn into the class struggle with all men, who share not only a biological identity but also a political and social one. The collective political interests of men are referred to as "patriarchy." Patriarchy is the systematic and structural oppression of women in politics and culture, which is supported by capitalism. Radical feminism incorporates such Marxist/socialist ideas as "surplus labor" through which one class is said to use the free market in order to commit economic theft upon another class. An example of surplus labor in radical feminism would be housework that is unsalaried. Men (not merely capitalists) wield the free market and other institutions as a means to control women. The classification "male" becomes so significant that it predicts and determines how the individuals within that class will behave. Radical feminists can level accusations of "rapist" at nonviolent men because they are presumed to be beneficiaries of "the rape culture" established by patriarchy.

To prevent the oppression of women, it is necessary to deconstruct the institutions through which men control women—institutions such as the free market and the family. The law must act to benefit historically disadvantaged "woman" at the expense of historically oppressive "man."

This class analysis makes no sense within the theoretical framework of ifeminism that declares all human beings have the same interest in life, liberty, and the pursuit of happiness. All human beings share the same natural rights just as they share a basic biology.

Nevertheless, individualism has a long tradition of class analysis that does categorize people according to a salient political factor. That factor is: does an individual use force to achieve her goals? Does she acquire "goods" such as wealth or power through merit and productivity? Or does she use aggression, often in the form of law, to expropriate wealth and power from others? Expressed in the most basic form, ifeminism's form of class analysis asks, are you a member of the political or productive (economic) class? Do you use the political or the economic means to further your interests?

Another key difference between radical and ifeminist class analysis is that the latter does not predict the behavior of individuals. Both men and women can use political means. An individual can change her class affiliation at will, abandoning the use of force and adopting economic means instead. Classes within ifeminist analysis are fluid. This is not true of radical feminist analysis that is based on biology.

To radical feminism, biology is the factor that fixes an individual into a class. To ifeminism, the use of force is the salient factor and an individual can cross class lines at any point. The only way to prevent fluidity is to establish classes by force. That is, to use laws or other coercive means to cement class advantages into the fabric of society, thus establishing legally static classes. In other words classes become static only when legal barriers are raised to prevent social, political, or economic mobility.

The fluidity of classes in ifeminist theory implies that there is no necessary conflict between the genders. The fact that men have oppressed women in the past says nothing necessary about whether they will oppress them in the future. Whether an individual man is an oppressor or a friend of women depends on whether he uses political means and this is a matter of conscious choice.

The concept of "class" is only one of many areas of intellectual contention between radical and individualist feminism. The two traditions also define other essential concepts, such as "equality" and "justice," in different manners. However, my purpose here is simply to render a sense of how deep the ideological division runs.

Liberty for Women

Liberty for Women applies the theory of ifeminism to specific issues that confront women in the twenty-first century. It does not attempt to establish dogma, but to sketch a broad theoretical framework within which many answers are possible. For example not all ifeminists agree on such key issues as abortion: a small but significant minority are pro-life. As long as this stance is a personal belief and not one imposed upon others through law, there is no conflict with ifeminism. No personal belief or peaceful choice can conflict because the theoretical framework is that of choice itself. It is "a woman's body, a woman's right" in every decision a human being can make, with one exception. No one can rightfully decide to initiate force and, thus, deny a similar range of choice to another.

With such a broad framework, ifeminism naturally accommodates a wide range of opinion. Discussion and debate are encouraged as the intellectual wellspring that is necessary to sustain a vigorous movement. The essays that comprise "Foundations," *Liberty for Women's* preliminary section, display such a dialogue. Richard Epstein expresses a more conservative view of government than the Introduction. He believes that limited government is not a violation of individual rights. As an individualist anarchist as well as an ifeminist, I argue for voluntary cooperation as the proper basis of society.

In an article originally written for a perhaps hostile audience of British feminists, Camille Paglia offers a perspective on the last generation of feminism and the need for change. As is typical of Paglia, it is insightful, iconoclastic, and stylish.

After "Foundations," *Liberty for Women* is divided into five parts: "Women and Sex"; "Women and the Family"; "Women and Work"; "Women and Violence"; and "Women and Technology."

"Women and Sex" is the first category addressed, not only in *Liberty for Women* but usually within the feminism tradition itself. After all, the biological differences between men and women lie at the heart of why feminism arose. Moreover it is important to immediately address two of the most contentious issues of twentieth-century feminism in order to dispel a common misconception. Ifeminism is sometimes misidentified as a conservative tradition because it champions free-market solutions rather than governmental ones. But it also defends every choice between consenting adults, including pornography and prostitution. The key words in analyzing any issue are "consenting adults." Are the people who are involved in a situation capable of informed consent and have they actually said "yes." If so, the situation is consensual and a private matter. If not, it is coercive and third parties are justified in intervening.

Three essays comprise the section "Women and Sex": "On Pornography" by Nadine Strossen; "For Their Own Good" by Norma Jean Almodovar; and "Whether from Reason or Prejudice" by Martha C. Nussbaum. Ms. Strossen's essay persuasively examines the dangers of anti-pornography laws. Ms. Almodovar's essay blends cogent arguments for sex worker rights with the passionate rhetoric of one who has experienced the abuses being exposed. Ms. Nussbaum brings a philosophical and cultural sanity to the subject of taking money for bodily services.

The modern ifeminist defenses of pornography and prostitution are direct continuations of the free love tradition that coalesced around *Lucifer the Light Bearer* in the nineteenth century. Like the *Lucifer* circle, modern ifeminists consider a woman's claim to her own body and her right to behave in any peaceful manner she chooses as inviolate. Nussbaum's essay also recognizes the commonality between economic and sexual freedom which led nineteenth-century feminists to champion a laissez-faire approach to both. Both economic and sexual liberty are expressions of the fundamental ifeminist theme, "a woman's body, a woman's right," and of her right to contract freely with her own body.[34]

Collectively the essays constituting the second section reflect the same approach to family taken by the individualist feminists Lillian Harman and E. C. Walker in their nonchurch, nonstate marriage of 1887 for which the couple was arrested. Through the union and subsequent motherhood, Lillian expressed her commitment to "free marriage" and to having children thereby. Yet the ceremony also celebrated the unconditional right of a woman to her own body. When Moses Harman—Lillian's father—was called upon to "give the bride away," he responded, "I do not 'give away the bride,' as I wish her to be always the owner of her person."[35] The modern ifeminist celebration of marriage and family as a choice consistent with a woman's self-ownership continues the tradition expressed in the Harman-Walker union.

Three essays comprise the section "Women and the Family": "Chairing the Department" by Mimi Gladstein; "Fetal Protection and Freedom of Contract" by Ellen Frankel Paul; and Alexander Tabarrok on "Abortion and Liberty." Ms. Gladstein offers a delightful essay with a serious message: Housework is a superb training ground for the skills required by an academic career. Her essay may well be the first defense of housekeeping presented by a modern feminist anthology. Ms. Paul offers a much-needed free-market analysis of fetal rights and relevant evolving law. She places this legal concept into a framework of "freedom of contract." Mr. Tabarrok discusses abortion within the context of the right to choose.

Nineteenth-century ifeminists wished to break down the artificial barriers to work and education that had been established by law to the detriment of women. Earlier ifeminists raged against laws that shut women out of many professions, laws that assigned a married woman's wages to her husband—in short, against laws that crippled women in the business and financial world. They demanded equality under law that protected a woman's right to contract and they settled for nothing less. As a solution to the oppression, it became fashionable to champion labor laws that were said to protect women. Typically these laws restricted the age at which girls could begin work and the hours or conditions of labor. Nineteenth-century ifeminists opposed protective labor laws because they interfered with a woman's right to contract and placed her at a disadvantage in the labor force. The goal was not to be protected by a paternalistic state but to be granted equal status with men under laws that respected their rights. In the opening to her most famous essay, "Legal Disabilities of Women," the abolitionist Sarah Grimké declared, "There are few things which present greater obstacles to the improvement and elevation of woman . . . than the laws . . . which rob her of some of her *essential* rights."[36] Grimké went on to argue that a woman's independence requires her to have the same right to contract as a man.

Today women are no longer legally disadvantaged in the marketplace. Rather they are advantaged by such policies as affirmative action. Yet being legally privileged is no more just than being oppressed and both constitute an enforced inequality between the sexes that leads to gender conflict. Moreover as long as women's "rights" rest upon the favors of a paternalistic government, they can never be secure. Both as a matter of justice to men and respect for women's equal rights, modern ifeminists call for the repeal of all legal privileges based on sex.

Three essays comprise the section "Women and Work": "What Does Affirmative Action Affirm?" by Wendy McElroy; "Groping Toward Sanity" by Cathy Young; and "The Case Against Comparable Worth" by Ellen Frankel Paul. Ms. McElroy applies free-market principles to one of the most popular and destructive public policies of our generation: affirmative action. Ms. Young offers perspectives on sexual harassment, bringing her usual common sense to bear on an issue that has brought far more division among the sexes than justice. Ms. Paul analyzes one of the more totalitarian workplace measures suggested by contemporary feminism—comparable worth. She explains why that measure is not merely unworkable but badly flawed in its very conception.

When nineteenth-century ifeminists led a campaign to protect women against violence, society exacted a high price from them for doing so. Moses Harman, editor and publisher of *Lucifer the Light Bearer*, spent years in prison for publishing a letter that called for forced sex within marriage to be recognized as rape. Harman and the *Lucifer* circle wanted to strip away the social biases that clouded the issue of gender violence and deprived a woman—whatever her status—from exercising the right of self-protection.

Two essays comprise the section "Women and Violence": "Women and Violent Crime" by Rita J. Simon; and "Disarming Women" by Richard W. Stevens, Hugo Teufel III, and Matthew Y. Biscan. Ms. Simon corrects many of the errors and assumptions of feminist statistics on violence and women to reveal a more accurate picture. The essay by Mr. Stevens, Mr. Teufel, and Mr. Biscan cogently argues that women are better off empowering themselves through self-defense with firearms than they are relying on a government system that tragically fails millions of victims of violent crime every year.

More than a century ago, Gertrude B. Kelly embodied the twin positions that have come to define the individualist feminist attitude toward technology: as a medical doctor, she embraced its liberating possibilities; as an individualist anarchist, she rejected any state involvement in science. In a speech entitled "State Aid to Science" Kelly argued, "There is no means by which state aid can be given to science without causing the death of science." Men and women would continue to enjoy the bounty of science only as long as it was left to the innovation and energy of individuals.

Four essays comprise the section "Women and Technology": "Breeder Reactionaries" by Wendy McElroy; "I Am in Mourning" by Lois Copeland; "The Official Plan to Eliminate the Midwife 1899–1999," by Faith Gibson; and Janis Cortese on "The Third WWWave."

Ms. McElroy challenges the current feminist rejection of the new reproductive technologies. Instead she argues for the liberating nature of medical progress in this area. Ms. Copeland expresses her frustration at being unable to offer the best medical care and consultation to patients because of governmental interference. Ms. Gibson examines how male obstetricians conspired to eliminate competition from midwives through state control—despite the fact that midwives have always had better records of safety than obstetricians (a fact that continues to this day). Ms. Cortese provides a voice for third-wave feminism. She embodies the rebellious pro-technology, pro-sex new generation that will rejuvenate the existing feminist status quo.

Liberty for Women presents the fundamentals of ifeminist theory and applies it to a wide range of specific issues. It is not meant to be the final word on what constitutes individualist feminism. Ifeminism will be shaped by the continuing work of those who have contributed to this book and by many others. It is fitting that such a dynamic school of feminism is blossoming in a new century full of new possibilities.

Notes

1. Overviews of this key period for individualist feminism can be found in Lewis Perry, *Radical Abolitionism: Anarchism and the Government of God in Antislavery Thought* (Ithaca, N.Y., 1973); Blanche Glassman Hersh, *The Slavery of Sex: Feminist Abolitionists in America* (Urbana, Ill., 1978); and Wendy McElroy, *Freedom, Feminism and the State* (Oakland, 1991).

2. To say that American feminism arose from abolitionism—and was impacted by transcendentalism—is not to deny the clear impact of other traditions upon the movement. American feminism drew heavily upon British classical liberalism, including the work of British feminists such as Mary Wollstonecraft. Nevertheless American women organized around issues and historical events that were uniquely their own—for example, Puritanism, the American Revolution, and plantation slavery. A pivotal event was the Civil War. Maria Weston Chapman (1806–1885) helped to transmit British classical liberalism to America through her two volume *Harriet Martineau's Autobiography* (Boston, 1877). Chapman appended some 460 pages of tribute and reminiscence.

3. David D. Hall, ed., *The Antinomian Controversy 1636–1638: A Documentary History* (Durham, N.C., 1990), is an excellent collection of contemporaneous documents surrounding Hutchinson's trial and banishment. Selma R. Williams, *Divine Rebel: The Life of Anne Marbury Hutchinson* (New York, 1981), provides good biographical background.

4. Most of Abigail Adams's surviving correspondence is in the Adams Papers, Massachusetts Historical Society. A good selection of her letters can be found in Lester J. Cappon, ed., *The Adams–Jefferson Letters: The Complete Correspondence Between Thomas Jefferson and Abigail and John Adams* (Chapel Hill, N.C., 1959).

5. Between 1772 and 1805, Warren published five plays, three political satires, three books of poetry, a pamphlet critiquing the recently proposed Constitution and one of the most important histories of the American Revolution. Much of her literary work appeared in *Poems, Dramatic and Miscellaneous* (Boston, 1790). See *Plays and Poems of Mercy Otis Warren: Facsimile Reproductions Compiled and with an Introduction by Benjamin Franklin* (New York, 1980); *History of the Rise, Progress and Termination of the American Revolution, Interspersed with Biographical, Political, and Moral Observations* (Boston, 1805; Indianapolis, 1988). The largest body of Warren's manuscript material rests with the Massachusetts Historical Society. Mary Elizabeth Regan, *Pundit and Prophet of the Old Republic: The Life and Times of Mercy Otis Warren*, (Ph.D. dissertation, University of California, 1984), provides good biographical material.

6. The Grimkés' key works and speeches have been reprinted in *The Public Years of Sarah and Angelina Grimké: Selected Writings 1835–1839* (New York, 1989). The definitive biography is Gerda Lerner, *The Grimké Sisters from South Carolina: Rebels Against Slavery* (New York, 1971). The primary manuscript source is the Theodore Dwight Weld Collection, William L. Clements Library, the University of Michigan, Ann Arbor.

7. For details see Henry Mayer, *All on Fire: William Lloyd Garrison and the Abolition of Slavery* (New York, 1998), 290.

8. Fuller's classic feminist book *Woman in the Nineteenth Century* (New York, 1971), grew from an essay in the *Dial* and presaged the concept of "sisterhood." Fuller also worked as a literary critic for the *New York Tribune*; many of her articles were collected in *Papers on Literature and Art* (New York, 1846). See *Memoirs of Margaret Fuller Ossoli* (New York, 1972). Mason Wade, *Margaret Fuller: Whetstone of Genius* (New York, 1940) provides valuable biographical data. Bell Gale Chevigny, *The Woman and the Myth: Margaret Fuller's Life and Writing* (Old Westbury, N.Y., 1976); mixes biogra-

phy with reprints of Fuller's material. The range of her work is well represented in Mason Wade, ed., *The Writings of Margaret Fuller* (New York, 1941).

9. Peabody's *Record of a School* (New York, 1969) presented a transcendentalist view of moral education and established Bronson Alcott (the focus of her report) as an important figure in intellectual circles. In May 1849 the single issue of her periodical *Aesthetic Papers* introduced Henry David Thoreau's "Civil Disobedience." *Last Evening with Allston and Other Papers* (New York, 1975), is a collection of her work.

10. Theodore Stanton and Harriet S. Blatch (eds.), *Elizabeth Cady Stanton as Revealed in Her Letters, Diary and Reminiscences* (New York, 1922), 106.

11. Quoted in William L. O'Neill, *Everyone was Brave: A History of Feminism in America* (New York, 1971), 17.

12. The issue of whether women should vote was a matter of debate within the abolitionists themselves, with Garrison and the *Liberator* favoring suffrage for women. (Mayer, *All on Fire*, 319)

13. A notable exception was arguably the most important theorist in ifeminism, Voltairine de Cleyre (1866–1912), who worked in relative isolation. De Cleyre is best remembered for the essay "Anarchism and American Traditions," in which she argued that anarchism was the logical consequence of the principles of the American Revolution. The best source for de Cleyre's writing is Alexander Berkman, ed., *Selected Works of Voltairine de Cleyre*, with a biographical sketch by Hippolyte Havel (New York, 1972). The definitive biography is Paul Avrich, *An American Anarchist: The Life of Voltairine de Cleyre* (Princeton, N.J., 1978).

14. The best source for women in free thought is George A. MacDonald's two volume *50 Years of Freethought* (New York, 1929–1931), which centered on the periodical the *Truthseeker* (1873–present).

15. The primary individualist anarchist periodical *Liberty*, edited by Benjamin R. Tucker, was by no means a vehicle for feminism but it did provide an important forum for women's voices. Its contributors were a virtual honor list of individualist feminists, including Gertrude Kelly, Sarah E. Holmes, Bertha Marvin, Lillian Harman, Clara Dixon Davidson, Ellen Battelle Dietrick, Kate Field, Emma Schumm, Juliet Severance, Charlotte Perkins Stetson, Josephine Tilton, Helen Tufts, and Lois Waisbrooker.

16. Hal D. Sears, *The Sex Radicals* (Lawrence, Kans., 1977), 20.

17. Second in importance was *The Word*, subtitled "A Monthly Journal of Reform" (Princeton, Mass., 1872–1890, Cambridge, Mass., 1892–1893), edited by Ezra Heywood. *The Word* began as a labor paper but soon focused on free love issues such as birth control. Heywood's essay on birth control, *Cupid's Yokes: The Binding Forces of Conjugal Life: An Essay to Consider Some Moral and Physiological Phases of Love and Marriage, Wherein Is Asserted the Natural Right and Necessity of Sexual Self-Government* (Princeton, Mass., 1876), was the most controversial pamphlet in the history of ifeminism. Its distribution—estimated variously at 50,000 to 200,000—contravened the Comstock Laws, which outlawed birth control information as obscene. Heywood was imprisoned repeatedly for its publication. Many of Heywood's essays can be found in *The Collected Works of Ezra H. Heywood* (Weston, Mass., 1985). A microfilm run of *The Word* is available from the Massachusetts Historical Society and contains such gems as Angela Heywood's defense of abortion based on the idea of "a woman's body, a woman's right"—perhaps the first such defense in American feminism.

18. No less controversial than *Lucifer* or *The Word*, but less substantial in content, was the free love periodical *Woodhull and Claflin's Weekly* (1870–1876), edited by Victoria Woodhull (1838–1927) and her sister Tennessee Claflin (1845–1923). *The Victoria Woodhull Reader* (Weston, Mass., 1974), edited by Madeleine B. Stern, is the best

source for Woodhull's original work. Emanie Sach's biography *"The Terrible Siren": Victoria Woodhull (1838–1927)*, (New York, 1928) is the most valuable source of biographical material.

19. Nineteenth-century ifeminism had about as many male champions as female ones. Perhaps because individualist feminists never pinned their hopes on politics and did not feel deep betrayal over being excluded from the Constitution, they did not become embittered toward men. Another prominent male ifeminist was Stephen Pearl Andrews (1812–1886), author of the booklet *Love, Marriage and Divorce and the Sovereignty of the Individual* (Weston, Mass., 1975), an exchange of sorts between Horace Greeley and Andrews. Charles Shively, *The Thought of Stephen Pearl Andrews (1812–1886)*, (master's thesis, University of Wisconsin, 1960), deals with Andrews's views on sex, marriage, and the family.

20. During these confinements Lillian Harman (his daughter), Lillie D. White, and Lois Waisbrooker assumed editorship. Many individualist feminists, such as Celia B. Whitehead, Lillie D. White, and Lois Waisbrooker published in *Lucifer*. *Lucifer* and its staff produced many pamphlets. Moses Harman's include: *Love in Freedom* (Chicago, 1900); *Institutional Marriage* (Chicago, 1901); and *A Free Man's Creed: Discussion of Love in Freedom as Opposed to Institutional Marriage (Los Angeles, 1908)*.

21. "The Unconscious Evolution of Mutual Banking," *Liberty*, February 12, 1887, 7.

22. "The Wages of Sin is Death," *Liberty*, May 22, 1886, 5.

23. As quoted in McElroy, *Freedom, Feminism and the State*, 213.

24. As quoted in McElroy, *Freedom, Feminism and the State*, 51.

25. Lane's most famous work *The Discovery of Freedom: Man's Struggle Against Authority* (New York, 1972) is an overview of mankind's intellectual progress through history. It examines the struggle between freedom and authority. Roger Lea MacBride, ed., *The Lady and the Tycoon* (Caldwell, Ohio, 1972), provides a portion of Lane's correspondence. An interesting exchange of correspondence is captured in William Holtz, ed., *Dorothy Thompson and Rose Wilder Lane: Forty Years of Friendship 1921–1960* (Columbia, Mo., 1991). The best biographical source is *Rose Wilder Lane: Her Story* (New York, 1977). Some of Lane's papers are available at the Herbert Hoover Presidential Library in West Branch, Iowa.

26. Also valuable is Anne Klejment, *Dorothy Day and the Catholic Worker: A Bibliography and Index* (New York, 1986).

27. Nathaniel Branden and Barbara Branden, *Who is Ayn Rand?* (New York, 1964), provides a sense of Rand's circle, with its tendency to idolize her. Essays analyze the many facets of Rand and her impact. The definitive biography is Barbara Branden's *The Passion of Ayn Rand* (Garden City, N.Y., 1986).

28. It is not possible to both concisely and adequately chronicle the recent surge in ifeminism. Three items may be used as indicators of the richness of this now dynamic force. In addition to *Feminist Interpretations of Ayn Rand* (University Park, Pa., 1999), a pivotal organization, Association of Libertarian Feminists (www.alf.org), continues to have a strong presence thanks to the efforts of ifeminist Joan Kennedy Taylor. And in 1999 a new organization named ifeminists.com (www.ifeminists.com) emerged to serve as a portal for information on individualist feminism on the Internet and as a meeting place for ifeminists.

29. Henry Veatch, "Bibliographical Essay," *Literature of Liberty*, vol. 1, no. 4 (October–December, 1978), 13.

30. Joan Acker, *Doing Comparable Worth: Gender, Class, and Pay Equity* (Philadelphia, 1989), 22.

31. *Roe v. Wade*, 410 U.S. 179 (1973).

32. Perhaps the pivotal book in the development of radical feminism was Kate Millett, *Sexual Politics* (1970), which argued that women had been confined like animals by men who used them for pleasure and breeding stock. A series of works expanded radical feminist theory. In *Psychoanalysis and Feminism* (1974), Juliet Mitchell dovetailed feminism, Marxism, and psychoanalysis. Linda Gordon's anthology *Woman's Body, Woman's Right* (1976) provided a history of birth control and placed it within a socialist context. *Against Our Will* (1975) by Susan Brownmiller "gave rape its history"—a history in which all men were natural rapists. The list of books spinning out radical feminist ideology could fill pages.

33. Catharine A. MacKinnon, *Toward a Feminist Theory of the State* (Cambridge, Mass., 1987), 114.

34. A modern rephrasing of the aforementioned Sears quote—"The doctrine of free love was bound to develop as an ethical counterpart of laissez-faire economics"— might be "ifeminism is a conjoining of a woman's right to choose sexually and her being 'Free to Choose' economically."

35. Sears, *The Sex Radicals*, 85.

36. As quoted in McElroy, *Freedom, Feminism and the State*, 121.

Camille Paglia

❦

Libertarian Feminism in the Twenty-first Century

THE WOMEN'S MOVEMENT IS IN RADICALLY DIFFERENT STAGES IN DIFFERENT regions of the world. Many misunderstandings exist, even between British and American feminism, despite their mutual influence and support in the historical campaign for suffrage.

There are, in my analysis, two primary spheres of future action: first, basic civil rights and educational opportunity must be secured for Third World women; second, the education and training of Western women must be better designed to prepare them for leadership positions in business and politics. Women's studies programs, as structured in the United States, have not proved that feminist ideology helps women to understand life or to function in the real world, where men must be dealt with as friends or foes.

As a classroom teacher of nearly thirty years, I am committed to identifying and developing the factual material and practical strategies that the next generation of women will need to exercise power and, one hopes, to head nations. Military history, not feminist theory is required: without an understanding of war, few women will ever be entrusted with topmost positions in government. In the United States, for example, the president also serves as Commander-in-Chief and thus must win the confidence of the armed forces.

In the 1990s American feminism experienced cataclysmic changes. My wing of pro-sex feminism, which was ostracized and silenced through the long period ruled by anti-pornography activists such as Andrea Dworkin and Catharine MacKinnon, made a stunning resurgence. As a free speech militant, my thinking is grounded in the 1960s sexual revolution. Most of the positions for which I was pilloried when I came on the scene a decade ago, with the publication of my long-delayed first book, are now scarcely controversial at all, so sweeping has been the victory of libertarian feminism, which is in tune with a younger, sassier generation of feminists.

Popular culture, particularly rock 'n' roll, is no longer the enemy—as it was when I was at war with fellow feminists in the late 1960s for my admiration of the "sexist" Rolling Stones. Fashion and beauty are of interest again, instead of being automatically labeled as oppressive tools of patriarchy. Hormones and biological sex differences are slowly returning to the agenda, after a quarter century of rigid social constructionism.

Labyrinthian poststructuralist feminism is increasingly recognized as an ahistorical dead end. The disintegration of the Soviet Union undermined the fashionable Marxism of bourgeois intellectuals such as the propagandist Susan Faludi. Capitalism's central role in the modern emancipation of women is starting to be seen.

American campus feminists, who rode high for twenty years, have been gradually marginalized in this decade: few played much role in the public debates that have raged about sexual harassment in the workplace, a vital issue that swept away the late 1980s victim-obsessed date-rape hysteria. From the 1991 Clarence Thomas/Anita Hill hearings to the recent bitter quarrel over the president's affair with a young intern, the prominent campus feminists have been irresponsibly silent, demonstrating the inadequacies of conventional feminist theory when grappling with thorny contemporary questions.

The Clinton scandals have also exposed the political biases of women's groups such as the National Organization for Women: the obtrusive collusion of present and past presidents of NOW (plus Gloria Steinem) with the most liberal wing of the Democratic Party has seriously damaged the women's movement, which in my view should be a big tent that gathers in women of every political and religious affiliation. As a registered Democrat and a member of pro-choice groups such as Planned Parenthood, I contend that the women's movement should have no ideological litmus test about abortion or any other issue.

Most feminists abroad have little conception of the way American feminism veered toward tyranny after its early successes in the late 1960s. What looks like "anti-feminism" has really been a rebellion here by insurgents like myself who are equity feminists: that is, we believe that only equality of the sexes before the law will guarantee women's advance. We vigorously oppose all special protections of women—as in anti-pornography legislation—as inherently infantilizing. This is an old argument within feminism: Susan B. Anthony, for example, promoted the temperance movement (which demanded prohibition of the public sale of alcohol because drunken men impoverished and endangered women), thus endorsing a puritanical intrusion of the state into private life.

Though recent polls show that most American women refuse to describe themselves as feminists and often have a negative view of movement leaders, I am convinced that feminism, for all its internal dissension, is alive and well and will continue to be a major cultural force around the world in the twenty-first century.

Richard A. Epstein

❋

Liberty and Feminism

WHAT IS THE RELATIONSHIP BETWEEN THE STATUS OF WOMEN AND THE CAUSE of liberty in modern times? The question may appear to be anachronistic. After all, the major battles over the status of women in the United States were fought long ago. They were, as it is sometimes difficult to remember, battles over civil capacity (for example, during the nineteenth century the ability of married women to make contracts in their own right, to give evidence, and to serve on juries) and over political capacity (during the early twentieth century the right of women to vote in political elections and to stand for office).

At the time, the resistance to these simple and self-evident claims was so great that in retrospect it is hard to fathom the political turmoil generated by such modest reforms. The strife was at least as great as the present-day contention over civil rights and affirmative action. Of course the resolution of the major questions at issue by 1920 did not put an end to debates over the role and place of women in society. In this chapter I hope to give some sense of how the debate has progressed, and to indicate why the very arguments that rightly led to the legal reforms affecting the status of women during the nineteenth century militate against the demands for reform from the late-twentieth-century feminist movement. In stating this position, I do not mean to position myself in the vanguard of reaction. On the contrary I believe that the progressive ideals of the nineteenth century remain just as progressive today.

The issues of civil and political capacity concern the ability of individuals to enter into ordinary business and social transactions and to participate in the general political life of the nation. They are the sorts of rights that can be guaranteed to all individuals even if the state does not adhere to any single sound principle of regulation.

The basic point is that the ordinary definition of liberty gives one not only the capacity to move about freely but also the capacity to better oneself through voluntary transactions. The logic of those transactions is that of mutual gain through mutual consent. We can agree that individuals have complex visions of themselves and of what actions or states of affairs serve their self-interest. Still all can improve their lot by surrendering what they value less for what they value more. How could one defend a system that excludes any portion of the population from these advantages? In any particular case someone might be relieved by the exclusion from the economic arena of those perceived as competitors rather than trading partners. But if we consider the entrance of women into the marketplace (or of any other group previously subjected to systematic exclusion), the overall balance of convenience tilts sharply in favor of free entry. New entrants are not merely potential competitors; they are also potential co-workers, suppliers, customers, and consultants. When they assume those roles, the new entrants enhance the vitality of the social system as a whole.

Exclusions in this situation act as an internal barrier against free trade, with consequences no better (and arguably worse) than those arising from the formal exclusion of foreign goods and labor via taxes, tariffs, quantitative restrictions, quotas, and the like. The necessary consequence of the exclusion is that trade gains are blocked by the artificial barrier, leaving the sum of production possibilities reduced with no evident distributional advantages to offset that social loss. Moreover the classical prohibitions on women's contracting and women's suffrage gave rise to suspicion, distrust, and regret that could easily have been eliminated by removing the barriers to entry that frustrated the operation of competitive markets.

One reason why the nineteenth-century case for women's rights was (and is) so strong is that it dovetails neatly into any and all theories that recognize the limits as well as the uses of markets. For example the arguments for and against an anti-trust law that limits horizontal price-fixing or mergers scarcely touch upon this issue. One cannot conceive of a single argument in which the exclusion of women from the marketplace improves the resolution of such questions. Moreover, we can think of good reasons why systematic exclusion from the political process is likely to cause profound dislocations: what gain arises from a system in which all are bound by but only some participate in decision making? A dominant set of solutions leads all libertarians and utilitarians to support the progressive movements of an earlier age.

From Women's Liberation to Feminism

What has brought about today's split between the feminists and the free traders who march under the utilitarian and libertarian banners? The first point of separation pertains to the name of the movement. When the present wave of feminist activity burst on the scene during the 1960s, it was closely tied to the anti-war movement and the racial upheaval in the United States. For a time the movement gave recognition to its libertarian roots in its choice of name: women's liberation. The term hearkened back to the earlier crusades to remove the formal barriers to entry in both economic and political markets. But the name did not stick. It was always a bit too cute and refined for its purpose, and it projected a certain genteel quality inconsistent with the more hard-edged and programmatic tone of the modern movement.

The shift in nomenclature did not take place in a vacuum, given the parallelism between race and sex in the civil rights movement. The nineteenth-century version of the civil rights movement in race relations followed much the same path as the nineteenth-century women's movement. In order to allow slaves to assume the status of free individuals, one had only to abolish the institution of slavery. In the formative period of the women's movement, during the mid-nineteenth century, abolitionism was not a program to grant freed blacks full civil and political rights. As Andrew Kull writes, "There were a hundred arguments to be made against slavery before anyone would necessarily reach the idea—occupying, then as now, a relatively remote level of abstraction—that the law ought not to distinguish between persons on the basis of color."[1] One argument advanced in favor of the abolition of slavery was that it did not entail going further to embrace the ideal of the "equal protection of the laws." Rather the point was that whites could rid themselves of the moral stain of slavery and racial domination without having to grant blacks full political and civil equality. Once the blacks were free, they could still be excluded from the vote and from public office. Likewise with respect to the sexes. Objections to the capacity to contract were more easily overcome than uneasiness about giving (as only men could) women the vote, where the implications for the diffusion of political power were far greater.

Equality of Opportunity or Result

By the 1960s all legal obstacles to women's economic and political participation having been overcome, the dispute became focused on the true nature of equality. Within the earlier system there was little tension between liberty and equality. To insist that all persons have full civil and political capacity made liberty and equality perfectly consistent, just as the denial of some people's liberty to participate necessarily infringed on their entitlements.

One of the great advantages of the earlier system had been that, because it focused on what came to be called with some derision the "formal" aspects of the system, there was a straightforward legal program for correction of the status quo and implementation of powerful reforms. In every area of life, de jure discrimination is much easier to understand and to attack than de facto discrimination. For de jure discrimination, the sufficient legal cure is to remove the disabilities under which certain individuals previously labored, allowing them to participate on the same terms as others. Equality of social and economic outcomes was never a feature of the system; participation rights and successful outcomes had no necessary connection. There was only the weaker but more profound assumption that the older distributions of power and privilege could not easily survive a massive infusion of new players into the system. The whole enterprise thus comported with the Hayekian insight that new entry necessarily changes the patterns of behavior for incumbents by destabilizing their cozy institutional arrangements.

In the legal system, however, a fundamental transition is never as tidy as this philosophical program might make it appear. Questions arise as to whether the transition from the old to the new regime has been successful or whether some political friction, resistance, or hostility has limited the value of the newly created legal rights. When outcomes differed, some observers inferred that opportunities must actually have differed as well.

To me it seems obvious that equal opportunities will always yield unequal results. Nor will the differences in outcome be random within or across groups. Instead they will reflect powerful systematic tendencies. With respect to employment and social role differentiation by sex, the conclusion seems clear: a system of equal rights to participate in business and political life will result in differences of occupational choice and political behavior, among other things, as actual experience has amply confirmed.

In many cases the difference in outcomes has not been taken as a response to systematic differences in preferences between men and women. Rather it has been viewed as proof that the system itself does not operate in the proper fashion. One explanation is that "society" (often spoken of as some detached entity) distorts people's thinking so that the preferences underlying their behavior are not "authentic," no matter how deeply held. Instead those preferences spring from acculturation and upbringing, which themselves operate improperly. To the psychological concerns about distorted preference formation some critics have added the usual suspects for market imperfections—asymmetrical information and improper discounting of future values—as well as unconscious discrimination, illicit stereotyping, unfortunate path dependence, ingrained cognitive biases, and of course glass ceilings—those things we can feel but cannot see.

As these notions gained currency the pressure mounted for aggressive regulatory action. In the United States the first wave of so-called anti-discrimination regulation came with the 1963 Equal Pay Act and the 1964 Civil Rights Act. To the latter the prohibition against sex discrimination was added not quite as a joke, but as a dubious stratagem by Southern senators determined to show the absurdity of prohibiting private discrimination on the basis of race.

The language in which these interferences with market behavior were couched, however, was the language of opportunity and capacity, not that of equality of result. Supporters of the new regulatory efforts presumed that so long as private employers could indulge their taste for discrimination—notice how the term "taste" serves to trivialize the importance of the manifested preference—we would not really have a level playing field. (The implicit assumption seemed to be that all employer preferences operated in the same undesirable direction.) Laws were therefore required to make sure that each firm offered the same opportunities to all individuals.

The prohibition against discrimination by sex makes some sense in the public sphere—the state should not prohibit women from competing, nor should it subject them to differential taxes or other burdens—but now it was carried over to private parties without any regard for the traditional public-private distinction in the law. No longer would the obligation to provide equal opportunity be fulfilled by the removal of state obstacles to participation in markets. Now it extended to employers, landlords, and others, who would be required to operate essentially as if they were governmental entities or public utilities, even though they do not possess any monopoly power in labor markets.

Why this transformation? The answer has much to do with the perennial tension between equality of opportunity and equality of result. The former ideal is relatively uncontroversial as an abstract proposition. And, notwithstanding the derision heaped on a concern for mere "formal" equality, that conception helped fuel the most welcome nineteenth-century reforms. But the relationship between equality of results and equality of opportunity has always been problematic. Can we have confidence that the opportunities are equal when the results turn out to be quite different in the areas of overall wage levels, occupational distributions, and career paths?

The optimistic view of the early civil rights movement was that we would never have to face head-on the implications of the choice between these two standards of equality. Rather, because individuals were basically the same in their capabilities and interests, the removal of barriers to opportunities would quickly translate into an equalization of outcomes across the characteristics over which discrimination was forbidden, including sex. The optimism on that front proved to be misplaced in the case of both race and sex discrimination. Equality of opportunity did not translate into identical results in occupational choices or wage levels. Why not? And what, if anything, should be done about the disparities?

The initial approach was to treat the matter as a question of evidence. In the prevailing conception, to discriminate is to treat two individuals who are alike in critical respects differently because of some irrelevant consideration. To the extent that one expects (as I do not) that the elimination of irrelevant considerations leads to similar forms of behavior, then disparate choices and disparate degrees of success call at the very least for an explanation. So the early statutes made it appear that although the ultimate concern was the intent to engage in disparate treatment, such intent could be inferred from the observed differences in outcome.[2] Originally the inference was relatively weak, and in principle the charge could be dissipated if an employer could show that his practices did not involve any form of prohibited discrimination. Stated otherwise, the evidence as to actual practices could be used to overcome the inference from differential results.

That equilibrium was delicate, and with time the balance changed. The evidence about intention was slippery and, besides, it is commonly believed that people act on the strength of various stereotypes and subconscious preconceptions, some of which are said to be so ingrained that they continue to operate even after they are called to the attention of those who labor under them. So what is needed is a bright light to reveal the hidden discrimination and that revelation can be achieved only by treating the outcomes as proof of discrimination, wholly without regard to any direct evidence of intent to discriminate. The movement from treatment to impact defines one of the major aspects of the modern intellectual feminist movement.

Different Endowments, Different Behaviors
Recall again the premise of the argument: in equilibrium, similar distributions should exist for men and women over all relevant dimensions of em-

ployment. But why should we make that assumption? The issue here is not a moral question, the tacit implication being that those who deny the argument are misguided in their perceptions of how the world ought to be. Rather, the issue is a predictive question: do women and men choose similar career paths? The answer has to be no. I would be amazed if any voluntary sorting mechanism, such as the one operative in a market economy, ever produced such a result for any two population groups, let alone two that differ in some major and visible way, such as by sex.

To proceed with the argument, assume that both men and women seek to maximize their utility by finding the personal and occupational path that best suits their tastes and other natural endowments. The assumption here is that individual self-interest (suitably modified to take into account family and friends) drives and explains the behavior of individuals of both sexes. But the common commitment to self-interest, suitably defined, does not lead them to behave in the same way. The behavioral differences stem, in part, from differences in the endowments. These differences are manifestly physical, but also in many ways psychological. The physical differences seem too obvious to dispute. Nor can they be overcome by changes in diet or exercise; biology matters too much for such social responses to neutralize sex differences. Moreover why would we suppose that the psychological makeup of men and women is identical when their physical differences are manifest?

Of course all men are not identical, nor are all women identical in these characteristics. I mean to say only that their overall distributions differ in predictable ways along many dimensions. Within each sex individuals differ widely, and the distributions often differ by sex. Women have a longer life expectancy than men, but not all women outlive all men. Men are taller than women on average, but some men are shorter than most women. In both cases the differences are likely to be most pronounced at the extreme tails of the distributions. So it goes for any trait on which it is possible to array individuals, both within and across sex groups. But for present purposes the group differences, not the individual differences within groups, are decisive.

We should not expect any specific sex-linked difference in endowment to manifest itself in only a single dimension. Suppose that men are physically stronger than women. It would be odd if, notwithstanding their relative weakness, women were physically more aggressive than men. How would their interest be served by pursuing a course of action that exposed them to greater peril than men? There is no survival value in a mismatch of physical and psychological traits. Rather the sensible hypothesis is that evolution favors the emergence of personality traits that are organized and developed to complement physical traits in an integrated whole. Of course social influences also play a role. But socialization should reinforce the basic evolutionary tendencies. It is not in the interest of parents to guide their own children along the path to self-destruction. One may question the strength of the correspondences, but surely they are not nil. With differences across multiple dimensions reinforcing each other, we should expect to see fairly systematic differences overall, even though both groups contain certain notable exceptions. And so long as the largest payoffs go to individuals at one or both extremes, we should expect that these few cases will exert a disproportionate effect on the aggregate data, whether they pertain to influence or wealth.

That said, we should not neglect the middle of the distribution, either. With respect to the integration of home and work life, it seems indisputable that women, as a group, have to (and want to) devote a greater portion of their resources to childbirth and child rearing than men do. Pregnancy and nursing lie exclusively in the female domain. Although it is possible to substitute technology for parental care, such substitutions typically do not equalize the amount of child-care time given by each parent. The psychological dispositions should on average match the capacity to provide care, so that women would have a greater desire (or tolerance) for this activity than men do. Within families, that differential does not imply that women do all the child rearing and men none. But it does suggest that if couples optimize in making their trade-offs, women will do more child rearing than men, given women's tendency toward a greater fondness and ability for that activity. The egalitarian marriage therefore faces a systematic obstacle in that by demanding equal child care by husband and wife, it reduces the total "production" from marriage, which in turn reduces the gains from entering into that relationship. It is no accident that many people use the word "househusband" with a tinge of bemused disdain.

The effects of differential commitment are not confined to the division of responsibility in raising young children. It influences other occupational and educational choices that complement and depend on family choices. Women often leave the paid labor force or reduce their workloads there during the years that their children are young. There is no reason to suppose that their husbands have ordered them to do so. The more plausible explanation is that desires and functions align, as noted earlier, so that relative to men, women have a greater desire to remain at home for extended periods, even at the cost of some occupational and career advancement. In my view, that difference in career choices is voluntary in most cases. It is part-time work to make ends meet that many women regard as the distraction when they have young children at home. Most women who do not work full time do not want to work full time.

Once such a choice has been made, it influences the patterns of investments that people make in the workplace and in training for work. There arises a differential willingness to take jobs with high-risk characteristics. That in turn leads more women than men to work on a piecework basis with stable income, so that the residual risk bearers are disproportionately men. Over time this difference influences the earnings levels by sex, the nature of the professions into which women and men go, and, more critically, the roles they occupy within those professions. Even if all people were the same in every dimension but one, we would see major differentiation in career paths and outcomes arising from the principle of comparative advantage. As women gravitate toward flexible hours, men move more often into jobs that require long hours and extended travel. As men gravitate toward professions that require great physical strength, women gravitate toward other professions, including counseling and administration. If the differences express themselves across multiple dimensions (including the taste for risk), then we should see profound differences in occupational choices and career paths that will not abate even as women enter the workforce in ever greater numbers.

Victor Fuchs's informative 1988 study, *Women's Quest for Economic Equality*, makes the basic point. To be sure, large numbers of women have entered the professions—most notably law and medicine—in recent years. But the divergent career paths of men and women become most striking when one looks at the organization of subspecialties.[3] There are far more women in family law than in contingent-fee tort litigation; far more in pediatrics or obstetrics and gynecology than in neurosurgery or orthopedic surgery. Perhaps some part of these differentials could be explained by sex discrimination within the various specialties, but if so, such an explanation should be made by presenting proof of specific acts and policies, not merely by making assumptions based on the numbers. In any event it hardly follows that all forms of occupational differences can be explained by (improper or proper) behavior on the demand side. The selection effect works on the supply side as well. In choosing their career paths, women attach different weights to work and family than men do, and they take into account the differences in physiology and psychology between the sexes noted earlier. In this view there is no iron social law that designates certain positions as male and others as female. But differential pressures work at every stage of life in the choice of professions and of the roles played within the professions.

Private and Collective Preferences

The marketplace is only one arena. Public opinion is another. Nowadays social pressures tend to work against the traditional divisions of labor. Commonly women declare, and men agree, that greater female participation in certain professions and occupations would count as an unquestioned social good. Government programs pushing in that direction receive widespread support: hence the carrot of affirmative action programs, many of which go beyond what the law requires, and the stick of anti-discrimination laws, many of which are enforced by parties too eager to infer discrimination when none exists.

But matters operate differently at the individual level. The same woman who thinks the major investment banks should have more female partners makes a personal decision that she does not want to put in the hours needed to reach that goal. She may want to stay at home more with her children, or she may hate travel; she may dislike the grind and the constant confrontation of high-level negotiations. She may resist any suggestion that stereotypes are at work in this regard. Hers is just an individual judgment about herself; it is not one about the position of women in general, on which she takes the opposite view.

But careful psychological calibration hardly matters for these purposes. The operative question in all such cases is how often that same intellectual and emotional process leads to the same results. If most women go through the same process of thought and arrive at the same conclusion, the tyranny of small decisions is at work. The landscape of family and occupational choices reflects not the big-picture views on equality of the sexes but the composite of small-picture views of what is best for a woman and her family. This is a quasi-public-choice explanation for the disconnect between political attitudes and personal behavior that does not require us to assume the irrationality or instability of preferences. Voting in accordance with their general preferences, people can easily support laws that rest on the presumption that any imbalances in labor markets are produced by social forces of discrimination. So the politics of the nation moves to the left, for women more than for men.[4] But actual practices turn out to be more conservative than the rhetoric, because the sum of individual ground-level choices leads to behaviors that reinforce occupational and wage differences rather than undercut them. The long-term equilibrium is thus in tension. The sum of the private decisions will be treated as compelling evidence of discrimination that requires strong government remedies. But practices will prove resistant to such legal remedies because the dominant element consists of choices made by employees, not choices made by firms, as commonly supposed.

Why are women's politics systematically further to the left than men's and becoming more so? At first glance one suspects that the opposite should be the case. As women come to receive as much—or more—formal education as men, and as women enter the paid labor force in large numbers, their experiences should converge with those of men, and that convergence of experience should bring about a convergence of political views. But the opposite has happened. When women enter the paid labor force their experiences are often not the same as men's, and that difference prompts different responses to what they observe.

Take the hottest issue of the day: sexual harassment. Americans spend as much time today trying to figure out the optimal rules of conduct with regard to sexual harassment as Americans of the late nineteenth century spent dealing with the far more serious danger posed by industrial accidents—the loss of life or limb in the workplace. Yet the risks now seem largely to run in one direction. In principle, quid pro quo harassment (which, wholly apart from statutory prohibitions, could not survive under contract in the modern workplace) might take place with women as the aggressors and men as the victims. And in some cases it surely does. Yet, overwhelmingly, the publicized harassments run in the opposite direction. Similarly the legal complaints regarding a hostile workplace environment are virtually all brought by women against men or, more accurately, against corporate employers held accountable for the sins of male supervisors and co-workers.

Why not allow such interrelationships to be governed by the employment contract, which could stipulate the procedures and penalties for various forms of violations? Because the political forces that call discrimination in general a social problem will not relent with respect to practices that, if anything, look more like personal aggression than a refusal to deal for reasons of sex. Forces of political economy press in the same direction. The established women in the workforce may like the anti-harassment rules and benefit from the protection they afford. The women who are willing to take the risks of harassment for the gains of employment are not allowed to compete by agreeing to work on different terms.

Yet who has the political influence? Surely it is those who belong to powerful organized groups. Perhaps we have here a clear conflict of interest between women belonging to different groups, similar to the conflicts that often divide men. Or perhaps other forces are at work as well to reinforce women's left-leaning political alignment. Women may easily identify with the lack of power and believe that government intervention is needed to offset the advantage that men possess. But even that factor does not explain why on all sorts of other issues women as a group favor higher levels of political intervention, usually to offset differences in wealth or advantages. Part of the explanation may stem from women's generally greater (perhaps for biological reasons) aversion to risk. In their private lives, women are more likely than men to believe that cooperation works better than competition, so why not in government as well?

No single explanation can account for all the political differences between men and women, but a number of particular differences may reinforce each other. The persistent differences between the sexes lead to both behavioral and attitudinal differences. The effects are not cabined into some tiny area of human life—they influence all our experiences and interactions. We must oppose the common view that equality of opportunity, rightly conceived, necessarily and properly brings about equality of results. More specifically we should not try to tinker with the outcomes of markets by imposing the strong norm of equality of results, which we cannot and should not achieve, given the differences of preferences and abilities of men and women. The existing patterns are not driven by exploitation (which, like the ether of classical mechanics, becomes ever more difficult to detect). They are driven in the main by informed choices at the micro level. To legitimize outcomes, we must revert back to the older libertarian theories of justice, which Robert Nozick described as leading to a distrust of all pattern principles of justice.[5] Rather than posit our knowledge of what the ends should be, we should let the process run as it will, taking care to see that no major impediments interfere with bargaining and career choice.

The nineteenth-century program that abolished formal legal impediments to entry was roughly consistent with that normative view, which is no surprise inasmuch as Nozick's own theory of justice—justice in acquisition, justice in transfer, and justice in rectification—corresponds closely with traditional theories of property, contract, and tort, of which he had little direct knowledge. Of course in individual cases we should be alert to the risks of duress, misrepresentation, and incapacity that can skew contractual preferences in untoward ways. But these small perturbations, of immense complexity in litigation, do not matter much in understanding the broader patterns of society, for they operate in only a small fraction of cases, and even then in ways that are independent of the concerns about male-female differences in education, income, occupation, and career path. Having opened the way for unimpeded bargaining, we can conclude with confidence that outcome differences are a source of social strength and a sign of a free society. It is when we see the lockstep progression of men and women (or indeed of any groups, whether defined by race, religion, national origin, or other identifiers), that we should infer that government mischief has interfered with the interplay of autonomous choices through voluntary exchange and association—choices that remain critical for the preservation of a free society.

Notes

1. Andrew Kull, *The Color-Blind Constitution* (Cambridge, Mass., 1992), 27.

2. See, for example, *McDonnell Douglas v. Green*, 411 U.S. 792 (1973), 804: "Statistics as to [the employer's] employment policy and practice may be helpful to a determination of whether [his] refusal to rehire [a dismissed employee] in this case conformed to a general pattern of discrimination against blacks." A similar logic has been applied in cases of alleged sex discrimination.

3. Victor Fuchs, *Women's Quest for Economic Equality* (Cambridge, Mass., 1988) chapter 3. Mr. Fuchs also notes that the gap in self-employed income is as great as in employee income, and that differences between the sexes in tips and commissions track the differences in wages. Discrimination by employers cannot explain these strong correlations.

4. John R. Lott, Jr. and Larry Kenny, *How Dramatically Did Women's Suffrage Change the Size and Scope of Government?* Manuscript, 1988.

5. Robert Nozick, *Anarchy, State, and Utopia* (New York, 1974).

WOMEN
and
SEX

Nadine Strossen

❧

On Pornography
Lessons from Enforcement

In a male supremacist society the only obscenity law that will
not be used against women is no law at all. . . . How long will
it take oppressed groups to learn that if we give the state
enough rope, it will end up around our necks?
—Ellen Willis[1]

The master's tools will never dismantle the master's house.
—Audre Lorde[2]

THE FUNDAMENTAL PREMISE IN THE PROCENSORSHIP FEMINISTS' PHILOSO-
phy—that our entire societal and legal system is patriarchal, reflecting and
perpetuating the subordination of women—itself conclusively refutes their
conclusion that we should hand over to that system additional power. The
procensorship feminists cannot have it both ways. If, as they contend, governmental power is inevitably used to the particular disadvantage of relatively disempowered groups, such as women, it follows that women's rights
advocates should oppose measures that augment that power, including
Dworkin-MacKinnon-type laws. As columnist George F. Will observed:
"For someone who so strenuously loathes American society, which she
says is defined by pornography, MacKinnon is remarkably eager to vest in
this society's representative government vast powers to regulate expression."[3]

The Conspicuous Absence of Sexual Speech in Repressive Regimes

> Under patriarchy, no woman is safe to live her life, or to love, or to mother children. Under patriarchy, every woman is a victim, past, present, and future. Under patriarchy, every woman's daughter is a victim, past, present, and future. Under patriarchy, every woman's son is her potential betrayer and also the inevitable rapist or exploiter of another woman.
>
> —Andrea Dworkin[4]

> [I]t is the state—not free speech—that is the oppressor of women. It was the state, not pornography, that burned women as witches. It was 18th and 19th century law, not pornography, that defined women as chattel. . . . It is the state, not pornography, that has raised barriers against women. It is censorship, not freedom, that will keep the walls intact.
>
> —Wendy McElroy[5]

Sexual expression is an integral aspect of human freedom. Throughout history the suppression of sexually explicit speech has characterized regimes that repress both free speech and human rights in general. Measures to suppress sexual expression consistently have targeted views that challenge the prevailing political, religious, cultural, or social orthodoxy.

Sexually explicit speech has been banned by the most repressive regimes, including Communism in the former Soviet Union, Eastern bloc countries, and China; apartheid in South Africa; and fascist or clerical dictatorships in Chile, Iran, and Iraq. Conversely, recent studies of Russia have correlated improvements in human rights, including women's rights, with the rise of free sexual expression. Pete Hamill explains the connection:

> Recent history teaches us that most tyrannies have a puritanical nature. The sexual restrictions of Stalin's Soviet Union, Hitler's Germany and Mao's China would have gladdened the hearts of those Americans who fear sexual images and literature. Their ironfisted Puritanism was not motivated by a need to erase inequality. They wanted to smother the personal chaos that can accompany sexual freedom and subordinate it to the granite face of the state. Every tyrant knows that if he can control human sexuality, he can control life.[6]

In places where real pornography is conspicuously absent, tellingly, works of political dissent are labeled as such. Laws banning obscene or pornographic expression have been used to suppress all kinds of expression, and the pejorative terms "obscene and pornographic" have been used to condemn a wide range of views, far beyond the legal or dictionary definitions of those terms, and even altogether outside the realm of sexuality. The Communist government of the former Soviet Union denounced dissenting political views as pornographic and obscene and suppressed political dissidents under obscenity laws. In August 1987, when the Chinese Communist government dramatically increased its censorship of books and magazines with Western political and literary messages, it condemned them as "obscene," "pornographic," and "bawdy." The white supremacist South African government banned black writing as "pornographically immoral." In Nazi Germany and the former Soviet Union, Jewish writings were reviled as "pornographic," as were any works that criticized the Nazi or Communist parties, respectively.[7]

Even in societies that generally respect human rights, including free speech, as we have seen, the term "pornography" tends to be used as an epithet to stigmatize expression that is politically or socially unpopular. Accordingly, the freedom to produce or consume anything called "pornography" is an essential aspect of the freedom to defy prevailing political and social mores. Pornography is not just the samizdat of individuals who are oppressed or dissident sexually, to paraphrase Stanford law professor Kathleen Sullivan; it is also the samizdat of those who are oppressed or dissident in any respect.

Legal scholar Kenneth L. Karst provides intriguing insights into the link between sexual freedom, including free sexual expression, and freedom from discrimination:

> The suppression of unreason is rooted in the same fears that produce group subordination: men's fear of the feminine, whites' fear of blackness, heterosexuals' anxiety about sexual orientation. Historically, all these fears have been closely connected with the fear of sexuality. It is no accident that the 1960s, a period of sexual "revolution," also saw the acceleration of three movements that sought major redefinitions of America's social boundaries: the civil rights movement, the gay liberation movement, and the women's movement.[8]

Like all groups who seek equal rights and freedoms, women and feminists have an especially important stake in securing free speech. Throughout history, free speech consistently has been the greatest ally of those seeking equal rights for groups that have been subject to discrimination. Correspondingly, censorship measures have consistently been used to the particular detriment of the relatively unpopular and powerless.

Hating Speech

The pattern of disempowered groups being disproportionately targeted under censorship schemes extends even to censorship schemes that are allegedly designed for their benefit. This phenomenon is vividly illustrated by the enforcement record of laws against "hate speech"—speech that expresses racial, sexist, religious, and other forms of invidious discrimination. Since feminist-style anti-pornography laws are simply a specific kind of anti-hate-speech law, it is important also to examine such laws' historical enforcement record. This record demonstrates, once again, that pro-censorship feminists posit a false choice between free speech and equality values. As Justice Hugo Black noted in his dissent from a 1952 Supreme Court decision upholding a hate-speech law (which has been implicitly overturned by subsequent decisions), "If there be minority groups who hail this holding as their victory, they might consider the possible relevancy of this ancient remark: 'Another such victory and I am undone.' "[9]

The first individuals prosecuted under the British Race Relations Act of 1965, which criminalized the incitement of racial hatred, were black power leaders. Their overtly racist messages undoubtedly expressed legitimate anger at real discrimination, yet the statute drew no such fine lines, nor could any similar law possibly do so. Rather than curbing speech offensive to minorities, this British law instead has been used regularly to curb the speech of blacks, trade unionists, and anti-nuclear activists. Perhaps the ultimate irony of this law, intended to restrain the National Front, a neo-Nazi group, is that it instead has barred expression by the Anti-Nazi League.

The British experience is typical. None of the anti-Semites who were responsible for arousing France against Captain Alfred Dreyfus was ever prosecuted for group libel. But Emile Zola was prosecuted for libeling the French clergy and military in his classic letter "J'Accuse," and he had to flee to England to escape punishment.

Similarly, University of Michigan Law School professor Eric Stein has documented that although the German Criminal Code of 1871 punished offenses against personal honor, "The German Supreme Court . . . consistently refused to apply this article to insults against Jews as a group—although it gave the benefit of its protection to such groups as Germans living in Prussian provinces, large landowners, all Christian clerics, German officers, and Prussian troops who fought in Belgium and Northern France."[10]

That the foregoing examples simply illustrate a long-standing global pattern was documented in a 1992 book published by Article XIX, the London-based International Centre Against Censorship (which takes its name from the free speech guarantee in the Universal Declaration of Human Rights) and the Human Rights Centre at the University of Essex in Great Britain, which draws upon contemporary analyses of the situations in fourteen different countries with various laws punishing racist and other hate speech. According to Sandra Coliver, Article XIX's legal director:

> The flagrant abuse of laws which restrict hate speech by the authorities . . . provides the most troubling indictment of such laws. Thus, the laws in Sri Lanka and South Africa have been used almost exclusively against the oppressed and politically weakest communities. . . . Selective or lax enforcement by the authorities, including in the UK, Israel and the former Soviet Union, allows governments to compromise the rights of dissent and inevitably leads to disaffection and feelings of alienation among minority groups.[11]

The international pattern also holds true in specific, localized contexts—namely, on university and college campuses, where anti-pornography feminists have made some headway. Again, the British experience is instructive. In 1974, in a move aimed at the National Front, the British National Union of Students (NUS) adopted a resolution that representatives of "openly racist and Fascist organizations" were to be prevented from speaking on college campuses "by whatever means necessary (including disruption of the meeting)."[12]

The rule had been designed in large part to stem an increase in campus anti-Semitism. But following the United Nations' cue, some British students deemed Zionism a form of racism beyond the bounds of permitted discussion, and in 1975 British students invoked the NUS resolution to disrupt speeches by Israelis and Zionists, including the Israeli ambassador to Great Britain. The intended target of the NUS resolution, the National Front, applauded this result. The NUS itself, by contrast, became disenchanted by this and other unintended consequences of its resolution and in 1977 repealed it.

The British experience parallels what has happened in the United States, judging from the campus hate speech codes for which enforcement information is available.[13] One such code was in effect from April 1988 until October 1989 at the University of Michigan. Because the American

Civil Liberties Union brought a lawsuit to challenge the code (which resulted in a ruling that the code was unconstitutional), the university was
forced to disclose information that otherwise would have been unavailable
to the public about how it had been enforced.[14] This enforcement record,
while not surprising to anyone familiar with the consistent history of censorship measures, should come as a rude awakening to any who believe
that anti-hate-speech laws will protect or benefit racial minorities, women,
or any other group that has traditionally suffered discrimination.

During the year and a half that the University of Michigan rule was in
effect, there were more than twenty cases of whites charging blacks with
racist speech. More importantly the only two instances in which the rule
was invoked to sanction racist speech (as opposed to other forms of hate
speech) involved the punishment of speech by or on behalf of black students. The only student who was subjected to a full-fledged disciplinary
hearing under the Michigan rule was an African-American student accused of homophobic and sexist expression. In seeking clemency from the
punishment that was imposed on him after this hearing, the student asserted that he had been singled out because of his race and his political
views.

Others who were punished at Michigan included several Jewish students accused of engaging in anti-Semitic expression (they wrote graffiti,
including a swastika, on a classroom blackboard; they said they intended it
as a practical joke) and an Asian-American student accused of making an
anti-black comment (his allegedly "hateful" remark was to ask why black
people feel discriminated against; he said he raised this question because
the black students in his dormitory tended to socialize together, making
him feel isolated). Likewise the student who in 1989 challenged the University of Connecticut's hate-speech policy, under which she had been penalized for an allegedly homophobic remark, was Asian American. She
claimed that other students had engaged in similar expression, but that
she had been singled out for punishment because of her ethnic background. Representing this student, the ACLU persuaded the university to
drop the challenged policy.[15] And the first complaint filed under Trinity
College's then-new policy prohibiting racial harassment, in 1989, was
against an African-American speaker who had been sponsored by a black
student organization, Black-Power Serves Itself.

The hate speech lesson from enforcement? Watch what you say about
others, depending on not only who those others are, but also who you are.
If you are a member of a group that has traditionally suffered discrimination, including women, restrictions on hate speech are especially likely to

be wielded against your speech. In fact all forms of censorship have consistently been used to suppress speech of and for women.

Women in the Wake of Censorship

> Censorship has been throughout history the single most widely used patriarchal tool for "protecting" women—from birth control, abortion, sexual satisfaction, and nonheterosexual relationships. Without free speech we can have no feminist movement.
> —National Organization for Women of New York State[16]

> I believe that censorship only springs back against the givers of culture—against authors, artists, and feminists, against anybody who wants to change society. Should censorship be imposed. . . . Feminists would be the first to suffer.
> —Erica Jong[17]

Although we "babes" have "come a long way," as the saying goes, could we have come further, faster without the "help" of censorship? Here the lesson from enforcement is that women should go slow on censorship, because censorship consistently has been used to slow our search for equal status.

Until recently, the "gag rule," in effect from 1988 until 1993, banned the dissemination of information about abortion at federally funded family-planning clinics. (In the fall of 1994, more than three hundred republican congressional candidates pledged to reinstate the gag rule.) As columnist Anna Quindlen observed, "What the gag rule has taught us is that reproductive freedom is not possible without free speech."[18] That lesson should have been learned from the steady use of censorship, throughout our history, to fetter women's reproductive freedom.

Of particular note, laws permitting the suppression of sexually oriented information have often been used to suppress information that is essential not only for women's reproductive rights, but also for other aspects of the women's rights cause. Anti-obscenity laws consistently have been used to suppress information about contraception. Dr. Charles Knowlton, author of the first known medical work about contraception in the United States, *Fruits of Philosophy; or, The Private Companion of Young Married People*, was prosecuted in 1839 under the Massachusetts anti-obscenity law.

Likewise the first federal anti-obscenity statute, passed in 1873, criminalized the interstate mailing of both sexually oriented material and material related to contraception or abortion. This statute, which is generally known as the Comstock law in honor of the leading anti-obscenity crusader, Anthony Comstock, who had lobbied for it, provided:

> No obscene, lewd, or lascivious book, pamphlet, picture, paper, print, or other publication of an indecent character, or any article or thing designed or intended for the prevention of conception or procuring of abortion, nor any article or thing intended or adapted for any indecent or immoral use or nature . . . shall be carried in the mail.[19]

Each violation of the law could be punished with a fine up to five thousand dollars or imprisonment at hard labor for one to ten years. Twenty-four states enacted legislation that was modeled on this federal law, prohibiting not only the intrastate transportation of obscene materials, contraceptives, and abortifacients, but also their advertisement or publications about them. Moreover fourteen state anti-obscenity statutes also enjoined speech about contraception and abortion.

Armed with this legislation, Comstock, the longtime director of the Society for the Suppression of Vice, as well as his successor, John Sumner, zealously prosecuted feminists and pioneering birth control advocates who tried to distribute information about women's sexuality and reproduction. Among those Comstock persecuted, at least fifteen women committed suicide, including Ida Craddock, who was imprisoned in 1902 for writing advice manuals on conjugal relations.

In her 1992 biography of Margaret Sanger, the leading early birth control champion, Ellen Chesler, noted that the Comstock-inspired anti-obscenity laws all but banned any discussion of contraception, even between doctors and patients and within the medical community.[20] Because these laws suppressed much scientific, accurate information about contraception and abortion, the only "information" readily available was in underground publications by quacks and charlatans.[21]

Sanger was persecuted under the anti-obscenity laws throughout her career. Her campaign to convey accurate sexual information began in 1912 with two articles in a New York City newspaper. The first, entitled "What Every Mother Should Know," ran without incident, but the United States Post Office barred the second, "What Every Girl Should Know." The article contained no information on birth control, but postal officials were offended by Sanger's explanation of venereal disease and her use of words such as "gonorrhea" and "syphilis." Consequently the newspaper's next issue contained the following announcement: "What Every Girl Should Know: 'NOTHING!' By order of the Post Office."[22]

In 1913 Anthony Comstock prosecuted Sanger for her writings on sexuality and birth control. She was criminally prosecuted again in 1917 and served thirty days in a workhouse for having operated a birth control clinic in Brooklyn. Sanger also served time in jail in Portland, Oregon, for distributing information about birth control. In 1929 she was banned in Boston.

Margaret Sanger had the dubious distinction of being one of the first victims of a new form of censorship that was applied to a then-new medium early in this century. The Supreme Court had ruled in 1915 that movies were not protected "speech" under the First Amendment, and one of the first films banned under that decision was *Birth Control*, a 1917 picture produced by and featuring Margaret Sanger.[23] The New York Court of Appeals held that this movie, a dramatization of Sanger's family planning work, could be censored "in the interest of morality, decency, and public safety and welfare."[24]

This episode underscores several significant themes: the close connections between sex and politics (and between sexual and political repression) and the bad tendencies of the former "bad tendency" rationale for suppressing speech (that speech may be censored because it might tend to bring about some future harm), which pro-censorship feminists are seeking to revive. The court stressed that the film "tends to ridicule the public authorities and the provision of . . . the Penal Law forbidding the dissemination of contraceptive knowledge," and therefore held that it could be barred, even for adult-only audiences, because it "may engender a desire to obtain" birth control information, and thus might "lead to violations of the law."

The banning of films concerning birth control and other sexual-political subjects of particular interest to women and feminists continued into the second half of the twentieth century. In support of his argument that "women who are claiming their equal citizenship should think twice about pressing the argument that pornography is not protected speech," UCLA law professor Kenneth Karst noted that, until the 1950s New York censors routinely banned films that treated themes of particular concern to women's rights advocates: pregnancy, venereal disease, birth control, abortion, illegitimacy, prostitution, miscegenation, and divorce.[25]

From 1873, when the Comstock Act was passed, through the 1930s, other feminists and health experts who tried to present information about women's sexuality and reproductive options were also plagued by obscenity laws. Charges were brought against Emma Goldman for giving information about birth control during a lecture in New York. Mary Ware Denett was convicted and sentenced to pay a three-hundred-dollar fine for her book *The Sex Side of Life: An Explanation for Young People*, which she had written for the education of her adolescent sons.[26] Marie Stopes's *Married Love*, which offered basic anatomical information and health advice to newly married couples, was prosecuted under American anti-obscenity laws, even though it was an established bestseller in Europe and had already been expurgated for the American market.[27] (The ACLU represented Dennett and Stopes, and on appeal succeeded in overturning Dennett's conviction and the U.S. Customs Service's ban on both their books.)

Edward Bliss Foote, a popular health writer, was convicted in a prosecution brought by Comstock and forced to eliminate all information about contraception from his published writings. Comstock also successfully prosecuted Ezra Heywood, who had distributed a journal that advertised contraceptives. A *Marriage Manual*, by Hannah Abraham Stone, was subjected to censorship efforts in 1935 when it was first published.

The gag has been loosened or tightened at various times, but never removed. In 1990 Janet Benshoof, director of the ACLU's Reproductive Freedom Project, was charged with the misdemeanor of "soliciting abortion" under the strict anti-abortion law that Guam had just passed. Her alleged crime? Benshoof said, during a speech at the Guam Press Club, that Guamanian women could still get legal, low-cost abortions in Hawaii, despite Guam's law criminalizing virtually all abortions, and she gave Guamanian women the address and phone number of Planned Parenthood in Hawaii.[28] This was eighty years after Margaret Sanger, Planned Parenthood's founding mother, was first prosecuted for providing similar information.

Women must go forward. The past is not as different from the present as the future must be. In Anna Quindlen's words:

> In the fight to keep women free it is important to remember this: freedom of speech is the bedrock of it all. Silence is what kept us in our place for too long. If we now silence others, our liberty is false. No more gag rules—that should be our goal. In clinics, in colleges, in lecture halls. Anywhere.[29]

Butler Did It: "Big Surprise" in Canada

Thanks to the Canadian Supreme Court's February 1992 decision in *Butler v. The Queen*, we have been able to observe the MacDworkinite regime in operation. As far as Canada is concerned, Erica Jong's prediction quoted earlier—that "feminists would be the first to suffer" under any newly imposed censorship—is, unfortunately, now a description.

Andrea Dworkin has said, "The *Butler* decision is probably the best articulation of how pornography, and what kinds of pornography, hurt the civil status and civil rights of women," and Catharine MacKinnon has en-thused, "[The *Butler* decision] is a stunning victory for women. This is of world historic importance. This makes Canada the first place in the world that says what is obscene is what harms women, not what offends our val-ues."[30] Others though they may agree about the decision's "world historic importance," offer dramatically different assessments:

> You presented a brief to the Supreme Court that has us in the shits right now. . . . [Y]ou handed them post-modern lan-guage. . . . The language that they had been looking for to come back after us, and now they are busting our bookstores.
> —Elaine Carol, performance artist addressing a feminist lawyer whose arguments were adopted in *Butler*[31]

> This law isn't protecting us; it is silencing us.
> —Liz Czach, member of the feminist caucus of the Ontario Coalition Against Film and Video Censorship[32]

> Andrea Dworkin has done more damage to women's culture in her tenure as darling of the media than anyone who is a leader of the right wing. She is morally responsible for what is happening to women's literature in Canada.
> —Pat Califia[33]

> *Butler* is just about morality. It's morality in the guise of pro-tecting women and children. And who needs the protection of the male patriarchy anyway, of the state?
> —Ellen Flanders[34]

The *Butler* decision has been a potent weapon to suppress free speech for all as well as the equality rights of various disempowered groups, in-cluding the very women whose rights it was supposed to enhance. As a 1993 article in the *Nation* commented, "This epidemic of censorship shows how 'progressive' controls on expression are bound to backfire." It con-cluded, "If Canada's border fiasco gives pause to MacKinnonites in other countries—the lobby for the Pornography Victims' Compensation Act in the United States, for example—maybe it will have been worth the absurd-ities."[35]

Because Canada's experience under *Butler* provides the only record of the actual impact of a Dworkin-MacKinnon-style law in operation, it is im-portant to examine that record in detail. At the very least, the Canadian experience imposes a heavy burden of proof on anti-pornography advocates to show that the enforcement trends in Canada would not be replicated here. That burden of proof seems to be insurmountable, though, since the Canadian enforcement trends result from two factors that transcend the U.S.-Canada border: the inherently vague concept of "subordinating" or "degrading" material that is at the heart of all MacDworkinite laws; and the homophobic, anti-feminist orientation that many Canadian officials share not only with their U.S. counterparts, but also with many private citizens in both countries.

In two important respects, the Canadian version of the feminist anti-pornography law is less sweeping than the original Dworkin-MacKinnon model. First, notwithstanding *Butler*'s incorporation of the MacDworkinite concept of pornography into the Canadian anti-obscenity law, that law continues to provide that no material will be deemed obscene if it has an artistic purpose or is part of the serious treatment of a sexual theme. This is similar to the provision in the U.S. Supreme Court's definition of obscenity that excludes any material with serious literary, artistic, political, or scientific value. The Dworkin-MacKinnon model law, though, contains no comparable limitation.

Second, the Canadian obscenity law, again parallel to American obscenity law, applies only to works considered as a whole. Therefore a work cannot be suppressed just because isolated passages meet the obscenity definition. Under the Dworkin-MacKinnon law, by contrast, even an isolated sexually explicit, subordinating depiction would warrant suppressing an entire work, regardless of its overall value.

The spring 1993 issue of *Feminist Bookstore News*, a Canadian publication, contained the following description of Canada's first year of experience with the anti-pornography definition that was supposed to be such a boon to feminists: "The *Butler* decision has been used . . . only to seize lesbian, gay and feminist material."[36] Within the first two and a half years after the *Butler* decision, well over half of all Canadian feminist bookstores had had materials confiscated or detained by customs. From Quebec to Victoria, Canadian bookstore managers had the same comment: that *Butler* increased censorship in Canada by customs, police, and lower courts, and that the predominant targets have been gay, lesbian, and women's literature.

Even those Canadian feminists who championed the *Butler* decision—working through the Women's Legal Education and Action Fund (LEAF), which MacKinnon co-founded—have been forced to acknowledge that it has become an engine for oppressing feminist, gay, and lesbian expression. Karen Busby, a lawyer who worked on the LEAF brief, made the following confession in the fall of 1993 at a symposium in Toronto:

> Before the ink was dry on *Butler* . . . the Toronto police raided
> Glad Day Bookshop, a lesbian and gay bookstore, and confis-
> cated *Bad Attitude*, a lesbian erotic magazine. . . . It was a
> shocking raid. Police ignored representations made by men and
> women in most cities across Canada, including . . . Toronto . . .
> and yet the one thing that they raid is this one magazine that
> sells about forty copies every two months in Canada when it
> comes out. It is hardly a threat to women's equality and yet
> that's the magazine that they chose.[37]

To add insult to injury, while Glad Day's owner and manager were arrested for selling *Bad Attitude*, a nearby mainstream bookstore that also
sold it was left alone.

Bad Attitude is a magazine published by and for women—specifically,
lesbian women. Its editor has explained that the magazine "is called *Bad
Attitude* because that's what women who take their sexuality into their own
hands (so to speak) are told they have."[38] Nonetheless, the judge who
ruled in the Glad Day case found that this feminist, lesbian publication
harmed women, and he therefore convicted the Glad Day principals. His
ruling was based on a story (told just in words, with no photographs or il-
lustrations) in the magazine about a sex fantasy, entitled "Wunna My Fantasies," by San Francisco writer Trish Thomas. The story is about a woman
who surprises another woman in a shower, grabbing her, tying her, slap-
ping her, and pulling her hair. While the showering woman initially resists
her assailant's sexual advances, she ultimately succumbs, and they both
end up enjoying their sexual encounter. Thomas has said that when she
does public readings of her stories about this kind of lesbian fantasy, with
some sadomasochistic elements, she is "amazed by not just the numbers of
women that come up to me . . . to tell me that they've had these fantasies,
but the diversity of women—very conservative women too."[39]

Despite the fact that women enjoy the type of fantasy described in
"Wunna My Fantasies," the male judge who found it "degrading" and "demeaning," Claude Paris, explained that its fatal flaw was that it described
"enjoyable sex after subordination by bondage and physical abuse at the
hands of a total stranger." He dismissed the fact that the fantasy's aggressor is female as "irrelevant." Taking his cue from the Canadian Supreme
Court in *Butler*, Judge Paris ruled that the ultimately consensual nature of
the sex the story describes is not enough to absolve it of the criminalizing
"degrading" label. He stated: "The consent . . . far from redeeming the material, makes it degrading and dehumanizing."[40]

A second lower court decision enforcing *Butler* also resulted from
seizures of homosexual erotica from Glad Day Bookshop and also held ho-

mosexual expression to be "degrading." This decision, issued by Judge F. C. Hayes, held all thirteen of the confiscated gay publications to be "degrading and dehumanizing," explaining only that they showed sexual encounters without any "real, meaningful human relationship."[41] As Karen Busby of LEAF acknowledges, Judge Hayes's decision "[is] clearly homophobic. . . . He said that sex between men in and of itself was degrading and dehumanizing."[42] Chris Bearchell, a lesbian feminist journalist in Canada, commented:

> Before Hayes's ruling some people no doubt hoped that the Butler decision might bring more enlightened obscenity rulings because of the court's declaration that its role was to protect women and children from harm. . . . Now they are probably wondering just what pictures and descriptions of consenting men having sex with each other have to do with violence against women and children.[43]

Despite the boasting of Dworkin, MacKinnon, and (at least initially) their LEAF allies that *Butler* ushered in a brave new era of pro-feminist censorship, Judge Hayes's ruling makes clear instead that *Butler* simply allows censorship on traditional moralistic grounds. Indeed, precisely that interpretation of *Butler* has been made by "Project P," the anti-obscenity squad of the Ontario Provincial Police. According to a spokesman, Project P interprets *Butler* to permit explicit sexual expression only if it includes romance and a story line.[44] This prompted Susan Ditta, former curator of the National Gallery of Canada and now the media arts officer at the Canada Council, to comment, "As someone who's spent a great deal of time writing about the deconstruction of narrative in contemporary video art practice, I got really worried about there having to be a story line."[45]

The fact that *Butler* merely provides a new gloss on an old notion of obscenity is underscored by its lack of any impact on the detailed regulations that Canadian Customs officials had previously followed in enforcing the obscenity law at the border. After *Butler*, government lawyers reviewed those regulations and concluded that not one word needed to be changed. As stated by Jacques Boivin, a Canadian artist, this "just goes to show that the reputedly 'feminist' definition of 'degradation' is not a departure but . . . a further reformulation of paternalistic control. Same old baloney with a recycled label."[46] Lawyer Brenda Cossman, who teaches at Canada's York University, calls the new label "sexual morality in drag."[47]

Another aspect of the Glad Day case, the singling out of publications, publishers, distributors, and stores that are relatively small and powerless, also heralded what has been a continuing enforcement pattern under *But-*

ler. In 1993 Inland Books, a New York–based small-press book distribution company and the largest U.S. exporter of lesbian and gay literature to Canada, had 73 percent of its shipments to Canada detained. In one of the biggest book detentions in its history, Canadian customs detained a 1993 shipment of hundreds of titles from Inland to thirty-six Canadian stores, including university bookstores, literary bookshops, and even a religious bookstore. The distributors that serve lesbian and gay bookstores often carry political publications other than those targeted specifically for the lesbian and gay audience. Because it was part of such a shipment, a September 1993 issue of the *Nation* was detained by Canadian Customs officials.

The *Butler* decision has been used preponderantly against publications with a feminist or lesbian/gay orientation. More mainstream-oriented materials that tend to be sold in mainstream establishments have been undistributed, benefiting from an apparent double standard in the enforcement of *Butler*. A prominent example is Madonna's *Sex*, which was published by a major commercial house and was sold in large, chain bookstores. (The book's sexually explicit contents, including scenes of rape and bestiality, were deemed sufficiently degrading by MacDworkinites that they publicly ripped it to shreds at a 1992 feminist pro-censorship conference at the University of Chicago Law School.) Likewise, since *Butler*, Canadian authorities have not interfered with the importation or sale of Bret Easton Ellis's *American Psycho*, which contains extremely violent, sexually graphic accounts of the mutilation of women.

The *Toronto Star* has reported that, in many further instances, books destined for nonmainstream bookstores have been seized and banned by customs while the big chain stores are allowed to sell the very same books. Small bookstores are thus suffering substantial economic hardships. The Toronto-based *Globe and Mail* estimated that 75 percent of shipments to Glad Day and similar stores are "opened, delayed, lost, forgotten and occasionally sent back without more than a handful of Canadian citizens knowing about it."[48] According to the *Toronto Star*, "Books dealing with homosexual activities are seized regularly and often times for months, quite literally in an attempt to close down the offending stores."[49] Notes Bruce Walsh, a spokesperson for the Canadian anti-censorship coalition CENSORSTOP, "[E]very gay bookseller in this country has attempted to sell their bookstores, but nobody wants to buy them."[50]

One lesbian bookstore has fought back against the Canadian government's selective suppression of lesbian sexual expression. The Little Sister Book and Art Emporium in Vancouver brought a lawsuit claiming that it had been subjected to government harassment. After the lawsuit was instituted—and some critics charge, specifically to blunt its allegations—Canadian officials broadened their enforcement efforts to include feminist bookstores, university bookstores, and radical bookstores.

CENSORSTOP has charged that the officials who are implementing *Butler* are "really interested in controlling radical dissent."[51] When Le Dernier Mot (LDM) bookstore published and sold transcripts of a telephone conversation that was politically embarrassing to the Canadian government, and that the government had attempted to ban from publication, customs authorities immediately began to seize books that were being shipped to LDM as allegedly violating the *Butler* obscenity standard. Prior to this incident, no LDM books had ever been seized. Likewise just one week after Pages Bookstore in Toronto had installed a provocative anti-censorship display, customs seized allegedly obscene books being shipped to it.

Whether or not Canadian officials have actually exercised their discretionary authority under *Butler* to target political dissent, it is indisputable that the Canadian Supreme Court's adoption of the Dworkin-MacKinnon anti-pornography standard has given officials a powerful weapon which they could easily aim at dissent, should they wish to do so.

Recalling that *Butler*'s supposed rationale is to protect women from works that harm them, it is difficult to understand how the feminist writings that have been seized under *Butler* would harm women. Some material has been suppressed under *Butler* on the grounds that it is allegedly degrading and harmful not to women, but to men. For example, Canadian Customs has seized a book entitled *Weenie-Toons! Women Artists Mock Cocks* because of its alleged "degradation of the male penis."[52] Similarly, customs' banned list includes a lesbian feminist magazine entitled *Hothead Paisan*, even though it portrays no sexual activity, because it is purportedly "sexually degrading to men."[53] This comic book–style magazine depicts the adventures of a lesbian terrorist who will not take any guff from men, and who makes those who give her trouble disappear.

In one of the condemned *Hothead Paisan* strips, a white man wearing a business suit chains himself to a statue of Christopher Columbus (on which is engraved, "I found it, it is mine, kill those people") and declares, "Women will have the right to choose over my dead body!" In response, the magazine's heroine, the lesbian avenger "Hothead," springs into action. Crying "Now that's an engraved invitation!" she beats this anti-choice demonstrator into the ground.[54] In addition to turning the tables on the incapacitating woman-as-victim stereotype, this strip conveys messages about other political issues, including colonialism and reproductive freedom. What a travesty that it has been suppressed in the name of feminism, under a feminist-advocated law!

And of course two books written by Andrea Dworkin herself, *Pornography: Men Possessing Women* and *Women Hating*, were seized at the U.S.-Canadian border. According to customs, they "illegally eroticized pain and bondage."[55] Dworkin's graphic, sexually explicit descriptions of men committing violent and degrading acts against women are presumably provided for purposes of persuading society to mobilize against misogynistic violence and discrimination. But neither the *Butler* decision nor any other version of the Dworkin-MacKinnon anti-pornography law contains any exception for subordinating sexually explicit depictions that are part of a feminist presentation. Nor could any such exception possibly be added without compounding the law's already overwhelming subjectivity.

At least one other book that described sexual violence expressly for the purpose of condemning it and aiding people to resist it was also, ironically, among the first targets of *Butler*'s censorial regime. It was a novel by Robert Lally, a retired Canadian psychologist who had worked with child molesters. He wrote the book to mobilize the public to take serious action against pedophiles. Its main character, based on a composite of Lally's patients, was designed to show laypeople how pedophiles think and operate. In Lally's words, the book "was supposed to disgust people and frighten the hell out of them, so they would say, 'Let's do something about pedophiles.'" Lally sent one copy of his manuscript to a literary agent in the United States. When she returned it to him, Canadian Customs officials intercepted the manuscript pursuant to the *Butler* ruling. As Mary Williams Walsh wrote in the *Los Angeles Times*:

> Lally's project would . . . appear to be just the sort of undertaking the anti-pornography lobby would applaud: In his own way, he wanted to protect society from sex crimes. But the plan backfired. Under *Butler*, Lally's opus itself was found to be obscene. Three Mounties and a Customs officer raided his house and seized his only other copy of the manuscript. Then they clapped their alleged porn kingpin into the back of their squad car.[56]

It is quite possible that Canadian Customs confiscated Dworkin's *Woman Hating* purely on the basis of its title. And just as Ohio law enforcement officials went after Debbie Reynolds's exercise video *Doing It Debbie's Way* because of its "provocative" title, Canadian Customs recently confiscated *Hot, Hotter, Hottest*,[57] apparently for the same reason; this is a cookbook containing recipes for spicy cuisine. Laughable as these incidents may be, they illustrate the frightening force of the feminist anti-pornography law to suppress a limitless range of materials that are valued by diverse audiences.

Although the primary target of Canada's post-*Butler* enforcement efforts have been feminist, lesbian, and gay materials, *Butler* also has emboldened customs officials to seize other works, including serious mainstream books. Canadian Customs seized thirty copies of Marguerite Duras's novella *The Man Sitting in the Corridor* that had been ordered by Trent University. This novella by the respected writer was detained because it includes several scenes in which a woman is beaten after passionate sex; in the last such scene, she dies. Canadian Customs also has seized books by critically acclaimed authors such as Kathy Acker, Ambrose Bierce, Langston Hughes, David Leavitt, Audre Lorde, Anne Rice, and Oscar Wilde. It has barred *Weird Smut Comics*, a publication dealing with the evils of censorship, the political journal *Lies of Our Times*, and the illustrated collection of essays published by the feminist Anti-Censorship Taskforce, *Caught Looking*.

In 1993 customs detained a shipment of fifteen hundred copies of *Black Looks: Race and Representations*, by black feminist academic bell hooks, that were en route to several Canadian universities. Although all of the other books were seized pursuant to *Butler*, *Black Looks* was detained under a Canadian law prohibiting hate speech more generally, which the pro-censorship feminists also support.

Canadian authorities have not enforced *Butler* against the type of violent, misogynistic heterosexual materials that its advocates had hoped they would proscribe. Catharine MacKinnon appeared to concede that enforcement of the decision had not advanced women's interests in a telephone conversation she had in September 1993 with Leanne Katz, executive director of the National Coalition Against Censorship. MacKinnon noted that the Canadian government authorities were not going after the kind of violent, heterosexual materials that had been involved in the *Butler* case itself, to which Leanne Katz replied, "Big surprise." MacKinnon echoed, "Big surprise."[58]

And an Even Bigger Chill
As if direct government censorship of allegedly degrading sexually oriented materials under *Butler* were not damaging enough to free speech and equality values, *Butler* has also spurred two indirect, even more expansive forms of censorship. Like all censorial schemes, it has led to self-

censorship, and it also has created a "slippery slope," encouraging the adoption of additional censorship measures.

The massive self-censorship among Canadians, triggered by *Butler*, was described in a February 1994 report by the Free Expression Project of Human Rights Watch:

> The indirect effect of daily customs seizures and police raids is self-censorship by the bookstores, video stores and private citizens who for financial reasons, cannot afford to mount legal challenges. Oxford University Press refused to distribute *Gay Ideas: Outing and Other Controversies*, a Beacon Press book by Canadian philosopher Richard Mohr, rather than incur the wrath of Customs. Many publishers send page proofs to the Prohibited Importations Unit in Ottawa prior to printing their Canadian editions. The Unit's staff go through the various magazines, whiting out text and replacing offending photos with black dots. Customs has even deleted safe-sex information in U.S. publications imported for Canadian gay men.[59]

The second spillover effect of *Butler* has been that Canadian government officials have been emboldened to pass other measures that suppress an even broader range of expression. As a September 1993 *Los Angeles Times* article noted, *Butler* led the Canadian House of Commons and provincial legislatures to write sweeping new laws against controversial expression, including a prohibition on serial killer trading cards and a law making it a crime to make, print, publish, import, distribute, or sell—and in some cases even possess—any depiction of a sexual act by anyone under eighteen years old, even in fiction or art, and even though Canadian law recognizes that people as young as twelve may legally engage in sexual acts.[60]

The first prosecution under the draconian, *Butler*-inspired law barring sexual depictions of young people illustrates its dangerous overbreadth. Charged in the case was a twenty-six-year-old Toronto artist, Eli Langer, whose paintings and drawings were seized from the Mercer Union, one of Toronto's most respected artist-run galleries. The works portray both children and adults engaging in sexual behavior. Langer says his works were made not from models, but from his imagination. Moreover these paintings explore the impact of child sexual abuse. In response to pressure from the arts community, the government decided not to prosecute Langer.

Although the law banning sexual depictions of young people contains an exemption for works with artistic merit (as well as educational, scientific, or medical value), it puts the burden of proof on the accused. In light of the ten-year prison sentence and fines that could be opposed following a conviction, no doubt many serious artists, scientists, and others will avoid all sexual descriptions or depictions of people under eighteen. One wonders whether Shakespeare would have written *Romeo and Juliet* or whether Nabokov would have written *Lolita* had they faced such a law. And what of Judy Blume's novels about and for adolescents? (The law contains no special provision that would exempt any of these authors—or, in the case of deceased writers, anyone who continues to circulate their works—from its general terms.)

Unavailing Apologetics

The Canadian government's use of *Butler's* feminist anti-pornography analysis in a discriminatory and harassing fashion has been so blatant and persistent that even LEAF, which had worked with MacKinnon to promote that analysis, has been forced to recognize the great damage it has done. In June 1993, a group of LEAF leaders and anti-censorship activists met and issued a joint news release that "unanimously condemned the use of the *Butler* decision to justify discriminatory use of law to harass and intimidate lesbians and gays and sex trade workers." The LEAF signatories further conceded that "[s]ince . . . *Butler* . . . Canada Customs, some police forces . . . and some government funders have exploited obscenity law to harass bookstores, artists, and AIDS organizations, sex trade workers, and safe sex educators."[61]

In light of the abysmal experience with Canada's version of the feminist anti-pornography law, the law's feminist defenders have been unable to explain away its devastating impact on free speech and equality, on women and lesbians and gay men. As Leanne Katz remarked, "Nearly ten percent of *Only Words* is devoted to a rhapsodic analysis of *Butler's* acceptance of her ideology. Yet MacKinnon's book says not a word about the real life consequences of her Pyrrhic victory. Only words, indeed."[62]

When, in October 1993, I debated Kathleen Mahoney, the law professor who co-authored the LEAF brief in *Butler* (in collaboration with Catharine MacKinnon) and who argued LEAF's position in the Canadian Supreme Court, she conceded that *Butler* has been used discriminatorily to harass lesbian and gay publications, but, maintained that this fact was no basis for criticizing the ruling. Specifically, Mahoney argued that the post-*Butler* enforcement record simply reflected the pre-existing homophobia on the part of Canadian law enforcement authorities. She said: "We have as many homophobic police officers, I'm sure, as you do maybe even more, as well as customs officials. . . . [P]olice activity against gays . . . has always been going on."[63]

Of course. And it always will as long as they—or their feminist allies— keep coming up with new tools to play with.

Rather than condemning the Canadian attacks on feminist and lesbian publications, Dworkin and MacKinnon apparently condone at least some of them. Referring to the conviction of Glad Day Bookshop based on the short story in *Bad Attitude*, Dworkin declared: "Lesbian porn is an expression of self-hatred. . . . When it is trafficked in the world, it becomes a social reality, and the hatred that it spreads then is not [sic] longer a hatred only of self, but becomes a hatred of the group."[64] Likewise in a 1994 letter to the *New York Times*, MacKinnon wrote that, "maybe the publications" that had been targeted under *Butler* "do harm on the basis of sex. . . . [T]he *Bad Attitude* publication . . . contained sex between a young girl and a nurse-caretaker."[65]

Aside from apologizing for some of the Canadian censorship under *Butler*, Dworkin and MacKinnon have made three arguments we could expect if their anti-pornography law were to be enforced in the United States. First they sound their familiar and wrongheaded argument that the Canadian law that *Butler* interpreted is significantly different from their model law because it is criminal, rather than civil. Second, they note that some of the seizures by Canadian Customs have involved temporary detentions, rather than permanent confiscations. Third, they contend that the customs officials are following different standards from those laid down in *Butler*.[66] All three arguments are unsound.

Dworkin and MacKinnon's observation that some customs detentions of materials have "only" been temporary shows a similar failure to come to grips with reality. For all practical purposes, just as "justice delayed is justice denied," so too, delivery delayed is denied, especially when the materials in question are periodicals.[67] The Canadian press has reported that, under *Butler*, customs officials have seized and held magazines for weeks or months, often rendering them out-of-date and unsalable. In addition, books as well are made unsalable because they are returned in damaged condition. According to the Canadian anti-censorship organization CENSORSTOP, "Customs destructively treats materials seized, ranging from minor damages to 'accidental loss.'"[68]

Damaging as even a temporary customs detention may be, it is important to realize that many such "detentions" are in fact permanent, and thus amount to outright confiscations. Although detention decisions may be appealed, the rulings are seldom reversed unless there is a rash of adverse publicity—as there was, for example, concerning the seizures of Dworkin's books. The only alternative is court action, which is both expensive and slow. Since many booksellers cannot afford to mount such challenges, the ostensibly temporary detention, imposed by the importations bureaucracy, becomes a permanent ban.

Yet another reason why customs detentions have devastating consequences, unacknowledged by Dworkin and MacKinnon, is that these detentions have led to more self-censorship by Canadian booksellers. As reported by the Free Expression Project Human Rights Watch:

> A bureaucratic appeals process often deters even the most committed challengers. Rather than face costly delay and interference, retailers censor their own orders of books and videos, limiting anything remotely suspect. In doing so they limit their consumers' access to alternative viewpoints. . . . Even though magazines are supposed to be reviewed on an issue-by-issue basis, [bookstores] no longer buy the magazines that have been the subject of litigation or publicity. "*Bad Attitude* and *On Our Backs* [lesbian erotic magazines] have effectively been banned in Canada," said Janine Fuller [bookbuyer for Little Sisters bookstore]. Insidiously, *Butler* has also affected the number of titles bookstores order. "Where I used to buy thirty-six copies by a famous lesbian author," said Fuller, "I now order maybe two."[69]

Dworkin and MacKinnon similarly ignore reality when they assert that the customs seizures are carried out under an independent legal authority, not the *Butler* decision. The customs legislation on obscenity incorporates Canadian courts. After the *Butler* decision, Canadian government lawyers reviewed existing customs regulations to bring them into conformity with *Butler*, and found that the regulations did not need to be revised. Customs now has renewed carte blanche, not a new carte blanche.

What Have We Learned?

The enforcement record of the MacDworkinite anti-pornography law in Canada, and the consistent enforcement record of other censorial measures, teaches a clear lesson: women should beware of any such measure.

Any scheme for censoring would suppress many works that are valuable to women and feminists; would be enforced in a way that discriminates against the least popular, least powerful groups in our society, including feminists and lesbians; would perpetuate demeaning stereotypes about women, including that sex is bad for us; would perpetuate the disempowering notion that women are essentially victims; would harm women who voluntarily work in the sex industry; and would reinforce the political power of factions with a patriarchal agenda. By undermining free speech, censorship would deprive feminists of a powerful tool for advancing women's equality. Since sexual freedom and freedom for sexually explicit expression are essential aspects of human freedom, censoring such expression would undermine human rights more broadly.

In contrast to these significant costs that any pornography censorship scheme would impose on feminist goals, pro-censorship feminists rely on only one asserted benefit of such a scheme: that it would reduce violence and discrimination against women. This purported benefit is at best merely speculative.

Because reducing misogynistic discrimination and violence is so important, some feminists might be tempted to conclude that censorship would be justified by the possibility that it might advance this goal.

This point is highlighted by considering some other factors, aside from pornography, that are alleged to contribute to misogynistic discrimination and violence. These include women's improving legal and economic status, women's expanding sexual options, and the associated rise of the women's movement. Susan Faludi's *Backlash: The Undeclared War Against American Women* cites evidence that one of the causes of the 1980s backlash against the women's rights movement was women's increased employment outside the home, which has led to anxiety, depression, and loss of self-esteem among men.[70] Likewise, some research indicates that advances in women's rights may cause some male sexual aggression against women.[71] Furthermore, some feminist theorists and other scholars maintain that sexual assaults (as well as the consumption of pornography) have increased as a result of the women's movement and the misogynistic reactions that some men have to that movement. Andrea Dworkin herself has asserted this causal connection.[72]

Presumably Dworkin, as well as most other feminists, would resist any effort to curb advances in women's rights, even if that effort were premised on the rationale that advances in women's rights contribute to anti-female violence. This would be a clear case of cutting off one's nose to spite one's face. As we have seen, the same is true of censoring pornography.

In an apparent nod to the dearth of evidence that pornography causes the harm she ascribes to it, Catharine MacKinnon has attempted to bolster her censorial crusade by declaring, "There is no evidence that pornography does no harm."[73] In light of the appalling Canadian experience with MacKinnon's censorship scheme, and the other consequences of enforcement we have seen, her own phrase should be recast: "There is substantial evidence that censoring pornography does substantial harm."

Notes

1. Ellen Willis, "An Unholy Alliance," *New York Newsday*, February 25, 1992.

2. Audre Lorde, "The Master's Tools Will Never Dismantle the Master's House," in *Sister Outsider: Essays and Speeches* (San Francisco, 1984), 110–113.

3. George F. Will, "Pornography Scare," *Washington Post*, October 28, 1993.

4. Andrea Dworkin, *Our Blood: Prophecies and Discourses on Sexual Politics* (New York, 1976), 20.

5. Wendy McElroy, "The Unholy Alliance," *Liberty*, February 1993, 53.

6. Pete Hamill, "Women on the Verge of a Legal Breakdown," *Playboy*, January 1993, 189.

7. Alan Dershowitz, "What is Porn?" *ABA Journal*, November 1, 1986, 36.

8. Kenneth L. Karst, "Boundaries and Reasons: Freedom of Expression and the Subordination of Groups," *University of Illinois Law Review*, 1990, 103–104.

9. See Laurence H. Tribe, *American Constitutional Law*, 2nd ed. (Mineola, N.Y., 1988), 926–927. *Beauharnais v. Illinois*, 343 U.S. 250, 275 (1952) (dissenting).

10. Eric Stein, "History against Free Speech: The New German Law against the 'Auschwitz'—and Other—'Lies,'" *Michigan Law Review* 85 (November 1986), 286.

11. Sandra Coliver, "Hate Speech Laws: Do They Work?" in Sandra Coliver, ed., *Striking a Balance: Hate Speech, Free Speech, and Non-Discrimination* (Essex, England, 1992), 373–374.

12. Aryeh Neier, *Defending My Enemy* (New York, 1979), 155–157.

13. Nadine Strossen, "Regulating Racist Speech: A Modest Proposal?" *Duke Law Journal*, 1990, 554–555.

14. *Doe v. University of Michigan*, 721 F. Supp. 852 (E.D. Mich. 1989). The ACLU also successfully challenged a hate speech code at the University of Wisconsin. *UWM Post, Inc v. Board of Regents of University of Wisconsin System*, 774 F. Supp. 1163 (E.D. Wis. 1991).

15. *Wu v. University of Conn.* (No. Civ. H89–649 PCD) (D. Conn. 1989).

16. NOW-New York State, "Canada Sounds Death-Knell for Free Speech," press release, February 28, 1992.

17. Quoted in Mary Kay Blakely, "Is One Woman's Sexuality Another Woman's Pornography?" *Ms.*, April 1985, 37–38.

18. Anna Quindlen, "The Gag Rules," *New York Times*, October 7, 1992.

19. Quoted in Margaret A. Blanchard, "The American Urge to Censor: Freedom of Expression versus the Desire to Sanitize Society—From Anthony Comstock to 2 Live Crew," *William and Mary Law Review* 33 (1992), 766.

20. Ellen Chesler, *Woman of Valor: Margaret Sanger and the Birth Control Movement in America* (New York, 1992), 70.

21. *Ibid.*

22. Cited in Blanchard, "The American Urge to Censor," 766.

23. *Mutual Film Corp. v. Industrial Commission*, 236 U.S. 230 (1915). This decision was reversed by *Winters v. New York*, 333 U.S 507 (1948) and *Joseph Burstyn, Inc. v. Wilson*, 343 U.S. 495 (1952).

24. *Message Photo-Play Co. v. Bell*, 166 N.Y.S. 338 (1917).

25. Karst, "Boundaries and Reasons," 114, n. 79.

26. Mary Ware Dennett, *The Sex Side of Life: An Explanation for Young People* (New York, 1928).

27. *U.S. v. One Obscene Book Entitled "Married Love,"* 48 F. 2d 821 (S.D.N.Y. 1931).

28. Tamar Lewin, "Guam's Abortion Law Tested by A.C.L.U. Lawyer's Speech," *New York Times*, March 21, 1990.

29. Quindlen, "The Gag Rules."

30. Quoted in Tim Kingston, "Canada's New Porn Wars: 'Little Sister' Gay/Lesbian Bookstore Battles Canadian Customs," *San Francisco Bay Times*, November 4, 1993. Quoted in Tamar Lewin, "Canada Court Says Porn Harms Women," *New York Times*, February 28, 1992.

31. Elaine Carol, in *Ideas—Feminism and Censorship*, transcript from the Canadian Broadcasting Company (Toronto, 1993), 16.

32. Quoted in Rashida Dhooma, "Gay Demo Rakes Pornography Charges," *Toronto Sun*, n.d.

33. Quoted in Kingston, "Canada's New Porn Wars."

34. Ellen Flanders, in *Ideas—Feminism and Censorship*, 9.

35. Carl Wilson, "Northern Closure: Anti-Pornography Campaign in Canada," *Nation*, December 27, 1993, 788.

36. "Canada Customs Hits Feminist Stores and Others," *Feminist Bookstore News*, March/April 1993, 21.

37. Karen Busby, "LEAF and Pornography: Litigating on Equality and Sexual Representations," unpublished, 1993, 17.

38. Quoted in Camilla Gibb, "Project P Targets Lesbian Porn," *Quota*, May 1992, 5.

39. Trish Thomas, in *Ideas—Feminism and Censorship*, 15.

40. *Her Majesty The Queen against John Bruce Scythes, Thomas Frank Ivison, and Ontario Corporation #620704 Operating as Glad Day Bookshop, Inc.*, Ontario Court of Justice (Provincial Division), (February 16, 1993), C H. Paris, j.

41. *Glad Day Bookshop v. Deputy Minister of National Revenue for Customs and Excise* (DMVR), Ontario Court of Justice (General Division), (July 14, 1992).

42. Busby, "LEAF and Pornography," 17.

43. Chris Bearchell, "Gay Porn Is Getting Skinned Alive," *Toronto Star*, January 15, 1993.

44. Susan Ditta, in *Ideas—Feminism and Censorship*, 15.

45. *Ibid.*

46. Jacques Boivin, letter to Leanne Katz, November 17, 1993.

47. Brenda Cossman, in *Ideas—Feminism and Censorship*, 16.

48. Editorial, "Reading Between the Borderlines," *Toronto Globe and Mail*, June 30, 1992.

49. Pierre Berton, "How Otto Jelinek Guards Our Morals," *Toronto Star*, May 29, 1993.

50. Quoted in Bill Redden, "O for Christ's Sake Canada," *PDXS* (Portland, August 30–September 12, 1993).

51. Berton, "How Otto Jelinek Guards Our Morals."

52. "Canada Customs Hits Feminist Stores and Others." *Feminist Bookstore News*.

53. Redden, "O for Christ's Sake Canada."

54. Diane DiMassa, *Hothead Paisan: Homicidal Lesbian Terrorist* (San Francisco, 1993), 120–121.

55. Sara Scott, "Porn Police: Who Decides What to Ban at the Border," *Montreal Gazette*, April 14, 1993.

56. Mary Williams Walsh, "Chill Hits Canada's Pornography Law," *Los Angeles Times*, September 6, 1993.

57. Kingston, "Canada's New Porn Wars."

58. Leanne Katz, memo to Roz Udow, September 23, 1993. See also letter from

Catharine A. MacKinnon to Leanne Katz, November 11, 1993, expressing MacKinnon's disagreement with some aspects of Katz's description of the telephone call, but not the aspect described in the text.

59. Human Rights Watch Free Expression Project, *A Ruling Inspired by US Anti-Pornography Activists Is Used to Restrict Lesbian and Gay Publications in Canada*, February 1994, 8–9.

60. NCAC Working Group on Women, Censorship, and "Pornography," "MacKinnon/Dworkin 'Theories' Flunk Reality Test," press advisory, November 10, 1993; Mary Williams Walsh, "Chill Hits Canada's Porn Law," *Los Angeles Times*, September 6, 1993. Act of June 30, 1987, ch. 24, 1987 Statute of Canada 633 (Can.) sec. 139.(2) Sexual Offenses: exception. 1994 Tremear's Criminal Code Section 163.1.

61. LEAF, "Historic Gathering Condemns Targeting of Lesbian and Gay Materials and Sex Trade Workers," news release (Toronto, June 21, 1993).

62. NCAC Working Group on Women, Censorship, and "Pornography," "MacKinnon/Dworkin 'Theories' Flunk Reality Test."

63. Kathleen Mahoney, panel and group discussion at the Nineteenth Annual Olin Conference, Washington University, St. Louis, Mo., October 20, 1993.

64. Quoted in Kingston, "Canada's New Porn Wars."

65. Catharine MacKinnon, letter to *New York Times* opinion page editor Mitchel Levitas, January 1, 1994.

66. The three arguments were presented in the following: MacKinnon letter to Mitchel Levitas; MacKinnon answers to questions at National Press Club, November 22, 1993; Dworkin-MacKinnon press release, August 26, 1994; MacKinnon letter to Leanne Katz.

67. Attributed to William Ewart Gladstone, 1809–1898 in John Bartlett and Justin Kaplan, eds., *Bartlett's Familiar Quotations*, 16th ed. (Boston, 1992), 446.

68. CENSORSTOP, "Canada Customs Evades Little Sister's Trial Action . . . Again," press release, September 29, 1993.

69. Human Rights Watch, *A Ruling Inspired by U.S. Anti-Pornography Activists*, 9.

70. Susan Faludi, *Backlash: The Undeclared War Against American Women* (New York, 1991), 40–41.

71. Larry Baron and Murray A. Straus, "Sexual Stratification, Pornography, and Rape in the United States," in Neil M. Malamuth and Edward Donnerstein, eds., *Pornography and Sexual Aggression* (Orlando, Fla., 1984), 185, 205–206.

72. Faludi, *Backlash*, xxi; Jeffrey Weeks, *Sexuality and Its Discontents* (New York, 1986), 233; Alan Sobel, *Pornography: Marxism, Feminism, and the Future of Sexuality* (New Haven, Conn., 1986), 82, 84; Naomi Wolf, *The Beauty Myth: How the Images of Beauty Are Used Against Women* (New York, 1991); Andrea Dworkin, "Why So-Called Radical Men Love and Need Pornography," in Laura Lederer, ed., *Take Back the Night* (New York, 1980), 148, 153.

73. Catharine MacKinnon, *Only Words* (Cambridge, Mass., 1993), 37.

Norma Jean Almodovar

❦

For Their Own Good

The Results of the Prostitution Laws as Enforced by Cops, Politicians, and Judges

On May 25, 1998, headlines in the Los Angeles *Daily News* declared, "Mexico blasted in rape response":

Sexism and apathy have hindered Mexican police investigations into the cases of more than 100 women raped and killed in the border city of Ciudad Juarez, the federal human rights panel said Sunday.

The frequently grisly assaults, dating to 1993, have terrified residents of the industrial city south of El Paso, Texas. They fear a serial killer—or even copycat killers—may be on the loose. . . .

In an open letter Sunday to Chihuahua state officials, the National Human Rights Commission said the assumption by local officials that some of the victims were prostitutes had slowed investigations into the killings.

ANYONE CONCERNED WITH HUMAN RIGHTS SHOULD BE OUTRAGED AS THEY read the preceding article. It is unconscionable that there are law enforcement agents anywhere in the world who do not investigate the rapes and murders of some of its citizens because they may have been prostitutes. We, in the United States, are of course more concerned about our marginalized citizens and have passed laws against prostitution so we can protect our women from exploitation.

The laws that prohibit prostitution are enacted to protect our "basic human rights" and "preserve our dignity" for "our own good," and to prevent all women from being exploited, are they not?

That is the purpose of the laws, asserts Dr. Janice G. Raymond, co-executive director of "Coalition Against Trafficking in Women." In the Report to the Special Rapporteur she states:

> There may be a small number of women that 'choose' to enter prostitution. We do not doubt that some women say that they have chosen it, especially in public contexts orchestrated by the sex industry. In the same way, some people choose to take dangerous drugs such as heroin, under conditions they did not choose originally and might not choose now, if offered something different.
>
> However, even when some people choose to take dangerous drugs, we still recognize that drug use is harmful. In this situation, it is harm to the person, not the consent of the person, that is the governing standard. We cannot allow the sex industry, or even non-governmental organizations, to rationalize the existence of prostitution based on this opportunistic use of consent and deny the harm to women and girls. . . .
>
> Some treat prostitution as a personal choice, ignoring the sexual exploitation of prostitution while at the same time announcing that the worst thing about prostitution is stigmatization. But the worst thing about prostitution is its violation of and violence against women and children.
>
> While emphasizing the harm that is done to actual women and children in prostitution, we must also note that the sexual exploitation of prostitution is harmful to all women. The sexual violation of any women is the sexual degradation of all women. . . . Prostitution is a practice that violates the human dignity and integrity guaranteed to all persons in the Universal Declaration of Human Rights. This Declaration proclaims that all human persons are born free and equal in dignity and rights. Any form of sexual exploitation, including prostitution, abrogates this human dignity.

But what about women who, ungrateful to their more knowledgeable feminist sisters such as Dr. Raymond, do not accept the premise that their work in prostitution is a violation of their human dignity? As Broward County, Florida, NOW chapter president Shayna Moss so poignantly interpolates in the article below, it is the opinion of some feminists that prostitutes lose all rights if we continue to allow ourselves to be exploited.

> She calls herself "Jane Roe II" and says she was a prostitute for
> the rich and famous. . . . Now the Palm Beach County woman
> wants . . . to make prostitution legal. . . .
>
> She cites *Roe vs. Wade* and argues; If a woman has the right
> to an abortion, should not she also have the right to sell her
> body for sex? . . .
>
> Asked about Jane Roe II's argument linking abortion and
> prostitution, Shayna Moss, president of the Broward County,
> Fla. chapter of the National Organization for Women, says, I
> don't see a connection between the two. I don't think a hooker
> has rights.

It is widely accepted then, in reputable circles, that prostitutes are
without rights or standing before the law. It is therefore not much of a
stretch to conclude that our deaths are meaningless and it is not necessary
to expend the energy to investigate our murders. The following quotes
make it chillingly clear that those of us who choose for whatever reason to
engage in commercial sex are no longer considered a part of the human
race.

> These were "misdemeanor murders," biker women and hook-
> ers . . . sometimes we'd call them "NHI"—no humans involved.

> Since 1985 at least 45 women have been sexually assaulted
> and brutally murdered in San Diego County. These women, des-
> ignated by law enforcement as prostitutes, drug addicts and
> transients, have been associated with the police term, "NHI—no
> humans involved." NHI is an in house rhetorical discounting of
> crimes against individuals from marginalized sectors of our soci-
> ety. This nonhuman classification, as well as the personal in-
> volvement of police officers with a number of the victims, has
> hindered public awareness and a full-scale investigation of these
> murders.

If this is truly the conviction of our own law enforcement agencies and
feminist upholders of our human rights, how could we expect our neigh-
bors to the south to be more empathetic than we are toward raped and
murdered women who were probably nothing more than prostitutes? The
Mexican police who appeared negligent in their duties toward the one
hundred or so women raped and killed in the border city of Ciudad Juarez
are looking less and less culpable and barbaric, and more like our very own
police.

Articles chronicling police abuses toward prostitutes appear with alarming frequency. If viewed individually, it is easy to dismiss each abuse as an aberration, perhaps out of character for the police. However when viewed with other such incidents occurring nationally, it is impossible not to see a pattern of abuse. And it is impossible not to draw the conclusion that the laws that are supposed to protect women from the "exploitation" and degradation of prostitution are abused by those who are supposed to uphold them.

Exactly what behavior is requisite to nullify a woman's rights so she is no longer considered "human"? In most states, prostitution is "any lewd act for money or other consideration." "Lewd" is defined as the touching of male genitalia and buttocks and female genitalia and breasts for the purpose of sexual arousal and gratification. Early American case law had a much broader definition of prostitution. A woman offering her body for sexual intercourse for hire or for indiscriminate sexual intercourse without hire was also legally a prostitute (or non-human).

Of course it is no longer an exclusively female crime; men can and are being prosecuted for prostitution, although the number of arrests of male prostitutes is disproportionately less than female prostitutes. There are several reasons for this. First, because it is considered less of a social problem than female prostitution, and second, because male police officers are reluctant to pose as homosexuals and potential customers of male hustlers. These law enforcement agents have no similar compunctions about posing as customers of female prostitutes and, in some cases, having sex with them prior to arresting them.

At the beginning of the twenty-first century, the unresolved issues of self-determination and human sexuality that have torn our nation apart remain far from resolution. While we wage verbal war with ourselves over who is a victim and what constitutes degradation, women's lives are being destroyed by police officers who have the power to arrest them for choosing to accept money from men with whom they voluntarily engage in sexual acts that are not inherently illegal. This unequivocal opportunity to exert control over some women's lives results in the most heinous and inhumane victimization of an invisible segment of society, prostitutes. The police, usually male, vagariously decide which woman will get arrested on any particular day and which woman will go to jail, based only on the willingness of the woman to cooperate with the law enforcement agent entrusted to protect her from being exploited.

Unquestionably there is a split in the women's movement over the issue of prostitution and pornography. Some feminists are even willing to abridge the First Amendment in order to prevent the production of sexually explicit material. Since prostitution is already illegal in most states, there is even a movement to link the constitutionally protected speech of pornography with illegal prostitution in order to prohibit it. There are some very angry women who truly believe that it is acceptable to abrogate the freedom of other women to prevent a greater harm to women as a whole.

Yet these very same women champion a woman's right to "choice" as long it is abortion that is being discussed. If indeed a woman has a right to "choice," there must be some fundamental reason that one can make that claim. Without a sound underlying premise or axiom for one's postulation-argument, no claim of rights can be established which cannot be invalidated by another group making its own proclamation.

Prostitution (and pornography) must be considered the same issue for feminists as abortion. It is the right to choice. The right for a woman to control her own sexuality, with whom she will have sex, when, and under what circumstances.

The concept of "self-ownership" coincides with the concept of liberty (ostensibly the underlying principle in the formation of our country), and seems to fit the bill as a suitable foundation for making such an argument. If you "own" your own body, certainly you can choose to do what you will with it, and since slavery was abolished in this country, no individual or group can claim that someone's body (life) arbitrarily belongs to anyone else.

If one claims the "self-ownership" premise to establish the argument that a woman has the right to choose an abortion, then the perimeters of the concept "choice" cannot be limited to abortion. Either an individual has a right to "choice," defined as the act of "deciding," which includes any and all options—good, bad, moral or immoral—available to an individual, or the claim to the right to choice is baseless and therefore meaningless.

If pro-choice advocates claim the right to choose, based on no other premise than they have the right to choose, it is equally acceptable for anti-abortion advocates to state that no such rights exist and pass laws that support their assertion.

Some feminists maintain that pornography and prostitution are degrading and harmful to all women and justify their desire to abolish these things as a means to protect women from being exploited. If such arguments to prohibit the choices voluntarily made by some women have any validity at all, then anti-abortion activists could assert the same claims regarding the degrading and emotionally deleterious effects that abortion has on women and demand that women be protected from such harm through the prohibition of abortion.

I cannot deny that some women and girls—perhaps even quite a few—are in prostitution against their will. Further some prostitutes may find the work emotionally taxing or disagreeable and may have violent confrontations with their clients or their pimps. Some of these lamentable conditions are shared by women who are in violent noncommercial relationships and abusive marriages; those who are forced to work in sweatshops or to clean toilets; those who are sexually exploited by their boss; and generally anyone who is in a personal relationship or working situation which is not of their choosing. Nevertheless it would be imprudent to suggest that society resolve the unpleasantness of any coercive situation by prohibiting the basic activity such as marriage or relationships, clothing manufacturing, janitorial professions, or the coed workplace.

The threat of arrest and all that accompanies it, including extortion and forced sex with the police, is more emotionally damaging than the exchange of money for otherwise lawful activity. So long as the sex is consensual it should not matter to anyone outside the relationship how many times the sexual activity occurs, or with how many sexual partners, or for whatever mutually agreed upon price. If mutual agreement is not present in any relationship, there already exists an abundance of applicable laws specifically relating to coercion. Laws against prostitution are extraneous and do not protect women from anything.

Since the laws prohibiting prostitution were first enacted at the turn of the twentieth century, there has been a collusion between the police officers, judges, politicians, pimps, and madams, in which the enforcement of the law depends upon the cooperation of the players. In exchange for extorted sex, money, and information from the prostitutes or their agents, the police and the courts will turn a blind eye to the illegal activities.

For some women failure to continue to cooperate with the police can result in an early death, as seems to be the case with Donna Gentile, a street prostitute and police informant in San Diego. Gentile grew weary of being extorted by the cops and blew the whistle on those who demanded free sex and information from her. For her efforts the cops who had been involved in the sex and extortion scheme were fired and demoted, and her body was later found beaten and strangled; the killer or killers have not been caught. Others, like Alex, the Beverly Hills Madam, maintain their lucrative business with the full knowledge and consent of the LAPD, as long as they remain informants. In Madam Alex's case, when she outlived her usefulness to the police after twenty years, she was arrested. However her defense was her status as a valuable police informant, and with the witnesses and evidence she produced for the judge, she successfully avoided going to prison under the mandatory sentencing law.

Why the disparity in enforcement? Why permit some prostitutes to continue to be exploited as long as they cooperate with the police? If encouraging prostitution is, as former chief Los Angeles prosecutor Ira Reiner claims, worse than rape or robbery in terms of its emotional impact upon the victim, why be lenient with some panderers because they provide valuable information? What possible information gathered from pimps and panderers could be so valuable that law enforcement agents would allow the continued exposure of unsuspecting young women to a lifetime of shame and degradation which robs them of their bodily integrity, personal privacy, self-respect, and reputation?

District Attorney Ira Reiner further alleges that, whereas rape is accomplished by one act of force, pandering can cause a woman to be pressured into an endless series of acts of indiscriminate sexual intercourse which progressively rape her spirit, character, and self-image. Unlike rape, pandering is a cold-blooded, calculating profit-seeking criminal enterprise. He concludes: It is clearly a vicious practice.

He fails to mention that indiscriminate sexual intercourse without the exchange of money or other consideration is not a crime, nor is arranging it against the law. One can conclude that multiple indiscriminate sexual encounters have no significant impact upon women as long as no money is exchanged. Shame and degradation are the only possible results for the victim brazen enough to charge for it. If a woman gives it away for free, there is no problem and no crime. The government cares not if a woman loses her reputation. Let her charge for sex and the government will be right there to take the money away from her in the form of fines and jail sentences and give her a criminal record to boot. This will absolve the shame from her act?

This prostitute-as-victim theory now so deeply imbedded into law, which is espoused by so-called feminists such as Catharine MacKinnon and Andrea Dworkin, involves the irrational belief that all women except for themselves and their peers are inherently incapable of self-determination and need "big sister" protection. This protection is not from men who would exploit women for "free," but from men who know their value and pay them accordingly. How are women protected by being led to jail in handcuffs and having their freedom taken away?

And though the law is gender neutral, it is almost always the woman who is prosecuted, fined, and imprisoned. Here feminists agree with us; male prostitutes do not get arrested in the same numbers or with the frequency and intensity that female prostitutes do. They pat us on the head and insist that they do not want the police to continue to arrest us, only our customers. This proposal is so patently absurd that one wonders if its promoters could have given any thought to the obvious flaws of such a policy.

Would the police be required to arrest all clients of prostitutes, or only those potential customers of streetwalkers they can entrap through the use of police decoys, leaving alone the vast number of customers who use the services of call girls, escorts, and massage therapists?

If police are expected to arrest every customer, the question arises, how would this be possible? The police have not yet been successful in arresting and incarcerating every prostitute (to prevent them from being exploited). This is surprising considering all the legal advantages the police have with ever-increasing criminal penalties; major technological advances in surveillance; court decisions and laws which permit all manner of otherwise unconstitutional statutes; police behavior such as legalized entrapment and being able to arrest someone for merely possessing the "intent to commit prostitution"; and being legally permitted to have sex with a suspected prostitute.

There must be at least ten customers for every prostitute or a prostitute cannot earn a living. Multiply the number of suspected prostitutes around the world by ten, throw in a few more one-time-only clients and without coming close to the actual number of customers, it becomes apparent that unless the police are willing to lock up any able-bodied male with a dollar in his pocket, it would not be possible to arrest every customer. Thus the police would be left in the untenable position of selectively enforcing the law.

So how will they decide which customers to arrest? An arbitrary enforcement policy leads to predictable police behavior—extortion, coercion, and intimidation. No longer able to threaten to arrest the prostitute if she fails to cooperate and give the nice officer sex, money, or information, the police instead threaten to arrest her clients if she fails to cooperate. Naturally it would not be to her advantage to have her clients arrested, so, with her livelihood still at stake, she necessarily capitulates to the officers' demands. Lest one think that this scenario is implausible, one need only review the plethora of news articles from the turn of the last century to the present, in which police and other law enforcement officials have been caught with their pants down, literally.

Should police departments reallocate their scarce resources and, at the expense of domestic violence cases, rapes, assaults, robberies, homicides, and other violent crimes, deploy officers to arrest the nonviolent clients of prostitutes when no complaint against them has been made?

Apparently this is already the policy of the Los Angeles Police Department in regard to the arrest of prostitutes. Enforcement of the prostitution laws in Los Angeles has escalated since former Police Chief Willie Williams retired.

In a letter dated October 10, 1997, responding to an editorial piece in the *Los Angeles Times* written by COYOTE attorney Edward Tabash, Los Angeles Police Chief Bernard C. Parks argues his case for the continued criminalization of prostitution:

> In response to your article in the *Los Angeles Times* regarding the legalization of prostitution, I would like to address some issues that are of concern to me. . . .
>
> It is estimated that 95 percent of all prostitutes who work in the City of Los Angeles are working for a pimp or madam. These individuals (the prostitutes) earn only a small part (approximately 20 percent) of the income derived from their prostitution activities. Those who exploit prostitutes prey on the young males and females who are vulnerable to the controlling influence of drugs and physical/sexual abuse. The average age of a person—male or female—who becomes involved in prostitution is 15 to 18 years old. By the time these individuals reach the age of 25 to 30, they are of marginal use to their pimps or madams and are no longer employable. With no skills, they often become involved in other illegal activity or survive on the largess of society. . . .
>
> It has been shown statistically that there is a direct correlation between prostitution and other serious crimes in areas where high levels of streetwalking prostitution are allowed to occur.
>
> I would like to point out that laws prohibiting prostitution are not merely . . . to protect women from being exploited by pimps and panderers. Laws are generally enacted to deter people from certain behavior which society deems contrary to its quality of life. . . .
>
> Whether one advocates arresting and incarcerating prostitutes to protect them from exploitation or because their conduct is offensive to society, the undeniable fact remains that the act itself is indicative of a greater problem that will not be solved by approving the practice.

His two-page letter concludes, "I appreciate your opinion and hope this correspondence will assist you in understanding the position of the Los Angeles Police Department." Interestingly the arguments he offers for the continued criminalization of prostitution are chapter and verse the arguments made in the Robert Ferguson book *The Nature of Vice Control in the Administration of Justice*, used in police training courses throughout the country.

The sad thing is that none of the arguments justify the continued use of valuable scarce resources to arrest and incarcerate men and women who work as prostitutes or their clients, unless and until other crimes are committed which violate the rights of others through the use of force, the threat of force, or fraud.

Those prostitutes who are truly the victims of violence within their work environment are denied access to help because they are outside the law. Furthermore, help is not available because the police department is too busy making prostitution arrests of women who are not 15 to 18; have no pimp; do not work on the streets; keep all the money they make (except for that which they have to pay to attorneys to defend themselves); do not have drug habits; are not abused by anyone other than the police officers who demand sexual favors or money from them; and are not committing any other "criminal activity."

Although the "estimates" and assertions made by Chief Parks are wholly and incredibly inaccurate, let us examine each as if it were true. These claims are fairly typical of all of the arguments made by those who do not want prostitution decriminalized.

First, Police Chief Parks alleges that "95 percent of all prostitutes who work in the City of Los Angeles are working for a pimp or madam." Even if it were true that we all worked with pimps or madams (which we do not), it does not justify arresting us. The coercion which sometimes exists in the prostitute's relationship with a pimp or madam can be dealt with without making prostitution illegal. When the Mafia takes over the docks, the police do not arrest the dock workers for unloading the ships. Similarly, there is no reason to arrest prostitutes when we are victimized by pimps. When prostitutes are exiled from the benefits of the legal system the violence they face increases.

Coercion is not inherent to the profession of prostitution but is a result of criminalization. Just as the drug trade has been made much more violent by the war on drugs the prostitutes' trade has been made more violent by the war on prostitution. Manufacturing alcohol was a violent profession during prohibition but is not so today when the sale of alcohol is legal. In the United States where selling drugs is illegal, drug selling is a violent profession. In Holland, where selling many drugs is de facto legal, drug sellers are mild-mannered shop owners.

Second, Police Chief Parks states that "These individuals (the prostitutes) earn only a small part (approximately 20 percent) of the income derived from their prostitution activities"—meaning that pimps and madams supposedly take 80 percent of the monies that we make. To the extent that this argument is true it makes a good case for legalization or decriminalization so that prostitutes could more easily choose their managers in a competitive marketplace. But what exactly is this argument supposed to prove? If prostitutes kept 80 percent of their income and paid only 20 percent to their pimps and madams would Chief Parks stop arresting them? In what way is the prostitute helped by arresting him or her for only keeping 20 percent of his or her earnings? Will Chief Parks next be examining the wages of models, realtors, or auto salespeople to see how much of their income they pay to their managers?

Third, Chief Parks declares, "Those who exploit prostitutes prey on the young males and females who are vulnerable to the controlling influence of drugs and physical/sexual abuse." It would seem that he has not heard that there are counterparts to those predators in sports and show business, to name only two, and that drug use is prevalent in those professions. Has he never heard of the casting couch on which vulnerable young men and women, arriving fresh off the Greyhound buses from farming communities in the Midwest, are exploited by unscrupulous people who demand sexual favors in exchange for movie and television roles? Should we criminalize sports and show business to prevent potential exploitation or possible drug use? Are prostitutes more deserving of protection than the vulnerable young people who want to enter those professions?

And what about the horrible abuse that occurs in some marriages, including within the marriages of many police officers? Should prostitutes be protected from such potential abuse but not wives? Would anyone suggest that spousal abuse is less of a problem for women than the abuse that might occur in a prostitute-client relationship? If prohibition of prostitution is a proven effective method to protect women, should we not support the criminalization of marriage as a way to combat the social scourge of spousal abuse? And, if we advocate the arrest of prostitutes' customers for no other reason than that they are customers and therefore are violating our human dignity, would it not be prudent to arrest husbands who do not abuse their wives and have never shown a propensity to violence, on the outside chance that they might someday hit their spouse in a fit of anger?

In his fourth point, Parks continues, "The average age of a person—male or female—who becomes involved in prostitution is 15 to 18 years old." Surely he is aware that there are already laws which would allow the police to arrest the adult individual who has sex with a minor, regardless of money involved. How does it help the cases of fifteen- to eighteen-year-olds to arrest adults in their twenties, thirties, and forties who are working as prostitutes? Would it not be more effective to utilize scarce police resources to pursue those who hire underage people? The argument that arresting adult prostitutes discourages clients from engaging in sex with minors is ludicrous. Men who want to have sex with minors are not interested in hiring someone in their twenties or beyond.

Fifth, Parks asserts, "By the time these individuals reach the age of 25 to 30, they are of marginal use to their pimps or madams and are no longer employable." Most of the people who are being arrested for prostitution are well into their adulthood, and well past the age at which it is alleged we are "no longer employable" in our profession. Turning again to the similarities in sports, the majority of athletes have a very short term career after which they are of marginal use to their manager or team. Would anyone suggest that all those who have become unemployable as a result of their age, physical disabilities, or other condition outside of their control be incarcerated?

Sixth, "With no skills, they often become involved in other illegal activity or survive on the largess of society." Again this is an argument for decriminalization. By giving us an arrest record for prostitution, we are virtually guaranteed to be unemployable when we want to leave the profession. It is the criminalization of prostitution, not the profession itself, which can lead to difficulties when a prostitute retires. Moreover Parks's argument proves too much. When middle-aged women get divorced—those who married young, have several children, and did not pursue a higher education—many have no job skills, do not have the youth and looks that are required by today's job market, and are forced to "survive on the largess of society." Should we arrest women if they have no job skills; if they get divorced and become a financial drain on society; or if they are abused by their spouses and seek outside help? Should we prohibit them from getting married in the first place, a relationship that can lead directly to the above scenario?

As a seventh statement, Parks maintains, "It has been shown statistically that there is a direct correlation between prostitution and other serious crimes in areas where high levels of streetwalking prostitution are allowed to occur." It is not clear if Chief Parks is talking about other countries when he states "where high levels of streetwalking prostitution are allowed to occur," because streetwalking and other forms of prostitution are illegal in California, thus they are never "allowed" to occur. If he is referring to the crime statistics in other countries where it is lawfully permitted to occur, he should check the facts before making such statements.

Let's re-state the above argument with a few minor changes. "It has been shown statistically that there is a direct correlation between bank robberies and other serious white collar crimes in areas where banks are allowed to exist." Or how about: "It has been shown statistically that there is a direct correlation between hold-ups and other serious crimes in areas where there are liquor stores and 7-11's." If we were to close down banks, we would not have to worry about any bank-related crimes. Closing 7-11 and liquor stores would eliminate most convenience-store related crimes, too. It is irrational to continue to criminalize prostitution because of the ancillary crimes that occur solely because prostitution is illegal.

Next Parks argues, "Laws are generally enacted to deter people from certain behavior which society deems contrary to its quality of life." "Quality of life" is a subjective concept and the least impressive argument for the continued harassment, arrest, and incarceration of a group of people who are trying to improve their quality of life by earning a living. The current enforcement of prostitution laws goes well beyond any justifiable prevention or expurgation of inappropriate public activity which would concern "society." Sting operations such as the one conducted by a consortium of law enforcement agencies to arrest Heidi Fleiss and her employees do not result in an improved "quality of life" for anyone other than the officers who get to ogle semi-naked women, drink alcohol while on the job, rent fancy hotel rooms, and order expensive room service. No one is safer because Heidi Fleiss or anyone like her is behind bars.

Parks concludes, "Whether one advocates arresting and incarcerating prostitutes to protect them from exploitation or because their conduct is offensive to society, the undeniable fact remains that the act itself is indicative of a greater problem that will not be solved by approving the practice." Neither, of course, is it solved by the continued incarceration of prostitutes. "Society" does not have to approve of a practice in order for it not to be a crime. Does "society" approve of homosexuality, abortion, or divorce? Undoubtedly many parts of "society" do not but in most of the United States homosexuality, abortion, and divorce are not and should not be illegal.

Not that long ago laws prohibiting homosexuality were actively, though selectively, enforced. Well-meaning people believed that a stint behind bars would convince homosexuals to modify their offensive, immoral behavior. Usually the arrest and subsequent incarceration destroyed the life of the individual, but it was for his or her own good, not to mention the good of the collective sensibilities of "society." The question is, who determines whose values, opinions, and preferences become law in this "society"? Who decides what is offensive to us all? If there is a sufficient number of people who do not like gays, and there are, and they are vocal enough, should we return to incarcerating homosexuals because they offend "society"? If there are enough born-again Christians to whom abortion is offensive and contradictory to their Christian beliefs, is it appropriate to once again criminalize women for terminating the lives of their unborn babies? Should divorce be illegal?

When private acts, like the ones mentioned above involving consenting adults, are criminalized, the police are forced to resort to intrusive and often unconstitutional methods to garner an arrest and obtain a conviction. Further, the laws regulating adult human sexuality are so difficult to enforce without using selective prosecution, that many states have repealed most so-called moral laws against sodomy and oral copulation. The California Constitution explicitly grants an "absolute right to privacy," and accords to its citizens that as long as no coercion is involved, any private consenting adult activity is none of the government's business—except when private activity involves money.

It would seem the government believes that money is the root of all evil, particularly if the government thinks it is not getting any of it.

In order to combat the "evils" of prostitution, law enforcement agents needed more effective "legislative tools." Thanks to the proliferation of prostitutes' rights organizations, prostitutes were becoming far too savvy. They knew what a police officer was legally permitted to do and what he could not do to make an arrest. So, a few years ago in California, a law was enacted that amended the penal code to allow a police officer to "legally entrap" a person suspected of prostitution. The nickname for the new law was the "use a smile, go to prison" law, because the law states "A person agrees to engage in an act of prostitution when, with specific intent to so engage, he or she manifests an acceptance of an offer or solicitation to so engage, regardless of whether the offer or solicitation was made by a person who also possessed the specific intent to engage in prostitution." No longer are words necessary to commit this crime of which the prostitute is the "victim." Facial expressions such as smiling or winking, or even body gestures are sufficient to violate the law.

And if that law was not adequate to make an arrest, a new law went into effect on January 1, 1996, that gave police unlimited power to arrest anyone they suspect of "possessing the intent" to commit prostitution. Liberal Democrat State Assemblyman Richard Katz's law made it a misdemeanor to "loiter in any public place in a manner and under circumstances manifesting the purpose and with the intent to commit prostitution." It is now a crime to harbor thoughts about breaking the law without actually violating the law. According to the law's author, "It is the intent of the Legislature to assist law enforcement in controlling prostitution related activities and to minimize the adverse effect these activities have upon local communities." The legislature finds and determines that loitering for the purposes of engaging in a prostitution offense constitutes a public nuisance which, if left unabated, adversely affects a community's image, public safety, and residential and business development, and tends to encourage further criminal activity. Furthermore, prostitution-related activities consume an inordinate amount of limited law enforcement resources. So, in order to reduce the expense of actually having to catch someone in the act of soliciting for an act of prostitution, the legislature wants the cops to be able to circumvent our constitutional rights and arrest us for merely possessing an intent to break the law.

The law defines "loitering" as "to delay or linger without a lawful purpose for being on the property and for the purpose of committing a crime as opportunity may be discovered." A "public place" is defined as an area "open to the public or exposed to public view and includes streets, sidewalks, bridges, alleys, plazas, parks, driveways, parking lots, automobiles, whether moving or not, and buildings open to the general public, including those which serve food or drink or provide entertainment, and the doorways and entrances to buildings or dwellings and the grounds enclosing them."

The law further states that "among the circumstances" that can be considered in determining whether a person loiters with the intent to commit prostitution are:

> (1) The person repeatedly beckons to, stops, engages in conversations with or attempts to stop or engage in conversations with passersby.
>
> (2) Repeatedly stops or attempts to stop motor vehicles by hailing the drivers, waving arms or making any other bodily gestures, or engages or attempts to engage the drivers or passengers of the motor vehicles in conversation. [An innocent "Hi, how are you, can you help me fix my car? I need a ride to a service station," becomes criminal conversation.]
>
> (3) Has been convicted of violating this section, subdivision (a) or (b) of Section 647, or any other offense relating to or involving prostitution within five years of the arrest under this section.
>
> (4) Circles an area in a motor vehicle and repeatedly beckons to, contacts, or attempts to contact or stop pedestrians or other motorists. [Is one breaking the law if they are looking for a parking space—go around the block a couple of times, stop and ask someone in a parked car if they are leaving?]
>
> (5) Loiters in an area that is known for prostitution activity.

(6) Has engaged, within six months prior to the arrest under this section, in any behavior described in this subdivision, with the exception of paragraph (3), or in any other behavior indicative of prostitution activity. [Which means, they can arrest you for the intent, and then, arrest you later because they arrested you before.]

If the above law were applied to any group of people other than prostitutes, undoubtedly the ACLU and other civil rights organizations would protest loudly. But the voices of these tireless defenders are strangely silent. Could it be that they believe some "anti-decrim" activists who allege that "most prostitutes" do not want prostitution legalized or decriminalized? Do they actually believe that anyone would prefer to go to jail than to work as a prostitute? Anyone who contends that we do should spend a few hours behind bars and rethink this nonsense. Do these busybody feminists believe that it is necessary to erode the constitutional rights of all members of society just to get us prostitutes to quietly accept their protection and shuffle off to jail where we will realize how exploited we are when we accept money for what we could otherwise legally give away?

Most prostitutes do not want to get arrested and go to jail. But as long as prostitution remains illegal, for whatever reason, the police will continue to take away our freedom. That is why the laws must change. Most activists within the prostitutes' rights movement favor a decriminalized system rather than a legalized one. Legalization is a system whereby the state regulates, taxes, and licenses whatever form of prostitution is legalized, and often involves the establishment of special government agencies to deal with prostitution. It means that the government enacts new laws that put the control of prostitution in the hands of the police or the state. The police department (or the criminal justice system) has no business running or regulating prostitution, any more than it should run restaurants or grocery stores or the movie industry. These are all businesses, subject to business regulations, and under civil authority. Prostitution is a business, a service industry. It should be run as a business, subject only to the same kinds of business laws and regulations as other businesses.

Decriminalization would allow this to happen. It would repeal all existing criminal codes from noncoercive adult commercial sex activity, and related areas, such as management and personal relationships. It would involve no new legislation to deal with prostitution per se, because there are already plenty of laws which cover problems such as fraud, force, theft, negligence, and collusion. Those laws could be enforced against anyone who violated them, just as they are now, when force of fraud is used in any other profession. As Priscilla Alexander points out in "California NOW, Working on Prostitution," "decriminalization offers the best chance for women who are involved in prostitution to gain some measure of control over their work. It would also make it easier to prosecute those who abuse prostitutes either physically or economically, because the voluntary, nonabusive situations would be left alone."

A woman's body belongs to her and not to the government. The U.S. Constitution is the supreme law of the land, and we believe that the Constitution protects the individual's rights to own, use, and enjoy his or her body in any manner that he or she deems appropriate, as long as the rights of others are not violated. Everyone has a right to make moral decisions about his or her life and property (including the use of his or her body) that others may find disagreeable, disgusting, or immoral.

Until we return the control of all individual choices to the individual, the presumably unintended consequences of protectionist legislation will be the continued victimization of those the laws were designed to protect. The devastation to the lives of those unfortunate enough to be "protected" by the law enforcement officers charged with upholding the law is enormous and should outrage anyone who claims to be concerned with the well-being of the "less fortunate." As Peter McWilliams said in his book, *Ain't Nobody's Business If You Do*, "What the enforcement of laws against consensual activities does to the individuals is nothing short of criminal. The government is destroying the very lives of the people it is supposedly helping and saving."

Whether or not we as individuals find the notion of prostitution repugnant, immoral, sexist, or degrading, it is not in the best interest of women to continue to allow the use of the criminal justice system to remedy so-called social ills. Jerome Lawrence and Robert E. Lee—authors of *Inherit the Wind*, wrote these lines, "I say that you cannot administer a wicked law impartially. You can only destroy. You can only punish. I warn you that a wicked law, like cholera, destroys everyone it touches—its upholders as well as its defilers." The prohibitions against prostitution are wicked laws. For the sake of all women, we must repeal them.

Martha C. Nussbaum

❁

Whether from Reason or Prejudice
Taking Money for Bodily Services

> Taking leave of Binod, Durga slowly, deliberately walks towards the shack of Sukhlal the contractor, who stared at her even yesterday and flashed ten-rupee notes.
>
> What else can one do, she argues to herself, except fight for survival? The survival of oneself, one's loved ones, and the hopes that really matter.
>> —Manik Bandyopadhyay, *A Female Problem at a Low Level* (1963)

> If the story is about the peasant wife selling her body, then one must look for the meaning of that in the reality of peasant life. One can't look at it as a crisis of morality, in the sense one would in the case of a middle-class wife.
>> —Manik Bandyopadhyay, *About This Author's Perspective* (1957)[1]

ALL OF US, WITH THE EXCEPTION OF THE INDEPENDENTLY WEALTHY AND THE unemployed, take money for the use of our bodies.[2] Professors, factory workers, lawyers, opera singers, prostitutes, doctors, legislators—we all do things with parts of our bodies, for which we receive a wage in return.[3] Some people get good wages and some do not; some have a relatively high degree of control over their working conditions and some have little control; some have many employment options and some have very few. And some are socially stigmatized and some are not.

The stigmatization of certain occupations may be well founded, based on convincing well-reasoned arguments. But it may also be based on class prejudice or stereotypes of race or gender. Stigma may also change rapidly, as these background beliefs and prejudices change. Adam Smith, in *The Wealth of Nations*, writes that there are "some very agreeable and beautiful talents" that are admirable so long as no pay is taken for them, "but of which the exercise for the sake of gain is considered, whether from reason or prejudice, as a sort of publick prostitution." For this reason, he continues, opera singers, actors, and dancers must be paid an "exorbitant" wage to compensate them for the stigma involved in using their talents "as the means of subsistence." "Should the publick opinion or prejudice ever alter with regard to such occupations," he concludes, "their pecuniary recompence would quickly diminish."[4] Smith was not altogether right about the opera market, but his discussion is revealing for what it shows us about stigma.[5] Today few professions are more honored than that of opera singer; yet only two hundred years ago that public use of one's body for pay was taken to be a kind of prostitution. Looking back at that time, we now think that the judgments and emotions underlying the stigmatization of singers were irrational and objectionable, like prejudices against members of different classes and races. Nor do we see the slightest reason to suppose that the unpaid artist is a purer and truer artist than the paid artist. We think it entirely right and reasonable that high art should receive a high salary. If a producer of opera should take the position that singers should not be paid—on the grounds that receiving money for the use of their talents involves an illegitimate form of commodification and even market alienation of those talents—we would think that this producer was a slick exploiter, out to make a profit from the ill treatment of vulnerable and impressionable artists.[6] On the whole we think that, far from cheapening or ruining talents, the presence of a contract guarantees conditions within which the artist can develop.[7]

It is widely believed, however, that taking money or entering into contracts in connection with the use of one's sexual and reproductive capacities is genuinely bad. Feminist arguments about prostitution, surrogate motherhood, and even marriage contracts standardly portray financial transactions in the area of female sexuality as demeaning to women and as involving a damaging commodification and market alienation of women's sexual and reproductive capacities.[8] The social meaning of these transactions is said to be both that these capacities are turned into objects for the use and control of men and also that the activities themselves are being turned into commodities, and thereby robbed of the type of value they have at their best.

One question we shall have to face is whether these descriptions of our current judgments and intuitions are correct. But even if they are, what does this tell us? Many things and people have been stigmatized in our nation's history, often for very bad reasons. An account of the actual social meaning of a practice is therefore just a door that opens onto the large arena of moral and legal evaluation. It invites us to raise Smith's question: are these current beliefs the result of reason or prejudice? Can they be defended by compelling moral arguments? And, even if they can, are these the type of moral argument that can form a basis for a legal restriction? Smith, like his Greek and Roman Stoic forebears, understood that the evaluations that ground emotional responses and ascriptions of social meaning in a society are frequently corrupt—deformed by self-interest, resentment, and mere unthinking habit. The task he undertook, in *The Theory of Moral Sentiments*, was to devise procedures and strategies of argument through which one might separate the rationally defensible emotions from the irrational and prejudiced. In so proceeding, Smith and the Stoics were correct. Social meaning does no work on its own: it offers an invitation to normative moral and political philosophy.

Here we will investigate the question of sexual "commodification" by focusing on the example of prostitution.[9] I shall argue that a fruitful debate about the morality and legality of prostitution should begin from a broader analysis of our beliefs and practices with regard to taking pay for the use of the body and from a broader awareness of the options and choices available to poor working women. The former inquiry suggests that at least some of our beliefs about prostitution are as irrational as the beliefs Smith reports about singers; it will therefore help us to identify the elements in prostitution that are genuinely problematic. Most, though not all, of the genuinely problematic elements turn out to be common to a wide range of activities engaged in by poor working women. The second inquiry will suggest that many of women's employment choices are so heavily constrained by poor options that they are hardly choices at all. This should bother us. The fact that a woman with plenty of choices becomes a prostitute should not bother us, provided that there are sufficient safeguards against abuse and disease, safeguards of a type that legalization would make possible.

The most urgent issue raised by prostitution is that of employment opportunities for working women and their control over the conditions of their employment. The legalization of prostitution, far from promoting the demise of love, is likely to make things a little better for women who have too few options to begin with.[10] The really helpful thing for feminists to ponder, if they deplore the nature of these options, will be how to provide more options for these women, through education, skills training, and job creation. These unsexy topics are insufficiently addressed by feminist philosophers in the United States, but they are inevitable in any practical project dealing with real-life prostitutes and their female children.[11] This suggests that at least some of our feminist theory may be insufficiently grounded in the reality of working-class lives, and too focused on sexuality as an issue in its own right, as if it could be extricated from the fabric of poor people's attempts to survive.

Why were opera singers stigmatized? Two common cultural beliefs played a role. First, throughout much of the history of modern Europe—as, indeed, in ancient Greece—there was a common aristocratic prejudice against earning wages. The ancient Greek gentleman was characterized by "leisure"—meaning that he did not have to work for a living. Aristotle reproved the Athenian democracy for allowing such base types as farmers and craftsmen to vote since, in his view, the unleisured character of their daily activities and their inevitable preoccupation with gain would pervert their political judgment, making them grasping and small-minded.[12] The fact that the Sophists typically took money for their rhetorical and philosophical teaching made them deeply suspect in the eyes of such aristocrats.[13] Much the same view played a role in the medieval church, where it was controversial for one to offer philosophical instruction for pay.[14] Bernard of Clairvaux, for example, held that taking fees for education is a "base occupation" (*turpis quaestus*). (Apparently he did not think this true of all wage labor, only where it involved deep spiritual things.)

Such views about wage labor remained closely linked to class privilege in modern Europe, and exercised great power well into the twentieth century. Any reader of English novels will be able to produce many examples of the view that a gentleman does not earn wages, and that someone who does is overpreoccupied with the baser things in life, therefore base himself. Such views were a prominent source of prejudice against Jews, who, not having the same land rights as Christians, had no choice but to earn their living. Even in this century, in America, Edith Wharton shows that these attitudes were still firmly entrenched. Lily Bart, impoverished heroine of *The House of Mirth*, discusses her situation with her friend Gus Trenor. He praises the investment tips he has gotten from Simon Rosedale, a Jewish Wall Street investments expert whose wealth has given him entry into the world of impoverished aristocrats who both use and despise him. Trenor urges Lily to encourage Rosedale's advances: "The man is mad to know the people who do not want to know him, and when a fellow's in that state, there is nothing he won't do for the first woman who takes him up." Lily dismisses the idea, calling Rosedale "impossible," and thinking silently of his "intrusive personality." Trenor replies: "Oh, hang it—because he's fat and shiny and has a shoppy manner! . . . A few years from now he'll be in it whether we want him or not, and then he won't be giving away a half-a-million tip for a dinner!"[15] In the telling phrase "a shoppy manner" we see the age-old aristocratic prejudice against wage work, so deeply implicated in stereotypes of Jews as pushy, intrusive, and lacking in grace.

To this example we may add a moment in the film *Chariots of Fire* when the Jewish sprinter hires a professional coach to help him win. This introduction of money into the gentlemanly domain of sport shocks the head of his college, who suggests to him that as a Jew he does not understand the true spirit of English athletics. Genteel amateurism is the mark of the gentleman, and amateurism demands, above all, not earning or dealing in money. It may also imply not trying too hard, not giving the impression that this is one's main concern in life, but this attitude appears to be closely related to the idea that the gentleman does not *need* the activity, has his living provided already; so the rejection of hard work is a corollary of the rejection of the tradesman. (Even today in Britain such attitudes have not totally disappeared. People from aristocratic backgrounds frequently frown on working too hard at one's scholarly or athletic pursuits, as if this betrays a kind of base tradesman-like mentality.)

What is worth noting about these prejudices is that they do not attach to activities themselves, but, rather, to the use of these activities to make money. To be a scholar, to be a musician, to be a fine athlete, to be an actor even, is fine so long as one does it as an amateur. But what does this mean? It means that those with inherited wealth can perform these activities without stigma, and others cannot.[16] In England in the nineteenth century, it meant that the gentry could perform those activities, and Jews could not. This informs us that we need to scrutinize all our social views about moneymaking and alleged commodification with extra care; for they are likely to embed class prejudices that are unjust to working people.

Intersecting with this belief, in the opera singer example, is another: that it is shameful to display one's body to strangers in public, especially in the expression of passionate emotion. The anxiety about actors, dancers, and singers reported by Smith is surely of a piece with the more general anxiety about the body, especially the female body, that has been a large part of the history of quite a few cultures. Thus, in much of India until very recently (and in some parts still), it is considered inappropriate for a woman of good family to dance in public; when Rabindranath Tagore included middle-class women in his theatrical productions early in this century, it was a surprising and somewhat shocking move. In a similar manner, in the West, the female body should be covered and not displayed, though in some respects these conditions could be relaxed among friends and acquaintances. Female singers were considered unacceptable during the early history of opera; indeed, they were just displacing the castrati during Smith's lifetime, and they were widely perceived as immoral women.[17] Male actors, singers, and dancers suffered too, and clearly Smith means to include both sexes. Until very recently such performers were considered to be a kind of gypsy, too fleshy and physical, unsuited for polite company. The distaste was compounded by a distaste for, or at least a profound ambivalence about, the emotions that it was, and is, the business of these performers to portray. Such attitudes betray an anxiety about the body, and about strong passion, that we are now likely to think irrational, even though we may continue to share these attitudes at times. In any case we are not likely to think them a good basis for public policy.

When we consider our views about sexual and reproductive services, then, we must be on our guard against two types of irrationality: aristocratic class prejudice and fear of the body and its passions.

Prostitution is not a single thing. It can only be well understood in its social and historical context. Ancient Greek *hetairai* such as Pericles' mistress Aspasia have very little in common with a modern call girl.[18] Even more important, within a given culture there are always many different types and levels of prostitution: in ancient Greece, the *hetaira*, the brothel prostitute, the streetwalker; in modern America, the self-employed call girl, the brothel prostitute, the streetwalker (and each of these at various levels of independence and economic success). It is also evident that most cultures contain a continuum of relations between women and men (or between same-sex pairs) that have a commercial aspect—ranging from the admitted case of prostitution to cases of marriage for money or expensive dates at the end of which sexual favors are expected. In most cultures, marriage itself has a prominent commercial aspect: the prominence of dowry murder in contemporary Indian culture, for example, testifies to the degree to which a woman is valued, above all, for the financial benefits one can extract from her family.[19] Here we will focus on contemporary America, on female prostitution only, and on explicitly commercial relations of the sort that are illegal under current law.

We will consider the prostitute by situating her in relation to several other women who take money for bodily services:

1. A factory worker in the Perdue chicken factory who plucks feathers from nearly frozen chickens.

2. A domestic servant in a prosperous upper-middle-class house.

3. A nightclub singer in middle-range clubs who often sings songs requested by the patrons.

4. A professor of philosophy who gets paid for lecturing and writing.

5. A skilled masseuse employed by a health club (with no sexual services on the side).

6. A "colonoscopy artist" who gets paid for having her colon examined with the latest instruments in order to test out their range and capability.

By considering similarities and differences between the prostitute and these other bodily actors, we can more easily identify the distinctive features of prostitution as a form of bodily service.

We will not address the issue of child prostitution or nonconsensual prostitution (e.g., young women sold into prostitution by their parents, forcible drugging and abduction, and so forth). We will look only at the type of choice to be a prostitute that is made by a woman over the age of consent, frequently in a situation of great economic duress.

1. *The prostitute and the factory worker.* Both prostitution and factory work are usually low-paid jobs; but in many instances a woman faced with the choice can (at least over the short haul) make more money in prostitution than in factory work. (This would probably be even more true if prostitution were legalized and the role of pimps thereby restricted, though the removal of risk and some stigma might at the same time depress wages, to some extent offsetting that advantage for the prostitute.) Both face health risks, but the health risk in prostitution can be very much reduced by legalization and regulation, whereas the particular type of work the factory worker is performing carries a high risk of damage to the nerves in the hands, a fact about it that appears unlikely to change. The prostitute may well have better working hours and conditions than the factory worker, especially if prostitution were legalized. She has a degree of choice about which clients she accepts and what activities she performs, whereas the factory worker has no choices—she must perform the same motions again and again for years. The prostitute also performs a service that requires skill and responsiveness to new situations, whereas the factory worker's repetitive motion exercises relatively little human skill and contains no variety.[20]

The factory worker, however, is unlikely to be the target of violence, whereas the prostitute needs—and does not always get—protection from violent customers. (Again, this situation can be improved by legalization: prostitutes in the Netherlands have a call button wired up to the police.) The factory worker's occupation, moreover, has no clear connection with stereotypes of gender—though this might not have been the case. In many parts of the world, manual labor is strictly segmented by sex, and more routinized, low-skill tasks are given to women.[21] The prostitute's activity does derive some of its attraction from stereotypes of women as sluttish and immoral, and it may in turn perpetuate such stereotypes. The factory worker suffers no invasion of her internal private space, whereas the prostitute's activity involves such (consensual) invasion. Finally the prostitute suffers from social stigma, whereas the factory worker does not—at least among people of her own social class. For all these reasons, many women, faced with the choice between factory work and prostitution, choose factory work, despite its other disadvantages.

2. *The prostitute and the domestic servant.* In domestic service as in prostitution, one is hired by a client and one must do what that client wants or fail at the job. In both, one has a limited degree of latitude to exercise skills as one sees fit, and both jobs require the exercise of some developed bodily skills. In both, one is at risk of enduring bad behavior from one's client, though the prostitute is more likely to encounter physical violence. Certainly both are traditionally professions that enjoy low respect, from society and from the client. Domestic service on the whole is likely to have worse hours and lower pay than (at least many types of) prostitution but it probably contains fewer health risks. It also involves no invasion of intimate bodily space, as prostitution (consensually) does.

Both prostitution and domestic service are associated with a type of social stigma. In the case of domestic service, the stigma is related to class: it is perceived as an occupation only for the lowest classes.[22] Domestic servants are in a vast majority of cases female, so the occupation is socially coded by sex. In the United States domestic service is very often racially coded as well. Not only in the South but also in many parts of the urban North African-American women often hold these low-paying occupations. In my home in suburban Philadelphia in the 1950s and 1960s, the only African Americans we saw were domestic servants, and the only domestic servants we saw were African American. The perception of the occupation as associated with racial stigma ran very deep, producing difficult tensions and resentments that made domestic service seem to be incompatible with dignity and self-respect. (It needn't be, clearly; and I shall return to this.)

3. *The prostitute and the nightclub singer.* Both of these people use their bodies to provide pleasure, and the customer's pleasure is the primary goal of what they do.[23] This does not mean that a good deal of skill and art

is not involved, and in both cases it usually is. Both have to respond to requests from the customer though (in varying degrees depending on the case) both may also be free to improvise or to make suggestions.

How do they differ? The prostitute faces health risks and risks of violence not faced by the singer. She also allows her bodily space to be invaded, as the singer does not. It may also be that prostitution is always a cheap form of an activity that has a higher better form, whereas this need not be the case in popular vocal performance (though of course it might be).[24] The nightclub singer, furthermore, does not appear to be participating in, or perpetuating, any type of gender hierarchy—though in former times this would not have been the case, singers being seen as "a type of publick prostitute" and their activity often associated with anxiety about the control of female sexuality. Finally, there is no (great) moral stigma attached to being a nightclub singer, though at one time there certainly was.

4. *The prostitute and the professor of philosophy*. These two figures have a very interesting similarity: both provide bodily services in areas that are generally thought to be especially intimate and definitive of selfhood. Just as the prostitute takes money for sex, which is commonly thought to be an area of intimate self-expression, so the professor takes money for thinking and writing about what she thinks—about morality, emotion, the nature of knowledge—all parts of a human being's intimate search for understanding the world and herself. It was precisely for this reason that some medieval thinkers saw philosophizing for money as a moral problem: it should be a pure spiritual gift and is degraded by the receipt of a wage. The fact that we do not think that the professor (even one who regularly holds out for the highest salary offered) thereby alienates her mind or turns her thoughts into commodities—even when she writes a paper for a specific conference or volume—should put us on our guard about making similar conclusions in the case of the prostitute.

In both cases the performance involves interaction with others, and the form of the interaction is not altogether controlled by the person. In both cases there is at least an element of producing pleasure or satisfaction (note the prominent role of teaching evaluations in the employment and promotion of professors), though in philosophy there is also a countervailing tradition of believing that the goal of the interaction is to produce dissatisfaction and unease. (Socrates would not have received tenure in a modern university.) It may appear at first that the intimate bodily space of the professor is not invaded—but we should further explore this idea. When someone's unanticipated argument goes into one's mind, is this not both intimate and bodily? (And far less consensual, often, than the penetration of prostitute by customer.) Both performances involve skill. It might plausibly be argued that the professor's involves a more developed skill, or at least a more expensive training—but we should be cautious here. Our culture is all too ready to think that sex involves no skill and is simply "natural," a view that is surely false and is not even seriously entertained by many cultures.[25]

The professor's salary and working conditions are usually a great deal better than those of all but the most elite prostitutes. The professor has a fair amount of control over the structure of her day and her working environment, but she also has fixed mandatory duties, as the prostitute, when self-employed, does not. If the professor is in a nation that protects academic freedom, she has considerable control over what she thinks and writes, though fads, trends, and peer pressure surely constrain her to some extent. The prostitute's need to please her customer is usually more exigent and permits less choice. In this way, she is more like the professor of philosophy in Cuba than like her American counterpart—but the Cuban professor appears to be worse off, since she cannot say what she really thinks even when off the job.[26] Finally, the professor of philosophy, if female, both enjoys reasonably high respect in the community and also might be thought to bring credit to all women, in that she succeeds at an activity commonly thought to be the preserve only of males. She thus subverts traditional gender hierarchy, whereas the prostitute, while suffering stigma herself, may be thought to perpetuate gender hierarchy.

5. *The prostitute and the masseuse.* These two bodily actors seem very closely related. Both use a skill to produce bodily satisfaction in the client. Unlike the nightclub singer, both do this through a type of bodily contact with the client. Both need to be responsive to what the client wants, and to a large degree take direction from the client as to how to handle his or her body. The bodily contact involved is rather intimate, though the internal space of the masseuse is not invaded. The type of bodily pleasure produced by the masseuse may certainly have an erotic element, though in the type of "respectable" masseuse considered here, it is not directly sexual.

The difference is primarily one of respectability. Practitioners of massage have fought for, and have to a large extent won, the right to be considered as dignified professionals who exercise a skill. Their trade is legal, it is not stigmatized, and practitioners generally do not believe that they degrade their bodies or turn their bodies into commodities by using their bodies to give pleasure to customers. They have positioned themselves alongside physical therapists and medical practitioners, dissociating themselves from the erotic dimension of their activity. As a consequence of this successful self-positioning, they enjoy better working hours, better pay, and more respect than most prostitutes. What, then, is the difference?

One is having sex, and the other is not. But what sort of difference is this? Is it a difference we want to defend? Are our reasons for thinking it so crucial really reasons, or are they simply vestiges of moral prejudice? These questions call up a number of distinct beliefs: the belief that women should not have sex with strangers; the belief that commercial sex is inherently degrading and makes a woman a degraded woman; the belief that women should not have to have sex with strangers if they do not want to; and the general belief that women should have the option to refuse sex with anyone they do not really choose. Some of these beliefs are worth defending and some are not. (I shall argue that the issue of choice is the really important one.) We need to sort them out and to make sure that our policies are not motivated by views we are not really willing to defend.

6. *The prostitute and the colonoscopy artist.* This hypothetical occupation is included for a reason that should now be evident: it involves the consensual invasion of one's bodily space. (The example is not so hypothetical: medical students need models when they are learning to perform internal exams, and young actors do earn a living playing such roles.[27]) The colonoscopy artist uses her skill at tolerating the fiber-optic probe without anaesthesia to make a living. In the process, she permits an aperture of her body to be penetrated by another person's activity—far more deeply penetrated than is generally the case in sex. She runs some bodily risk, since she is being used to test untested instruments, and she will probably have to fast and empty her colon regularly enough to incur some malnutrition and some damage to her excretory function. Her wages may not be very good—for this is probably not a profession characterized by what Smith called "the beauty and rarity of talents," and it may also involve some stigma, given that people are inclined to be disgusted by the thought of intestines.

Yet, on the whole, we do not think that this is a base trade or one that makes the woman who does it a fallen woman. We might want to ban or regulate it if we thought it was too dangerous, but we would not be moved to ban it for moral reasons. Why not? Some people would point to the fact that it neither reflects nor perpetuates gender hierarchy, and this is certainly true. (Even if being a woman is crucial to a person's selection for the job—they need to study, for example, both male and female colons—it will not be for reasons that seem connected with the subordination of women.) Surely a far greater part of the difference is that most people do not think anal penetration by a doctor in the context of a medical procedure is immoral, whereas lots of people do think that vaginal or anal penetration in the context of sexual relations is (except under special circumstances) immoral.[28] A woman who goes in for that is therefore an immoral and base woman.

Prostitution has many features that link it with other forms of bodily service. It differs from these other activities in many subtle ways but the biggest difference consists in the fact that it is more widely stigmatized. Professors no longer get told that selling their teaching is a *turpis quaestus*. Opera singers no longer get told that they are unacceptable in polite society. Even the masseuse has won respect as a skilled professional. What is different about prostitution? Two factors stand out as sources of stigma. One is that prostitution is widely held to be immoral; the other is that prostitution is frequently bound up with gender hierarchy—with ideas that women and their sexuality are in need of male domination and control, and the related idea that women should be available to men to provide an outlet for their sexual desires. The immorality view would be hard to defend today as a justification for the legal regulation of prostitution, and perhaps even for its moral denunciation. People thought prostitution was immoral because they thought nonreproductive and especially extramarital sex was immoral. The prostitute was seen, typically, as a dangerous figure whose whole career was given over to lust. But female lust was and often still is commonly seen as bad and dangerous, so prostitution was seen as bad and dangerous. Some people would still defend these views today, but it seems inconsistent to do so if one is not prepared to repudiate other forms of nonmarital sexual activity on an equal basis. We have to grant that the most common reason for the stigma attached to prostitution is a weak reason, at least as a public reason: a moralistic view about female sexuality that is rarely consistently applied and that seems unable to justify restriction on the activities of citizens who have different views of what is good and proper. At any rate, it seems difficult to use the stigma so incurred to justify perpetuating the stigma through criminalization, unless one is prepared to accept a wide range of morals laws that interfere with chosen consensual activities—something that most feminist attackers of prostitution rarely wish to do.

More promising as a source of good moral arguments might be the stigma incurred by the connection of prostitution with gender hierarchy. Only a small minority of people view prostitution in a negative light because of its collaboration with male supremacy; for only a small minority of people at any time have been reflective feminists, concerned with the eradication of inequality. Such people will view the prostitute as they view veiled women, or women in *purdah*: with sympathetic anger as victims of an unjust system. This reflective feminist critique does not explain why prostitutes are held in disdain—both because it is not pervasive enough and because it leads to sympathy rather than to disdain.

Gender hierarchy actually explains stigma in a very different way, a way that turns out in the end to be just another form of the immorality charge. People committed to gender hierarchy, and determined to ensure that the dangerous sexuality of women is controlled by men, frequently have viewed the prostitute—a sexually active woman—as a threat to male control of women. They therefore become determined either to criminalize the occupation or, if they also think that male sexuality needs such an outlet (and that this outlet ultimately defends marriage by giving male desire a safely debased outlet) to keep it within bounds by close regulation. Criminalization and regulation are not straightforwardly opposed; they can be closely related strategies. In a similar manner, prostitution is generally conceived as not the enemy but the ally of marriage: the two are complementary ways of controlling women's sexuality. The result is that social meaning is deployed in order that female sexuality be kept in bounds carefully set by men. The stigma attached to the prostitute is an integral part of such bounding.

A valuable illustration of this thesis is given by Alain Corbin's fascinating and careful study of prostitutes in France in the late nineteenth century.[29] Corbin shows that the interest in legal regulation of prostitution was justified by the alleged public interest in reining in and making submissive a female sexuality that was always potentially dangerous to marriage and social order. Kept in carefully supervised houses known as *maisons de tolérance*, prostitutes were known by the revealing name of *filles soumises*, a phrase that most obviously designated them as registered, "subjugated" to the law, but that also connoted their controlled and confined status. What this meant was that they were controlled and confined, so that they themselves could provide a safe outlet for desires that threatened to disrupt the social order. The underlying aim of the regulationist project, argues Corbin was "the total repression of sexuality."[30] Regulationists tirelessly cited St. Augustine's dictum: "Abolish the prostitutes and the passions will overthrow the world; give them the rank of honest women and infamy and dishonor will blacken the universe."[31] In other words: stigma has to be attached to prostitutes because of the necessary hierarchy that requires morality to subjugate vice, and the male to subjugate the female. Separating the prostitute from the "good woman," the wife whose sexuality is monogamous and aimed at reproduction, creates a system that maintains male control over female desire.[32]

This attitude to prostitution has modern parallels. One instructive example is from Thailand in the 1950s, when Field Marshal Sarit Thanarat began a campaign of social purification, holding that "uncleanliness and social impropriety . . . led to the erosion of social orderliness."[33] In theory Thanarat's aim was to criminalize prostitution by the imposition of prison terms and stiff fines, in practice the result was a system of medical examination and "moral rehabilitation" that shifted the focus of public blame from the procurers and traffickers to prostitutes themselves. Unlike the French system, the Thai system did not encourage registered prostitution; but it was similar in its public message that the problem of prostitution is a problem of "bad" women, and in its reinforcement of the message that female sexuality is a cause of social disruption unless tightly controlled.

Sex hierarchy commonly causes stigma not through feminist critique but through a far more questionable set of social meanings, meanings that anyone concerned with justice for women should call into question. For it is these same meanings that are also used to justify the seclusion of women, the veiling of women, and the genital mutilation of women. Together, the social meanings uphold the view that women are essentially immoral and dangerous and can be controlled by men only if men carefully engineer things so that women do not get out of bounds. The prostitute, seen as the uncontrolled and sexually free woman, is perceived as particularly dangerous as she is both necessary to society and in need of constant subjugation. If she is seen as an honest woman, a woman of dignity, she will destroy society. If she is marginalized, she may be tolerated for the service she provides (or, in the Thai case, she may provide an engrossing public spectacle of "moral rehabilitation").

All this diverts attention from some very serious crimes, such as the use of kidnapping, coercion, and fraud to entice women into prostitution. For these reasons international human rights organizations, such as Human Rights Watch and Amnesty International, have avoided taking a stand against prostitution as such, and have focused their energies on the issues of trafficking and financial coercion.[34]

It appears, then, that the stigma associated with prostitution has an origin that feminists have good reason to connect with unjust background conditions and to decry as both unequal and irrational, based on a hysterical fear of women's unfettered sexuality. There may be other good arguments against the legality of prostitution, but the existence of widespread stigma all by itself does not appear to be among them. So long as prostitution is stigmatized, people are injured by that stigmatization, and it is a real injury to a person not to have dignity and self-respect in her own society. But that real injury, as with the comparable real injury to the dignity and self-respect of interracial couples, or of lesbians and gay men, is not best handled by continued legal strictures against the prostitute. It can be better dealt with by fighting discrimination against these people and taking measures to promote their dignity. As the Supreme Court determined in a mixed-race custody case, "Private biases may be outside the reach of the law, but the law cannot, directly or indirectly, give them effect."[35]

Pervasive stigma itself does not appear to provide a good reason for the continued criminalization of prostitution, any more than it does for the illegality of interracial marriage. Nor does the stigma in question even appear to ground a sound *moral* argument against prostitution. This is not the end of the issue: for there are a number of other significant arguments that have been made to support criminalization. With our six related cases in mind, we will examine those arguments in turn.

1. *Prostitution involves health risks and risks of violence.* To this we can make two replies. First, insofar as this is true the problem is made much worse by the illegality of prostitution, which prevents adequate supervision, encourages the control of pimps, and discourages health checking. As Corbin shows, regimes of legal but regulated prostitution have not always done well by women: the health checkups of the *filles soumises* were ludicrously brief and inadequate.[36] But there is no reason why one cannot focus on the goal of adequate health checks, and some European nations have done reasonably well in this area.[37] The legal brothels in Nevada have had no reported cases of AIDS.[38] Certainly risks of violence can be far better controlled when the police serve as the prostitute's ally rather than her oppressor.

To the extent to which risks remain an inevitable part of the way of life, we must now ask what general view of the legality of risky undertakings we wish to defend. Do we ever want to rule out risky bargains simply because they harm the agent? Or do we require a showing of harm to others, as might be possible in the case of gambling, for example? Whatever position we take on this complicated question, we will almost certainly be led to conclude that prostitution lies well within the domain of the legally acceptable: for it is probably far less risky than boxing, another activity in which working-class people try to survive and flourish by subjecting their bodies to some risk of harm. There is a stronger case for paternalistic regulation of boxing than of prostitution, and externalities, such as the glorification of violence as example to the young, make boxing at least as morally problematic, probably more so. And yet very few Americans would defend the criminalization of boxing. Sensible regulation of both prostitution and boxing, by contrast, seems reasonable and compatible with personal liberty.

In the international arena, many problems of this type stem from the use of force and fraud to induce women to enter prostitution, frequently at a very young age and in a strange country where they have no civil rights. An especially common destination is Thailand, and an especially common source is Burma, where the devastation of the rural economy has left many young women an easy mark for promises of domestic service elsewhere. Driven by customers' fears of HIV, the trade has focused on increasingly young girls from increasingly remote regions. Human rights interviewers have concluded that large numbers of these women were unaware of what they would be doing when they left their country and are kept in Thailand through both economic and physical coercion. In many cases, family members have received payments which then become a "debt" that the girl has to pay off.[39] These circumstances, terrible in themselves, set the stage for other forms of risk and violence. Of the women and girls interviewed by Human Rights Watch, 50 to 70 percent were HIV positive; discriminatory arrests and deportations are frequently accompanied by abuse in police custody. All these problems are magnified by the punitive attitude of the police and government toward these women as prostitutes or illegal aliens or both, though under both national and international law trafficking victims are exempt from legal penalty and are guaranteed safe repatriation to their country of origin. This situation clearly deserves both moral condemnation and international legal pressure but it is made worse by the illegality of prostitution itself.

2. *The prostitute has no autonomy; her activities are controlled by others.* This argument does not serve to distinguish prostitutes.[40] The factory worker does worse on the scale of autonomy, and the domestic servant no better. This point expresses a legitimate moral concern: a person's life seems deficient in flourishing if it consists only of a form of work that is totally out of the control and direction of the person herself. Karl Marx rightly associated that kind of labor with a deficient realization of full humanity, and, invoking Aristotle, persuasively argued that a flourishing human life probably requires some use of one's own reasoning in the planning and execution of one's own work.[41] But that is a pervasive problem of labor in the modern world, not a problem peculiar to prostitution as such. It certainly does not help the problem to criminalize prostitution—any more than it would be to criminalize factory work or domestic service. A woman will not exactly achieve more control and "truly human functioning" by becoming unemployed. What we should instead think about are ways to promote more control over choice of activities, more variety, and more general humanity in the types of work that are actually available to people with little education and few options. That would be a lot more helpful than removing one of the options they actually have.

3. *Prostitution involves the invasion of one's intimate bodily space.* This

argument does not seem to support legal regulation of prostitution, so long as the invasion in question is consensual: the prostitute is not kidnapped, fraudulently enticed, a child beneath the age of consent, or under duress against leaving if she should choose to leave. In this sense prostitution is quite unlike sexual harassment and rape, and far more like the activity of the colonoscopy artist. Prostitution is not to everyone's taste, and it involves a surrender of bodily privacy that some will find repellant. But it is not for that reason necessarily bad, either for self or others. The argument does not even appear to support a moral criticism of prostitution, unless one is prepared to make a moral criticism of all sexual contact that does not involve love or marriage.

4. *Prostitution makes it harder for people to form relationships of intimacy and commitment.* This argument is prominently made by Elizabeth Anderson, in defense of the criminalization of prostitution.[42] The first question we should ask is, is this true? People still appear to fall in love in the Netherlands and Germany and Sweden. They also fell in love in ancient Athens, where prostitution was not only legal but also probably publicly subsidized.[43] One type of relationship does not appear to remove the need for the other—any more than a Jackie Collins novel removes the desire to read Proust. Proust has a specific type of value that is by no means found in Jackie Collins, so people who want that value will continue to seek out Proust, and there is no reason to think that the presence of Jackie Collins on the bookstand will confuse Proust lovers into thinking that Proust is really like Jackie Collins. So too, one supposes, with love in the Netherlands: people who want relationships of intimacy and commitment continue to seek them out for the special value they provide and they do not have much trouble telling the difference between one sort of relationship and another, despite the availability of both.

Second, one should ask which women Anderson has in mind. Is she saying that the criminalization of prostitution would facilitate the formation of love relationships on the part of the women who were, or would have been, prostitutes? Or is she saying that the unavailability of prostitution as an option for working-class women would make it easier for romantic middle-class women to have the relationships they desire? The former claim is implausible, since it is difficult to see how reinforcing the stigma against prostitutes, or preventing some poor women from taking one of the few employment options they might have, would be likely to improve their human relations.[44] The latter claim might possibly be true (though it is hardly obvious) but it seems a repugnant idea, which I am sure Anderson would not endorse, that we should make poor women poorer so that middle-class women can find love. Third, one should ask Anderson whether she is prepared to endorse the large number of arguments of this form that might plausibly be made in the realm of popular culture and, if not, whether she has any way of showing how she could reject those as involving an unacceptable infringement of liberty and yet allowing the argument about prostitution that she endorses. For it seems plausible that making rock music illegal would increase the likelihood that people would listen to Mozart and Beethoven; that making Jackie Collins illegal would make it more likely that people would turn to Joyce Carol Oates; that making commercial advertising illegal would make it more likely that we would appraise products with high-minded ideas of value in our minds; that making television illegal would improve children's reading skills. We would and do utterly reject those ideas because we do not want to live in Plato's *Republic*, with our cultural options dictated by a group of wise guardians, however genuinely sound their judgments may be.[45]

5. *The prostitute alienates her sexuality on the market; she turns her sexual organs and acts into commodities.*[46] It seems implausible to claim that the prostitute alienates her sexuality just on the grounds that she provides sexual services to a client for a fee. Does the singer alienate her voice, or the professor her mind? The prostitute still has her sexuality; she can use it on her own, apart from her relationship with the client, just as the domestic servant may cook for her family and clean her own house.[47] She can also cease to be a prostitute, and her sexuality will still be with her, and hers, if she does. So she has not even given anyone a monopoly on those services, far less given them over into someone else's hands. The real issue that separates her from the professor and the singer seems to be the degree of choice she exercises over the acts she performs. But even this is not a special issue for the prostitute, any more than it is for the factory worker or the domestic servant or the colonscopy artist—all of whom choose jobs in which they will not have a great deal of say over what they do or how they do it. Freedom to choose how one works is a highly desirable luxury but a feature of few jobs that nonaffluent people perform.

As for the claim that the prostitute turns her sexuality into a commodity, we must ask what that means. If it means only that she accepts a fee for sexual services, then that is obvious. Nothing further has been said that would show us why this is a bad thing. The professor, the singer, the symphony musician—all accept a fee and it seems plausible that this is a good state of affairs. Professors are more free to pursue their own thoughts now, as moneymakers, than they were in the days when they were supported by monastic orders; symphony musicians playing under the contract secured by the musicians union have more free time than nonunionized musicians, and more opportunities to engage in experimental and solo work that will enhance their art. In neither case should we conclude that the existence of a contract has converted the abilities into things to be exchanged and traded separately from the body of the producer. They remain human creative abilities, securely housed in their possessor. So if, on the one hand, to "commodify" means merely to accept a fee, we have been given no reason to think that this is bad.

If, on the other hand, we try to interpret the claim of "commodification" using the narrow technical definition of "commodity" used by the Universal Commercial Code, the claim is plainly false.[48] For that definition stresses the "fungible" nature of the goods in question, and "fungible" goods are, in turn, defined as goods "of which any unit is, by nature or usage of trade, the equivalent of any other like unit." While we may not think that the soul or inner world of a prostitute is of deep concern to the customer, she is usually not regarded as simply a set of units fully interchangeable with other units.[49] Prostitutes are probably somewhat more fungible than bassoon players, but not totally so. Corbin reports that all *maisons de tolérance* standardly had a repertory of different types of women to suit different tastes. What seems to be the real issue is that the woman is not attended to as an individual, not considered as a special unique being. But that is true of many ways people treat one another in many areas of life and it seems implausible that we should use that kind of disregard as a basis for criminalization. It may not even be immoral: for surely we cannot deeply know all the people with whom we have dealings in life, and many of those dealings are just fine without deep knowledge. So our moral question boils down to the question, is sex without deep personal knowledge always immoral? It seems officious and presuming to use one's own experience to give an affirmative answer to this question, given that people have such varied experiences of sexuality.

There appears to be nothing baneful or value-debasing about taking money for a service, even when that service expresses something intimate about the self. Professors take a salary, artists work on commission under contract—frequently producing works of high intellectual and spiritual value. To take money for a production does not turn either the activity or the product into a commodity in the baneful sense in which that implies fungibility. If this is so, there is no reason to think that a prostitute's acceptance of money for her services necessarily involves a baneful conversion of an intimate act into a commodity in that sense. If the prostitute's acts are less intimate than many other sexual acts people perform, that does not seem to have a great deal to do with the fact that she receives money, given that people engage in many intimate activities, such as painting, singing, and writing, for money all the time without loss of expressive value. Her activity is less intimate because that is its whole point. And it is problematic, to the extent that it is, neither because of the money involved nor because of the nonintimacy but because of features of her working conditions and the way she is treated by others.

Here we are left with an interesting puzzle: for the above argument about professors and painters certainly seems to imply that there is no reason, in principle, why the most committed and intimate sex cannot involve a contract and a financial exchange. So why does it not, in our culture? One reply is that it quite frequently does. People often form committed relationships that include an element of economic dependence, whether one-sided or mutual; marriage has very frequently had that feature, not always for the worse. But to the extent that we do not exchange money for sex, why do we not? In a number of other cultures courtesans, both male and female, have been somewhat more common as primary sexual partners than they are here. Unlike quite a few cultures, we do not tend to view sex in intimate personal relationships the way we view an artist's creation of a painting, namely as an intimate act that can nonetheless be deliberately undertaken as the result of an antecedent agreement. Why not? Sex, however prolonged, still takes up much less time than writing an article or producing a painting. Furthermore, it is not possible to do it too often, its natural structure is that it will not very often fill up the entire day. One may therefore conduct an intimate sexual relationship in the way one would wish, not feeling that one is slighting it, while pursuing another line of work as one's way of making a living. Artists and scholars sometimes have to pursue another line of work but they prefer not to. They characteristically feel that to do their work in the way they would wish they ought to spend the whole day doing it. So they naturally gravitate to the view that their characteristic mode of creative production fits very well with contract and a regular wage.

This still fails to explain cultural differences. To begin to grapple with these we need to mention the influence of our heritage of romanticism, which makes us feel that sex is not authentic if not spontaneous, "natural," and to some degree unplanned. Romanticism has exercised a far greater sway over our ideas of sex than over our ideas of artistic or intellectual production, making us think that any deal or antecedent arrangement somehow diminishes that characteristic form of expression.

Our romantic ideas about the difference between sex and art are problematic to the extent that they make people think that sex happens naturally, does not require complicated adjustment and skill, and flares up and down uncontrollably.[50] Insofar as they make us think that sex fits badly with reliability, promise-keeping, and so forth, these ideas are certainly subversive of Anderson's goals of "intimacy and commitment," which would be better served, probably, by an attitude that moves sex in intimate personal relationships, and especially marriages, closer to the activity of the artist or the professor. Romantic views also promote Anderson's goals to some degree, insofar as they lead people to connect sex with self-revelation and self-expression, rather than prudent concealment of self. Many current dilemmas concerning marriage in our culture stem from an uneasy struggle to preserve the good in romanticism while avoiding the dangers it poses to commitment.

6. *The prostitute's activity is shaped by, and in turn perpetuates, male dominance of women.*[51] The institution of prostitution as it has most often existed is certainly shaped by aspects of male domination of women. As I have argued, it is shaped by the perception that female sexuality is dangerous and needs careful regulation; that male sexuality is rapacious and needs a "safe" outlet; that sex is dirty and degrading, and that only a degraded woman is an appropriate sexual object.[52] Nor have prostitutes standardly been treated with respect, or given the dignity one might think proper to a fellow human being. They share this with working-class people of many types in many ages, but there is no doubt that there are particular features of the disrespect that derive from male supremacy and the desire to lord it over women—as well as a tendency to link sex to female defilement that is common in the history of Western European culture. The physical abuse of prostitutes and the control of their earnings by pimps—as well as the pervasive use of force and fraud in international markets—are features of male dominance that are extremely harmful and that do not have direct parallels in other types of low-paid work. Some of these forms of conduct may be largely an outgrowth of the illegality of the industry and closely comparable to the threatening behavior of drug wholesalers to their—usually male—retailers. So there remains a question how far male dominance as such explains the violence involved. But in the international arena, where regulations against these forms of misconduct are usually treated as a joke, illegality is not a sufficient explanation for them.

Prostitution is hardly alone in being shaped by, and reinforcing, male dominance. Systems of patrilineal property and exogamous marriage, for example, certainly do more to perpetuate not only male dominance but also female mistreatment and even death. There probably is a strong case for making the giving of dowry illegal, as has been done since 1961 in India and since 1980 in Bangladesh, though with little success.[53] It can be convincingly shown that the institution of dowry is directly linked with extortion and threats of bodily harm and ultimately with the deaths of large numbers of women.[54] It is also obvious that the dowry system pervasively conditions the perception of the worth of female children: they are a big expense, and they will not be around to protect one in one's old age. This structure is directly linked with female malnutrition, neglect, noneducation, even infanticide, abuses that have caused the deaths of many millions of women in the world.[55] The governments of India, Bangladesh, and Pakistan are rightfully concerned about the dowry system since it seems difficult to improve the bad economic and physical condition of women without some structural changes. Pakistan has recently adopted a somewhat quixotic remedy, making it illegal even to serve food at weddings. Dowry is an institution affecting millions of women, determining the course of almost all girls' lives pervasively and from the beginning. Prostitution as such usually does not have either such dire or such widespread implications. It is frequently the product of the dowry system, when parents take payment for prostituting a female child for whom they would otherwise have to pay dowry. The case for making it illegal on grounds of subordination seems weaker than the case for making dowry, or even wedding feasts, illegal. Yet these laws are themselves of dubious merit and would probably be rightly regarded as involving undue infringement of liberty under our constitutional tradition. Significantly, Human Rights Watch, which has so aggressively pursued the issue of forced prostitution, takes no stand one way or the other on the legality of prostitution itself.

More generally, one might argue that the institution of marriage as it has most frequently been practiced both expresses and reinforces male dominance. It would be right to use law to change the most inequitous features of that institution—protecting women from domestic violence and marital rape, giving women equal property and custody rights, and improving their exit options by intelligent shaping of the divorce law. But to rule that marriage as such should be illegal on the grounds that it reinforces male dominance would be an excessive intrusion upon liberty, even if one should believe marriage irredeemably unequal. So too with prostitution: what seems right is to use law to protect the bodily safety of prostitutes from assault, to protect their rights to their incomes against the extortionate behavior of pimps, to protect poor women in developing countries from forced trafficking and fraudulent offers, and to guarantee their full civil rights in the countries where they end up—to make them, in general, equals under the law, both civil and criminal. But the criminalization of prostitution seems to pose a major obstacle to that equality.

Efforts on behalf of the dignity and self-respect of prostitutes have tended to push in exactly the opposite direction. In the United States, prostitutes have long been organized to demand greater respect, though their efforts are hampered by prostitution's continued illegality. In India the National Federation of Women has adopted various strategies to give prostitutes more dignity in the public eye. On National Women's Day they selected a prostitute to put a garland on the head of the Prime Minister. In a similar manner, UNICEF in India's Andhra Pradesh has been fighting to get prostitutes officially classified as "working women," so that they can enjoy the child-care benefits local government extends to that class. Giving workers greater dignity and control can gradually change both the perception and the fact of dominance.

7. *Prostitution is a trade that people do not enter by choice; therefore the bargains people make within it should not be regarded as real bargains.* We must distinguish between three cases. First is the case where the woman's entry into prostitution is caused by some type of conduct that would otherwise be criminal: kidnapping, assault, drugging, rape, statutory rape, blackmail, or fraud. Here we may certainly judge that the woman's choice is not a real choice, and that the law should take a hand in punishing her coercer. This is a terrible problem currently in developing countries. International human rights organizations are right to make it a major focus.[56]

Closely related is the case of child prostitution. Child prostitution is frequently accompanied by kidnapping and forcible detention. Even when children are not stolen from home, their parents have frequently sold them without their own consent. Even where it is not, we should judge that there is an impermissible infringement of autonomy and liberty. A child (and because of clients' fears of HIV brothels now often focus on girls as young as ten) cannot give consent to a life in prostitution.[57] Lack of information and of economic options, if parents collude in the deal, in addition to the lack of adult political rights makes such a "choice" no choice at all.

Different is the case of an adult woman who enters prostitution because of bad economic options: because it seems a better alternative than the chicken factory, because there is no other employment available to her, and so forth. This too is a case where autonomy has been infringed, but in a different way. Consider Joseph Raz's vivid example of "the hounded woman," a woman on a desert island who is constantly pursued by a man-eating animal.[58] In one sense, this woman is free to go anywhere on the island and do anything she likes. In another sense she is quite unfree. If she desires to stay alive, she has to spend all her time and calculate all her movements in order to avoid the beast. Raz's point is that many poor people's lives are nonautonomous in just this way. They may fulfill internal conditions of autonomy, being capable of making bargains, reflecting about what to do, and so forth. But none of this counts for a great deal, if in fact the struggle for survival gives them just one unpleasant option, or a small set of unpleasant options.

This seems to be the truly important issue raised by prostitution. Like work in the chicken factory, it is not an option many women choose with alacrity, when many other options are available.[59] This might not be so in some hypothetical culture, in which prostitutes have legal protection, dignity, and respect, and the status of skilled practitioner, rather like the masseuse.[60] But it is true now in most societies, given the reality of the (albeit irrational) stigma attached to prostitution. But the important thing to realize is that this is not an issue that permits us to focus on prostitution in isolation from the economic situation of women in a society generally. Certainly it will not be ameliorated by the criminalization of prostitution, which reduces poor women's options still further. We may grant that poor women do not have enough options, and that society has been unjust to them in not extending more options, while nonetheless respecting and honoring the choices they actually make in reduced circumstances.

Here are some things that have actually been done in India, where prostitution is a common last-ditch option for women who lack other employment opportunities. First, both government and private groups have focused on the provision of education to women to equip them with skills that will enhance their options. One group in Bombay focuses in particular on skills training for the children of prostitutes, who are at especially high risk of becoming prostitutes themselves unless some action increases their options. Second, nongovernmental organizations have increasingly focused on the provision of credit to women in order to enhance their employment options and give them a chance to "upgrade" in the domain of their employment. One such project that has justly won international renown is the Self-Employed Women's Association (SEWA), centered in Ahmedabad in Gujerat, which provides loans to women pursuing a variety of informal-sector occupations, from tailoring to hawking and vending to cigarette rolling to agricultural labor.[61] With loans they can get wholesale rather than retail supplies, upgrade their animals or equipment, and so forth. They also get skills training and, frequently, the chance to move into leadership roles in the organization itself. Such women are far less likely to need to turn to prostitution to supplement their income. Third, they can form labor organizations to protect women employed in low-income jobs and to bargain for better working conditions—once again making this work a better source of income and diminishing the likelihood that prostitution will need to be selected. This is the other primary objective of SEWA, which is now organizing hawkers and vendors internationally. Fourth, they can form groups to diminish the isolation and enhance the self-respect of working women in low-paying jobs. This is a ubiquitous feature of both government and nongovernment programs I visited in India and a crucial element of helping women deliberate about their options, if they wish to avoid prostitution for themselves or their daughters.

These steps are the real way to address the problem of prostitution. Feminist philosophers do not talk a lot about credit and employment; they should do so far more.[62] It seems a dead end to consider prostitution in isolation from the other realities of working life of which it is a part, and one suspects that this has happened because prostitution is a sexy issue and getting a loan for a sewing machine appears not to be. But philosophers and intellectuals had better talk more about getting loans, learning to read, and so forth, if they want to be relevant to the choices that are actually faced by working women, and to the programs that are actually doing a lot to improve such women's options.

The stigma traditionally attached to prostitution is based on a collage of beliefs most of which are not rationally defensible and which should be especially vehemently rejected by feminists: beliefs about the evil character of female sexuality, the rapacious character of male sexuality, the essentially marital and reproductive character of "good" women and "good" sex. Worries about subordination more recently raised by feminists are much more serious concerns but they apply to many types of work poor women do. Concerns about force and fraud should be extremely urgent concerns of the international women's movement. Where these conditions do not apply, feminists should view prostitutes as (usually) poor working women with few options, not as threats to the intimacy and commitment that many women and men seek. This does not mean that we should not be concerned about ways in which prostitution as currently practiced, even in the absence of force and fraud, undermines the dignity of women, just as domestic service in the past undermined the dignity of members of a given race or class. But the correct response to this problem seems to be to work to enhance the economic autonomy and the personal dignity of members of that class, not to rule off-limits an option that may be the only livelihood for many poor women and to further stigmatize women who already make their living this way.

In grappling further with these issues, we should begin from the realization there is nothing *per se* wrong with taking money for the use of one's body. That is the way most of us live and formal recognition of that fact through contract is usually a good thing for people, protecting their security and their employment conditions. What seems wrong is that relatively few people in the world have the option to use their body in their work in what Marx would call a "truly human" manner of functioning, by which he meant having some choices about the work to be performed, some reasonable measure of control over its conditions and outcome, and also the chance to use thought and skill, rather than just to function as a cog in a machine. Women in many parts of the world are especially likely to be stuck at a low level of mechanical functioning, whether as agricultural laborers, as factory workers, or as prostitutes. The real question is how to expand the options and opportunities such workers face, how to increase the humanity inherent in their work, and how to guarantee that workers of all sorts are treated with dignity. In the further pursuit of these questions, we need, on balance, more studies of women's credit unions and fewer studies of prostitution.

Notes

1. Both the story and the extract from the critical work are translated from the Bengali by Kalpana Bardhan. See *Of Women, Outcastes, Peasants, and Rebels: A Selection of Bengali Short Stories* (Berkeley, Calif., 1990), 19, 157. Bandyopadhyay (1908–1956) was a leading Bengali writer who focused on peasant life and issues of class conflict.

2. I am grateful to the students in my seminar on sexual autonomy and law for all that their discussions contributed to the formulation of these ideas, to Sibyl Schwarzenbach and Laurie Shrage for discussions that helped me think about how to approach this topic, and to Elizabeth Anderson, Gertrud Fremling, Richard Posner, Mark Ramseyer, Eric Schliesser, Elizabeth Schreiber, Steven Schulhofer, Alan Soble, and Cass Sunstein for valuable comments on an earlier draft of this article.

3. Even if one is a Cartesian dualist, as I am not, one must grant that the human exercise of mental abilities standardly requires the deployment of bodily skills. Most traditional Christian positions on the soul go still further: Thomas Aquinas, for example, holds that souls separated from the body have only a confused cognition and cannot recognize particulars. So my statements about professors can be accepted even by believers in the separable soul.

4. Adam Smith, in R. H. Campbell, and A. S. Skinner, eds. *An Inquiry into the Nature and Causes of the Wealth of Nations* (Indianapolis, 1981), I.x.b.25. In Adam Smith, in J. C. Bryce, ed., *Lectures on Rhetoric and Belles Lettres* (Oxford, England, 1983), ii.230, Smith points out that in ancient Greece acting was "as creditable . . . as it is discreditable now."

5. He expresses the view that the relevant talents are not so rare and that when stigma is removed many more people will compete for the jobs, driving down wages; this is certainly true today of acting, but far less so of opera, where "the rarity and beauty of the talents" remains at least one dominant factor.

6. Such arguments have often been used in the theatre; they were used, for example, in one acting company of which I was a member in order to persuade actors to kick back their (union-mandatory) salaries to the owners. This is fairly common in theater, where the union is weak and actors are so eager for employment that they are vulnerable to such arguments.

7. The typical contract between major U.S. symphony orchestras and the musicians' union, for example, guarantees year-round employment to symphony musicians, even though they do not play all year; this enables them to use summer months to play in low-paying or experimental settings in which they can perform contemporary music, chamber music, do solo and concerto work, and so forth. It also restricts hours of both rehearsal and performance during the performing season, leaving musicians free to teach students, attend classes, work on chamber music with friends, and otherwise enrich their work. It also mandates blind auditions (that is, players play behind a curtain)—with the result that the employment of female musicians has risen dramatically over the past twenty or so years since the practice was instituted.

8. See Elizabeth Anderson, *Value in Ethics and Economics* (Cambridge, Mass., 1993); Elizabeth Anderson, "Is Women's Labor a Commodity?" *Philosophy and Public Affairs* 19 (1990), 71–92; Margaret Jane Radin, *Contested Commodities: The Trouble with the Trade in Sex, Children, Bodily Parts, and Other Things* (Cambridge, Mass., 1996); Margaret Jane Radin, "Market-Inalienability," *Harvard Law Review* 100 (1987), 1849–1937; Cass R. Sunstein, "Neutrality in Constitutional Law: With Special Reference to Pornography, Abortion, and Surrogacy," *Columbia Law Review* 92 (1992), 1–52; Cass R. Sunstein, *The Partial Constitution* (Cambridge, Mass., 1993), 257–290. For contrasting feminist perspectives on the general issue of contract, see Jean Hampton, "Feminist Contractarianism," in *A Mind of One's Own: Feminist Essays on Reason and Objectivity* (Boulder, Colo., 1993), 227–255; Susan Moller Okin, *Justice, Gender, and the Family* (New York, 1989).

9. I shall use the terms "prostitution" and "prostitute" throughout because of their familiarity, although a number of international women's organizations now avoid it for reasons connected to those in this article, preferring the term "commercial sex worker" instead. For one recent example, see *Reproductive Health in Developing Countries: Expanding Dimensions, Building Solutions*, report of the Panel on Reproductive Health, National Research Council, Amy O. Tsui, Judith N. Wasserheit, and John G. Haaga, eds. (Washington, D.C., 1997), 30, stressing the wide variety of practices denoted by the term "commercial sex," and arguing that some studies show economic hardship as a major factor, but some do not.

10. Among feminist discussions of prostitution, my approach is close to that of Sibyl Schwarzenbach, "Contractarians and Feminists Debate Prostitution," *New York University Review of Law and Social Change* 18 (1990–1991), 103–129, and to Laurie Shrage, "Prostitution and the Case for Decriminalization," *Dissent*, Spring 1996, 41–45, in which Shrage criticizes her earlier view expressed in "Should Feminists Oppose Prostitution?" *Ethics* 99 (1989), 347–361.

11. To give just one example, the Annapurna Mahila Mandel project in Bombay offers job training and education in a residential school setting to the daughters of prostitutes; they report that in five years they have managed to arrange reputable marriages for one thousand such girls.

12. Aristotle, *Politics* VII, 9–10.

13. One can find evidence for this in the attitudes evinced by characters in Platonic dialogues such as, *Apology*, *Protagoras*, and *Gorgias*.

14. I have profited here from reading an unpublished paper by Dan Klerman, "Slavery, Simony and Sex: An Intellectual History of the Limits of Monetary Relations," unpublished manuscript, University of Chicago, March 30, 1990.

15. Edith Wharton, *The House of Mirth* (New York, 1964), 86–87.

16. Or those supported by religious orders.

17. Elizabeth Billington, who sang in Thomas Arne's *Artaxerxes* in London in 1762,

was forced to leave England because of criticisms of her morals; she ended her career in Italy. Another early diva was Maria Catalani, who sang for Handel, for example, in *Samson*. By the time of the publication of *The Wealth of Nations*, female singers had made great headway in displacing the castrati, who ceased to be produced shortly thereafter. For Smith's own attitudes to the female body, see Adam Smith, in D. D. Raphael and A. L. Macfie, eds., *The Theory of Moral Sentiments* (Indianapolis, Ind., 1948), I.ii.1.3, where he states that as soon as sexual passion is gratified it gives rise to "disgust" and leads us to wish to get rid of the person who is its object, unless some higher moral sentiment preserves our regard for (certain aspects of) this person. "When we have dined, we order the covers to be removed; and we should treat in the same manner the objects of the most ardent and passionate desires, if they were the objects of no other passions but those which take their origin from the body." Smith was a bachelor who lived much of his life with his mother and did not have any lasting relationships with women.

18. Aspasia was a learned and accomplished woman who apparently had philosophical and political views; she is said to have taught rhetoric and to have conversed with Socrates. But she could not perform any of the functions of a citizen both because of her sex and because of her foreign birth. Her son Pericles was subsequently legitimated and became a general. More recently, some scholars have questioned whether Aspasia was in fact a *hetaira*, and some now think her a well-born foreign woman. But other *hetairai* in Greece were well educated and had substantial financial assets; the two women recorded as students in Plato's Academy were both *hetairai*, as were most of the women attested as students of Epicurus, including one who was apparently a wealthy donor.

19. See Martha Nussbaum, "Religion and Women's Human Rights," in Paul Weithmann, ed., *Religion and Contemporary Liberalism* (Notre Dame, Ind., 1997), 93–137.

20. It is probably, however, a developed skill to come to work regularly and to work regular hours each day.

21. Consider, for example, the case of Jayamma, a brick worker in Trivandrum, Kerala, India (discussed by Leela Gulati, *Profiles of Female Poverty* (Oxford, England, 1981), 35–62), whom I met on March 21, 1997, when she was approximately sixty-five years old. For approximately forty years, Jayamma worked as a brick carrier carrying heavy loads of bricks on her head all day from one place to another. Despite her strength, fitness, and reliability, she could never advance beyond that job because of her sex, whereas men were quickly promoted to the less physically demanding and higher-paying tasks of brick molding and truck loading.

22. This appears to be a ubiquitous feature: in India, the mark of "untouchability" is the performance of certain types of cleaning, especially those dealing with bathroom areas. Mahatma Gandhi's defiance of caste manifested itself in the performance of these menial services.

23. This does not imply that there is one thing, pleasure, varying only by quantity, that they produce. With Mill (and Plato and Aristotle), I think that pleasures differ in quality, not only in quantity.

24. This point was suggested to me by Elizabeth Schreiber. I am not sure whether I endorse it: it all depends on whether we really want to say that sex has one highest goal. Just as it would have been right, in an earlier era, to be skeptical about the suggestion that the sex involved in prostitution is "low" because nonreproductive, so too it might be good to be skeptical about the idea that prostitution sex is "low" because it is nonintimate. Certainly nonintimacy is present in many noncommercial sexual relationships and is sometimes desired as such.

25. Thus the *Kama Sutra*, with its detailed instructions for elaborately skilled performances, strikes most Western readers as slightly comic since the prevailing romantic ideal of "natural" sex makes such contrivance seem quite unsexy.

26. We might also consider the example of a skilled writer who writes advertising copy.

27. See Terri Kapsalis, *Public Privates: Performing Gynecology from Both Ends of the Speculum* (Durham, N.C., 1997); Terri Kapsalis, "In Print: Backstage at the Pelvic Theater," *Chicago Reader*, April 18, 1997, 46. While a graduate student in performance studies at Northwestern, Kapsalis made a living as a "gynecology teaching associate," serving as the model patient for medical students learning to perform pelvic and breast examinations.

28. The same goes for vaginal penetration, according to Kapsalis. She says that the clinical nature of the procedure more than compensates for "society's queasiness with female sexuality." (Kapsalis, "In Print," 46).

29. Alain Corbin, *Women for Hire: Prostitution and Sexuality in France After 1850*, Alan Sheridan, trans. (Cambridge, Mass., 1990).

30. See Corbin, *Women*, 29. Representative views of the authors of regulationism include the view that "debauchery is a fever of the senses carried to the point of delirium; it leads to prostitution (or to early death . . .)" and that "there are two natural sisters in the world: prostitution and riot" (373).

31. Augustine, *De ordine* 2.4.12.

32. For a more general discussion of the relationship between prostitution and various forms of marriage, see Richard Posner, *Sex and Reason* (Cambridge, Mass., 1992), 130–133.

33. Sukanya Hantrakul, "Thai Women: Male Chauvinism à la Thai," *Nation*, November 16, 1992, cited with further discussion in *A Modern Form of Slavery: Trafficking of Burmese Women and Girls into Brothels in Thailand*, Asia Watch Women's Rights Project (New York, 1993).

34. See *A Modern Form of Slavery: The Human Rights Watch Global Report on Women's Human Rights* (New York, 1995), 196–273, especially 270–273. The pertinent international human rights instruments take the same approach, including the International Covenant on Civil and Political Rights, the Convention on the Elimination of All Forms of Discrimination Against Women, and the Convention for the Suppression of Traffic in Persons and the Exploitation of the Prostitution of Others.

35. *Palmore v. Sidoti*, 466 U.S. 429 (1984).

36. In Paris Dr. Clerc boasted that he could examine a woman every thirty seconds and estimated that a single practitioner saw four hundred women in a single twenty-four-hour period. Another practitioner estimated that the average number of patients per hour was fifty-two. See Corbin, *Women*, 90.

37. For a more pessimistic view of health checks, see Posner, *Sex and Reason*, 209. He points out that they frequently have had the effect of driving prostitutes into the illegal market.

38. See Richard Posner, *Private Choices and Public Health: The AIDS Epidemic in an Economic Perspective* (Cambridge, Mass., 1993), 149, with references.

39. See *A Modern Form of Slavery*, Human Rights Watch, 1–7.

40. See Anderson, *Value in Ethics and Economics*, 156: "Her actions under contract express not her own valuations but the will of her customer."

41. This is crucial in the thinking behind the "capabilities approach" to which I have contributed in *Women, Culture, and Development*, Martha Nussbaum and Jonathan Glover, eds., (Oxford, England, 1995) and other publications. For the connec-

tion between this approach and Marx's use of Aristotle, see my "Aristotle on Human Nature and the Foundations of Ethics," in J. E. J. Altham and R. Harrison, eds., *World, Mind, and Ethics: Essays on the Philosophy of Bernard Williams* (Cambridge, England, 1993).

42. See Anderson, *Value in Ethics and Economics*, 150–158. Anderson pulls back from an outright call for criminalization, concluding that her arguments "establish the legitimacy of a state interest in prohibiting prostitution, but not a conclusive case for prohibition," given the paucity of opportunities for working women.

43. See Kenneth J. Dover, *Greek Homosexuality*, 2nd ed. (Cambridge, Mass., 1978); and David Halperin, "The Democratic Body," *One Hundred Years of Homosexuality and Other Essays* (New York, 1990), 88–112. Customers were all males but prostitutes were both male and female. The evidence that prostitution was publicly funded is uncertain since it derives from comic drama; but it is certain both male and female prostitution enjoyed broad public support and approval.

44. For a similar point, see Radin, "Market-Inalienablity," 1921–125; Radin, *Contested Commodities* 132–136. Anderson refers to this claim of Radin's apparently as the source of her reluctance to call outright for criminalization.

45. I would not go as far as John Rawls, however, in the direction of letting the market determine our cultural options. He opposes any state subsidy to opera companies, symphony orchestras, museums, and so forth, on the grounds that this would back a particular conception of the good against others. We could defend such subsidies, within limits, as valuable because they preserve a cultural option that is among the valuable ones and that might otherwise cease to exist. Obviously much more argument is needed on this entire question.

46. See Radin, *Contested Commodities*. Anderson, 156: "The prostitute, in selling her sexuality to a man, alienates a good necessarily embodied in her person to him and thereby subjects herself to his commands."

47. On this point, see also Schwarzenbach, "Contractarians and Feminists," with discussion of Marx's account of alienation.

48. See Richard Epstein, "Surrogacy: The Case for Full Contractual Enforcement," *Virginia Law Review* 81 (1995), 2327.

49. Moreover, the Uniform Commercial Code does not cover the sale of services, and prostitution should be classified as a service rather than a good.

50. It is well known that these ideas are heavily implicated in the difficulty of getting young people, especially young women, to use contraception.

51. See Shrage, "Prostitution and the Case"; Andrea Dworkin, "Prostitution and Male Supremacy," *Life and Death* (New York, 1997).

52. An eloquent examination of the last view, with reference to Freud's account, which endorses it, is in William Miller, *The Anatomy of Disgust* (Cambridge, Mass., 1997), chapter 6.

53. The Dowry Prohibition Act of 1961 makes both the taking and giving of dowry illegal; in Bangladesh, demanding, taking, and giving dowry are all criminal offenses. See Nussbaum, "Religion and Women's Human Rights."

54. It is extremely difficult to estimate how many women are damaged and killed as a result of this practice. It is certainly clear that criminal offenses are vastly underreported, as is domestic violence in India generally, but that very problem makes it difficult to form any reliable idea of the numbers involved. See Indira Jaising, *Justice for Women* (Bombay, 1996), and Nussbaum, "Religion and Women's Human Rights."

55. See Amartya Sen and Jean Drèze, *Hunger and Public Action* (Oxford, England, 1989), 52 and chapter 1. Kerala, the only Indian state to have a matrilineal property tra-

dition, also has an equal number of men and women (contrasted with a 94:100 sex ratio elsewhere) and 97 percent both male and female literacy, as contrasted with 32 percent female literacy elsewhere.

56. See, for example, *A Modern Form of Slavery: Trafficking of Burmese Women and Girls into Brothels in Thailand*; *A Modern Form of Slavery: The Human Rights Watch Global Report on Women's Human Rights*, 1273–1296; *Human Rights are Women's Rights*, Amnesty International (London, 1995), 53–56.

57. On Thailand, see *A Modern Form of Slavery: The Human Rights Watch Global Report on Women's Human Rights*, 197.

58. Joseph Raz, *The Morality of Freedom* (Oxford, England, 1986), 374.

59. See Posner, *Sex and Reason*, 43, on the low incidence of prostitution in Sweden, even though it is not illegal. His explanation is that "women's opportunities in the job market are probably better there than in any other country."

60. See Schwarzenbach, "Contractarians and Feminists."

61. An extremely high proportion of the labor force in India is in the informal sector. The Self-Employed Women's Association was first directed by Ela Bhatt, who is now involved in international work to improve the employment options of informal-sector workers. For a valuable description of the movement, see Kalima Rose, *Where Women Are Leaders: The SEWA Movement in India* (Delhi, India, 1995).

62. But see, here, Schwarzenbach, "Contractarians and Feminists"; and Shrage "Prostitution and the Case for Decriminalization." I have also been very much influenced by the work of Martha Chen, *A Quiet Revolution: Women in Transition in Rural Bangladesh* (Cambridge, Mass., 1983) and "A Matter of Survival: Women's Right to Work in India and Bangladesh," in *Women, Culture, and Development*. Bina Agarwal, *A Field of One's Own: Gender and Land Rights in South Asia* (Cambridge, England, 1994) and "'Bargaining' and Gender Relations: Within and Beyond the Household," *Feminist Economics* 3 (1997), 1–51.

WOMEN
and the
FAMILY

Mimi Gladstein

❦

Chairing the Department
A Matriarchal Paradigm

"WE DON'T HIRE HOUSEWIVES."[1] THAT WAS THE RETORT TO MY INITIAL INQUIRY about the possibility of joining the faculty of the English Department at the University of Texas at El Paso. It was the mid-sixties and the chairman could not have been more taken aback at my temerity in suggesting I might join his faculty. What would it take for me to be hired, I inquired? You must get a Ph.D. from another university, he explained, sure that such a solution was out of the realm of possibility in those "Father Knows Best" and "Leave it to Beaver" days, when it was father who left the house and mother was never pictured without her ever-present apron. But teaching was what I loved and did best and teaching at a university was what I wanted to do. It seemed only rational to me that I go away to school. I had internalized many of Ayn Rand's precepts against self-sacrifice and her call to be the best that one can be. The community was scandalized. My parents were appalled. The next chairman, who in the meantime had hired me for part-time work because of burgeoning enrollments, was censorious. Although he was in the midst of divorce from his wife of twenty-two years in order to marry a student younger than his daughter, he thought it his prerogative to advise me that going away to work on my Ph.D. might jeopardize my marriage. When I did quit—male colleagues were given leaves-of-absence—to pursue the terminal degree, the chairman at the time warned: "We have our Chaucer man; we have our Shakespeare man; we have our eighteenth- and nineteenth-century men. If you want to return here, you'll have to find another area."

Like most women who joined university faculties during the late sixties and early seventies, I found an entrenched masculinist system, not only in the department but also throughout the university administration. How sweet it was those many years later, to be the chair who presided over the retirement party for the man who did not hire housewives. And since the department had its Chaucer, Shakespeare, and Melville men, I am fond of explaining that I found an appropriate area, one they did not have covered when I left for graduate school. I became the department's "women's man," teaching the first women's studies courses, leading the battles for equity.

The subsequent struggles to change pervasive inequities were instructive. Without realizing it, prior to joining the faculty, I had internalized some of the prevailing mind-set that being a housewife and working in women's organizations was of a lesser worth than man's work. Conventional wisdom held that my household responsibilities prevented my being as professional and dedicated as my male colleagues. I wondered then why it was that though I was still a wife and mother when I returned, I managed to complete my degree sooner than the three ABD unmarried males who were hired at the same time I was. Revelations continued when I could not get male colleagues to a committee meeting because Wednesday afternoon was their regular golf tee time. Unlike these colleagues who had followed the traditional and continuous path from the best colleges through prestigious graduate schools to a job, my education had been sporadic; I had three children while pursuing my master's degree, barely making the six-year time limit. It was often a close race between what would come first, the baby or the end of the semester. My advanced state of pregnancy was the source of some anxiety for my male professors. Few women taught the graduate courses in those days. It was also a battle fighting the perceptions that somehow pregnancy disintegrated the mind, doing housework ossified the intellect. My thesis director could not assimilate the seeming paradox that I could bake fabulous cakes and cookies and still set the curve in his classes.

But my purpose here is not to recount horror stories about the routes many women took to assume leadership positions in our professions. It is, instead, to share certain discoveries I made as a university administrator, particularly during the two times I chaired the university's largest department—discoveries which cause me to question conventional wisdom about the necessary qualities and preparation for being an effective manager or chairperson. Extrapolating the universal from the individual and personal, I would like to suggest that though one reads volumes about women's lack of preparation for administrative positions, all I really needed to know about chairing a department I learned by being a Jewish mother. Being a feminist also helped.

Let me clarify one term at the onset. What we stereotype as the "Jewish mother" is not so different from the Italian, Irish, Mexican, or African-American mother. The universality of the type was made clear to me during a class discussion of *Portnoy's Complaint*. A group of irate women were up in arms about what they saw as Philip Roth's pejorative characterization of Jewish mothers when a young man got up to speak. "My name is George Kelley," he said, "and that is my Mexican-Irish mother." Clarence Brown, whose family hailed from the formerly all-black community of Vado was sure that his grandmother had provided the model. Mothering everywhere fosters certain archetypal qualities. And for a future chairperson, those attributes can prove most valuable.

"Few chairpersons bring a managerial perspective to their work," conjectures David B. Booth in his description of shared dilemmas of academic administrators.[2] That may be because few chairpersons are mothers first. When one has balanced the needs of home and family and a professional life, one does not survive unless one develops sound managerial skills. Of course Booth is referring to people who have followed the traditional path to department administration. Sounding a similar note, Allan Tucker bemoans the lack of national and regional workshops to help department chairpersons with their new responsibilities.[3] Most new chairpersons have not had to set up the scheduling of carpools for three children in two different schools, plus get them to after-school religious studies, music and dance lessons, gymnastics and sports events, as well as to doctor and dental appointments, while doing the planning and shopping for healthy and nutritious breakfasts and dinners, keeping the family budget, getting the bills paid, and teaching a four-course load of freshman and sophomore English. That usually falls to mothers to do.

No one-day, two-day, or even weeklong workshop, with its homilies and abstractions about time management can begin to provide the same preparation that mothering provides. The principle is clearly established in freshman English. Abstractions and generalizations are most effective when supported with specifics and examples. The workshop's leaders exhort one to "set priorities and budget time accordingly." But that abstraction is no help or preparation when the dean requests that you prepare and return, in one week, a prospectus, justification, and budget for a desired new program. Nor does it help to know that your work may be an exercise in futility, never used. But still, it must be ready, just in case certain funds become available as a result of the legislature's latest deliberations. This, of course, during a week when the department is hosting two candidates for important positions and has its annual student writing awards program with a major writer invited to present the awards and give a reading. Set priorities and budget time indeed! On the other hand, if one has gone through the experience of waking to a child with a 102-degree fever on a day when one is scheduled to present crucial lectures in several classes, plus chair a certain important committee meeting and pick up one's visiting mother-in-law at the airport, one has experienced a "baptism of fire" which creates a hardened veteran at juggling and prioritizing.

John A. Shtogren, who as president of the Higher Education Leadership and Management Society, wrote extensively about problems of university and college administrators who, like myself, came to administration through literary studies.[4] That, he explains, is why he uses images and metaphors to describe the job. Water imagery was his theme, mothering metaphors are mine. Shtogren identifies the job of chair, as one who "creates an environment where faculty can grow to their greatest potential and teaching and learning are optimal" or in management jargon, one who optimizes human resources.[5] Any conscientious mother knows that one of her main roles in life is to create an environment in which each child develops his or her talents and potential. Why else would a sane person listen to hours of squeaky violin practice, sit through the hundredth performance of "The Nutcracker," or give up every Tuesday and Thursday afternoon to soccer drills? So the conscientious chair, who is not particularly interested in poetry, attends the readings of her faculty and various other poets brought in on an NEA grant, reads the latest esoteric take on Medieval troubadour tales published by her colleague, and though her area be twentieth-century American fiction, she watches the mail for conferences and announcements that might create professional opportunities for her faculty in fields from professional writing to Caribbean literature.

The paradox is that though the individual faculty member is encouraged to specialize, to make oneself an expert in a small field, the chair is expected to enlarge the scope of her interests, to be a Jill-of-all-trades. Shtogren declares that the question of what a chair is supposed to do is answered by one word: "everything."[6] In his analysis, the task is: "formidable."[7] True, but anyone whose training was in being wife/mother/professor is used to doing "everything," to being faced with "formidable" tasks. To be a mother is to be an educator, doctor and nurse, playmate and disciplinarian, chief cook and bottle washer, finance manager, nutritional expert, and target for all the complaints and dissatisfactions of the family. A word about this latter quality. Mothers, in this century, have gotten used to being blamed for everything from not allowing their sons to grow up, thus creating the great American boy-man (Philip Wylie defined it as Momism), to driving their children relentlessly to stage and screen success. Bette Midler is one in a line of actresses to recreate the role of Rose, the quintessential stage mother, in *Gypsy*. We mothers are used to being blamed for all the failures in the family, so it is not a great shock to adapt to the chair's role as lightning rod for all the department's ills. If Professor X's fall schedule does not suit him, never mind that it was the one he asked for last spring, the chair is trying to make life difficult for him. If her class has low enrollment, Professor Y accuses the chair of poor scheduling. When I was a little girl, I thought my mother stayed up all night planning things to aggravate me. My children thought the same. Faculty sometimes behave as if they think my time is spent figuring out how to make things difficult for them.

I am not the only one who has noted analogies between the family and the department. Allan Tucker has also noted the parallels between departmental and domestic situations. In elaborating on the special character of the chair's challenges, he notes that the chair, unlike the dean, has to live with the results of any administrative decisions. Pointing out deans' distances from the day-to-day encounters with faculty impacted by their decisions, Tucker explains: "they do not have to maintain a family relationship with their faculty members. The department chairperson, on the other hand, does. He or she must be acutely aware of the vital statistics of each family member—births, deaths, marriages, divorces, illnesses, and even private financial woes."[8] He goes on to explain: "This intimate relationship is not duplicated anywhere else in the college or university because no other academic unit takes on the ambience of a family, with its personal interaction, its daily sharing of common goals and interests (with frequent contention over how those goals are to be pursued) and its concern for each member."[9]

This concern for each family member, this mothering, can have positive results. In *Women of Academe* the authors quote a professor whose tenure experience was enhanced by a nurturing chair: "I was very lucky to have a female chairperson who took me through tenure the way you would want a mother to stand by you as a guide, who cared about you but wanted you to have your own independence."[10] My tenure as chair was greatly enhanced by the number of untenured faculty I mentored to affirmative tenure decisions. And one morning I was bemused to find on my desk a mug which reads: "Everyone needs a Jewish Mother." One of those professors, of Catholic school education, currently a vice president, still jokingly refers to me as her Jewish mother.

Another way that having been a Jewish mother prior to being chair taught me skills that were useful in my administration was in learning the techniques for getting maximum reception repasts for the minimum monetary output. *De rigueur* behavior for Jewish mothers is belonging to and being active in any number of volunteer charitable organizations such as Hadassah, National Council of Jewish Women, Sisterhood, and B'nai B'rith Women. One learns in these organizations to operate on minimum overhead. Unlike large charity organizations who hire professional money-raisers, who work out of lavishly furnished offices with paid staff, Hadassah women are their own staff. Every donated dollar must go to the cause, not to expenses. So we learn early the fine art of "schnorring," defined by Leo Rosten in *The Joys of Yiddish* as begging. In other words, rather than take money out of donations for food for our fundraising events, we learn to convince merchants who we patronize and who support our causes to donate. Using my "schnorring" skills while chair of the department, I was able to encourage restaurants, habitually frequented by our faculty and often hired to cater university and department events, to occasionally donate elegant foods for a reception after a major reading. Thus discretionary department funds were kept for more lasting investments, such as computers and CD players.

Of course, there are pitfalls in the paradigm. If a person tries to be supermom and do it all alone, she is setting herself up for psychological and physical exhaustion. The wise mother trains her family to assume responsibility for part of her formidable job. This also teaches coping and home management skills, essential for raising competent adults. It occurred to me, both as feminist and working mother, that there was no reason that I should be responsible for all the meals in the house. We all had full days, my husband at his job, my children at school and their various extracurricular activities. Why should I be the one to do all the cooking and cleaning? So we divided the responsibilities. Each child kept his or her own room clean. And each child was assigned a day to be responsible for dinner. On those days the ones who did not cook cleaned up after dinner. My husband, whose repertoire is primarily soups and salads, chose Sunday night. The children cooked on Tuesday, Wednesday, and Thursday. Saturday was designated as "do your own thing" night. My one bow to convention was to assume responsibility for two nights, Monday and Friday, when we had our traditional family Sabbath meal. Every Sunday we planned the week's menus and made the shopping list accordingly. Simple meals were planned for the youngest to prepare; the eldest asked for my recipes for certain dishes that he wanted to try. This way the boys learned menu planning and meal preparation as well as clean-up duties. More than that they learned to see themselves as as responsible for that aspect of home management as their sister or me. It is called "equality."[11] In a department all faculty need to see themselves as responsible, according to their abilities, for the smooth running of the department. When everyone is asked to contribute, burnout is lessened. Certain jobs, the cooking and cleaning of the department, should not always fall on the same shoulders. In later years, as an associate dean, I jokingly castigated the male chair of the history department, whose excuse for not having coffee ready for a Saturday workshop was that the secretary was not there. I told him I thought that the ability to make coffee should be requisite for chairing a department. A good CEO can do all the jobs in his company.

The paradigm is not limited to the academic world. I am not the only woman who took the lessons I learned in doing undervalued work and made them work to my advantage. Examples abound of women who translated their homemaking skills into lucrative businesses. The name Martha Stewart comes immediately to mind.[12] But before there was Martha Stewart, a homemaking empire in herself, there were women such as Bette Graham. Using her kitchen mixmaster, in 1951 Bette Graham invented Liquid Paper. When IBM declined her offer to sell them the product—after all, male scientists in a laboratory did not invent it—she started her own business, a business she sold in 1979 for 47.5 million dollars.[13] Marlene Conway, without any background in science or chemistry, came up with a process for separating a diaper's wood pulp from its superabsorbent polymer and reusing both. She did this by experimenting with her son's soiled diapers.[14] An article in *Director* tells the story of Carol Bowhill, whose success is described as the "triumph of enthusiasm and house-wifely common sense over management theory." Without business training, and while raising three children, she has built a rental-property business that employs tweny-seven people and makes some four million dollars a year.[15] An even more cheering story is of Ela Bhatt, whose Self-employed Women's Association bank lends money to illiterate women with no training except in homemaking.[16] These women, who could not get conventional credit, have a 95 percent repayment rate.

But it was not only mothering that provided me with the necessary administrative and management skills to be an effective administrator. Working in the women's movement and in women's volunteer organizations also teaches useful management skills. As a feminist working with women's groups, I learned the value of the matriarchal paradigm, a horizontal organizational pattern of shared responsibility and authority, rather than the vertical organizational charts favored in the patriarchal system. In the English department in the early 1970s, we formed a women's group to research and combat gender-related inequities in salary, promotion, and tenure. All shared equally in the work of that group and it was one of the best experiences in our lives. It was not only the camaraderie that made it so but also our efficacy in changing department culture. I can sense some reader's hackles being raised at what could be perceived as collectivism. But an activity can be called by different names depending on who is doing the naming. I saw it as making each woman take individual responsibility. No one was idle and then benefited from the work of the others. Later, when we formed a women's studies program, the administrative unit of that program was headed not by a chair, but by a coordinator who worked with a coordinating committee. The position of coordinator was rotated among the members of the coordinating committee. And members of the coordinating committee served four-year terms and were replaced by new members on a revolving schedule. The result was a large number of faculty who were invested in the success of the women's studies program and who also understood the work necessary to assure the effectual functioning of the program. In later years, the original group was, interestingly enough, dissipated because the women were tapped for important leadership roles in their departments and in the college.

Translating my experience in women's studies to running the department, I found that the more different people who participated in critical decision-making functions of the department, the better it was for department morale. One example was the personnel committee, which in our department is responsible for determining the merit evaluations and rankings as well as recommendations for promotions and tenure of the whole department. People who had not served on that committee often imagined some kind of cabal and complained that they had been unfairly judged. Through suasion and inducement I was able to bring about the election to that committee of people who had never before served. The effect was an education for those people and a reduction of the suspicions surrounding the procedure. When one must judge the comparative accomplishments of faculty then one can see the rationale behind ratings. Evaluations are still painful but not in quite the same way. There is a better overall understanding of why some colleagues receive large merit raises and others do not.

Another instance of feminist organization was in my appointment of the administrative staff of the department. As it worked out, in the first year of my term the colleagues I asked to be assistant chair, director of literature, director of creative writing, director of graduate studies, and director of composition were all women. Only the director of English-education was male. I say "as it worked out" because my choices were a result of selecting the best people for the jobs and not because I was excluding men. The department ran smoothly and harmoniously with an overwhelmingly female staff. When my three-year term was over, the male-majority department asked me to serve again. Those women I had appointed were asked to stay on by subsequent chairs. Much of the feminist tone of my term came from divesting myself of some of the supposed "powers" of the chair. The various directors did all the scheduling and an elected committee did the evaluating. Of course, all of their work was subject to my approval. But it is a rare occasion when rational beings, working together, cannot agree.

So much of this is a matter of semantics. Let me illustrate. Feminist linguistic studies are full of examples of the different names that men and women associate with similar behaviors. Assertive behavior is called ambitious in men, pushy in women. A sexually active man is called a "playboy" or "macho," whereas similar behavior in a woman brings the pejorative epithets of "promiscuous" or "nymphomaniac." So it is with the techniques I am advocating. What I have called mothering or feminism may be called by other names in the works of other scholars. One text on academic administration calls it "participatory management."[17] Old-time tomes call it "division-of-labor." I have seen it referred to as democratic executive style. In another instance the behavior was described as collaborative leadership. I imagine some of the more fundamentalist individualists could recoil at what they would call collectivism. I call it effective administration. In Juliet's words, "A rose by another name would smell as sweet." It obviously worked; at the end of my term as chair, the president of the university asked me to take over as executive director of the university's Diamond Jubilee celebration. That job allowed me to use my housewifery skills to create and manage events as diverse as football half-times, city-wide street festivals, physics fairs, student retention programs, Vietnam War Memorial dedications, city and university planning commissions, and a year-long program of nationally and internationally renowned speakers. And that is just a sample of what the job entailed. My administrative assistant, marveling at the clock-work management of these events and the creation of photogenic contexts, had no idea that I had learned those skills giving parties and being a hostess for my husband's business events in my younger days as a housewife in suburbia.

Call it what you will. Whenever I think back to that misguided chairman who did not hire housewives, I wonder how many effective administrators he lost for the department.

Notes

1. Parts of this essay were published originally in the *Proceedings of the Women in Higher Education Conference* (Orlando, Fla., 1994).

2. David B. Booth, "Administrative Development of Chairpersons and Departments," in John A. Shtogren, ed., *Administrative Development in Higher Education*, (Richmond, Va., 1978), 157.

3. Allan Tucker, *Chairing the Academic Department: Leadership Among Peers* (New York, 1984), 1.

4. Shtogren, *Administrative Development*, 171.

5. *Ibid.*, 172.

6. *Ibid.*, 173.

7. *Ibid.*, 174.

8. Tucker, *Chairing*, 5.

9. *Ibid.*

10. Nadya Aisenberg and Mona Harrington, *Women of Academe: Outsiders in the Sacred Grove* (Amherst, Mass., 1988), 47.

11. I take it as a given that the more self-maintenance skills any human knows, the more independent that human can be. But, in the days I am describing, men who learned to cook, clean, do the laundry, and sew were in short supply.

12. Eva MacSweeney, "Martha Stewart," *Harper's Bazaar*, August 1998, 164–168. While I use homemaking metaphors to describe academic work, MacSweeney uses academic language to depict Stewart. She describes her as having "Ph.D. level knowledge of every conceivable area of homemaking." Her contention is that Stewart is restoring to women the "right to take pleasure and pride in the household arts."

13. The mixmaster is now part of the traveling exhibit: "Texas Women: A Celebration of History."

14. "If You Have a Lemon, Make Lemonade," *Canadian Business* 69 (September 11, 1996), 48–54. She has enlarged her focus from diapers to turning other environmental nightmares into corporate opportunities.

15. Phoebe Corke, "French Connector," *Director* 49:8 (March 1996), 19–20. Bowhill rents French properties to British vacationers. This article describes her as a "Hampshire housewife."

16. Caitlin Kelly, "Micro-banker," *Worldbusiness* 2:2 (March/April 1996), 46.

17. David R. Powers and Mary F. Powers, *Making Participatory Management Work*, (San Francisco, 1983).

Ellen Frankel Paul

❧

Fetal Protection and Freedom of Contract

THE ATTEMPT BY SOME MANUFACTURERS TO LIMIT OR PROHIBIT THE EMPLOY-
ment of fertile or pregnant women in jobs which unavoidably use dangerous chemicals in their production processes has run squarely into
anti-discrimination law, specifically Title VII of the Civil Rights Act of 1964
and its amendment by the 1978 Pregnancy Discrimination Act (PDA). A recent Supreme Court decision, *International Union, UAW v. Johnson Controls*, has galvanized vocal advocacy groups and focused public attention
on such "fetal protection policies."[1] Anti-discrimination suits turn on ar-
cane issues of statutory interpretation, burdens of proof, judicially constructed theories and tests, and jesuitical readings of the precedents, and
this case is no exception. All of this legal minutia usually serves to insulate
these issues from public scrutiny and confine whatever debate there is to
legal experts and their epigones in the more refined media. But the issue
of fetal protection lends itself rather easily to exploitation, and the debate
has played itself out on television talk shows of the most sensationalist
sort. Bedraggled business lobbyists have proven no match for representatives of women's groups or the American Civil Liberties Union (ACLU) accompanied by a working woman sterilized in order to retain her job.

What has been lost in both the public hoopla and the debate over legal
niceties by judges and commentators is a regard for the principle of freedom of contract and its centrality to both individual liberty and the free
market. For autonomous individuals who are subject to no person's will
but their own, contractual freedom is the outward expression of their ownership of their own bodies, of their liberty to dispose of their labor and its
fruits as they see fit. This Lockean insight, capturing as it does the inti-

mate connection between personal autonomy and economic behavior, was embraced by our Founders and incorporated in Article I, Section 10.1 of the Constitution, which declares that "No State shall . . . pass any . . . Law impairing the Obligation of Contracts." Although restricted to only retroactive application by an early Supreme Court decision, protection of freedom of contract enjoyed particular judicial favor during the heyday of the much-maligned "Old Court" (from roughly the last decade of the nineteenth century to the mid-1930s).[2] Contractual freedom was read into the due process clauses of the Fifth and Fourteenth Amendments and used to overturn prospective legislation that interfered with various terms and conditions of employment, such as restrictions on hours, minimum wages, and bans on "yellow dog contracts." Since the New Deal this judicial oversight of economic liberties has been nearly universally condemned until quite recently when a handful of commentators have attempted to revitalize the due process clauses.

Freedom of contract is, also, imperative to the smooth functioning of a market economy, for without a stable regime of contract with appropriate laws and a judiciary to arbitrate disputes, a society would be reduced to barter or plunder. Perhaps the importance of a regime of contract is most evident where it is lacking, namely in the former Soviet Union where all market manifestations and the laws and institutions that made them possible were ruthlessly extirpated, and their re-creation is proving a daunting task, one which in the interim leaves much economic activity on either a barter or "mafia" basis.

Fetal Protection Policies: The Social Background

During the past quarter-century, women in ever increasing numbers have entered the U.S. workforce. No longer just secretaries, teachers, or nurses, they have invaded traditionally male preserves—police stations, firehouses, coal mines, and unionized, highly paid manufacturing jobs. This feminization of the workforce is the result of many social forces and lifestyle changes, easily enumerated but not easily quantifiable. Among these forces are changes in the law that made divorce easier and alimony less likely, and which forced many women, even those with young children, into becoming self-sufficient.[3] In addition, twenty years of increasing taxes and low economic growth have made a middle-class family lifestyle virtually insupportable without two wage earners. The sexual revolution of the late 1960s and the women's rights movement also encouraged women to seek independence from men and to alter their dreams from the traditional marriage. Finally, anti-discrimination laws with their affirmative action interpretations have encouraged women to enter nontraditional occupations and gave businesses an additional incentive—liability avoidance—to employ them.

Two million working women become pregnant in the United States each year, which means that 71 percent of pregnancies occur in working women. This makes pregnancy an important—and costly—management problem for businesses employing significant numbers of female workers. These management problems, however, have not been left exclusively to employers to handle, for the Pregnancy Discrimination Act explicitly defined the Civil Rights Act's Title VII ban on employment discrimination on the basis of sex to include pregnancy. Many longstanding practices in the marketplace were no longer permissible, such as firing a woman once her pregnancy became known, denying employment to a pregnant woman, or treating pregnant women differently from other employees who suffer temporary disabilities with respect to medical insurance, fringe benefits, or disability leave.

While Title VII itself mandated that employers ignore differences between men and women as long as the women can fulfill the requirements of the job, the PDA went a step further by in effect demanding that employers likewise ignore pregnancy or treat it as they do all other (nonvoluntary) disabilities. The PDA states that within Title VII:

> The terms "because of sex" or "on the basis of sex" include, but are not limited to, because of or on the basis of pregnancy, childbirth, or related medical conditions and women affected by pregnancy, childbirth, or related medical conditions shall be treated the same for all employment-related purposes . . . as other persons not so affected *but similar in their ability or inability to work*.[4]

One difference between men and women that some employers found increasingly difficult to ignore is the heightened susceptibility of fetuses to dangerous chemicals in the workplace, fetuses that by nature—irrespective of law—only women can carry. Companies whose manufacturing processes could not eliminate the use of harmful chemicals or could not bring their use within safe limits for fetuses responded with fetal protection policies, some more restrictive than others. Whether motivated by a moral regard for the welfare of future generations (as Johnson Controls contends) or out of a self-interested desire to avoid future tort liability for damaged offspring, or, even more insidiously, to bar women from lucrative male jobs (as Johnson's detractors argue), these policies did not sit well with female employees banned from their jobs or those denied employment, nor with women's advocacy and civil liberties groups.[5]

Johnson Controls' policy, which was adopted in 1982, triggered lawsuits in both federal and state courts.[6] It replaced an earlier, more lenient policy put in place by the previous owner (Globe Union) of what would become in 1978 Johnson's battery division. With the existing technology the production of batteries requires the use of lead, a chemical particularly harmful to young children and fetuses. Since 1978 the use of lead paints in homes has been banned in the United States and there is pressure in Congress today to go even further than this and mandate that all houses built before that date be inspected on resale and that warnings be provided to buyers. There is abundant evidence, and scientific agreement, on the harmfulness of lead to young children who might ingest large quantities of it through chipped paint and suffer mental impairment as a result.

Johnson Controls after exploring its options decided that the previous policy, adopted by Globe Union in 1977, was no longer sufficient in light of the additional scientific evidence that had emerged on the danger of lead exposure to fetuses. Fetal exposure to lead could result in miscarriage, premature delivery, stillbirth, low birth weight, developmental problems, and other central nervous system disfunctions. The previous policy included warning women of the dangers of lead exposure to fetuses, advising them that the company recommended that fertile women not work with lead if they were considering having children, and requiring that those still wishing to work with lead sign a statement acknowledging that they had been advised of the risks.

Johnson Controls concluded that despite its best efforts—expenditure of $15 million on lead-reduction technology since acquiring the battery division, its adherence to government-approved safety limits for lead exposure for adults set by the Occupational Safety and Health Administration (OSHA) and its insistence on showers, the use of respirators, and other safety devices for workers exposed to high levels of lead—a ban on the assignment of fertile women to high-exposure parts of the plant was necessary to protect their potential offspring. The company was concerned, too, that under the previous policy eight women with excessive lead levels had given birth between 1979 and 1982 and that one of their children also had an excessive level. The 1982 policy bars women of childbearing capacity from being hired for high-exposure jobs or for jobs that would lead in the normal course of promotion to such jobs. Women already in such jobs were "grandfathered in," that is, they were permitted to retain their jobs if their blood lead levels remained below thirty micrograms per deciliter (the level considered safe by OSHA for workers considering having families). Those transferred from such jobs retained their previous salaries, even if their new jobs were at lower wage rates. Women whose inability to bear children was medically documented could remain in high-exposure jobs or be hired for them. The company maintained that it was not its intention to force fertile women into being sterilized, though some women, including one of the plaintiffs who sued Johnson Controls, did claim that they were forced to choose between sterilization and loss of their jobs and that they in fact chose sterilization. One plaintiff claimed that her compensation was lowered upon removal from a high-lead exposure position.[7]

Johnson Controls is not unique in its adoption of fetal protection policies. The Equal Employment Opportunity Commission (EEOC) cited a 1979 estimate that 100,000 jobs were at that time affected by such policies, and another much-quoted estimate put the number of jobs that might be affected in the future at between 15 and 20 million.[8] Such prominent companies as B. F. Goodrich, General Motors Corp., Monsanto Co., and E. I. duPont de Nemours & Co. maintained similar policies.[9] The danger that such policies might spread to other industries, and that they might be extended beyond jobs exposing women to harmful chemicals to jobs requiring, perhaps, heavy lifting, is what prompted women's rights groups and the ACLU to view such policies as a danger to women's rights and opportunities almost on a par with restrictions on abortion. Isabelle Katz Pinzler, the ACLU's director of women's rights, argues that, "Since time immemorial, the excuse for keeping women in their place has been because of their role in producing the next generation. The attitude of Johnson Controls is: 'We know better than you. We can't allow women to make this decision. We have to make it for them.'"[10]

The public debate, both before and after the Supreme Court handed down its decision in *Johnson Controls*, has been framed in starkly contrasting images. On the women's rights side of the debate, as the quotation from Pinzler indicates, the issues are: a woman's right to decide what employment is best for her and for her actual and potential children, with the claim that she is in the best position to balance all factors of health as well as economics; preserving the employment gains of women by fighting policies that would shrink their opportunities; opposing policies that force women to choose between destroying their fertility or losing their jobs; and fighting the reimposition of paternalistic policies, whether government enforced or adopted by individual companies. On management's side the pre-eminent issue, at least as posed for public consumption, is viewed as a moral one: protecting those who cannot choose for themselves, namely potential fetuses, from workplace hazards that might significantly impair them. In the words of Stanley S. Jaspan, Johnson Controls' lawyer before the Supreme Court, "It violates common sense to require an employer to damage unborn children. A manufacturer that creates a hazard has an obligation to protect against injury for that hazard."[11] The critics of fetal protection policies tend to view statements such as Jaspan's as mere pretexts for reimposing the old-boy exclusivity on the plant floor.

Fetal Protecton Policies—The Legal Quagmire

If we wish to see how an anti-discrimination statute can decimate freedom of contract, then Johnson Controls is exemplary. The tortured history of the case as it wended its way from federal district court through two levels of appeal, first the Seventh Circuit and then the U.S. Supreme Court, is also a nearly perfect example of how laws that seem fairly simple and straightforward to their framers can become twisted, distorted artifacts after years of exposure to creative counsel, judicial massaging, and unanticipated applications. Examining a fairly clear statute and a short amendment to it, the trial court judge and a majority of the judges on the Seventh Circuit found Johnson Controls' pleadings, replete with expert medical evidence, so compelling that they granted summary judgment *for the company*. The Supreme Court found the grant of summary judgment insupportable, the medical evidence debatable, and fetal protection policies on their face violative of anti-discrimination law. The lower courts embraced one paradigm of Title VII adjudication in reaching their conclusions, and the Supreme Court another.

The purpose, here, is not to examine this legal morass for its own sake but rather as an illustration of the danger of interfering with the marketplace in the name of civil rights. *Johnson Controls* bears close scrutiny not only for its effect on freedom of contract but also for the damage it inflicts on another principle of critical importance to a free market and a free society. That principle is the rule of law, and one of its requirements is that individuals or companies not be held liable under one law for obeying the stipulations of another. This is a requirement that the Supreme Court likely transgressed by placing civil rights and tort liability on a collision course. Another component of the rule of law is that legal rules ought to be predictable in their application and readily comprehensible to those subject to them, features that the law as interpreted in *Johnson Controls* conspicuously lacks.

Johnson Controls' initial victory was won in the United States District Court for the Eastern District of Wisconsin.[12] Chief Judge Warren framed the issue succinctly: "whether a fetal protection policy which prohibits women who are capable of bearing children from working in jobs where there is a likelihood that their blood lead level will rise above 30 micrograms violates Title VII of the 1964 Civil Rights Act."[13] After a review of the submissions of both parties and the law, he would conclude that it did not and grant summary judgment to Johnson Controls.[14]

In reaching his decision, the chief judge conceded that fetal protection policies do not fit neatly into the usual two paradigms applied to Title VII cases by the courts, a problem recognized by other judges who have wrestled with the few similar cases.[15] In order to make such cases come out the way the judges desire, they have had to be creative with the two Title VII paradigms, bending here, snipping there, cobbling together a rationale that will reach the right end, even if doctrinally messy. A brief overview of how judges have treated charges of, primarily, racial and sexual discrimination under Title VII will be necessary in order to see just how creative judges have been in dealing with challenges to fetal protection policies. Title VII reads in relevant part:

> It shall be an unlawful employment practice for an employer—
> (1) to fail or refuse to hire or discharge any individual, or otherwise to discriminate against any individual with respect to his compensation terms, conditions, or privileges of employment, because of such individual's race, color, religion, sex, or national origin; or (2) to limit, segregate, or classify his employees or applicants for employment in any way which would deprive or tend to deprive any individual of employment opportunities or otherwise adversely affect his status as an employee, because of such individual's race, color, religion, sex, or national origin.[16]

As Title VII cases progressed in the courts during the 1970s, judges articulated two paradigms for analyzing them—*disparate treatment* and *disparate impact*—both ultimately endorsed by the Supreme Court. *Disparate treatment* is intimately linked to the language of Title VII. One sort of problem that it addresses is facially discriminatory employment policies, that is, policies that merely in the stating of them violate some provision of Title VII. Employers can defend such policies only by showing that they fall within a narrow exception permitted under Title VII which has come to be known by an acronym: BFOQ. Discrimination is permissible "in those certain instances where religion, sex, or national origin is a *bona fide occupational qualification* reasonably related to the normal operation of that particular business or enterprise."[17] A BFOQ is a difficult defense to successfully mount, because the Supreme Court has read it narrowly to restrict it to job-related skills.

Given the difficulty of mounting a successful defense of fetal protection policies if an employer can only defend them as a BFOQ, and given

many judges' inclinations to uphold such policies as reasonable and socially justifiable in the interest of protecting the welfare of future generations, it is no wonder that judges have sought to squeeze these cases into
the contours of a more appealing paradigm. A *disparate impact* theory of
Title VII, the only other paradigm available, has had to serve those judges
eager to uphold fetal protection, even though the fit is an uneasy one. Disparate impact is a wholly created judicial artifact. It is aimed at facially
neutral policies that work to the detriment of protected groups, policies
"fair in form, but discriminatory in operation."[18] Policies successfully challenged under the disparate impact theory have included various objective
hiring tools such as standardized intelligence tests, height and weight standards, and educational-attainment requirements. Unlike disparate treatment cases, in which *intentional* discrimination must be proven (as Title
VII explicitly requires), disparate impact requires no showing of intentional discrimination. Plaintiffs usually build their cases under this theory
by showing evidence of statistical disparities between the employer's workforce and the available minority or female workers in the area. They must
point to a particular employment practice—seemingly neutral—that works
an unintentionally discriminatory effect. Employers can defend their policies by arguing *business necessity*, a somewhat broader category than disparate treatment's defense of BFOQ, thus an easier defense for businesses
to make. Plaintiffs must then prove that this defense is spurious and even
if they cannot, they can still prevail if they can show that a policy with a
less onerous effect on minorities or women would also serve the employer's legitimate business interest.

Fitting fetal protection policies on the Procrustean bed of disparate
impact theory is no simple task. It requires considerable ingenuity for the
judge must argue that a policy that explicitly only applies to females is a facially neutral policy when it practically screams out that it is not. Acknowledging that the policy is explicitly discriminatory would drive it back under
the inhospitable umbrella of disparate treatment from which it could not
emerge unscathed, as the Supreme Court would eventually and defini-
tively establish. Both Judge Warren and the majority of the Seventh Circuit Court of Appeals labored valiantly to twist Johnson Controls' fetal
protection policy into a facially neutral one with a disparate impact, and
then to argue that business necessity justified its adoption. Their labors do
not make a pretty picture though for good measure, the Seventh Circuit
majority did argue that even if they had considered the policy under the
disparate treatment theory it would still pass muster as a bona fide occupational qualification. It is difficult to reproduce their argument for the neu-

trality of this seemingly nonneutral policy since it was so blatantly contrived to reach the desired outcome, but what they seemed to be saying is that Johnson Controls was genuinely concerned with protecting fetal health and their concern led them to articulate a policy that affected only women because only women can carry fetuses. It is fair to say that their reasoning was outcome driven. They found the medical evidence of potential fetal damage from lead exposure so compelling, the medical evidence of damage to male reproductive capacity from lead exposure so scant, any alternative policy to protect fetuses as unlikely to achieve that objective (because lead stays in the blood, tissues, and bones for long periods after maternal exposure), that they were convinced that Johnson Controls' policy was reasonable and should be upheld. Therefore they massaged the niceties of standard Title VII interpretation to secure this outcome.

Three dissents were lodged by four judges of the Seventh Circuit, two of them quite forceful, and somewhat curiously, penned by staunch conservatives, former professors at the University of Chicago Law School, and Reagan appointees to the court. They found the majority's manipulation of Title VII paradigms unacceptable, with one, Judge Posner, arguing that the case should have gone to trial, that the appropriate paradigm was disparate treatment, and that the company should have had to defend itself under the BFOQ. Judge Easterbrook, taking an even harder line and adhering to strict statutory interpretation, saw Johnson Controls' policy as "sex discrimination, forbidden unless sex is a 'bona fide occupational qualification'—which it is not."[19] He was much concerned that the fetal protection policy treated an "employee not as an individual but as a woman,"[20] and that if such policies were judicially condoned more companies would adopt them and women might lose twenty million jobs. The threat that such policies held of consigning women to low-paying "women's work" led him to declare that this case "is likely the most important sex-discrimination case in any court since 1964, when Congress enacted Title VII."[21] Because such a policy assumes "that women are less able than men to make decisions," and since prenatal injuries had not occurred at Johnson Controls' battery operations, the policy could not be justified as a BFOQ, for such a defense can only be established when "all or substantially all women would be unable to perform safely and efficiently the duties of the job."[22] It is mere "word play," he argued, "to say that 'the job' at Johnson is to make batteries without risk to fetuses."[23] Judge Easterbrook considered and also found wanting the possibility of tort liability since Title VII bars employers from considering the additional costs involved in employing female workers.[24] "Title VII," he emphasized, "applies even when—*especially* when—discrimination is rational as the employer sees things."[25] Defining tolerable risks and promulgating standards to protect future generations is, he thinks, properly the job of Congress or OSHA, and not of an individual company bent on enforcing zero risk on women exclusively. Women should be entitled to consider their net risks when deciding to take higher paying jobs with medical and other benefits that would expose them or their fetuses to dangerous chemicals, rather than lower paying jobs with the attendant risks of no prenatal care and no medical benefits.

When *Johnson Controls* reached the Supreme Court, Judge Easterbrook's arguments proved more persuasive than those of the Seventh Circuit's majority. With all justices concurring in the judgment of reversal, the Court held that Title VII as amended by the Pregnancy Discrimination Act precludes sex-specific fetal protection policies.[26] Justice Blackmun, delivering the Court's opinion, found obvious bias in Johnson Controls' policy; men, but not women, were given a choice about whether they wished to risk their reproductive health for a job exposing them to high levels of lead, thus the policy "explicitly discriminates against women on the basis of their sex . . . [and] creates a facial classification based on gender."[27] The Court rejected the lower court's selection of the disparate impact paradigm, finding that the policy fell squarely within disparate treatment analysis, but even here rejecting the appeals court's assertion that the policy could be justified as a BFOQ as well as the looser standard of disparate impact's business necessity. Reading the BFOQ narrowly, as the Court had in the past, Justice Blackmun pointed out that in order to qualify as a BFOQ a policy would have to relate to the "essence" of the job, that is, to the "central mission of the employer's business."[28] Concern for future children, however, is not an "essential aspect of batterymaking,"[29] because a woman's potential to bear children does not interfere with her ability to perform the job. Since the Pregnancy Discrimination Act's standard precludes discrimination against pregnant women unless they differ in their "ability or inability to work," the Court concluded that Johnson Controls could not discriminate against potentially pregnant women unless this reproductive potential interfered with their performance of the job, which nothing in the record showed that it did. Therefore, Justice Blackmun had "no difficulty in concluding that Johnson Controls cannot establish a BFOQ."[30] His opinion ended with these words, emphasizing the importance to the Court of a woman's right to choose:

> It is no more appropriate for the courts than it is for individual
> employers to decide whether a woman's reproductive role is

more important to herself and her family than her economic role. Congress has left this choice to the woman as hers to make.[31]

Before reaching this ringing declaration of women's rights, Justice Blackmun did respond to the tort liability issue that concerned Judge Posner of the Seventh Circuit and Supreme Court Justices White, Rehnquist, and Kennedy in their concurring opinion, even though the issue was not before the Court. He concluded that without negligence, a court would have great difficulty in finding an employer liable for damage to a newborn. If Title VII bans fetal protection policies, as the Court now held that it did, and the employer informs the woman of all risks, and the employer had not acted negligently, "the basis for holding an employer liable seems remote at best."[32] Justice White and his two sympathizers did find this tort liability issue more troubling. Justice White is far less certain than Justice Blackmun that state courts will not be hospitable to claims of prenatal damage. He states the following reasons for his concern: (1) that compliance with Title VII might not insulate defendants from tort liability in state courts;[33] (2) warnings may preclude claims by injured employees, but women cannot waive the claims of their children; (3) it will be difficult for employers to know beforehand what will constitute negligence, because even compliance with OSHA standards has been held not to preclude state tort or criminal liability; (4) and as an additional worry, employers may be held *strictly liable* (a standard much more deleterious to defendants than the negligence standard) if their manufacturing process is considered "abnormally dangerous."

As we emerge from the legal quagmire, several essential arguments need to be kept in mind. The judges and justices who found fetal protection policies illegal under Title VII and the PDA placed great emphasis upon issues of women's autonomy, women's equal right with men to freedom of choice in employment, and their equal capacity to weigh benefits and costs of particularly dangerous jobs. They also found unpersuasive arguments of additional costs of employing women in jobs that exposed them to dangerous chemicals, particularly the speculative cost of future tort liability to prenatally injured offspring. Of great concern to them, in addition, was the specter of similar fetal protection policies spreading to other sorts of jobs, with Judge Easterbrook even raising the specter of prohibitions against female taxi drivers for fear of the noxious fumes or accidents to which their fetuses might be exposed.

Fetal Protection, Anti-discrimination, and a Free Economy

Despite the lower courts' determination to view fetal protection within the disparate impact model, which at least held out the possibility that the policy could pass muster, it seems fairly clear that the Supreme Court's insistence that the policy is discriminatory on its face is more in harmony with Title VII precedents. But having said this, it is also fairly obvious why many judges found the disparate treatment paradigm unappealing. If there is a real danger of fetal harm from maternal exposure to lead in the workplace, and if lead lingers in the body for an appreciable period of time, and if batteries can only be produced with lead as a component—all hypotheses borne out by a preponderance of the expert testimony—then it is no wonder that judges wished to give Johnson Controls the leeway to protect fetuses, simply because it seemed reasonable to them to do so. That Title VII, as judicially interpreted for the last twenty years, leads logically to the rejection of fetal protection policies says something very revealing about Title VII. If the additional costs of employing women cannot be considered by employers even when it appears rational for them to consider such costs, then Title VII requires companies not to be rational calculators but to systematically ignore a whole category of costs in making economic calculations. As Judge Easterbrook pointed out, it is in precisely those instances in which discrimination is rational that the anti-discrimination law acts to forbid employers from taking such costs into account. With the Supreme Court's decision in *Johnson Controls*, companies cannot ban fertile women from exposure to hazardous chemicals in the workplace, and as Justice White observed in his concurrence, it is possible that with this ruling companies may not be able to prevent even pregnant women from engaging in such work.[34]

Tort Liability, Conflicts of Law, and the Rule of Law

One of the more puzzling implications of the Supreme Court's decision in *Johnson Controls* is that companies, in complying with a ban on fetal protection policies, will be exposing themselves to potential tort liability in state courts for children prenatally exposed to dangerous chemicals and suffering lifelong impairments because of such exposure. Companies, under the Supreme Court's reading of Title VII, cannot take such potential costs into account. But turning a blind eye to such potential liability forces companies into systematic miscalculations about their costs of production. Even more fundamentally, the Court has, rather cavalierly, placed employers in a Catch-22 situation where they are damned by the anti-discrimination law if they restrict fertile women from jobs that expose them to hazardous chemicals or possibly damned by the tort law if they do permit women to work around dangerous substances and their fetuses are harmed. While the Court dismissed the likelihood of successful tort cases brought by impaired offspring, to do so they had to dismiss over three decades of liability law expanded by judges eager to compensate even negligent victims at the expense of "deep pocket" defendants. As Justice White adumbrated, to dismiss such a possibility, as the majority did, is to ignore the shift from a negligence standard to a strict liability standard.[35] Further it leaves employers open to unknown and, therefore, incalculable risks of exposure to liability even when the standard remains negligence but with its precise contours unknown. If adherence to Title VII will not insulate an employer from state tort liability, nor will a good faith adherence to OSHA's standards for workplace exposure to hazardous substances—both hypotheses that seem plausible, as Justice White observed—then the Court, by insisting that employers ignore such considerations in their employment policies, has thereby forced employers to act irresponsibly and irrationally.

One wonders how to account for the Supreme Court's blithe dismissal of the liability issue. Can it be attributed to ignorance of the expansion of tort liability or, rather, to a hope that by expressing their belief that such suits would be unwinnable that they would send a message to state court judges that they ought not look sympathetically upon such suits when they arise? The first alternative seems implausible, since the expansion of tort liability has become a highly controversial political issue. Several states have already legislated limits on punitive damages, and similar legislation has been proposed on the federal level. The defendants' bar and many commentators have condemned the expansion of strict liability, joint and several liability, and the explosion of punitive damage awards. The justices could not have been oblivious to all of this; they heard a punitive damage case recently themselves. The second explanation seems more likely: that by stating the wish it will become a reality. A third alternative does suggest itself—that the justices acted out of a cynical disregard for the likely effects of their decision, certainly a possibility too repugnant to contemplate.

Regardless of how one interprets the justices' casual dismissal of the liability issue, it is all too likely that juries when confronted with a brain-damaged, mentally and physically impaired youngster will be eager to reach down into a "deep pocket." Appeals courts may trim the punitive damage awards but may also expand the traditional concepts of liability even further to allow for recovery. That is the history of tort liability, and companies that ignore such potentially staggering costs do so at their peril. But ignoring such costs is precisely what the Supreme Court mandated that companies do. That is the lesson of *Johnson Controls*.

A free market depends upon a basic structure of law. Without consistency, predictability, and impartiality in the law—all components of the concept of the "rule of law"—a market system would be precarious. *Johnson Controls* threatens all three of these constituents of the rule of law. Consistency precludes conflicts of law but that is precisely what adherence to Title VII may trigger, in the form of tort liability; predictability requires that one know in advance what sorts of actions will trigger liability, but the Court merely hopes that companies will not be exposed to liability for adherence to the anti-discrimination law; and finally, impartiality implies that all parties must be treated equally before the law. *Johnson Controls'* implication is that some people are more equal than others and can thrust the costs of their imprudence on a "deep pocket" corporate defendant.

Equal Rights and Freedom of Contract

A free-market system depends, most directly, on freedom of contract: on voluntary bargains between individuals who both benefit from the transaction. But anti-discrimination laws of the type just examined make some traders more equal than others, and they do so in an Orwellian quest to secure equality for all. What Title VII demands is that employers hire women (and members of other so-called protected groups) whom as rational calculators they might not voluntarily hire. It requires that employers ignore any additional costs that hiring women may involve and by dint of the Equal Pay Act of 1963 that they pay women and men the same wages for doing essentially the same jobs. To further remove the labor bargain from the ideal of a voluntary exchange, the Pregnancy Discrimination Act commands that employers in addition ignore the actual or potential pregnancy of women applicants and employees. The Americans with Disabilities Act insists that employers ignore the increased insurance costs of hiring the disabled when they make employment decisions and mandates that the same insurance must be provided for the disabled as for all other employees. Thus by government fiat the terms of trade have been altered and whole categories of perfectly rational business considerations rendered illegal. No longer can one assume that an offer of employment is freely entered into by an employer because the employer has a gun to his head, and that gun is the threat of an EEOC filing or a discrimination lawsuit.

To make matters even worse, Title VII has not been interpreted as a protection for *all* employees, as its neutral language would imply and as Judge Easterbrook kept insisting, but rather as in effect a results-orientated calculation of whether or not an accused employer has hired the right mix of "protected" workers, such as blacks, Hispanics, American

Indians, women, Eskimos, and Aleuts.[36] That is the whole point of the typical disparate impact case: to demonstrate that a firm failed to employ the right percentage of blacks or women in comparison to their availability in the geographic area or their proportion of the applicants or potential applicants.

In order to insulate themselves from discrimination charges and suits, employers must act irrationally from the perspective of a strictly rational actor. And since the labor market can no longer be considered a free, voluntary market, one can never know after a bargain has been struck whether it is advantageous to both parties. Women and other "protected" workers will reap unearned rewards—or as the economists like to call them "rents"—as beneficiaries of government coercion. Rather than achieving equal rights for all—the self-professed objective of anti-discrimination laws—some workers are made more equal than others, while all employers are forced to trade on terms that they may or may not have agreed to had their trades been left voluntary.

As a further illustration of how the search for equality by government fiat can take on ever more bizarre twists, it is worth perusing Mary E. Becker's "From *Muller v. Oregon* to Fetal Vulnerability Policies," an influential law review article.[37] Becker deplores the Supreme Court's former paternalistic attitude toward women as expressed in their opinions from the early decades of this century. In cases such as *Muller v. Oregon* (1908),[38] the "Old Court," roundly condemned in our era for its tenderness toward laissez-faire and freedom of contract, nevertheless upheld restrictive labor legislation when it affected women (and children, too). The Court allowed such interventions in the marketplace out of a desire to "protect" the weaker sex and insure healthy offspring. *Muller* upheld a ten-hour limitation on the number of hours that women could work each day, while in another case the Court approved a minimum wage for women, all practices declared violations of freedom of contract (under due process clauses of the U.S. Constitution) when applied by legislatures to men. Becker deplores such "protective" legislation and the Court decisions that upheld them as paternalistic, and she views fetal protection policies by employers as embracing the same kind of paternalistic attitude toward women, an attitude that implies that women are not capable of making decisions for themselves and has the effect of limiting women's opportunities to compete with men for the most lucrative jobs. If ever fetal protection policies are necessary, and she seriously doubts that they would be, Becker prefers that regulation should come from Congress rather than from employers.

Becker condemns paternalism of the old sort, but seems inured to a new-style paternalism implicit in anti-discrimination statutes favoring women as a "protected group." If these laws as interpreted by the courts bar employers from taking certain factors unique to women into account—such as their susceptibility to certain chemicals in the workplace—in their calculations about employment decisions, this implies that women cannot compete on equal terms with men in the market but must be given special treatment. If women are at a competitive disadvantage as a result of biological differences, their brief should be against God or Nature, rather than employers who simply make rational calculations based on the way things actually are, rather than on how we wish them to be.

Becker's preference for congressional or executive-agency regulation of fetal protection over policies set by employers—who presumably know their own industries better than regulators—is also curious. If the public-choice literature of Buchanan, Tullock, and their heirs teaches us anything, it is that regulators are far from disinterested actors, that they are often captured by the very industries that they regulate, and that their self-interest and proclivity to avoid blame leads them to empire-building and overregulation, without consideration of social cost and benefit. Yet, her seeming obliviousness to the lessons of the public choice literature is not the most noteworthy aspect of her second-best scenario (i.e., in the event that fetal protection proves irresistible). What is remarkable is her admonition that if Congress sees fit to regulate for fetal protection, Becker wants women to be compensated for their exclusion. Either through affirmative action programs or through a scheme of more direct compensation, she wants to transfer the costs of natural differences between men and women onto employers and society. Becker's prescription smacks of a paternalism similar to that which inspired the Old Court's willingness to accept restrictions on the hours of women's labor. Becker condemns the old sort of paternalism and then suggests that women be given special benefits to compensate them for natural differences. Just because women are different from men by nature, feminists who otherwise commendably argue for the equality of the sexes should not abandon this ideal when it is to women's disadvantage, and they ought not to encourage women to seek special dispensations from mostly male legislators. A demand for compensation seems nothing more than paternalism in a new guise.

Becker's willingness to preclude by law employers from adopting fetal protection policies illustrates the pitfalls of Title VII's and the PDA's insistence that members of some groups be made more equal than others in the name of achieving equality. In contrast to a government-enforced anti-discrimination regime, a free-market system grounded on freedom of contract has several advantages: all transactions are voluntary; no one comes to the employment marketplace with a government-guaranteed right to make the other party disregard rational, business calculations or face a lawsuit; trades, as a result, are mutually beneficial.

Fetal protection policies are just one illustration of the sort of voluntary behavior that is perfectly acceptable in a free-market system but taboo in a regime that attempts to impose equality by government decree. Anti-discrimination laws by their very nature render many kinds of voluntary behavior illegal and impinge on vital liberty rights. The problem is not just that the Supreme Court may have erred in deciding *Johnson Controls*, but rather that our anti-discrimination laws by their very nature adversely affect individual liberty. It is not only "economic" liberties such as freedom of contract that are abridged by an anti-discrimination regime: freedom of association is impaired when private clubs fall afoul of anti-discrimination law for using "sexist" or "racist" criteria in selecting their members; freedom of speech is truncated when verbal harassment codes are promulgated by state universities and students penalized for expressing indelicate racial sentiments, telling "sexist" jokes, or trying to discuss in class theories that explain behavioral differences between the sexes or sexual preferences as the result of biology. A free-market system and anti-discrimination laws are on a collision course. As time progresses and new wrinkles are added to these laws, freedom is diminished as government inserts itself into nearly every employment decision, empowering one party and blindfolding the other.

A new sort of paternalism is replacing the old: judges declare in effect that women's rights matter, but not employers', that women's autonomy and women's freedom of choice matter, but not employers'. The new paternalism, in a twist on the old, wants women to be equal to men in the results of the employment process, and to achieve this *equality of results* it insists that employers ignore differences between men and women, differences that any rational business would consider. The old paternalists thought that they were protecting women from exploitation in the marketplace, not that they were handicapping women in competing for the best jobs, as we now in our more enlightened age view the results of their efforts.[39] The new paternalists think that they are empowering women and treating them as equals, but in an even more enlightened age this attitude may be seen as the logical outgrowth of the old paternalism, sharing with it the same premise that women are a special class who cannot be left to fend for themselves on a free market. Such a more enlightened age may leave all people—men and women, blacks and whites—free to make their own deals without Leviathan throwing its weight on either side of the bargaining table.

Notes

1. 111 S. Ct. 1196 (1991). The Johnson case involved the production of batteries. Fetal protection policies have also been introduced in the petrochemical industry, the electronics industry, and hospitals. No accurate studies of the prevalence of such policies have been made, according to Joan E. Bertin, a lawyer for the American Civil Liberties Union, as quoted in "High Court to Review Plans on Fertile Women at Work," *New York Times*, March 27, 1990.

2. *Ogden v. Saunders* 25 U.S. (12 Wheat.) 212 (1827). For an intriguing discussion of Article I of the Constitution, its subsequent interpretation by the Court, and Chief Justice Marshall's heated dissent in this case, see: Bernard Siegan, *Economic Liberties and the Constitution* (Chicago, 1980), 62–66.

3. Even more important than the entry of divorced women into the marketplace was the increased desire of married women to maintain careers as an insurance policy against possible divorce.

4. Pregnancy Discrimination Act of 1978, 42 U.S.C. 2000e(k). Emphasis added.

5. A point conceded by Johnson Controls' spokesmen in comments to the media. John P. Kennedy, general counsel for Johnson Controls, stated that the company was concerned with third-party lawsuits from neurologically damaged children exposed to lead in the womb. "That's a legal liability a mother cannot waive," he is quoted as saying. "Fetal Protection Policies Spark Intense Feelings from Women," *The Blade*, October 7, 1990. A similar statement was made by an unnamed company spokesman who said that the company was concerned about stockholder financial exposure to such suits. "Who Decides Who Works at Jobs Imperiling Fetuses?" *New York Times*, September 2, 1990.

6. Johnson Controls' fetal protection policy did not fare well in a state court. A woman denied employment in one of its battery manufacturing plants in California challenged her denial as an act of sex discrimination under California's Fair Employment and Housing Act. The state appeals court considered a refusal to hire on the basis of a future possibility of pregnancy to be gender-based discrimination. *Johnson Controls v. California Fair Employment and Housing Commission*, California ct. App. 4th Dist., No. G007029, 2/28/90.

7. This account of Johnson Controls' policy is drawn from the majority opinions in both the Circuit Court of Appeals and the Supreme Court. There are differences in emphasis between the two and even differences in the rendition of the facts (with the Supreme Court, for one example, not noting that Johnson Controls acquired a previously existing battery manufacturer and that the old policy was put in place by that company, and for another example, the appeals court found six pregnancies and the Supreme Court eight). The citations are: for the circuit court, *International Union, UAW v. Johnson Controls, Inc.*, 886 F. 2d 871, 875–879 (7th Cir. 1989); and for the Supreme Court, *International Union, UAW v. Johnson Controls*, 111 S. Ct., 1200. The latter is much sketchier than the circuit court's opinion on the facts in the case and the details of the fetal protection policy.

In "Who Decides Who Works," one woman who was transferred from stacking lead plates to the company laundry was still paid at the higher salary attached to her former position, though she did complain about lost bumping rights for day-shift work. It appears that Johnson Controls did make an attempt in some instances to live up to its stated policy of transferring women without loss in salary. So the record is, to say the least, somewhat contradictory, with some women claiming loss in salary upon transfer and others not.

8. The precise source of this estimate is not made clear in the EEOC citation, since the agency cited a book which in turn cited the *Washington Post*, without further identifying the original source for this estimate. The 15 to 20 million figure for the potential jobs that could be affected by such policies is cited in the same EEOC footnote but here the source is identified as a Bureau of National Affairs special report issued in 1987, entitled "Pregnancy and Employment." Both the 100,000 and the 20 million figures are widely cited but usually without clear attribution, or attribution to the EEOC. See: "EEOC: Policy Statement on Reproductive and Fetal Hazards Under Title VII," October 8, 1988, n. 2.

9. A study on such policies by the University of Massachusetts and the Massachusetts Department of Public Health identified four substances known to cause fetal harm—glycol ethers, lead, organic mercury, and inorganic mercury—and eight additional substances suspected of causing reproductive damage but for which scientific proof remains scanty—arsenic or arsine gas, benzene, carbon disulfide, formaldehyde, methylene choride, vinyl chloride, trichloromethane or trichloroethylene, and toluene. As cited in: "The Battle over Fetal Protection—What's an Employer to Do?" *Fair Employment Practices*, Bureau of National Affairs, June 7, 1990, 67–68. The study also found that of the 198 companies out of 232 that responded, only one had removal and transfer policies that applied to men.

10. "Who Decides Who Works."

11. "Justices Hear Arguments in Fetal-Protection Case," *New York Times*, October 11, 1990.

12. *International Union v. Johnson Controls, Inc.*, 680 F. Supp.309 (E. D. Wis. 1988).

13. *Ibid.*, 310.

14. "Summary judgment is properly entered in favor of a party when the opposing party is unable to make a showing sufficient to prove an essential element of a case on which the opposing party bears the burden of proof." *Johnson Controls*, 886 F. 2d, 887. Granting summary judgment to Johnson Controls precluded a trial.

15. There have only been a handful of such cases. *Wright v. Olin Corporation*, 697 F. 2d 1172, at 1182 (4th Cir., 1982). This was a challenge to a fetal protection policy, similar to *Johnson Controls*, which banned fertile women from jobs involving contact with known abortifacient or teratogenic agents. The court noted that the policy did not fit "with absolute precision any of the developed theories," and it selected the disparate impact/business necessity paradigm that would later be accepted by the Seventh Circuit in *Johnson Controls*. *Wright* set out a three-pronged business necessity inquiry: (1) is there a substantial risk to the health of the fetus; (2) is that hazard transmitted only through women; (3) can the harm be prevented by a less discriminatory alternative. The Seventh Circuit in *Johnson Controls* would follow this mode of analysis, only differing from *Wright* in imposing the burden of persuasion on the plaintiff for all three steps. The Fourth Circuit sustained the fetal protection policy in *Wright. Hayes v. Shelby Memorial Hospital*, 726 F. 2d 1543 (11th Cir. 1984). Here, an x-ray technician challenged her termination once her pregnancy was discovered. The court adopted a similar paradigm to *Wright*'s of disparate impact/business necessity and the three-pronged test. The plaintiff prevailed in this case, for the court held that her firing violated Title VII because her exposure would not have risen above a limit for fetal exposure established by a congressional advisory panel. *Zunigan v. Kleberg County Hospital*, 692 F. 2d 986 (5th Cir. 1982). This was another case of an x-ray technician fired as a result of her pregnancy; here, too, a business necessity defense was adopted by the court. After the Seventh Circuit decision and after the Supreme Court granted

certiorari in *Johnson Controls*, the Sixth Circuit reversed a district court grant of summary judgment to a company with a policy similar to Johnsons', rejecting the disparate impact paradigm and viewing the only available defense as the more stringent BFOQ (see discussion in the text). (*Grant v. General Motors Corp.*, 908 F. 2d 1303 (1990).

16. Civil Rights Act of 1964, Section 703(a); 42 U.S.C. 2000e-2(a).

17. Title VII, 703(e)(1).

18. *Griggs v. Duke Power Co.*, 401 U.S. 424 (1971). This is the leading case on disparate impact, setting out the theory, the elements to be proven, and the shifting burdens of proof. Recently the Supreme Court has had another stab at refining the disparate impact theory, and its attempt has not pleased civil rights groups for it made proving disparate impact more difficult by placing the burden of proof for all elements squarely upon the plantiff. *Wards Cove Packing Co. v. Atonia*, 109 S. Ct. 211S (1989). In 1990 and 1991 attempts were made in Congress to define the shifting burdens back to where they were in *Griggs*, and thus make these cases easier for plaintiffs to win. In the Civil Rights Act of 1991 the effort finally succeeded.

19. *Johnson Controls*, 886 F. 2d at 908 (Easterbrook, J. dissenting).

20. *Ibid.*, 909.

21. *Ibid.*, 920.

22. *Ibid.*, 913.

23. *Ibid.*

24. Various courts have held that such additional costs of employing women as higher pension costs, or medical insurance, or more days off for sickness, or higher turnover are excluded from consideration under Title VII. See *Johnson Controls*, 910.

25. *Ibid.*, 914.

26. Concurring opinions were filed by Justice White (joined by Chief Justice Rehnquist and Justice Kennedy) and by Justice Scalia. All of the members of the Court, however, concurred in the judgment of reversal. In Justice White's concurrence he found erroneous the Court's holding that the BFOQ defense can "never justify a sex-based fetal protection policy." *Johnson Controls*, 111 S. Ct., 1210 (White, J. concurring).

27. Johnson Controls, 111 S. Ct., 1202.

28. *Ibid.*, 1205.

29. *Ibid.*, 1206.

30. *Ibid.*, 1207.

31. *Ibid.*, 1210.

32. *Ibid.*, 1208.

33. Tort cases of this sort would be heard in state courts and there have been cases in which adherence to federal law has not prevented defendants from losing in state courts. Justice White, in his concurrence, lists cases in which state tort claims were not preempted by adherence to federal laws. See: *Johnson Controls*, 1211 n. 2 (White, J. concurring). Justice White disagreed with the Court's holding that the BFOQ defense is so narrow that a fetal protection policy could never be justified. An example of what might qualify as a BFOQ, he argued, is a showing by an employer that in order to avoid substantial tort liability the exclusion of women from dangerous jobs is reasonably necessary.

34. *Johnson Controls*, 111 S. Ct., 1214 (White, J. concurring).

35. *Ibid.* For an excellent account of the transformation of tort liability see: Peter H. Huber, *Liability: The Legal Revolution and its Consequences* (New York, 1988).

36. Quaintly, Judge Easterbrook repeated several times the refrain that Title VII looks to the protection of individuals rather than groups. *Johnson Controls*, 886 F.2d, 910–911. The judicial history of Title VII, lamentably, speaks entirely in the other direc-

tion, with group equality replacing individual equality as the standard. For an excellent discussion of how this came about see: Herman Belz, *Equality Transformed: A Quarter-Century of Affirmative Action* (Rutgers, N.J., 1991).

37. Becker, "From *Muller v. Oregon* to Fetal Vulnerability Policies," University of Chicago Law Review S3 (1986), 1219.

38. 208 U.S. 412 (1908).

39. Many women's groups supported such legislation in the early part of this century out of a desire to protect women from harsh conditions and long hours of labor in the workplace. Mary Becker recognizes this in "From *Muller v. Oregon*", 1222. Judge Easterbrook expresses the modern view of the old paternalism: *Johnson Controls*, 886 F. 2d, 912–913.

Alexander Tabarrok

❦

Abortion and Liberty

MANY WRITERS HAVE ATTEMPTED TO ANSWER THE ETHICAL, LEGAL, HISTORI-cal, and economic questions raised by abortion but few have integrated their answers into a well-developed body of thought.[1] As a result, abortion is usually discussed without the rich context that imbues a consistent meaning to terms such as "the right to choose." Liberals, for example, will eloquently discuss the importance of individual rights and controlling one's own biology when discussing abortion but they drop such talk when the discussion turns to the validity of self-defense through gun owner-ship.[2] Conservatives are pro-choice when it comes to educational vouchers but not when it comes to the fundamental right of a woman to choose or not choose motherhood.

By contrast, classical liberals and libertarians (the terms are used here interchangeably) consistently value the right to choose. From the libertar-ian perspective, abortion rights—i.e., the right to control one's own body and to contract freely with those who provide abortions—are direct appli-cations of a larger political philosophy. The libertarian philosophy includes not only theories of rights but also an understanding of law, history, and economics—all of which weigh heavily in favor of abortion rights.

Abortions and the Women Who Have Them
Abortion is the deliberate termination of a pregnancy. In general terms, the termination occurs in one of three manners: In the earliest stage, "morning after pills" can prevent implantation of a fertilized egg in the uterus; shortly after implantation, drugs such as mifepristone (RU 486) can cause abortions similar to spontaneous miscarriages; in the first trimester (one to twelve weeks) and thereafter surgical techniques can re-move the developing fetus from the womb.[3] In the United States, as of

1997, almost 90 percent of abortions are performed in the first trimester (more than 50 percent in the first eight weeks or less) and about 10 percent are performed in the second trimester. Third trimester abortions are rare. About 1.4 percent of abortions occur later than twenty weeks.[4]

Abortion was illegal in the first half of this century in almost every part of the world.[5] Between 1950 and 1985 most countries in the developed world liberalized their abortion law as did a handful of developing nations. Today abortion is legal in most developed nations of the world—86 percent of the women in the developed world live in countries with liberal abortion laws. Restrictions on abortion are more common in developing countries.

An estimated 46 million women, or 35 of every 1,000 women of child-bearing age, have an abortion every year. Legal abortions account for 26 million of the total, implying that 20 million illegal abortions occur each year. Although statistics on illegal procedures are subject to uncertainty, death or disability for women due to unsafe abortions is highest in poor countries where abortion is illegal.

Around the world abortion rates for women who are pregnant are highest among women who are either young or old. That is, women who feel they are too young to care for a child or who may already have children are more likely to undergo the procedure. In the United States, 80 percent of women who have an abortion are unmarried, 20 percent are teenagers, and 50 percent are younger than twenty-five.[6] Sixty percent of women who have an abortion say they cannot afford a(nother) child.[7] In short, women in the United States who have abortions are typically young, unmarried, and often poor—sound reasons not to have a child.

Rights-based Arguments for Reproductive Liberty

As a social movement Western feminism is often dated from the late eighteenth century in England and the early nineteenth century in the United States.[8] The English tradition of feminism resulted from an extrapolation of the principles of classical liberalism as first developed by such thinkers as Adam Smith, David Hume, and John Locke. Following in this tradition, thinkers such as Mary Wollstonecraft, John Stuart Mill, and Harriet Mill argued that women had the same natural rights as men. In America feminism, as a self-conscious movement, sprang from the radical anti-slavery movement known as abolitionism: it came into being when abolitionist women asked themselves, "Are we fighting only for the rights of black male slaves, or for the rights of women as well?" In neither England nor in America did the issue of abortion receive much attention from the nascent movements, perhaps because the procedure was largely unregulated, especially in the early stages.[9]

Modern libertarian arguments for abortion rights generally fall into two categories that are associated with the political theorist Murray Rothbard, who focuses on rights theory, and with the novelist/philosopher Ayn Rand, who integrates ethics into her argument.[10] Rothbard and Rand both defend natural law in the Thomistic tradition, which they view as supporting a politics of individual rights and the corollary economics of laissez-faire capitalism. For Rothbard and Rand abortion rights represent a small aspect of a larger philosophy of liberty. Their extensive writings on liberty will not be discussed here, however, except as they tie directly to the issue of abortion. Nevertheless, it is important to emphasize that the power of their arguments springs from their consistent application of the principles of a broader philosophy to all social issues, not merely to abortion.

Rothbard approaches the issue of abortion from the perspective of the "right to self-ownership" rather than the "right to life," partly because he believes the latter term to be hopelessly ambiguous. By contrast, the "right to self-ownership" is clearly defined as the underlying principle that gives meaning to all other rights. Self-ownership is the fundamental right that every human being has to his or her own body and to the exercise of his or her capacities for self-realization. Self-ownership is a universal right, which means that every human being possesses it to the same degree: no one can rightfully infringe upon the equal self-ownership of another by initiating force. Any other position would imply that some form of slavery is acceptable.

From self-ownership, Rothbard argues that the mother's right to control her body is absolute: "The proper groundwork for analysis of abortion is in every man's absolute right of self-ownership. This implies immediately that every woman has the absolute right to her own body, that she has absolute dominion over her body and everything within it."[11] Most fetuses continue to the point of birth because the pregnant woman consents to their presence. If a woman does not consent, however, she has an unquestioned right to expel the fetus from her body. No one, not even a fetus, has the right to use another person's body against his or her will.[12]

Rothbard's position is similar to that of the philosopher Judith Jarvis Thomson.[13] Thomson poses the following thought experiment:

> You wake up in the morning and find yourself back to back in bed with an unconscious violinist. A famous unconscious violinist. He has been found to have a fatal kidney ailment, and the Society of Music Lovers has canvassed all the available medical records and found that you alone have the right blood type to help. They have therefore kidnapped you, and last night the vio-

linist's circulatory system was plugged into yours, so that your kidneys can be used to extract poisons from his blood as well as your own. The director of the hospital now tells you, "Look, we're sorry the Society of Music Lovers did this to you—we would never have permitted it if we had known. But still, they did it, and the violinist now is plugged into you. To unplug you would be to kill him. But never mind, it is only for nine months. By then he will have recovered from his ailment, and can safely be unplugged from you."[14]

There is no question that the violinist is a rights-bearer. But neither the violinist nor the Society of Music Lovers has a right to force you to stay tied to him, even to save his life. If the violinist does not possess such a right, then *a fortiori* an embryo does not have a right to have his mother carry it to term. According to Thomson, neither the need of the recipient nor the burden of the giver entitle the recipient to any portion of the giver's life.

An objection quickly arises in response to this analysis. Namely, the fetus, unlike the violinist, is in a position of dependency due to the actions of the pregnant woman. Even if this objection has some validity, it cannot apply to women who become pregnant due to rape. But to the abortion opponent, the resulting fetus is still an innocent human being and abortion is still murder. The anti-abortionist is caught in an internal contradiction. If he agrees that terminating a "rape" pregnancy is justified, then he abandons the moral objection to killing an innocent person. If he maintains that abortion is not justified, then he declares the issue of responsibility to be irrelevant to his argument. Whether or not the woman is responsible, he believes abortion is wrong and should be prohibited.

Moreover the dependency argument is factually incorrect. Most women who have had an abortion did not decide to get pregnant one day and change their minds the next. Instead a majority were actively trying not to get pregnant during the month they had sex.[15] If the woman was trying to avoid pregnancy, then the dependency argument loses all force. Thomson gives an appropriate analogy, if a woman leaves a window open and a burglar enters it would be absurd to argue that the burglar has a right to the use of her house because the woman was partly responsible for the burglar entering.[16]

Furthermore, the dependency argument presupposes that the fetus has a right to life. Rothbard and Thomson argue that even if the fetus has a right to life it does not have a right to use the mother's body. But neither indicates that they accept that the fetus has a right to life.[17]

Ayn Rand argues that the fetus does not have a right to life. Rand's views on abortion are complex and flow from both her theory of rights and her theory of moral virtue which themselves are closely linked. Rand's ethical theory emphasizes the virtue of rationality. Crucially for Rand, rationality is an attribute of the virtuous individual. To think is to think for one's self. Independence is thus a corollary of rationality and rights are desirable so that the independence necessary for virtue in a social context is protected. Rand writes that:

> Rights are a moral concept . . . the concept that preserves and protects individual morality in a social context—the link between the moral code of a man and the legal code of a society, between ethics and politics.

> "[A right is] a moral principle defining and sanctioning a man's freedom of action in a social context. . . . Thus, for every individual, a right is a moral sanction of a positive—of his freedom to act on his own judgment, for his own goals, by his own *voluntary, uncoerced* choice."[18]

From these two passages, it becomes clear that the concept of rights does not apply to a fetus because it has no freedom of action to define or sanction. The fetus cannot and does not act on its own judgment, it does not have its own "goals," it does not have the capacity for voluntary choice.[19] If we define coercion as the act of physically forcing someone to act against his or her will, then it is clear that a fetus cannot even be coerced as it has no will. Thus, for Rand, rights do not apply to fetuses because the context in which rights arise does not apply.[20]

A significant minority within libertarianism is pro-life. Sometimes the position is founded on religious faith and does not differ significantly from nonlibertarian religious arguments. Since such objections are not generally open to rational argumentation, they will not be discussed here. One organization in particular, however, does not base its objections to abortion on the grounds of religion but on the grounds of fetal rights. Libertarians for Life declare that abortion is not a right but "a wrong under justice." Doris Gordon, president of Libertarians for Life, argues that the non-aggression "principle" implies an anti-abortion position. She writes that, "The unalienable right not to be unjustly killed applies equally to all human beings. Day One in a human being's life occurs at fertilization— that is high school biology. If pregnant women are human beings, why not when they themselves were zygotes? A two-tiered legal policy on human offspring that defines a superior class with rights, and an inferior class without rights, is not libertarian."[21]

One difficulty with Gordon's argument is that the nonaggression principle is assumed as though it was a self-evident starting point for argument instead of the conclusion of a deeper argument.[22] The libertarian notion of aggression acquires meaning only within the context of a previously developed understanding of individual rights.[23] Gordon, however, does not develop a theory of individual rights. At several points Gordon cites Rand but, as we have seen, for Rand rights are a political concept created for the purpose of protecting a sphere of action in which individuals are free to use their own judgment. As fertilized eggs have no judgment in any meaningful sense of the word, there is no purpose for rights. Thus there is no context to give rise to rights and abortion is not aggression—the violation of rights—in a Randian or libertarian sense.[24]

For the purpose of ascribing rights, Gordon collapses the distinction between the potential and the actual, between a developing human being (the fetus) and an actual one (the pregnant woman). For Gordon a human being with full rights is present from the moment of conception onward. This seems utterly implausible as even children do not have full rights. Pro-choice advocates do not deny that the fertilized egg is a potential rights-bearer, merely that a potential is an actual.[25]

Since Rand's account of rights is closely connected with her account of morality, her argument for abortion is multifaceted and not limited to a syllogism. In ethics Rand advocates a form of egoism, rational self-interest, which proclaims a person's happiness properly to be his or her highest purpose.[26] Egoism contrasts sharply with altruism, the idea that service to others is the highest moral goal and virtue. Forcing women to carry fetuses to term would be forcing them to serve others at their own expense, which would be immoral. Rand finds servitude on behalf of the fetus especially galling because the fetus, as a potential human being, is so much less of a person than the woman. She writes:

> To equate a potential with an actual is vicious; to advocate the sacrifice of the latter to the former, is unspeakable. . . . The task of raising a child is a tremendous, lifelong responsibility, which no one should undertake unwittingly or unwillingly. Procreation is not a duty: human beings are not stock-farm animals. For conscientious persons, an unwanted pregnancy is a disaster; to oppose its termination is to advocate sacrifice, not for the sake of anyone's benefit, but for the sake of misery qua misery, for the sake of forbidding happiness and fulfillment to living human beings.[27]

Throughout history, the demands for self-sacrifice placed upon women have been much more onerous than those placed upon men. Women have been the victims of altruism par excellence.[28] To those who morally object to this victimization, the demand that a woman must place the interests of a fetus above her own may well be the height of immorality. Men are not required by law to make the sort of sacrifices that a woman who carries an unwanted pregnancy to term must accept.[29] The prohibition of abortion must be seen therefore in its broader context. It is not merely about the protection of fetal life: it is about the control and management of women.

A Brief History of Abortion in America

Abortion in the United States was basically legal until the 1820s, when some states began to prohibit abortion after the fourth month of pregnancy.[30] Even after the 1820s, abortion remained a widespread practice, remedies for menses were openly advertised in the popular press, and juries often acquitted abortionists. Abortion was considered to be a private matter between females, with obstetric care being provided by midwives who used herbal nostrums and other remedies for "restoring a woman's blood flow"—that is, for aborting a fetus. It was only after the Civil War that abortion came under concerted cultural attack and new legislation began to prohibit abortions except as "necessary to save the life of a woman."

One of the main thrusts behind the effective criminalization of abortion was the American Medical Association (AMA) which represented the interests of a relatively new professional group in the United States, physicians, who were almost exclusively male. In the 1830s and 1840s, a medical movement called Popular Health swept across America under the slogan "Every man his own doctor," and every woman as well. The movement constituted a wholesale rejection of medical licensing and the medical elitism of male physicians with their city practices among the upper and middle classes. Instead, Popular Health cried out for better personal hygiene, loose clothing for women, information on birth control, temperance, and a veritable flood of "cures" from whole grain cereal to electricity. A newly emerging feminism became associated with the Popular Health Movement, which generally advocated women's rights and certainly promoted women's health.[31]

Male physicians began to feel threatened by the democratization of health care and by the popularity of midwives who remained the most prevalent health providers by far in reproductive matters (see Gibson, this volume). In 1848 physicians formed the AMA—the first national organization of its kind—and started a relentless campaign to discredit nonlicensed health care providers as frauds and scam artists. At the same time male physicians lobbied for legislation that would ensure their position of privilege in medicine by severely regulating the services of nonlicensed competitors. Gradually obstetrics came under the control of male doctors and became less friendly toward a woman's right to prevent or to terminate a pregnancy. Still, abortionists and midwives advertised openly in newspapers and the *New York Times* estimated that there were two hundred full-time abortionists in New York City in 1870, with few health complications being reported. According to Linda Gordon, most complications arose from women who privately used internal medicines to induce miscarriages rather than from abortionists.[32]

Nevertheless, a variety of social factors aided the AMA in its crusade against midwives. As the biology of pregnancy became more sophisticated the point at which the fetus was legally considered to be alive—the point of quickening—changed from when movement could be felt to a much earlier stage. In addition the Civil War had devastated a generation of young men: both business and government wanted a population boom to rebuild the nation and expand into new territories. Although immigration swelled the population, a flood of foreigners only renewed the cry for a higher American birth rate in order to prevent "Yankee" stock from being overwhelmed. The Civil War left a wake of social disruption in which reformers thrived. Moralists preached against loose sexual attitudes and called for stronger social control over the nation's bedrooms; other reformers, including feminists, demanded access to birth control and the elimination of the state from the private matters of individuals.

In 1873 Congress passed the Comstock Act, so named in honor of Anthony Comstock, a founder of the New York Society for the Suppression of Vice and a crusader against vice, obscenity, and pornography. Obscene writings, as interpreted by Comstock, included writings on abortion, contraception, and women's rights pertaining to sexual relations—in addition, of course, to the usual list of works from Homer, Ovid, and Boccaccio as well as modern authors such as Walt Whitman (who was arrested for distributing *Leaves of Grass*). The act criminalized the publication, distribution, or possession of information about, or devices or medications for, "unlawful" abortion or contraception. Penalties under the act included fines and up to five years of imprisonment with hard labor. Even stronger penalties occurred if the mail was used to distribute such "obscene" material. As a special federal agent, Comstock worked diligently to enforce the act.

One of the earliest victims of Comstockery was the libertarian Ezra Heywood, publisher and editor of the *Word* (1872–1892). Heywood refused to abide by the restrictions imposed by the Comstock Act on the circulation of sexual information, especially birth control. For this, he endured years of legal persecution, much of which sprang from the distribution of his pamphlet "Cupid's Yokes" in which he advocated placing sexual urges under the control of reason rather than "animalism." Perhaps no other work was as influential as "Cupid's Yokes" in opening nineteenth-century America to a discussion of all forms of birth control.[33]

The prosecution of Heywood was far from an isolated event. Thousands were persecuted under the Comstock laws and Comstock publicly bragged about how many abortionists had committed suicide due to his persecution. Discussion of abortion and contraception was chilled even in medical textbooks and journals. Comstock lobbied successfully for the passage of strict state laws restricting birth control information. In his home state of Connecticut, he was responsible for the 1879 General Statutes of Connecticut, Section 6246: Use of drugs or instruments to prevent conception, which read: "Any person who will use any drug, medicinal article or instrument for the purpose of preventing conception shall be fined not less than fifty dollars or imprisoned not less than sixty days nor more than one year or be both fined and imprisoned."

By the late nineteenth century, abortion was effectively prohibited in the United States. The battle over birth control in all forms continued well into the twentieth century with President Theodore Roosevelt condemning such practices and the reformers, such as Margaret Sanger, battling to legalize them.[34] Often the battle was conducted on a state-by-state level. Between 1941 and 1959 in Connecticut, for example, no fewer than seventeen bills were introduced into the House. Those that passed were ultimately defeated in the Senate due to concerns over the impact on public morality. It was not until 1965 in *Griswald v. Connecticut*, that the Connecticut law restricting birth control was declared unconstitutional by the Supreme Court. By then, medical information had been denied to the people of that state for eighty-six years. By 1965 every state still banned abortion though some allowed the procedure in defined circumstances such as a pregnancy resulting from rape. This remained the status quo until 1970 when Alaska, California, Hawaii, New York, and Washington legalized abortion.[35] Under the separation of powers spelled out in the U.S. Constitution, abortion remained under state jurisdiction.

The legal turning point on abortion came in 1973 when the Supreme Court in *Roe v. Wade* declared most state abortion laws to be unconstitutional because they violated the right of privacy guaranteed by the Fourteenth Amendment.[36] The Supreme Court's decision gave women a right to privacy that included aborting a pregnancy in its early stages but it recognized the right of states to police the health of the woman and the fetus in later stages. Abortion was divided into trimesters: during the first three months, there were almost no restrictions; during the second trimester, the state could regulate abortion for health reasons; during the third trimester, abortions could be banned. Although the trimester system is no longer central to the court's reasoning and some first trimester restrictions such as twenty-four-hour waiting periods and parental consent laws have been ruled constitutional, the basic legality of abortion remains intact.

Abortion and the Social Context: Implications for Related Liberties

Historically, culturally, and legally, the issues of abortion (or, more generally, contraception) and a woman's role in society have been intimately linked. As noted above, the state has been so intrusive that it was only in 1965 that the Supreme Court ruled that a state had no power to prohibit married couples from using contraceptives.[37] As late as 1972 doctors were arrested and charged with illegally distributing contraceptives to unmarried women. Proponents of the classical liberal tradition would agree with Justice Brennan who wrote in the case overturning such laws that: "[i]f the right of privacy means anything, it is the right of the individual, married or single, to be free from unwarranted governmental intrusion into matters so fundamentally affecting a person as the decision whether to bear or beget a child."[38] It was this line of reasoning that led to the Supreme Court's decision in *Roe v. Wade*.

Many opponents of abortion argue that there is a categorical difference between abortion and some other forms of contraception, but the historical, cultural, and legal links are clear. The Catholic Church—perhaps the most prominent opponent of abortion—opposes most other forms of contraception. Furthermore, the question of what birth rate is desirable has always been connected to abortion policy. Indeed, a driving force behind state regulation of abortion has been population control. Abortion policy in totalitarian countries is especially illustrative.[39] In 1966 Romania, for example, banned all abortion and contraception.[40] To ensure compliance, women were closely monitored at work and periodically forced to submit to pregnancy tests and even to medical examinations for signs of having had an abortion. The goal was to increase population; it had nothing to do with "choosing life."[41] On the other extreme, China has long used financial incentives as well as coercion to increase the number of abortions and ease its perceived overpopulation.

Similarly some Western doctors argue that certain women should not have a right to reproduce because they cannot provide a suitable biological environment for a fetus, perhaps due to their age. In 1986 the American Fertility Society—which includes approximately ten thousand doctors and scientists—argued against a universal right to reproduce. Women who might not possess this right include those in overpopulated nations; those unable to provide adequate care; and those with genetic defects. Such pronouncements from authorities on reproductive rights remind us that the issue at hand is not abortion per se: it is the right of the individual to control his or her own reproductive decisions and to be free of state coercion in sexual matters. The right not to have an abortion is at least as important a right as the right to have an abortion.

"Quality" control of the population was a driving force in the criminalization of abortion in the United States.[42] One of the most frequent anti-abortion arguments in the middle to late nineteenth century (when many anti-abortion laws were put into place) was that the native-born population was being swamped by immigrants and their native-born children. As one anti-abortion activist said "the annual destruction of foetuses" had become so large among native women that "the Puritanic blood of '76 will be but sparingly represented in the approaching centenary."[43] A special committee of the Ohio legislature set up to investigate abortion was especially blunt, "Do [our native women] realize," asked the committee, "that in avoiding the duties and responsibilities of married life, they are, in effect, living in a state of legalized prostitution? Shall we permit our broad and fertile plains to be settled only by the children of aliens? If not, we must, by proper legislation, and by the diffusion of a correct public sentiment, endeavor to suppress a crime which has become so prevalent."[44] Note that the committee is concerned about abortion among married women of native stock, not about abortion per se. As Mohr writes, "There can be little doubt that Protestants' fears about not keeping up with the reproductive rates of Catholic immigrants played a greater role in the drive for anti-abortion laws in nineteenth-century America than Catholic opposition to abortion did."[45]

A further consequence of prohibiting abortion is the ever greater entanglement of medical care and the state. During the nineteenth-century prohibition in America, the duty of doctors to heal was sometimes overshadowed by their enforced duty to the state. For example the police arrested women suspected of having abortions and brought them before doctors to be examined. Few women, especially poor and minority women, had the resources to protest and fight against this invasion.[46] Leslie Reagan writes:

> It would have been virtually impossible for the state to enforce the criminal abortion laws without the cooperation of physicians. State officials won medical cooperation in suppressing

abortion by threatening doctors and medical institutions with prosecution or scandal. Physicians learned to protect themselves from legal trouble by reporting to officials women injured or dying as a result of illegal abortions. . . . The medical profession and its institutions acted as an arm of the state.[47]

If the fetus were accorded the legal status of personhood, the demand for medical reporting to the state would be exacerbated. Current law requires that every death be legally certified and logic would demand this requirement be extended to fetuses aborted through "miscarriage." Doctors would be put in the difficult position of judging whether the miscarriage had been spontaneous or induced. If a doctor gave a patient the benefit of the doubt, he might well become an accomplice to murder under the law because that is how an induced miscarriage would have to be classified.

To be consistent in their claims that the fetus is a person, pro-life advocates must call for charging the aborting woman with first degree, premeditated murder and subjecting her to whatever penalty exists under the law, up to and including the death penalty. A doctor who performs abortions would have to be treated in the same manner. If pro-life advocates back away from these scenarios, which are no more than a logical extension of their conclusions, then they are actually backing away from the personhood of the fetus.

Another factor that shaped, and continues to shape, the abortion debate in America are the indigenously Puritan views on sex and a woman's role in society. It is no accident that the first laws prohibiting abortion in America arose in the late nineteenth century just as the woman's suffrage movement was stirring and as property and divorce laws were being liberalized.[48] Nor is it a coincidence that Horatio Storer, one of the leading crusaders against abortion at the time, was also a leading opponent of allowing women to vote or to enter professions such as law and, of course, his own profession, medicine. The abortion laws were, in part, a backlash against women who wanted to expand their role in society beyond that of mother and wife.[49]

Reproductive and related rights appear reasonably secure in the United States today. Yet it would be foolish to believe that liberty cannot be lost. Until as late as 1997 the Comstock prohibitions against distributing information on "illegal" abortions remained Federal law.[50] Powerful forces worked to keep the law on the books despite the fact that since *Roe v. Wade* the law could not and has not been enforced. In 1994 anti-abortion forces managed to increase the fine for violating the Comstock law from $5000 to $250,000 and/or five years in prison.[51] Furthermore, a provision in section 507 of the Telecommunications Act of 1996 extended the Comstock prohibitions to the Internet.[52] It was only when free-speech advocates attacked the extension of Comstock-like restrictions to the Internet that the law was finally ruled unconstitutional. It is evident that politically powerful groups envision a time when abortion is criminalized and, following such an event, they stand ready to criminalize discussions of abortion.[53]

The extension of criminal law to include abortion would involve much more than restricting "reproductive" liberty. It would almost certainly lead to restrictions on free speech, monitoring of women, heavy sanctions against doctors, interference in the doctor-patient relationship, and enhanced federalization of power. All of these intrusions on liberty occurred prior to *Roe v. Wade*.[54] Given the use of abortion policy by governments in the past, it is also possible that the criminalization of abortion would extend to contraception and from there to other sexual materials or writings.

In considering the relationship between abortion and contraception, one should bear in mind not only the ethical, legal, and social connections but also the medical connection. The distinction between contraception and abortion is not clear-cut. The main function of oral contraceptives is to prevent ovulation and/or to thicken the cervical mucus thereby preventing sperm from fertilizing an egg. Oral contraceptives also prevent fertilized eggs from implanting.[55] Again, technically, pregnancy does not occur before implantation and, thus, such contraceptives do not cause an abortion.[56] Nevertheless, the logic of "a human life begins at conception" would also implicate oral contraceptives in at least some "abortions."

Apart from considerations of individual liberty, one of the great difficulties with using police powers to control abortion is that criminalization rarely "works." Even in totalitarian states, such as Romania, Nazi Germany, and Stalin's Soviet Union, illegal abortions occurred in large numbers and at relatively high rates.[57] In the United States in the years before abortion was legalized, there were an estimated 700,000 illegal abortions per year.[58] Estimates from a number of different studies suggest that 70 percent of the abortions that occur in the United States today would continue to occur if abortion were criminalized.[59] Many countries with severe restrictions on abortion have rates higher than the United States.[60]

The failure of abortion prohibition to greatly reduce the number of abortions is less surprising when considering similar failures of alcohol and drug prohibition. Alcohol, drug, and abortion prohibition each pits the individual's control of his or her own body against the attempt of others to assume control through the state.[61] The three prohibitions share important characteristics: public morals are often invoked and social control is posited as a solution. In each case, prohibition has failed to achieve its stated goal but it has increased state control and decreased individual liberty and the quality of life in society.[62]

Another general and dangerous feature of prohibition is that the quality of the prohibited good is reduced. Thus, alcohol poisonings increased during alcohol prohibition. Similarly, outlawing abortion would reduce the medical quality of the procedure, resulting in greater complications and more deaths.[63] Perhaps the most visible effect of criminalization is the dramatic increase in unsafe abortions that accompany such a measure. Typically the legalization of abortion results in an immediate 30 to 50 percent reduction in abortion-related maternal deaths.[64] Over a long time frame reductions in mortality can be even larger. A study by the Council on Scientific Affairs of the American Medical Association found that "between 1973 and 1985 there was more than a fivefold decline in the number of deaths per 100,000 legal-abortion procedures, most of which took place during the 1970s."[65] A large part of the decline was due to greater familiarity with abortion procedures among doctors and the trend toward earlier abortions that liberalization of abortion law helped to bring about.

The practical impossibility of the proposed abortion prohibition is made even more manifest by the existence of mifepristone (RU 486). Mifepristone is an anti-progestin: it interrupts pregnancy in the early stages by blocking the action of progesterone, a natural hormone that prepares the lining of the uterus for a fertilized egg. When administered within forty-nine days of a woman's last menstrual period and in combination with another drug, misoprostol, it is 95 percent effective at inducing an abortion.[66] Mifepristone is very safe.[67] Indeed, the mifepristone/misoprostol protocol is safe enough that a woman may have an abortion in the privacy of her own home. Banning the procedure did not work well even when the authorities could focus their enforcement efforts on doctors where the supply line is most vulnerable. It will be even less successful now that advanced medical training is not necessary to induce a safe abortion. Even if mifepristone were to be banned from the United States, it would still be available in dozens of countries around the world and could easily be smuggled into the United States.

Mifepristone is unlikely to be entirely banned in the United States, however, not only because of abortion rights activists but also because it has been shown to be useful in treating other conditions not related to pregnancy such as breast cancer, melingioma (cancer of the brain), and Cushing's disease. Mifepristone may also be effective as a daily contraceptive for both women and men.[68] Moreover, although mifepristone is the only FDA-approved drug for medical abortions, since the early 1980s other drugs such as methotrexate, an FDA-approved drug for the treatment of psoriasis and some cancers, have been used to induce early abortions.[69] It is legal to use an approved drug for a nonapproved ("off-label") indication so the use of methotrexate to induce abortions is not illegal. Doctors routinely prescribe drugs for nonapproved uses so the use of methotrexate off-label would not even be unusual.[70] Now that the potential has been shown, other drugs may be developed or tested for their potential as abortifacients.

If abortion is severely restricted in some states but not in others—a more likely scenario than absolute prohibition—the supply lines would become even more difficult to pierce. But scattered prohibitions would prevent some pregnant women from acquiring the drug soon enough for it to be effective. The accepted protocol requires that mifepristone be taken within seven weeks of the last menstrual period (effectiveness declines rapidly after eight to nine weeks). Currently one third of all abortions are performed at seven weeks or fewer and 50 percent at eight weeks or fewer, thus the scope for early abortion is large.[71] But it will take more time to find a source for mifepristone or other abortion services if abortion is prohibited. Regardless it is clear that mifepristone further limits the potential for abortion prohibition in the United States.

Utilitarian Considerations

Abortion has a number of social effects that are important but not directly connected with questions of liberty or rights. A brief survey of some of these effects is in order, to provide a full perspective on the debate. As noted above, 80 percent of women in the United States who have an abortion are unmarried, 20 percent are teenagers, and 50 percent are younger than twenty-five.[72] Often the women having abortions are poor. The social consequences of requiring poor, young, unmarried women to carry their pregnancies to term are generally negative. Certainly the consequences are negative for the mothers whose education, career, and marriage prospects are disrupted and diminished by the burden of having to raise a child.[73] The consequences, however, are also negative for other members of society including the prospective children of women who abort.

A large body of literature examines the consequences for children of being born to poor, young, and unmarried mothers. Moore, Morrison, and Greene find that the children of teenage mothers score lower in mathematics, reading recognition, and reading comprehension than the children of otherwise similar but older mothers.[74] Such deficits appear to last a long time as the children of teen mothers are less likely to complete high school than are children from otherwise similar backgrounds. Children of teen mothers are also more likely to be abused and end up in foster care than the children of adults.[75] Perhaps as a result of these deficits, the children of teen mothers are more likely to be incarcerated than the children of otherwise similar adults.[76] Sadly, the deficits may be passed on to a second generation as the children of teen mothers are themselves more likely to become teen mothers.[77]

One consequence of abortion access, as well as other forms of contraception, is that it lets young women delay childbearing to a time at which they are more capable, responsible, and desirous of children.[78] Note that if the children of teenagers who *choose* to give birth show a host of deficits, the consequences of requiring those teenagers who currently choose abortions to raise their children are likely to be even worse.

Studies have also shown a direct connection between abortion access and significant improvements in the birth weight and infant mortality for those fetuses that are carried to term.[79] These findings seem odd at first glance—how can access to abortion increase the birth weight and lower the infant mortality of those fetuses that are carried to term? On second glance, however, it is easy to see that the correlation between infant health and abortion access is a straightforward consequence of the fact that abortion increases the proportion of desired births.

Further evidence on the consequences to children of abortion access can be found by examining a natural experiment. A handful of states liberalized their abortion laws in 1970, three years before *Roe v. Wade* required the entire country to liberalize. By comparing children who were born between 1970 and 1973 in early liberalization states with children born at the same time in states that prohibited abortion, researchers estimated what the living conditions of children who were never born would have been had abortion been prohibited.[80] If abortion had not been available in the states that liberalized their abortion laws in 1970, the children who would have been born would have been 60 percent more likely than the average child to live in a single-parent family, 50 percent more likely to live in poverty, and 45 percent more likely to be on welfare. In addition the odds that these children would have died as infants would have been 40 percent higher than the average child.[81]

Critique of Anti-abortion Feminism

In the twentieth century, feminist thought has shown a disturbing tendency to jettison the individualist and classical liberal foundations that animated the movement in the late eighteenth and nineteenth centuries.[82] On issues such as free speech, economic liberty, sexual liberty, and "victimology" contemporary feminism has advocated approaches which individualist feminism rejects as contrary to the interests of both women and men. On the issue of abortion, however, feminist thought seemed to maintain its individualist roots. In the past, feminists of all stripes have proudly declared the libertarian principle of self-ownership, "a woman's body, a woman's right."

Yet, the libertarian underpinning of the right to abortion lies uneasily in the bed of thought of contemporary feminism that is increasingly collectivist and statist. Although the majority position within the current feminist movement is decidedly pro-choice, some prominent feminist voices have begun to criticize abortion and other forms of reproductive medicine and technology. For the anti-abortion feminists, abortion is, like everything else in society, a manifestation of the twin evils of patriarchy and capitalism.

Heather Menzies explains how even birth control—that apparent bastion of women's liberation—is part and parcel of women's oppression:

> I didn't immediately see the pill or the IUD as sinister in themselves; I began to see them, though, in context, as part of a larger system . . . they are part of a particular phrasing of the role of reproduction in society geared to production and consumption, and a particular phrasing of the problem of women's bondage to their own bodies.[83]

Another high profile radical-feminist, Gena Corea accuses modern abortion and contraception of "removing the process of reproduction itself from women."[84]

Catharine MacKinnon seems unconvinced that legal access to abortion was a victory for women. For one thing, *Roe v. Wade* legalized abortion as a privacy right and gender feminists are inherently suspicious of the private realm in which such perceived injustices as the free market and traditional marriage occur.[85] To gender feminists who rally around the slogan "the personal is political," privacy rights are a mask for patriarchy. MacKinnon writes:

> While the women's movement had . . . identified the private as a primary sphere of the subordination of women, *Roe v. Wade* had decriminalized access to abortion as a privacy right. A movement that knew that the private was a cover for our public condition was suddenly being told—and saying—that the abortion right was our right to the same privacy. If you forgot what this movement knew, this seemed like a good thing.[86]

To the hundreds of thousands of women who claim that *Roe v. Wade* benefited them as individuals, gender feminists acknowledge that an incidental benefit might have occurred but the main thrust of so-called abortion rights was to slot women into their place under patriarchy.

Twiss Butler comments:

> Granting women a sex-neutral right to privacy in reproductive matters was like granting women expensive, limited, and easily revocable guest privileges at the exclusive men's club called the Constitution. In contrast, men's membership in this club is a birthright, possibly retroactive to conception.[87]

Andrea Dworkin agrees:

> [T]he left says . . .'Little girls. . . . Well, what we'll do is that we will allow you to have an abortion right as long as you remain sexually accessible to us. And if you withdraw that accessibility and start talking this crap about an autonomous women's movement, we will collapse any support that we have ever given you. . . . Because if your abortion right is not going to mean sexual accessibility for us, girls, you can't have it.' And that's what they've been doing to us for the last fifteen years.[88]

Even some feminists who, as liberals, marched for abortion rights are questioning whether anything real was achieved. Barbara Katz Rothman epitomizes this drift in reflecting, "This emphasis on choice and information all sounded very logical at the time, sounded like women were going to get more and more control as first their access to information and then their choices expanded. I'm beginning to have second thoughts."[89]

There are at least three basic ideological reasons why some radical feminists are criticizing the pro-choice position. These reasons include:

1. The case for pro-choice rests on the individualistic principle of self-ownership: "a woman's body, a woman's right." And this principle is antagonistic to the collectivist agenda pursued by radical feminists who emphasize women's class rights and class interests. Self-ownership reduces the basic unit of social struggle to the level of individual rights, where every woman claims autonomy and choice—not as the member of an oppressed subclass, but as a full and free member of the human race.

2. Pro-choice is a call for reform, not a call for revolution, which is the goal of radical feminism which calls for nothing short of a total replacement of the current economic, political, and social system. In the sixties the campaign for abortion rights was expressed in terms of "repeal" or "le-

galization." Pro-choice aims at working with or through the system and does not maintain that patriarchal capitalism must be overthrown for women to control their own reproductive functions. Pro-choice advocates simply state that women must have the right to abort a fetus if they so wish. It is difficult to fit this reformist attitude into a revolutionary agenda.

3. For the anti-abortion feminists, and for many other feminist thinkers today, all issues concerning women, including abortion, are processed and analyzed according to the theory that women are always and everywhere oppressed by white male culture—patriarchy and capitalism. Oppression is said to permeate every aspect of society. Even women who do not think they are oppressed are victims (perhaps they are the most oppressed of all). Thus, the radical feminists' claim that unless patriarchy and capitalism are completely swept away, women will never be "free." The success of liberal feminism in securing abortion rights seems to contradict this claim. If liberal feminists did score an impressive victory without changing the current system, what happens to the radical claim? To maintain the ideology, any success that women appear to be making is said to be a mirage and a delusion created by the patriarchy to further cement its control.

The debate over abortion within feminism is a welcome opportunity for individualist feminists. They agree with the majority that abortion is a private matter that must be left to the conscience of those directly involved. But unlike liberal or radical feminists, individualist feminists can present an ideological challenge to the objections of anti-abortion feminists. The anti-abortion feminists argue that, for centuries, white male culture has dominated the field of reproduction which is now being used as yet another way to control women through procedures such as abortion (see also McElroy, "Breeder Reactionaries," in this volume). Individualist feminism maintains: technology is neither male nor female and the best health care for women, like the best quality in other commodities, is provided by a free and competitive marketplace.

To the objection that it is men who have "constructed the reality" in which birth control and abortion function, individualist feminists answer: women have been controlling their own bodies, including procuring abortions, for millennia. The issue is to keep the coercive apparatus of the state, often run by men or interest groups for their own purposes, out of the lives of individual women. Every woman must have the absolute right to determine her own reproductive destiny without legal barriers.[90]

The libertarian philosophy, of which individualist feminism is a part, strongly supports the right to choose, but it does so consistently. Mainstream "pro-choice" feminists consider the "right to an abortion" to be an entitlement for which others may legitimately be forced to pay. But one cannot defend the right to privacy and at the same time call for public funding of abortions. Ifeminism rejects all state funding of abortions. Pro-life advocates should not be forced to subsidize policies or practices which violate their conscience. State funding of abortions, which is limited by the Hyde amendment but still occurs, necessarily implicates pro-life believers in practices they reject and is one reason why the debate over abortion is so long-lasting. Ifeminism thus holds out the possibility of alleviating at least one aspect of the debate. Ifeminists call for the government to get out of reproductive decision-making altogether—to neither subsidize nor tax abortion or other contraceptive choices. Abortion should be a private decision privately funded.

The right to abort a fetus is part and parcel of a woman's natural right to her own body. A prohibition against abortion violates this natural right and encourages government control not only of women's bodies but also of speech, contraception, sexual freedom, and population. Abortion prohibition should be opposed by anyone with a concern for women or for liberty.

Notes

1. I thank Wendy McElroy for her extensive and helpful comments throughout the paper. I am especially indebted to her for permission to draw closely from McElroy (1996) in the last section of the paper. I would also like to thank Carl Close for comments. Responsibility for remaining errors and interpretations is soley my own.

Catholic thinking on abortion is one exception. It has a deep history that has evolved through time. In the thirteenth century, for example, Thomas Aquinas defined when a soul entered the body of a fetus and placed this standard into a Catholic framework.

2. Nicholas J. Johnson, "Principle and Passions: The Intersection of Abortion and Gun Rights," *Rutgers Law Review* 50 (1997), 97–197.

3. Technically pregnancy does not occur until implantation and thus the prevention of implantation is not an abortion. Nevertheless abortion opponents often argue that life or personhood begins at conception and consider the prevention of implantation an abortion.

4. Centers for Disease Control and Prevention, *CDC Surveillance Summaries MMWR* 1998: 48, no. SS-4 (July 30, 1999).

5. The information in the remainder of this section is drawn primarily from Alan Guttmacher Institute, *Sharing Responsibility: Women, Society & Abortion Worldwide* (New York, 1999). Available online at www.agi-usa.org. Accessed December 10, 2000.

6. Centers for Disease Control and Prevention, *CDC Surveillance Summaries MMWR*.

7. Alan Guttmacher Institute, *Sharing Responsibility*.

8. Parts of this section draw upon Alexander Tabarrok, "Rand the Moderate," *Journal of Ayn Rand Studies* 3:1 (2001).

9. Abortion was generally accepted in Western Europe in the early months of pregnancy until the mid- to late nineteenth century. Opinions began to change largely due to the absolute prohibition on abortion imposed in 1869 by the Roman Catholic Church.

10. Murray N. Rothbard, *The Ethics of Liberty* (New York, 1998); Ayn Rand, "A Last Survey: Part I," *The Ayn Rand Letter* 4 (1976), 1–4; Ayn Rand, "The Age of Mediocrity," *The Objectivist Forum* 2:3 (1981), 1–11; Ayn Rand, "Of Living Death," in L. Peikoff, ed., *The Voice of Reason: Essays in Objectivist Thought* (New York, 1988).

11. Rothbard, *Ethics*, 98.

12. Even granting for the sake of argument that a fetus possesses individual rights, it does not have the right to live off the bodily functions of another person.

13. Judith Jarvis Thomson, "A Defense of Abortion," *Philosophy and Public Affairs* 1:1 (1971), 47–66. Reprinted in J. Feinberg, ed., *The Problem of Abortion*, 2nd ed. (Belmont, Calif., 1984), 173–187.

14. *Ibid.*, 174.

15. Alan Guttmacher Institute, *Sharing Responsibility*. Rothbard argues that even if the woman wanted to get pregnant and changed her mind she cannot as a legal matter be justly forced to carry the pregnancy to term for the same reason that promises to marry or promises to work at a firm for ten years should be unenforceable in law.

16. More fancifully, Thomson imagines that people-seeds drift in the air like pollen. If you open your window and a seed drifts in and takes root there is surely no responsibility on your part to spend the next eighteen years raising the person.

17. Note also that neither Rothbard nor Thomson try to establish that abortion is always moral. Rothbard argues "not [for] the morality of abortion (which may or may not be moral on other grounds), but its legality, i.e., the absolute right of the mother to have an abortion" (*Ethics*, 98). The distinction is key. If the purpose of law is to protect the rights of individuals, rather than to enforce a particular vision of virtue, then the law should not concern itself with the morality of an action. The law should only ask whether it is a violation of rights.

18. Ayn Rand, "Man's Rights," in *The Virtue of Selfishness: A New Concept of Egoism* (New York, 1964) 192–193. Emphasis in original.

19. Having goals is not the same as acting in a goal-directed manner. Even the simplest of life-forms such as bacteria act in a goal-directed manner. Many nonliving things also act in a goal directed manner (a thermostat being the classic example).

20. See also Sharon Presley and Robert Cooke, "The Right to Abortion: A Libertarian Defense," Association of Libertarian Feminists Discussion Paper, 1979. They argue similarly to Rand that natural rights are based on "consciousness and choice."

21. Doris Gordon, "Abortion and Rights: Applying Libertarian Principles Correctly," *International Journal of Sociology and Social Policy* 19 (1999), 97–127. See also Gregory R. Johnson and David Rasmussen, "Rand On Abortion: A Critique," *Journal of Ayn Rand Studies* 1:2 (2000), 245–261; and the reply from Tabarrok, "Rand the Moderate."

22. Although Gordon claims that she is an atheist her argument has religious overtones. Gordon argues that the moment an egg is fertilized it is imbued with a "human nature," and therefore has natural rights. Substitute soul for human nature and we have the same argument from an explicitly religious perspective.

23. Libertarians regard taxation, product safety regulations, controls on international trade, and most other features of the modern state as "aggression." This term is

not being used in an ordinary dictionary sense and cannot be defined in the libertarian sense without a considerable background context.

24. Since Gordon's theory of aggression is without foundation it cannot answer why humans have rights but animals do not. Singer, *The Essential Singer: Writings On an Ethical Life* (New York, 2000) argues for animal rights.

25. Anti-abortionists often detail the physical development of the fetus, the development of toes and brainwaves, in order to give weight to the claim that it is an actual human being. But this development, by the standard defined by Gordon, is irrelevant to the issue of rights since rights exist at the moment of conception and are not increased thereby. The zygote with no visually discernible human characteristics claims the same individual rights as an eight-month-old fetus or a baby in the delivery room.

26. But note that Rand is not an ethical hedonist. Rand argues that happiness is a by-product of the pursuit and achievement of *rational* values and not something that can be pursued as a primary.

27. Rand, "A Last Survey," 2–3.

28. Rand's analysis of altruism provides a surprisingly unexamined link between her and sixties' feminists such as Betty Friedan. In *The Feminine Mystique*, Friedan argued that women were the victims of false values and delusions that led them to sacrifice their happiness and even their identity for the sake of their husbands and children. Friedan urged women to discard these false values and seek genuine, creative, and self-defining work, a message with which Rand agreed.

29. See, for example, Thomson, "Defense"; Laurence H. Tribe, *Abortion: The Clash of Absolutes* (New York, 1992); and Eileen McDonagh, *Breaking the Abortion Deadlock: From Choice to Consent* (Oxford, England, 1996), on the lack of "Good Samaritan" laws or morality that bind men. One of the implications of imbuing fetuses with rights is to burden the pregnant woman with restrictions on any behavior that could be called "fetal endangerment." Even today, women who take drugs or alcohol are often charged and vigorously prosecuted under "child abuse" laws. Yet men who physically attack women, in the process injuring a fetus, are only rarely charged with crimes against the fetus. See Jean R. Schroedel, Pamela Fiber, and Bruce D. Snyder, "Women's Rights and Fetal Personhood in Criminal Law," *Duke Journal of Gender Law and Policy* 7 (2000), 89–120.

30. The early laws did little more than codify what had long been true under common law. Early statutes "against" abortion (in the 1820s and 1830s) were poison-control laws by which the sale of certain commercial abortifacients was outlawed. See Leslie J. Reagan, *When Abortion Was a Crime* (Berkeley, Calif., 1997).

31. See Barbara Ehrenreich and Deirdre English, "Women and the Rise of the American Medical Profession," in Wendy McElroy, ed., *Freedom, Feminism, and the State* (Oakland, Calif., 1991), 193–208.

32. Linda Gordon, *Woman's Body, Woman's Right: A Social History of Birth Control in America* (New York, 1976), 53. According to Reagan, *Abortion*, the unsafe, backstreet abortions that are associated with criminalizing the procedure came into prominence in the 1940s and 1950s when doctors and clinics providing the service were forced to close.

33. The full title of the pamphlet is "Cupid's Yokes. The Binding Forces of Conjugal Life: An Essay to Consider Some Moral and Physiological Phases of Love and Marriage, Wherein Is Asserted the Natural Right and Necessity to Sexual Self-Government." Estimates of its distribution range up to hundreds of thousands, despite legal limitations placed on its circulation. The pamphlet led to the arrest of several prominent radicals who distributed it, including D. M. Bennett, editor of the *Truth*

Seeker, who was sentenced at age sixty to thirteen months of hard labor. For an excellent discussion of the drama surrounding "Cupid's Yokes," see Hal D. Sears, *The Sex Radicals: Free Love in High Victorian America* (Lawrence, Kans., 1977). Angela Heywood, Ezra's wife, wrote one of the first defenses of abortion on the grounds of a woman's body, a woman's right. See McElroy, *Freedom*.

34. In 1914 Margaret Sanger, the birth control and women's rights activist, founded the periodical, *The Woman Rebel*. *The Woman Rebel*'s motto was, "NO GODS. NO MASTERS," and proclaimed, "A Woman's Duty: To look the whole world in the face with a go-to-hell look in the eyes; to have an ideal; to speak and act in defiance of convention." Sanger was arrested for publication of *The Woman Rebel* and under threat of a forty-five-year sentence she jumped bail to England. Returning in 1915 she was put on trial; in 1916 the charges were dropped due to sympathetic public opinion and the authorities' fear that prosecuting her would make her into a martyr. Sanger continued to be arrested and sometimes jailed on related charges throughout her activist years. See E. Katz, et al., eds., *The Papers of Margaret Sanger* (Columbia, S.C., 1999) or adh.sc.edu. Accessed December 4, 2000.

35. Modest reforms had occurred in other states prior to 1970 but liberalization of abortion law did not occur until that year.

36. Although the reasoning in *Roe v. Wade* is based on the Fourteenth Amendment, the Ninth Amendment provides a far sounder foundation. The Ninth Amendment reads, "The enumeration in the Constitution of certain rights shall not be construed to deny or disparage others retained by the people." The Ninth Amendment was used appropriately in *Griswold v. Connecticut*, 381 U.S. 479 (1965). Conservatives who argue that the court invented privacy rights conveniently forget the Ninth Amendment. A proper understanding of original intent recognizes that the founding fathers believed in natural rights that were not limited to those listed in the Constitution.

37. In *Griswold v. Connecticut*.

38. In *Eisenstadt v. Baird* 405 U.S. 438 (1972).

39. Information in the next three paragraphs is drawn from Tribe, *Abortion*.

40. A woman with five children could apply for an abortion.

41. As a result of Romanian policy the orphanages were filled beyond capacity and many children were brought up in decrepit circumstances—a point not unrelated to the abortion controversy in the United States.

42. James C. Mohr, *Abortion in America* (Oxford, 1978).

43. Quoted in Mohr, *Abortion in America*, 167.

44. *Journal of the Senate of the State of Ohio* (Columbus, Ohio, 1867). Cited in Mohr, 208–209.

45. Quoted in Mohr, 167. More recently, pro-abortion activists have been accused of practicing racial policies since more black women abort fetuses per capita than white women. Both anti- and pro-abortion measures, when placed in the hands of the State, can be used for racist purposes.

46. See Reagan, *Abortion*, especially chapter 6 and the epilogue.

47. Reagan, *Abortion*.

48. Mohr, *Abortion in America*.

49. Mohr, *Abortion in America* and Reagan, *Abortion*.

50. Until 1971 the prohibition on distributing birth control information was not dropped.

51. 18 U.S.C. Section 1462.

52. See *Encyclopaedia Britannica* entry on Comstock Act (www.britannica.com).

See also materials available by search on abortion and Comstock at the Electronic Frontier Foundation website www.eff.org. Accessed December, 4, 2000.

53. The Alan Guttmacher Institute estimates that if *Roe v. Wade* were overturned today abortion would instantly be illegal in thirteen states due to existing laws.

54. Reagan, *Abortion*.

55. R. Hatcher, E. Guest, et al., *Contraceptive Technology*, 15th ed. (New York, 1990).

56. Used as a contraceptive, mifepristone (RU 486) also acts by preventing implantation. For a debate on whether the prevention of implantation is "abortion," see the correspondence section of the *New England Journal of Medicine* vol. 328, no. 5 (February 4, 1993).

57. Tribe, *Abortion*.

58. Mohr, *Abortion in America*, 254.

59. Gerald Rosenberg, *The Hollow Hope: Can Courts Bring About Social Change?* (Chicago, 1991), 355.

60. The U.S. abortion rate is below the world average.

61. Prostitution and homosexual activity also pit the individual's control of his or her own body against that of others acting through the State. See the essays by Almodovar and Nussbaum in this volume.

62. On the drug war and in particular the erosion of constitutional liberties see Richard L. Miller, *Drug Warriors and Their Prey* (Westport, Conn., 1996); William F. Shughart, *Taxing Choice: The Predatory Politics of Fiscal Discrimination* (Oakland, Calif., 1998); Mike Gray, *Drug Crazy* (New York, 2000); and Timothy Lynch, *After Prohibition* (Washington, D.C., 2000).

63. In the 1960s there were approximately two hundred maternal deaths a year due to illegal abortions in the United States (Council on Scientific Affairs, A. M. A., "Induced Termination of Pregnancy Before and After *Roe v. Wade*," *Journal of the American Medical Association* 208:22 (1992), 3231–3239). Around the world there are approximately 80,000 to 100,000 deaths due to induced abortions every year, most of them in developing countries where abortion tends to be more restricted (and thus illegal abortions are more common) than in the United States. See Alan Guttmacher Institute, *Sharing Responsibility*.

64. See Alan Guttmacher Institute, *Sharing Responsibility* and Reagan, *Abortion*.

65. Council on Scientific Affairs, "Induced Termination."

66. Data from the European studies indicate a 95 percent success rate, the experience in the U.S. clinical trials was slightly lower at 92 percent. Differences in success rates may be due to the lesser experience of the U.S. physicians, suggesting the rate will increase over time, or to slight differences in the way success was defined. See Population Council FAQ on Medical Abortion available at www.popcouncil.org/faqs/abortion.html. Accessed December 6, 2000.

67. Mifepristone has been used by more than 600,000 women in Europe with only one death (which was probably due to a different drug administered as part of the protocol and since removed in favor of safer alternatives) and it has been used by millions of women in Asia without notable problems. See Eric A. Schaff, Steven H. Eisinger, and Lisa S. Stadalius, "Weighting the Options in Medical Abortion," *Medscape Women's Health* 2:9 (1997), 1–15. Available online at www.medscape.com. Accessed December 5, 2000; Paul Blumenthal, Jane Johnson, and Felicia Stewart, "The Approval of Mifepristone (RU486) in the United States; What's Wrong With This Picture?" *Medscape Women's Health* 5:4 (2000), 1–4. Available online at www.medscape.com. Accessed December 5, 2000; and Population Council FAQ.

68. See Population Council FAQ.

69. See T. G. Stovall and F. W. Ling, "Single-dose Methotrexate: An Expanded Clinical Trial," *American Journal of Obstetrics and Gynecology* 168 (1993), 1759–1765. and Schaff, et al., "Weighting the Options."

70. For more on off-label drug prescribing, see Alexander Tabarrok, "Assessing the FDA Via the Anomaly of Off-Label Drug Prescribing," *The Independent Review* 5:1 (2000), 25–53.

71. CDC Surveillance Summaries.

72. *Ibid.*

73. Adoption is a substitute for abortion but an imperfect one. First, adoption requires that the pregnancy be carried to term—a significant financial, physical, and (sometimes) social burden. Second, it is not inconsistent for a woman to be willing to abort a fetus but not be willing to give away her baby. For some people it is difficult to give up responsibility for raising a child. Difficult and troubling questions will always arise: How is the child being treated? Is it loved? Opponents of abortion will argue that the alternative is much worse—the "death" of the child. Most women who have abortions see themselves as preventing the birth of a child in much the same way as birth control does. The woman who prefers an abortion to adoption is not being fickle or inconsistent.

74. See Kristin A. Moore, Donna R. Morrison, and Ansela D. Greene. "Effects on the Children Born to Adolescent Mothers," in R. A. Maynard, ed., *Kids Having Kids* (Washington, D.C., 1997), 145–180.

75. Robert M. Goerge and Joo L. Bong, "Abuse and Neglect of Children," in Maynard, *Kids*, 205–230.

76. Jeffrey Grogger, "Incarceration-Related Costs of Early Childbearing," in Maynard, *Kids*, 231–256.

77. Robert H. Haveman, Barbara Wolfe, and Elaine Peterson, "Children of Early Childbearers as Young Adults," in Maynard, *Kids*, 285–338.

78. On the margin, it is possible that mild restrictions on access to abortion can decrease teen births if pregnancies fall sufficiently. Severe restrictions on abortion access, however, will almost certainly increase teen births. See Thomas J. Kane and Douglas Staiger, "Teen Motherhood and Abortion Access," *Quarterly Journal of Economics* CXI:2 (1996), 467–506; compare with Jonathan Gruber, Phillip Levine, and Douglas Staiger, "Abortion Legalization and Child Living Circumstances: Who Is the 'Marginal Child,'" *Quarterly Journal of Economics* 456:1 (1999), 263–291 and Phillip B. Levine, Douglas Staiger, Thomas J. Kane, and David J. Zimmerman. "*Roe v. Wade* and American Fertility," *NBER Working Paper Series* (1996).

79. Michael Grossman and Steven Jacobowitz, "Variations in Infant Mortality Rates Among Counties of the United States: The Role of Public Policies and Programs," *Demography* XVIII (1981) 695–713; Hope Corman and Michael Grossman, "Determinants of Neonatal Mortality Rates in the U.S.: A Reduced Form Model," *Journal of Health Economics* IV (1985) 213–236; Theodore Joyce, "The Impact of Induced Abortion On Black and White Birth Outcomes in the United States" *Demography* XXIV (1987), 229–244; Michael Grossman and Theodore Joyce, "Unobservables, Pregnancy Resolutions, and Birth Weight Production Functions in New York City," *Journal of Political Economy* XCVII (1990), 983–1007.

80. Gruber, et al. "Abortion Legalization."

81. See also Carolyn T. Adams and Kathryn T. Winston, *Mothers At Work: Public Policies in the United States, Sweden, and China* (New York, 1980), who found that the children of Swedish mothers who were refused abortions had higher probabilities in

adulthood of being alcoholics and criminals. John J. Donahue and Steven D. Levitt, "The Impact of Legalized Abortion on Crime," *Quarterly Journal of Economics* CXVI:2 (2001), 379–420, argue that abortion legalization, beginning in 1970, is responsible for the decrease in crime rates beginning in the early 1990s.

82. I am grateful to Wendy McElroy for contributing to this section of the essay which is based closely on McElroy, *Freedom*, chapter 11.

83. Heather Menzies, "In His Image: Science and Technology," in S. Cream, ed., *Twist and Shout: A Decade of Feminist Writing in This Magazine* (Toronto, 1992), 157–158.

84. Gena Corea, Prologue, in P. Spallone and D. Steinberg Lynn, eds., *Made to Order: The Myth of Reproductive and Genetic Progress* (New York, 1987), 13.

85. Catherine MacKinnon, "Liberalism and the Death of Feminism," in D. Leidholdt and J. G. Raymond, eds., *The Sexual Liberals and the Attack On Feminism* (New York, 1990).

86. *Ibid.*, 6–7.

87. Twiss Butler, "Abortion and Pornography," in Leidholdt, *Sexual Liberals*.

88. Andrea Dworkin, "Woman Hating Right and Left," in Leidholdt, *Sexual Liberals*.

89. Barbara Katz Rothman, "The Meaning of Choice in Reproductive Technology," in R. Arditti, R. D. Klein, and S. Minden, eds., *Test Tube Women: What Future for Motherhood?* (Boston, 1984).

90. The assumed overwhelming power of patriarchy makes the victimology of much contemporary feminism more understandable. Who would not be a victim when every aspect of society operates to oppress? Concering abortion, sensitivity to a complex emotional and psychological event sometimes transforms into the idea that women who have abortions have been brainwashed—the proof positive of their brainwashing being that some women regret their decision to abort. Thus adult women are incapable of rendering informed consent and their "choices"—however articulately stated or documented—need not be taken seriously. Men have said this to women for centuries: it is disturbing to hear it from feminists. To undermine the right of a woman to be taken seriously when she says "yes" or "no" is to erase the progress for which feminists have fought for centuries.

WOMEN
and
WORK

Wendy McElroy

❀

What Does Affirmative Action Affirm?

AFFIRMATIVE ACTION IS AN ATTEMPT TO REDISTRIBUTE ECONOMIC POWER BY forcing employers to give preference to women.[1] As with all schemes of distributing justice, choice is taken from individuals and given to social planners. Affirmative action has been a debacle. It has not cured sex segregation in the workplace or closed the wage gap between men and women. More importantly it has hindered the institution that has done the most to benefit women economically: the free market.

Real Life

Last week I learned that a friend had been passed over for tenure at an Ivy League school. This was surprising to me. He had been teaching at the university for several years and was immensely popular, not only with the students but also within the department. With a book and several journal articles to his credit, his qualifications were in good order. So what was the problem?

He explained it to me: he was a white male in a department that needed more visible women and minorities. Never mind that the woman hired had less experience and fewer credentials. Never mind that the university had been grooming him for the position—the department head could not even look him in the eye while breaking the news. Never mind that my friend is now so embittered that he tells his male students to forget pursuing a degree in the humanities, because credentials and quality do not matter anymore. If they are white and male, he insists, there will be no place for them in academia.

I hope he is overstating the case. But I understand his bitterness: it is difficult not to rail against unfairness when there is next to no recourse against it.

If my friend were a woman, he could sue the university for unfair employment practices under Title VII of the Civil Rights Act of 1964. This section of the act states that it is unlawful for any employer:

> (1) to fail or refuse to hire or discharge any individual, or otherwise to discriminate against any individual with respect to his compensation, terms, or privileges of employment because of such individual's race, color, religion, sex or national origin.

But to bring such a suit he would have to belong to a class protected by Title VII: that is, he would have to be a woman or a minority. As a male from German-Irish ancestry, he is not simply excluded from protection; he is, in fact, the person against whom protection is being offered. Why is this protection necessary? My friend has always been sex-blind when it comes to his students and colleagues. Why, then, do women have to be shielded from him?

Because, it is argued, women have historically been discriminated against in employment. Since white males have benefited from this injustice as a class, they must now bear the brunt of adjusting the balance. This includes him.

Catharine MacKinnon explains why my friend is inescapably my oppressor: "the social relation between the sexes is organized so that men may dominate and women must submit and this relation is sexual."[2]

What is Affirmative Action?

The contradictory notion of "discriminating in order to obtain equal treatment" seems to violate common sense. This contradiction leads wayward feminists, like me, to ask: What exactly is affirmative action? And what is being affirmed?

Affirmative action, as a policy, is usually said to be in place when a company or an institution takes reasonable action to remedy any discriminatory behavior which has occurred in the past. On ethical grounds, most people would agree with such a policy though many would question the wisdom of enforcing the policy by law.

The spirit of affirmative action seems different from a literal interpretation of its words, however. To understand this spirit it is necessary to examine the roots of the issue in the context of the feminist movement from which affirmative action sprang.

First, it is necessary to acknowledge the truth of affirmative action's main claim: historically, women have been the victims of discrimination. During the nineteenth century, they were excluded from universities and unions, barred from professions such as medicine, and—upon marriage— often lost all title to whatever pittance they were allowed to earn. During the twentieth century, the legal barriers confronting women fell. Vestiges of legal inequality still exist but the instances are few—for example women and men often receive different sentences for the same crime. These differences are beginning to favor women at the expense of men.

The cry for affirmative action makes no sense if the goal is simply equal treatment before the law. Affirmative action is based on the concept of socio-economic equality, which became popular during the 1960s. Access to the basics was presented as the right of every American. The fact that the law was to allocate these goods on a favored basis to certain classes of Americans—blacks or women—was justified on two grounds. First, they were the victims of another class of Americans: white males. Second, only by assuring equal access to such consumer goods as education could the disadvantaged compete fairly.

What of women in this new world? Although legal barriers to women had largely fallen, it was argued that the ill effects of history still impacted modern women. The lingering injustice was especially blatant in the marketplace, which continued to undervalue women's work. The removal of legal barriers had not cured this exploitation; legal protection was required. It was necessary for the law to prefer women in order for the marketplace to treat them fairly.

Affirmative action prefers women through a wide range of measures which include: providing remedial training, accepting lower scores on tests for jobs or university admission, recruitment procedures aimed at women, and offering child-care facilities.

Why Should an Employer Accept These Measures?

Although affirmative action has seldom been mandated by law, administrative regulations and judicial rulings have often lent this policy the force of law. In 1965 President Lyndon B. Johnson established the Office of Federal Contract Compliance, which ensured that private businesses who did work for the federal government followed nondiscrimination requirements. With this a large block of the American economy adopted affirmative action. Under the Federal Guidelines of 1971, statistical representation became the litmus test of discrimination.

On a more local level, most states have Fair Employment Practice Laws and civil rights agencies who enforce them. Among the damages that can be awarded are: hiring or reinstatement; promotion; training; seniority; a pay increase; back pay, which is broadly defined to include pension and educational benefits; and legal fees.

The cost of swimming against affirmative action can be very high. In 1980 a court ordered the Ford Motor Company to give $13 million in back pay to women and minorities. Attorney fees alone can bankrupt a company. In a sex discrimination case against the University of Minnesota, the attorney fees came to $1,475,000. The successful plaintiff later abandoned academia to become a lawyer.

Even companies that rigidly implement affirmative action policies are not safe from the witch hunt surrounding this issue. Sears and Roebuck was among the first large companies to voluntarily evolve an affirmative action plan. They were also among the first to be sued by the government, who used Sears' own statistics to show that women were underrepresented as sales persons of such commodities as automobile tires. Sears was eventually exonerated. Ironically it became a target largely because its records on affirmative action were meticulously kept and available for inspection. Its attempt to comply backfired badly.

The marketplace—in self-defense—has adopted a de facto quota system that protects it against charges of discrimination. How, in the name of fairness, have we arrived at a system that openly discriminates on the basis of sex?

Arguments for Affirmative Action

Fundamentally, three arguments have been offered for affirmative action: social good; compensatory justice; and the ideal of equality.

The social good, or utilitarian, argument states that society will be enriched by advancing women. This is a relatively lightweight justification, since advocates of affirmative action themselves generally concede that they would push equality even if it lowered the overall good of society.

Moreover, it is easy to point out the disastrous long-term consequences to society of using a quota system rather than merit to allocate jobs. Affirmative action drives a wedge between individual worth and economic success: how does this benefit society?

Affirmative action might well increase the very evil it seeks to cure: prejudice. Dinesh D'Souza remarks on a strange phenomena happening on campuses across America.[3] Although student attitudes on race have grown more informed, incidents of racial hostility on campus seem to be increasing. D'Souza concludes that a new kind of racism is appearing—one that has been created by affirmative action, by the legal preference given to blacks. This is a racism that stems from the understandable resentment

felt by white or Asian students. It is a prejudice that springs not from ignorance but from experience.

Women in the workplace face a similar dilemma. In order to fill their
quotas, employers will promote women too quickly or into inappropriate
departments. When these women fail, it will be seen as confirmation of
the inadequacy of their sex. When other women succeed on their own, it
will be assumed that they were coddled along by preferential policies. And
what of the men who are discriminated against? Their understandable resentment might well be translated into a heightened sexism—just as my
friend's rejection has embittered him toward all of academia.

The black free-market economist Thomas Sowell has commented on a
bitter irony: blacks who had advanced through merit are being victimized
by preferential policies. They will not be given due credit for their accomplishments. The same is true of women in the marketplace.

In short, affirmative action is not what economists call "a zero sum
game," by which wealth and power are simply transferred from one group
to another. It is possible for everyone to lose in the exchange.

The argument from compensatory justice claims that anyone who
causes injury to an innocent person should remedy the damage. Affirmative action goes one step further, however, and claims that descendants of
the injured parties deserve compensation as well. There are two basic objections to this argument: the people receiving compensation are not the
victims and the people being forced to pay the compensation have done
nothing wrong.

Many of those forced to pay are also victims of historical prejudice.
Sowell comments on this further irony:

> The fact that some groups are poor because of historical injus-
> tices done to them has been taken by many as a blank check to
> consider all lower income groups victims of injustice. In many
> parts of the world, however, those initially in dire poverty have,
> over the generations, raised themselves to an above-average
> level of prosperity, by great effort and painful sacrifice. Now the
> deep thinkers come along and want to redistribute what they
> earn to others who were initially more fortunate but less hard
> working.[4]

The third most common argument for preferential treatment is a
moral one, based on the ideal of equality.[5] Yet government, in all its forms
and on an international basis, has an abysmal record in terms of favoring
equality. It was not Henry Ford who inscribed the institution of slavery
into the Constitution; it was politicians. Gary S. Becker emphasizes the

role of the government, and those who would use government, in oppressing minorities. He uses what is, perhaps, the most notorious case of discrimination to illustrate his point:

> Early in the twentieth century the government of South Africa already restricted the employment of blacks in mines, largely, it should be added, at the urging of the union of white miners.[6]

Becker goes on to give an impressive list of government-induced racism, including:

> the confiscation of some property of Japanese Americans in the United States during World War II, the restrictions legislated against Negroes in various Southern states, the limited amount of public education available to Jews in eastern Europe for several centuries, or the government imposed Apartheid in South Africa.[7]

A Good Word for Discrimination

Self ownership—a woman's body, a woman's right—requires the right to discrimination. To own something means to control its use, including the right of "freedom of association." The right to freely choose your friends and your employees on the basis of your own standards and judgment.

But freedom has risks. One of them is that people may choose to deal with women in a biased and offensive manner. As long as this "discrimination" is peaceful—that is, it involves no physical injury or threat of harm—it is not a violation of rights. Such discrimination is simply ignorant behavior, which shows incredibly poor taste. But both freedom of speech and freedom of association guarantee that people have the right to be wrong. To be offensive. To be prejudiced. Freedom of association requires the right to say "no" and to refuse to associate.

Discrimination—on some level—occurs in everyone's life. It is an inescapable part of forming preferences and tastes. As Becker observes:

> . . . discrimination and prejudice are not usually said to occur when someone prefers looking at a glamorous Hollywood actress rather than at some other woman; yet they are said to occur when he prefers living next to whites rather than next to Negroes.[8]

Everyone reaches their own conclusions about other people. And, in general, you associate with those you favor and avoid those you consider objectionable—for whatever reason. You invite friends into your home and bar those who are unpleasant. In the same manner, you have the right to hire whomever you consider appropriate. The decision may be biased. It may be "wrong," by society's standards. But a free society allows individuals to make their own judgments and allocate their own resources.

Discriminating on the basis of gender may well be unjust. But even in this case, women will benefit more from a free-market system than from government regulation. Even if a hefty percentage of society is misogynist, there will always be many others who want to profit by doing business with women. Any discrimination that is suffered will be random and escapable.

Richard Epstein observes:

> In a world in which 90 percent of the people are opposed to doing business with me, I shall concentrate my attention on doing business with the other 10%.[9]

He explains that—as long as individual rights are respected—racism or sexism will have only a limited impact:

> . . . as long as the tort law is in place, my enemies are powerless to block out mutually beneficial transaction by their use of force. . . . The critical question for my welfare is not which opportunities are lost but which are retained.[10]

The government's attempt to regulate the peaceful behavior and attitudes of society is doomed. It is ridiculous to suppose that the complex, ever-shifting interactions of society can be controlled. Even the most totalitarian of societies, the Soviet Union, was unable to prevent market forces and personal preference from erupting in the form of the black market.

The consequences of affirmative action cannot be controlled, or even predicted. This is because the individuals involved, both the perceived beneficiaries and losers, are not automatons. They are not, in Thomas Sowell's words, "blocks of wood passively placed where the policy dictates."

Unfortunately theorizing can bring little solace to my friend, who is debating whether or not to abandon the one career that has ever meant anything to him. There is no encouragement I can give him. What he says is true: no matter how good he is or how much he cares, doors are slammed in his face because he is a white male. I feel almost as outraged as he does.

Someone has to get blunt and tell these feminists to put up or shut up about equality and suffering and justice. Equality means "equal treatment," not privilege. Caring for those who suffer means caring for men as well as women. Justice requires that all human beings receive what they individually deserve. So far, all I have seen of affirmative action is institutionalized discrimination, and sloppy thinking. It is the sort of policy that gives feminism a bad name.

Notes

1. This essay is excerpted from *Sexual Correctness: The Gender-Feminist Attack on Women* (Jefferson, N.C., 1997).

2. Catharine MacKinnon, *Feminism Unmodified*, (Cambridge, Mass., 1987), 16.

3. Dinesh D'Souza, *Illiberal Education: The Politics of Race and Sex on Campus* (New York, 1991).

4. Thomas Sowell, *Compassion versus Guilt* (New York, 1987), 30.

5. See *Sexual Correctness*, chapter five, for in-depth treatment.

6. Gary S. Becker, *The Economics of Discrimination* (Chicago, 1971), 7.

7. *Ibid.*

8. *Ibid*, 13.

9. Richard Epstein, *Forbidden Ground: The Case Against Employment Discrimination Laws* (Cambridge, Mass., 1992), 30.

10. *Ibid.*

Cathy Young

❦

Groping Toward Sanity

Why the Clinton Sex Scandals Are Changing the Way We Talk About Sexual Harassment

"This is the death of sexual harassment," Susan Carpenter-MacMillan, the flamboyant adviser to Paula Jones, announced on television—meaning, of course, sexual harassment as a cause, not as a behavior, and referring to feminists' failure to support her protegé. That was a few days before Jones's sexual harassment suit against President Clinton was dismissed in 1998 on summary judgment. Since then there has been a good deal of talk about what the case will mean for the legal system and for the American workplace, with many conservatives in the unaccustomed role of lamenting that women will be discouraged from complaining and many feminists in the equally unaccustomed role of decrying frivolous lawsuits.

As legal precedent, the ruling by Judge Susan Webber Wright in *Jones v. Clinton* probably will not mean much. But the case and its ramifications may have a lasting effect on the cultural climate—an impact that could ultimately translate into legal change. If Anita Hill's testimony at the Clarence Thomas confirmation hearings in 1991 turned into a "teach-in" that mainstreamed much of the radical feminist ideology on sexual harassment, then the Clinton sex scandals may become a counter-teach-in that brings us a step closer to a more balanced view of the sexual dynamics between men and women in the workplace.

The concept of sexual harassment was around before Anita Hill. It was coined in the mid-1970s and soon gained recognition in the courts. In 1986 the Supreme Court gave its unanimous blessing to sexual harassment law in *Meritor v. Vinson*, a case in which a bank teller alleged that her supervisor pressured her into a sexual relationship. But the issue remained on the cultural periphery until the "national consciousness raising" of October 1991, when the country was riveted by Hill's claim that as her boss at the Equal Employment Opportunity Commission, Thomas had occasionally asked her out, talked about X-rated movies, and once joked about a pubic hair on a Coke can.

The "teach-in" succeeded: the Thomas-Hill episode established a dominant paradigm of sexual harassment. In this paradigm, any manifestation of sexuality in the workplace, from romantic pursuit to racy humor, is abusive if someone decides—perhaps long after the fact—that it was "unwelcome." Even if they do not mean harm, men who "just don't get it" bear all the blame for sexual conflicts. To question a charge of harassment is grossly insensitive, even if the behavior of the "victim," such as remaining friendly with the alleged harasser, seems to contradict her claims. Pennsylvania Republican Senator Arlen Specter had to work hard to live down his "grilling" of Anita Hill.

When the dust had settled, the new awareness of sexual harassment remained a part of the landscape. "Every time a man and a woman meet at the water cooler now, Anita Hill [is] right there between them," Wayne State University anthropologist Andrea Sankar told *Newsweek* a year after the hearings—and it speaks volumes about the social climate that this was supposed to be a *good* thing.

On Nexis, references to sexual harassment grew from fewer than fifteen hundred in 1990 to more than eight thousand in 1992 and nearly fifteen thousand in 1994. Every week, some new sexual harassment story was in the headlines. In 1993 New York state legislator Earlene Hill was able to cause a furor by revealing that a few years earlier a male colleague had failed to move to let her get to her seat and jocularly invited her to climb over his legs, while another had said "sex" instead of "six" while reeling off numbers in a speech and then joked, "Whenever I think of Earlene, I think of sex."

Yet from the moment former Arkansas state worker Paula Corbin Jones came forward in May 1994 with her claim of indecent advances by then-Governor Clinton, feminists were remarkably quick to abandon the Anita Hill paradigm. On CNN legal scholar and former Democratic strategist Susan Estrich declared that it was healthy for feminists to make the point that "not all women necessarily are telling the truth, and not every complaint deserves to be used in a way which destroys a man." Trying to neutralize charges of partisan hypocrisy, Estrich also noted, "Maybe we show it in the case of a friend of ours, but so be it."

Others who had supported wide-ranging definitions of sexual harassment in the past suggested that if Clinton indeed had Jones escorted to his hotel room, displayed his distinguishing characteristics, and asked for oral sex, it was no big deal. Katha Pollitt, the acid-tongued commentator for the *Nation*, noted that Jones lost no pay or promotions for rebuffing him. Eleanor Smeal, former head of the National Organization for Women and president of the Feminist Majority Foundation, opined that it was "a marginal sexual harassment case at best."

Many feminists feebly argued that Jones did not need their help. She was going to have her day in court, they said, whereas Anita Hill would not have been allowed to testify without feminist pressure. The dismissal of Jones's lawsuit took away this excuse; interestingly, some of the people who had used it, including former Representative Pat Schroeder (D-Colo.), applauded Judge Wright's ruling. On ABC's *This Week*, NOW President Patricia Ireland could not give a straight answer to the question, "If Paula Jones's allegations are true, was she harassed?" A number of feminist commentators asserted that a case of harassment must involve some economic or psychological harm to the plaintiff. In fact that has not been the law since 1993—though Wright did cite the absence of tangible damage in dismissing Jones's claim of outrage under Arkansas state law.

At the time Jones's suit was dismissed, allegations of sexual misconduct involving Clinton dominated the national scene as much as the Hill-Thomas circus did, with the post-Jones cases seemingly tailor-made for feminist outrage. Although White House intern Monica Lewinsky's Oval Office trysts were fully consensual by her own account, they appear to involve the sort of vast "power differentials" between participants that many feminists have argued preclude valid consent. In the topsy-turvy world of the Clinton scandals, it was left to conservatives such as Linda Chavez to take this position. The charge by volunteer Kathleen Willey that Clinton kissed and groped her when she came to see him about a job had overtones of a quid pro quo shakedown.

While Willey's *60 Minutes* appearance finally prompted strong words from Ireland, most feminists still took a "so what?" view of the whole thing. Gloria Steinem published an op-ed piece in the *New York Times* advancing what has become known as the "one free grope" theory: Clinton's alleged overtures to Jones and Willey, while boorish, did not amount to sexual harassment because he backed off when they said no.

It is getting more and more difficult to tell the feminists from critics of "sexual correctness" such as Katie Roiphe or Camille Paglia—the ones whom Susan Faludi derided a few years ago as "pod feminists," à la *Invasion of the Body Snatchers*. Susan Estrich scoffs that if every come-on in the workplace led to a lawsuit, "We'd all be in court all the time." Anita

Hill laments "the use of the term *sexual harassment* to describe any and every kind of sexually related transgression." Faludi herself seems to have been body-snatched. She writes that women who are true adults "acknowledg[e] that sexual encounters are often muddy and fumbled affairs and that, in the case of sexual harassment, the response should be nuanced and in scale to the offense," which sometimes means not reporting it.

The accusations of hypocrisy are well earned. Faludi, who now mocks the neo-Victorian view of working women as "shocked maiden[s]" horrified by a sexual advance, blames this image on paternalistic male pundits—though she herself once paid homage to that quintessential shocked maiden, Anita Hill. When Susan Estrich stresses that sex with one's subordinate may reflect poor judgment but is not against the law, she conveniently forgets to mention that in her 1991 Stanford Law Review article "Sex at Work" she argued that it should be against the law. But the ironic fact is that the new feminist perspective on men, women, and sex at work is mostly quite sensible.

Of course this is not systematic revisionism: most likely, Clinton's feminist apologists want a one-time exception for a president whom, despite reservations, they regard as supportive of their issues and who is under attack from conservatives. NOW spokeswomen are as hawkish as ever on sexual harassment, except when they hide behind an uncharacteristic deference to judicial decisions in the Paula Jones case. Steinem, who protests that feminists are not against sex in the workplace and certainly not against sex, recently gave a glowing endorsement to a sympathetic book about Andrea Dworkin, the feminist writer who is best known for her belief that all sexual intercourse subjugates women and whom Steinem called "one of the finest writers and minds of our time."

All this twisting and turning by feminists is likely to have a ripple effect they will not be able to control, as farsighted harassment hawks realize. Marie-Jose Ragab, president of a breakaway chapter of NOW in Virginia, said the national leadership's attitude was emboldening people to say that laws against sexual harassment have gone too far, a development she described as "inches away from hate speech." The *New York Times* editorial page warns that feminist excuses for Clinton may erode the effort to restrict "sexual talk or gestures by men in the workplace."

This much seems clear: The charges of hypocrisy and the dissension in the ranks are certain to undermine the feminists' authority to speak out on sexual harassment. Even Anita Hill's halo as the patron saint of this crusade has been badly tarnished. A standard that requires job-related repercussions for rebuffing unwanted sexual advances does not leave much of her case against Thomas.

Of course, as some have pointed out, it is not just feminists who are guilty of double standards when it comes to the Clinton sex scandals. The conservatives who discovered sexual harassment when they discovered Paula Jones are not far behind; though many conservatives, such as columnist Mona Charen, have warned against jumping on the sexual harassment bandwagon. Legal commentator Bruce Fein, who criticized the Supreme Court in 1993 for eliminating the requirement of economic or psychological damage in sexual harassment cases, assailed Wright for imposing such a requirement in *Jones v. Clinton*. John Whitehead, the president of the Rutherford Institute—which somehow went from defending the rights of Christians to championing Paula Jones—has compared the harassment endured by working women today to "the way blacks were treated in the twenties and thirties." The Independent Women's Forum, which has directed its share of barbs at harassment litigation, has joined forces with the dissident NOW chapter in Virginia to declare its abhorrence of sexual harassment.

The right-wing conversion to the cause may be driven by more than partisanship or Clinton hating. Some social conservatives—Irving Kristol, for one—have always been guardedly sympathetic to the feminist crusade against sexual harassment, viewing it, rather simplistically, as an effort to restore Victorian protections for the weaker sex. In *National Review*, Wendy Shalit, the newest member of the woman-as-victim school of conservatism, has warm words for Andrea Dworkin—one feminist who has cut Clinton no slack—and argues that feminism thrives by appealing to women's desire to be sheltered from predatory male sexuality. That does not explain why, in post-Monica polls, women are more willing than men to dismiss Clinton's alleged misconduct as his private business. But conservatives, whatever their intentions, do not make very convincing activists against sexual harassment, if only because they are latecomers to the campaign. If anything, their posturing sends the message that harassment charges are easily used as a political weapon.

And whatever their intentions, the pro-Clinton feminists are making the culture safe for a backlash against the post–Anita Hill sexual regime— a backlash which has been at least as strong a factor in the forgiving public attitude toward the Clinton scandals as the relatively strong economy. Judging from what talk-show callers say, people may not approve of a middle-aged, married man carrying on with a young subordinate, but they find it at least as outrageous that a sexual harassment complaint should open the way to invasive questions about a consensual affair.

They are also quite willing to recognize that accusers may have ulterior motives and that encounters subsequently labeled as "harassment" may involve complex, reciprocal dynamics: Most people in a poll taken after Willey's television interview thought neither Clinton nor Willey had told the complete truth. With no feminist thought-police to suppress these heresies, even making fun of a woman who claims sexual harassment is no longer politically incorrect. On MSNBC Wendy Murphy, a staunch feminist victims' advocate, caustically observed that it was ridiculous to "ask for $3 million merely because you saw a penis!"

Cultural attitudes are not the only determining factor in how we approach sexual harassment. The follies and excesses of the crusade against sexual harassment are also a product of bad laws and policies. But perhaps it was only in the cultural climate created by the October 1991 teach-in that these laws and policies could have flourished.

Current harassment law is grafted onto Title VII of the 1964 Civil Rights Act, under the theory—conceived by Catharine MacKinnon—that sexual advances on the job are a form of sex discrimination, depriving women as a class of equal opportunity. Whatever one thinks of the legitimacy of laws banning discrimination in private employment, these laws were never meant to create protections from sexual overtures on the job, which are not "based on sex" in the same sense as the refusal to hire or promote women and which—as the judges who rejected early civil rights suits for sexual harassment pointed out—could be made by a man to other men.

Oncale v. Sundowner, the case in which the Supreme Court affirmed earlier this year that Title VII covers "hostile environment" behavior between heterosexuals of the same sex, highlights the absurdity of the discrimination model—so much so that the *Washington Post* urged Congress to uncouple sexual harassment from sex discrimination. The mistreatment Joseph Oncale allegedly suffered at the hands of his co-workers on an all-male oil rig—including an assault in the shower in which a soap bar was shoved between his buttocks—is horrible. But whatever the reason he was singled out for such abuse, it surely could not have been his gender.

Meanwhile in male-on-female "hostile environment" cases the charge of discrimination often rests not on differential treatment of women and men but on the premise that vulgar talk and crude behavior are uniquely harmful or offensive to women. This, University of Michigan law professor Kingsley Browne has noted, "seems like just the sort of stereotype that Title VII was intended to erase."

The brand of feminist ideology that underlies the crusade against sexual harassment is focused not on equality but on sexual dominance. The standard response to concerns about the anti-sexual animus of this crusade—"Sexual harassment is not about sex, it is about power"—is disingenuous. To these ideologues, *sex* is not about sex but about power. Mac-Kinnon, who played a key role in crafting harassment law and who has as-serted that feminist theory "treats sexuality as a social construct of male power," is hardly an isolated voice. "Because of the inequality and coercion with which it is so frequently associated in the minds of women, the ap-pearance of sexuality in an unexpected context or a setting of ostensible equality can be an anguishing experience," writes Boston University law professor Kathryn Abrams. "Treatment that sexualizes women workers"—any sort of sexual dynamic between men and women—"prevents them from feeling, and prevents others from perceiving them, as equals in the workplace." Sex is presumed, as it were, to equal sexism.

Many courts have endorsed this radical view. Abrams's ruminations on the perils of sexuality for women have been cited in several prominent cases, including *Robinson v. Jacksonville Shipyards*, in which a federal judge in Florida issued an injunction in 1991 banning not just the display but the possession of pictures or literature with sexual themes in the work-place. Two years later in a less prominent Florida case, *Cardin v. VIA Trop-ical Fruits*, another federal court upheld a claim of a sexually hostile environment based primarily on "pervasive" racy cartoons and written jokes at work. Some of this material was posted or circulated by women, and much of it made fun of male anatomy. One cartoon showed a woman peering under the sheets at her mate, with the caption, "Where's the beef?" The court conceded that the humor "depicted both men and women" but went on to explain, in pure MacKinnonite terms: "[V]erbal and visual sexual humor—particularly vulgar and degrading jokes and car-toons repeatedly disseminated in the workplace—may tend to demean women. This is because such joking defines women as women by their sex-uality, and consequently may create practical obstacles . . . in the work-place."

The problems with the discrimination model of harassment law are compounded by the notorious subjectivity of "hostile environment" sexual harassment—defined by the EEOC and by the Supreme Court as "verbal or physical conduct of a sexual nature" that has "the purpose or effect of unreasonably interfering with an individual's work performance or creating an intimidating, hostile, or offensive working environment." Official proclamations have not done much good.

According to a U.S. Department of Labor pamphlet, if someone at work "made sexual jokes or said sexual things that you didn't like," or dis-played a picture you consider offensive, it is illegal—at least if it is "making it hard for you to work." But does this mean that you dread going to work every day or that you are occasionally distracted? Does it mean that you are the sort of person who has a fit over a copy of *Esquire* with a cover photo of an actress coyly looking over her shoulder with her back to the viewer, buttoning up her bra? This really happened, prompting a full investigation and eventually costing the culprit his job at a wastewater treatment plant in Olympia, Washington.

"If I run a stop sign, I have broken the law even if I did not intend to," a male EEOC official said during the Hill-Thomas teach-in, defending the emphasis on the victim's response rather than the offender's intent. But while one may fail to see a stop sign, its reality is hardly "in the eye of the beholder." If traffic laws were modeled on harassment policies, there would be no stop signs—you could just be fined for failing to stop when someone thought you should have.

Nor does harassment law require any actual damage to the plaintiff, economic or psychological. All that is needed, the Supreme Court held in 1993 in *Harris v. Forklift*, is a "discriminatorily abusive work environment." While the ruling stressed "a middle path between making actionable any conduct that is merely offensive and requiring . . . tangible psychological injury," it gave few clues as to where the line should be drawn. In a concurring opinion that sounded more like a dissent, Justice Antonin Scalia cautioned that the court's decision "lets virtually unguided juries decide whether sex-related conduct . . . is egregious enough to warrant an award of damages." (He added that given the "inherently vague statutory language," he saw no alternative.) *Harris* was an example of the extent to which harassment litigation had descended into triviality: While the charges in *Meritor* involved repeated sexual assaults, Teresa Harris, a rental manager at a forklift company in Tennessee, was accusing her boss, Charles Hardy, of nothing more than crude humor—to which she did not object for two years, until Hardy stopped buying supplies from Harris's husband. By Harris's own account, when she finally told him she was offended by his antics, Hardy apologized profusely and told her he had no idea she had been upset.

By distinguishing between "threatening or humiliating" conduct and mere offensiveness, *Harris* did enable some courts to roll back harassment litigation. In 1995 the U.S. Court of Appeals for the Seventh Circuit reversed an award to a woman whose boss had acted crudely on a few occasions—grunting to express his appreciation of her skirt, making a remark about masturbation as a cure for his loneliness—and stressed that Title VII was not meant to "purge the workplace of vulgarity." More recently, in *Oncale*, Scalia pointed out that the law is not a "civility code"; he further stressed that normal "male-on-male horseplay or intersexual flirtation" should not be confused with harassment and urged "careful consideration of the social context in which particular behavior occurs."

But these admonitions are no substitute for actual standards, which remain vague and inconsistent—as evidenced by the confusion over the dismissal of Paula Jones's suit on summary judgment. The decision was well within the law, yet it easily could have gone the other way. Furthermore as Walter Olson, author of *The Excuse Factory: How Employment Law Is Paralyzing the American Workplace*, pointed out in a commentary on the ruling, victories for defendants "are hard to turn into reliable precedent," since current legal doctrine "encourages lower courts to look at the 'totality of the circumstances' in each case anew, rather than developing definite rules that clearly assign or reject liability given a particular pattern."

Not all "hostile environment" claims are merely about bad manners. A number involve egregious conduct, sometimes intended to chase female intruders off male turf. In one such case in the 1980s, three women quit their jobs with a road construction crew after a three-month reign of terror in which male co-workers forcibly groped them and urinated in their lunch boxes and water bottles.

Yet some petty claims go a long way. Debra Black, a former manager for the Cincinnati developer Zaring Homes, won a $250,000 judgment in 1995 over a few incidents of juvenile humor by her co-workers, such as suggestions of names like "Hooterville" and "Twin Peaks" for a lot next to a Hooter's restaurant; snickers at the mention of a property owner named Dr. Busam; and a comment by a manager who picked up a pastry at a breakfast meeting and said suggestively, "Nothing I like more in the morning than sticky buns." Black never complained until she was fired for attaching a sheet with the president's signature to a document he had not seen.

The same year, former Wal-Mart clerk Peggy Kimzey was awarded $50 million, later reduced by the judge to $5 million. Kimzey had quit her job when her boss was not disciplined despite her complaint about his yelling and name calling—nonsexual and directed at both sexes. (Kimzey had refused an offer of a position with a different supervisor.) The sexual harassment claim was based mainly on the fact that five years earlier, the same supervisor had made a couple of vulgar jokes about her body. Kimzey conceded that she was not particularly upset at the time; indeed, she had indicated in employee questionnaires that she liked the informal atmosphere on the job and had asked to come back to the same department after leaving for family reasons.

Nor is it clear that a single incident does not create a hostile environment unless it rises to the level of assault—the conclusion many have made from Wright's ruling against Paula Jones. After *Harris v. Forklift* was remanded to the lower courts, a judge ruled that, while the company owner's vulgar joking did not constitute sexual harassment before Harris told him she found it offensive, the plaintiff was entitled to a damage award of $130,000 on the basis of a single crude remark her boss made about a month after she asked him to stop.

The award to Debra Black was later thrown out, and Wal-Mart may yet win on appeal. Still even a victory is costly for the defendant. Most sexual harassment claims are settled—including some that would be very unlikely to hold up in court, such as a suit filed in 1993 by two female nurses at a hospital in Santa Rosa, California, charging that their female supervisor's penchant for ribald jokes and bawdy birthday cards created "an environment tainted with sexual harassment." Most companies prefer not to be sued in the first place. Since businesses can avoid liability by showing that they do not tolerate harassment, the incentive is to err on the side of proscribing any behavior that might be actionable. Business magazines have long advised that "sexual bantering" and "suggestive remarks" should be stamped out, with no reference to severity, pervasiveness, or even unwelcomeness.

While relatively few sexual harassment claims may end up in court, measures taken by employers as a direct result of harassment laws—the zero-tolerance policies on "sexual humor and innuendo," the rules at some companies requiring employees who start dating to sign a paper attesting that the relationship is "welcome" and nonharassing, the sexual harassment prevention workshops—affect tens of millions of people.

The "Sexual Harassment Prevention Game," designed by Seattle-based human resources consultant Chuck Hatten for prevention workshops and purchased by, among others, U.S. West, Boeing, McDonald's, and AT&T, is a striking but representative example of the mentality behind such programs. The board game, in which players move ahead or back depending on the answers they give to questions about hypothetical situations, includes a scenario in which a female janitor complains about locker-room pictures of scantily clad female bodybuilders put up by another woman as inspiration for her fitness goals. The solution: The pictures must go. In another vignette, male employees who meet for weekly lunches where they trade raunchy jokes must be told that they have to invite women and cut out the humor (that women might contribute some jokes of their own is not even an option). An example of what is not harassment is revealing as well: A man brings flowers to a woman who earlier turned him down for a date, and she accepts but tells him she wants to keep their relationship professional. He's in the clear—but only as long as he never again shows any sign of romantic interest in her.

Some of the worst abuses of the crusade against harassment happen "in the shadow of the law," in actions taken by private companies but traceable to the effects of sexual harassment litigation. Probably the best-known case of this kind was that of Miller Brewing Co. executive Jerold McKenzie, who won $26 million in damages for wrongful termination last year after he was fired for discussing a racy episode of *Seinfeld* with a female office worker. While such lawsuits may deter overreaction to harassment complaints, they place employers in a damned-if-you-do, damned-if-you-don't predicament. At Commonwealth Life Insurance a few years ago, a male manager was demoted with a pay cut and transferred to another office for a reciprocal exchange of off-color greeting cards with a female colleague who later cried harassment. Women who engage in office ribaldry usually benefit from a double standard, but the ax can fall on them too. In 1994 at a branch of United Jersey Bank, a few female tellers and managers shared some giggles over male nudes from *Playgirl* (with no customers in the bank at the time). A male teller decided to take offense, and the women were punished with unpaid suspensions and demotions.

Employers, of course, should have every right to restrict speech, forbid the display of pictures (sexual or not), or limit dating on the job. They should certainly have the right to require that employees treat each other with courtesy and respect, though different workplaces can be expected to have different cultures. But it is a different matter when the state and the courts impose these rules, which businesses adopt "voluntarily" to avert legal action. The current interpretation of Title VII has empowered federal judges, juries, and regulators to act as sex and speech police. Apart from the constitutional concerns this situation should raise, it leads to the usual consequences that follow when the state seeks to control private behavior: People are discouraged from resolving personal conflicts on their own and encouraged to snitch on others and to use laws and regulations to settle personal scores.

In the mainstream media, the response to the Blob-like spread of the sexual harassment concept has been ambivalent. There has been some ridicule directed at cases of harassment overkill, such as an esteemed theology professor ordered into counseling for a classroom discussion of a classic story from the Talmud that includes a sexual reference; an employee who was forced to take down from his desk a small photo of his wife in a bikini; and a six-year-old boy who was punished for "sexual harassment" after giving a girl a peck on the cheek. But the basic assumption that sex-related conduct in the workplace which is unwanted but is neither coercive nor assaultive is a proper area for litigation and regulation has gone largely unchallenged.

Surveys showing an "epidemic" of harassment—based on sweeping definitions that include jokes and unwelcome requests for dates—have received mostly uncritical media coverage. Articles in the popular press have advised men not to say or do anything to a female co-worker that they would not say or do to another man—"Would you tell another guy you like the way he does his hair?"—or "to Mom"; both tips imply that women at work must be treated as asexual. Harassment "experts" are still taken seriously when they assert that "what is sexual harassment to one person is not sexual harassment to another," or that "people should be able to arrive at work, do their job and go home without having to hear jokes, stories or comments of a sexual nature." Recently, guidelines to appropriate workplace behavior proposed by the advocacy group 9to5—among them, "Would I want to be seen on the national news saying or doing this?"— were cited by the Associated Press without a trace of irony; nor did the reporter notice the contradiction between this Orwellian precept and the assertion by 9to5 director Ellen Bravo that feminists are not seeking to create "an uptight work environment."

What do ordinary Americans make of all this? Most people with no ideological agenda surely recognize that women contribute a great deal to "sexualizing" the workplace. They probably are ambivalent about making it illegal for a man to pursue a female co-worker after she has told him she is not interested: Too many marriages started that way. Nevertheless the message that sexual harassment is A Very Serious Issue has sunk in. The confusion is evident in opinion polls. In a *Time*/CNN poll more than half of men and women agreed that "[w]e have gone too far in making common interactions between employees into cases of sexual harassment." In a *Washington Post* poll conducted around the same time, two-thirds of women and 42 percent of men agreed that "[t]he federal government should enact tougher laws against sexual harassment in the workplace." Nearly 80 percent of men and women, however, also thought that false complaints were common and many reported policing themselves because of the new rules—even avoiding social contact with co-workers of the opposite sex, as about one in four men said they did often or sometimes.

But perhaps the ho-hum reaction to the sexual charges against Clinton speaks louder than polls. One indication of how oppressed many people have felt by what one journalist called "the pressure-cooker politesse" of the post–Anita Hill era is the widely acknowledged sigh of relief when "Zippergate" suddenly made it acceptable to talk about sex and tell salacious jokes at the office—another way in which the Clinton sex scandals may help end the war on sexual harassment.

Is there a better way to handle real sexual coercion and abuse on the job without polarizing the sexes, rolling out the heavy artillery against trivial misbehavior, or empowering the state to act as the manners police?

In her 1998 *Yale Law Journal* article Yale law professor Vicki Schultz assails the emphasis on sex rather than discrimination in current sexual harassment doctrine. As a result of this focus, she argues, nonsexual discrimination and gender-based hostile acts—men denigrating a female co-worker's competence or sabotaging her work—go unnoticed, while the persecution of innocuous sexual jokes gives feminists a bad name. Schultz's ideas seem to be in vogue with the feminist left: The May 25, 1998 issue of the *Nation* featured an abridgement of her article and the May/June 1998 issue of *Ms.*—an issue devoted to sex in the office—included an interview with Schultz.

Schultz makes some good points in criticizing the MacKinnonite equation of sex with sexism. But her suggestion that discrimination without sexual elements is slighted in current litigation is incorrect. Many sexual harassment claims—such as the previously mentioned lawsuit against Zaring Co. by former manager Debra Black—are hitched to sex discrimination charges found worthless even by the court which upholds the harassment charge. Moreover, Schultz's approach would likely create more problems that it would solve. Her definition of harassment would require employers to proscribe politically incorrect comments about gender—for instance, that mothers with small children should stay home—and perhaps even comments questioning an individual woman's competence in a "masculine" job.

Other scholars and attorneys would get rid of the discrimination model altogether and deal with sexual misconduct in the workplace as a civil tort. Many acts alleged in serious harassment claims, from sexual battery to indecent exposure, are grounds not only for criminal charges but for civil action—including liability suits against a company which was negligent in failing to protect workers from being victimized on the job. In the mid-1970s there were also a few successful damage suits under tort and contract law for sexual impositions by superiors involving no force but the abuse of workplace authority.

In a 1990 article in the *Yale Law and Policy Review*, Ellen Frankel Paul argued for going back to the tort approach. Her proposed tort would cover quid pro quo propositions and sexual conduct that a reasonable person would find "outrageous and extreme"; it would require intentional or reckless wrongdoing by the harasser and "economic detriment and/or extreme emotional distress" to the victim; and the employer would be liable only if it knew of the misconduct but failed to act (or failed to provide a complaint mechanism). Many elements of Paul's approach, if not its legal underpinning, are reflected in the emerging new cultural consensus about what constitutes actionable sexual harassment—such as the idea that a legal claim should require either tangible job detriment or severe and demonstrable psychological harm.

That is heartening, since a tort approach, despite its advantages, is unlikely to be adopted in the near future. The harassment-as-discrimination model has become entrenched; the Supreme Court is unlikely to reconsider its unanimous rulings in *Meritor* and *Harris*. Even without such radical reform, a great deal would be achieved by changing hostile environment law so as to require actual hostile intent—that is, to change the current wording which refers to conduct that has "the purpose or effect" of impeding work performance or creating an offensive or hostile environment, to "purpose *and* effect."

Is it likely that Congress will take any steps that could be perceived as weakening protections against sexual harassment? Few politicians are eager to rise to the defense of people who tell dirty jokes at the office, even if they are victimized by draconian punishments. A few years ago, an attempt by the EEOC to draft "religious harassment" guidelines which would have imposed sexual harassment-style rules on religious expression in the workplace was abandoned after protests from Christian and Jewish groups and from members of Congress; it is difficult to imagine legislators taking such a stand in defense of less respectable kinds of expression.

But political and legal practicality is affected by the cultural climate. Currently there seems to be a great deal of public support for the view that an individual's noncoercive sexual behavior is no one else's business and that a lawsuit based on sexual misconduct should involve actual damage to the plaintiff. It is is a good time for critics of "sexual correctness" to go on the offensive, hold a consciousness raising of their own, and push for legislative change.

If the Clinton scandals end up negating the effects of the Hill-Thomas drama, it will be the ultimate irony: Clinton's 1992 campaign rode the momentum of the "Year of the Woman," which had its roots in the upheaval over Anita Hill. But maybe that is not bad for a Clinton legacy.

Ellen Frankel Paul

❦

The Case Against
Comparable Worth

IN THE 1980S COMPARABLE WORTH—THE NOTION THAT FEMALE-DOMINATED jobs can be equated to entirely different male-dominated jobs by expert evaluators, and that women should receive upward readjustments to their salaries based on such studies—scored its greatest successes. Some state governments applied its formulas to their employees and feminists rallied behind its banner. Critics mounted a counterattack that—combined with the upward mobility of women in the late-Reagan and post-Reagan years— stalled comparable worth's advance. Yet the notion was never completely vanquished, and one hears comparable worth's rumblings to this day. Reprising the debate and reappraising arguments from comparable worth's heyday from our vantage point at the dawn of the new century is worth- while, if only to arm ourselves anew against such statist follies.

The opponents of comparable worth, here called market advocates, re- lied principally upon economic arguments to discredit the concept. Their main charges against comparable worth were: that the market is not inher- ently discriminatory; that the asserted wage gap of 40 percent in the 1980s was grossly inflated; that it would be too expensive to implement; that it would disrupt the U.S. economy by increasing inflation, driving up unem- ployment, and making U.S. products less competitive on world markets; that it would harm women's employment by overpricing their services; that it would hurt blue-collar workers because comparable worth evaluation schemes favor education over manual labor; and that reading such a stan- dard into anti-discrimination legislation would penalize employers for wage-setting practices over which they have little control.[1]

Market advocates also tried to respond to the more theoretical claims of the comparable worth supporters. To the proponents' claim that the market is inherently discriminatory, the opponents responded with a description of the competitive marketplace à la neoclassical economics (a tradition that the comparable worth forces scorned.) While market advocates often conceded that the market and especially governmental policy may have in the past served to depress women's wages and opportunities, they tended to view the future in a more halcyon light. If only the market were left to work matters out—perhaps, with the concession that the Equal Pay Act of 1963 (mandating equal pay for the same job) and Title VII of the Civil Rights Act of 1964 (banning sex discrimination in employment) were legitimate and ought to remain in place—women's pay would over time approximate the pay of their male colleagues. Thus, comparable worth, which they saw as a radical departure from the United States' free-market heritage, would soon be as unnecessary as it was undesirable.

Comparable worth's coterie of remaining supporters continue to advance arguments that have changed little since their cause's halcyon years in the mid- to late 1980s. Their principal arguments ought to seem quite familiar, since they have been echoed so often in the media, usually with little or no skepticism. They argue: that the market is inherently discriminatory; that a wage gap exists between women's earnings and men's, with women receiving roughly 76 percent or less (in 1998) of the wages of men; that the workplace is sex-segregated to the disadvantage of women, with women filling the least desirable jobs with the shortest advancement ladders; and that women's work is undervalued precisely because women perform it.

Their solution then as now is to promote comparable worth—first in the governmental arena and next throughout the private domain. Comparable worth would be achieved through the use of job evaluation schemes that can, allegedly, both measure the extent of the disadvantage that women suffer in particular firms and indicate the amount of the monetary remedy necessary to eliminate the disparity. For many proponents of comparable worth, the ideal way of achieving it is through judicial interpretation; that is, by the courts reading a comparable worth standard of compensation equity into Title VII of the Civil Rights Act. Other avenues of advancement for comparable worth lie in new federal legislation, state legislation, and, on a less sweeping plane, collective bargaining. Many universities have contracted with consulting firms to perform such comparisons, particularly comparing salaries in female-dominated faculty departments to male-dominated departments.

Market advocates dissented from each of the four main contentions of the proponents and then went on to critically examine the chosen instrument of executing comparable worth: job evaluations. Naturally they opposed both reading a comparable worth remedy into Title VII and enacting federal or state legislation mandating comparable worth. Some, though the minority, were not averse to reaching comparable worth on a firm-by-firm basis through collective bargaining.

Is the Market Discriminatory?

For the proponents of comparable worth, wages set by the marketplace embody the discriminatory animus of employers against women. To pay women the prevailing wage rate for a particular occupation is merely to perpetuate this historical impediment under which women suffer. Comparable worth's critics, naturally, had a quite different view of the marketplace. The critics, many of whom were economists, embraced the positive view of the marketplace that is held by a strong contingent of their profession.

The market serves an essential coordinating function. It takes the innumerable desires of individuals for particular goods and services and matches them to the supply. A market for a particular good clears when, through bargaining, the market settles upon a price at which the quantity supply and demand are equal. If, for example, the suppliers of apples ask a price higher than the market-clearing price, apples will go unsold because—at that price—the demand falls short of supply. On a market unburdened by barriers to the free movement of prices, the price will fall until a price is reached at which supply will equal demand. Conversely if the price initially set by the apple growers is too low, buyers will gobble up the apples quickly, and the sellers will raise the price.

Another important function of a market is to give signals to producers about where they ought to expend their capital and productive energies. If there is a sudden disaster—say, an unseasonal freeze in Florida that wipes out much of the orange crop—the higher price for the remaining oranges will encourage others to enter the market, perhaps by importing more oranges from abroad than usual.

Comparable worth supporters frequently claimed that wages are kept artificially low for female-dominated occupations. They often contended that nurses' wages were kept low even when nurses were in short supply, by hiring nurses from foreign countries. Their free-market opponents responded that rather than counting as an indictment of the market, this state of affairs indicated its smooth functioning. The fact that employers, in general, seek to fill positions at the least cost does not indicate a discriminatory animus against women. Rather it illustrates the normal way in which markets operate.

The labor market, say the critics, is no different from the market for commodities. As George Hildebrand put it: "The correct view is that the labor market is a market for labor services, where those services are provided by free human beings who cannot be compelled to supply them for a single instant beyond their willingness to do so."[2] Potential employees bargain with employers to get the highest wage for the services that they have to offer. If employer X is willing to pay potential employee Y at a weekly rate of four hundred dollars, and employee Y would gladly work for three hundred dollars, then the bargain that they will strike lies somewhere between those two points, depending on the bargaining ability of the two parties. The employer will begin with a deliberately low offer, the worker will respond with a counter-bid at something above three hundred dollars, and the process will continue until they arrive at a mutually agreeable figure.

The labor market also provides clues to individuals about how they ought to invest their time and talents in developing marketable skills. Where shortages exist and jobs go unfilled, wages rise, thus encouraging people to acquire the skills necessary to fill those jobs.

What the market does not do is establish the value of jobs or rank jobs in any normative sense based on the wages those jobs receive. The wages for various types of labor are like the prices of potatoes and diamonds; no one assumes that potatoes are less valuable (in the sense of being nutritious and useful to sustaining life) than diamonds (which are relatively useless) just because a potato sells for a minute fraction of the price of a diamond.[3] The outcome of market forces at any point in time will not conform to any preconceived hierarchy of the worth of jobs. The pattern constantly shifts as demand changes and the costs of supplying goods and services change.

Perhaps our values are twisted as a society, and the comparable worth supporters undoubtedly think they are, but the market should not be faulted for mirroring the choices of individuals who freely choose how to spend their limited resources. The comparable worth forces demand too much from the market if they expect it to somehow validate the skills and attributes that women bring to their jobs. Women, just like men, must subject themselves to the impartial forces of the labor market as it constantly fluctuates to equate supply and demand for particular sorts of labor.

Economist June O' Neill, former head of the Congressional Budget Office, gives an intriguing example of how the market, free from any hint of discrimination, may reward two seemingly comparable jobs quite differently. She takes two jobs—a Spanish-English translator and a French-English translator—which would, presumably, be rated as identical on a comparable-worth job evaluation. Even though all of the job demands for the two positions that are typically measured in job evaluations might be nearly identical, the market might reward the jobs very differently. Nondiscriminatory reasons that could account for such a difference might include the fact that the demand for translators of one language exceeded the other and that the supply of one may be greater.

How all of these factors would ultimately resolve themselves into wages for the two jobs is impossible to predict. She seriously doubts that any job-evaluation scheme could arrive at the market-clearing wage. In contrast she views the market as an efficient mechanism for processing "the scarcity of talents, the talents of heterogeneous individuals and the demands of business and consumers in arriving at a wage."[4] To adopt comparable worth, O'Neill predicted, would be to disrupt the market by capriciously setting wages. What would result would be unintended shortages and surpluses—unemployment—of workers in different fields.[5]

O'Neill had a ready response to one example frequently given by the comparable worth forces. They questioned the equity of the market when it rewards zookeepers more highly than child-care providers. Are not our children more valuable to society than zoo animals? This apparent dilemma is revealed to be grounded on a fundamental misunderstanding about what markets do. For many people know how to take care of young children, while the number of people with the skills to attend to the needs of wild animals is much smaller. The zookeepers, due to scarcity of supply, command a higher wage. The market is not passing any judgment on the intrinsic worth of the two occupations.[6]

The free-market critics of comparable worth were not, of course, oblivious to certain factors that make the U.S. economy depart from the ideal market of pure economic theory. Such governmental impediments as minimum wage laws, immigration laws, and laws empowering unions to establish closed shops, among others, all serve to diminish the natural responsiveness of the market to changing times. To the extent that unions can raise the wages of their members above the market rate by, in effect, monopolizing the pool of labor for particular skills, those who are protected by the unions will benefit at the expense of the nonunionized workforce.[7] In recent years unions have been less successful in monopolizing labor and their membership has declined, except in the public sector.

Two factors relating to unions had an adverse impact on women's wages and access to traditionally male jobs. Unions have an historical legacy of discrimination against women, usually a result of having barred their entry to the union hall, thus preventing them from being hired in lucrative trades. Male occupations, mostly in heavy industry, were heavily unionized while traditionally female occupations, until recent times, had been predominantly nonunion.

The critics view these phenomena not as cause to indict the market, but rather as examples of how the natural tendency of markets to ameliorate the effects of discrimination over time can be hampered by governmental interferences that benefit the haves at the expense of the have-nots. In marked contrast to the supporters of comparable worth, the opponents had no desire to turn to more government action as a cure for whatever discrimination might have remained in the marketplace, but to less. In fact, the critics argued, governmental policies are more likely to be discriminatory than the market.

Market advocates pointed to larger, system-wide distortions as exemplars of governmental activity that perpetuated discrimination. South Africa's system of apartheid, finally abandoned in 1990, is one conspicuous example of government-imposed discrimination, with the marketplace and international economic sanctions eventually serving as potent forces in undermining that system. Another frequently mentioned example is the system of segregation practiced in the American South beginning in the late nineteenth century, which was embodied in the laws of the states and imposed upon recalcitrant employers. Slavery, wherever practiced, has almost always, except in the most primitive times, been enshrined in the laws of governments.[8]

The lesson that the critics drew from these examples was that the way of correcting past legislative interferences by U.S. federal and state government, which have served, intentionally or not, to perpetuate discrimination, is not to encumber the economy with a vast, untried, and theoretically dubious proposition such as comparable worth. The preferred course, instead, was to eliminate these legislative impediments and let the market operate more freely.

Economist Gary Becker's *The Economics of Discrimination* was enormously influential in shaping the thinking of those who opposed comparable worth.[9] It is still influential to this day, having influenced several generations of economists. While the book, originally published in 1957, was not written with the intention of providing ammunition against comparable worth—which was not really a live policy issue until more than two decades later—the thrust of his argument easily lends itself to such a purpose.

Becker provided a framework for analyzing discrimination in the marketplace because of race, religion, sex, or any other nonpecuniary reason. "Individuals are assumed to act," he hypothesized, "as if they have 'tastes for discrimination,' and these tastes are the most important immediate cause of actual discrimination." When an employer acts in a discriminatory manner toward an employee, the employer acts as if he incurs "nonpecuniary, psychic costs of production" by employing that person.[10]

Becker formulated the quantitative concept of a "discrimination coefficient" to measure the value placed by an employer (or a consumer, or a fellow employee) upon the nonpecuniary cost of employing a member of a minority group against which he had a "taste for discrimination." With the aid of this concept he analyzed the extent of discrimination against blacks in the North and the South, concluding that the taste for discrimination in the South was twice as large as in the North.[11]

Of more immediate relevance to the comparable worth debate, Becker found that employer discrimination was less in competitive industries than in monopolistic ones. Another theoretical implication of his theory is that employee discrimination is greater in unionized than in competitive labor markets.[12]

Also significant is his finding that discrimination by any group reduces the discriminators' own incomes as well as the incomes of the disparaged group, though the minority suffers more from the effects of such discrimination than the majority. The significance of this finding is that it contravenes the popular view that those who discriminate are benefited by such behavior, that is, that discrimination is in the self-interest (as self-interest is equated with pecuniary interest) of the majority.[13] Contrary to popular opinion, too, is his conclusion that capitalist employers are not the beneficiaries of discrimination by members of their dominant group.[14]

Market advocates derived some support and consolation from Becker's analysis, principally his findings that discrimination harms those who discriminate, that discrimination is lower in competitive, nonunion settings than in their opposites, and that discrimination does not maximize the self-interest of those who practice it.

For the market advocates, then, the market is to a great extent self-correcting, because it acts to penalize those who make business decisions in an unbusinesslike way, say by indulging in racial hatred or sexual stereotyping. Over the long run, such businesses will languish while their more meritocratic competitors will prosper. As economist Robert Higgs opines: "The most effective way to eliminate discrimination is to make all markets as competitive as possible. Competitive markets place costs of discrimination on discriminators far more readily than any other alternatives, certainly far more readily than a political alternative."[15]

By contrast, the establishment of comparable worth would mean that the government and its equal-opportunity regulators would remain forever enmeshed in the workplace, supplanting neutral market decisions with their own value judgments. One effect of imposing comparable worth standards rather than the market would be to, in effect, mandate a minimum wage for women's jobs. It would insruct employers that for women's jobs x, y, and z, which are judged comparable to men's jobs a, b, and c, they must pay set minimums for each.

Jennifer Roback argued that if women's wages were set above the market-clearing wage established in the market, women would suffer the same kind of deleterious consequences as black youths under minimum wage laws. While some women would be winners—garnering higher wages for the same job than they would have had on the market—others would be losers, when they simply could not find employment at the artificially inflated, mandated rate. Moreover by artificially increasing wages for women's jobs, comparable worth would increase the incentive for women to enter traditionally female occupations and decrease the incentive to experiment with nontraditional jobs. Consequently it would reinforce stereotypes and intensify the competition for traditionally female jobs.

One unpleasant side effect would be an oversupply of applicants in these traditional jobs. Under such circumstances, employers have a tendency to discriminate on factors other than the ability to do the job and to hire only those with the best credentials. Like black teenagers who suffer higher unemployment compared with white youths, Roback feared that under a comparable worth scenario college-educated women would get the now scarcer traditionally female jobs in preference to older, less-educated women reentering the labor force. Ironically, then, precisely those whom the women's movement ostensibly wishes to help would suffer under comparable worth.

To make matters even worse artificially inflated wages for women would encourage employers to substitute capital for labor—technology for secretaries, for example—thus further diminishing the pool of jobs.[16] A far better way to help older and working-class women, Roback believes, is to encourage them to enter nontraditional fields. Comparable worth, she concludes, "exaggerates all the problems the women's movement has been trying to change."[17]

Other critics viewed the effects of the implementation of comparable worth in even more dire terms. Philosopher Michael Levin, for one, argued that the only alternative to the market is state control and that comparable worth would entail endless government intervention. As long as individuals are left to enjoy their accustomed economic liberty, wages will be set at the market price; if they are deprived of such freedom, the only remedy is state control.

By implication, then, he saw no middle course, no halfway solutions like comparable worth. To close the wage gap as of 1983, he estimated that it would have cost $250 billion, or 15 percent of the entire wages paid in that year. Taking inflation into account but mitigating its effects by the decrease in the wage gap, the figure for today would likely be higher. In the long run, inflating women's salaries would have a disincentive effect on the work of both males and females: women would be getting more without having to work harder, while men's wages would be held down until the wage gap disappeared. He predicted a "crisis of extreme proportions," should comparable worth be adopted.[18]

According to political scientist Jeremy Rabkin, the implementation of comparable worth would present major difficulties. The theory would be difficult to limit, that is, it would spread beyond public employment. By logical implication, the theory could not be limited to women or even minorities, but it would ultimately reach white males and, thus, the entire workforce. In the final analysis, he contended, the theory would be applied to all occupations and the effect of this on the workforce would be incalculable.[19]

The critics argued that the marketplace more efficiently displaces any discrimination against women that might exist than would an extreme alternative, such as comparable worth. The supporters fundamentally misunderstand the nature of markets when they think relative wages indicate a societal judgment about the worth of jobs and the people who perform them. What the market does is to equate supply and demand; and this is precisely what comparable worth would fail to do.[20] The result of adopting comparable worth would be economic chaos, followed by massive state intervention. Unemployment would rise along with inflation, and government regulators would intrude into twelve million workplaces, a frightening prospect and one that would make the burden of regulation lie even heavier on U.S. industry.[21]

The Wage Gap

Comparable worth's detractors have attempted to dispute the inference that the proponents draw from the raw data on the wage gap, i.e., that the wage disparity between the sexes can only be explained by discrimination on the part of employers.

Writing in the mid-1980s, June O'Neill argued that the 64 percent wage differential between women's work and men's was a flawed measure for various reasons. For one, it was based on a definition of full-time employment as thirty-five hours or more, thus ignoring the fact that full-time women worked 9 to 10 percent fewer hours than men. She thinks a better statistic is hourly earnings in one's present job. On this basis, women in

1983 earned 72 percent of what men earned. However, as O'Neill pointed out, this figure may have masked some significant progress. Women in the twenty-to-twenty-four-year-old age bracket earned 89 percent of their male peers' earnings.

O'Neill further pointed out that this gap had narrowed, with women in this same age group in 1979 earning only 81 percent of the male average salary. Furthermore as Thomas Sowell pointed out, single women between the ages of twenty-five and sixty-four earned 91 percent of the income of men who were also single.[22] Single men and single women were more nearly alike in their earning power than married men and married women.

These phenomena lead O'Neill to speculate that factors other than discrimination accounted for the disparity in earnings between men and women. She enumerated several factors that went a long way toward explaining the wage gap in nondiscriminatory terms. These factors included the facts that women had lower investments in schooling and that employed women had worked 60 percent of their working lives, while men had worked almost continuously. These two factors alone explained about half of the remaining earnings differential between the sexes, O'Neill contended.

The impact of these two factors on dissolving such a large portion of the wage gap should be underscored, since both of these reflected choices that women made, mostly in response to their roles in the family, principally their child-bearing and childrearing responsibilities. While the proponents of comparable worth tend to view these factors as the result of societal discrimination and stereotyping of women, it would be difficult to deny that significant numbers of women do make both educational and employment decisions based on their responsibilities within the family.

O'Neill then examined data from the National Longitudinal Survey (begun in 1968) and measured the effect on the wage gap after accounting for the influence of certain measurable factors, including "male-female differences in work experience, job tenure, and schooling, as well as differences in plant size" and other job characteristics, such as years of training required to master a skill, the dangerousness of the occupation, and whether the occupation had a high concentration of women. After taking these factors into account, she concluded that the wage gap had narrowed to 12 percent.[23]

Was this residual, then, the result of discrimination? O'Neill found this question impossible to answer because of the difficulty of assessing other, more intangible qualities that may have differentiated female from male workers. Other factors that were difficult to quantify may have explained most of the rest of the wage gap: women's expectations were different from men's, particularly in regard to their roles in the family, with women in great numbers assuming that their wages would be the family's secondary income and that they would not be continuously in the workforce.[24]

Given these disparate roles in the family, women tend to take different courses in high school and college, courses less directly tied to future employment than those selected by men; this was particularly true of middle-aged women and older women. Once these choices had been made, for the middle-aged and older, the effect lingered on. But O'Neill was willing to concede that discrimination may have accounted for part of the residual and even that the residual itself might have underestimated discrimination if some of the quantifiable factors themselves were affected by discrimination.

As evidence for the contention that women's early expectations affected their present wage levels, she cited the National Longitudinal Study, which asked women between the ages of fourteen and twenty-four the following question: "What do you want to do when you're thirty-five? Do you expect to be predominantly a homemaker, or do you expect to have some kind of career?" While a minority expressed a desire to have a career, by the time the cohort reached the age of thirty-five, nearly 70 percent of them were employed. Those who intended all along to pursue careers tended to gravitate to math and science courses in school and to male-dominated professions once they graduated, but those who had intended to become homemakers were typically employed in traditionally female jobs. Her conclusion was that expectations are very important in explaining the wage gap, although the extent of their influence is difficult to measure. What was encouraging, though, for the long term was that women's career expectations had already begun to change, and the study revealed growing numbers of women who intended to pursue jobs rather than homemaking. In 1973, 57 percent of women between twenty-five and twenty-nine expected to work, while in 1978 that figure had risen to 77 percent.[25]

The persistence of the wage gap since the 1950s is a fact often cited by comparable worth supporters, with the gap even widening a bit in the mid-1970s. O'Neill thought this puzzling, too, as she found it implausible to suppose that discrimination had intensified over those decades, since such a supposition seemed to be at odds with the observable progress that women had made.

She tried to discover an explanation for the wage gap's seeming intractability. What she discerned was that in the 1950s women in the workforce had 1.6 years more education on average than their male co-workers.

As women flooded the marketplace during the 1960s and 1970s, this profile changed dramatically. The entry of these women—who have little job experience and no college education—into the labor force could more than account for the widening of the wage gap in the 1970s; in more precise terms, this change alone would add 7 percent to the wage gap. Another 2 percent would be added by the widening in the gap between male job tenure and female that took place between the early 1950s and the mid-1960s. She also discovered that the wage gap for women under thirty-five had narrowed significantly since 1965—a hopeful sign. Over the 1980s, she predicted that the gap would narrow even further as women's work roles would more closely mimic men's and as they would invest more in college education and increase their work experience.[26]

O'Neill proved a savvy prognosticator. In an article that she co-authored in 1993, she noted that between 1976 and 1989 the "gender gap in wages on average declined by about 1 percent per year."[27] This rather remarkable progress came on the heels of several decades of post–World War II stagnation, in which the wage gap hovered around the 40 percent range. By 1990, by contrast, the gap had shrunk to about 28 percent (declining further as the decade of the 1990s progressed). Examining data from the National Longitudinal Study and other statistical sources, the authors found that during the 1980s several factors contributed to the growing earning power of women relative to men. The principal factors that they noted were: the increasing work experience of women, their improvement in years of school attended, and other skills acquired. They noted that this rising return on human-capital investment "reflect[s] a deepening in women's training whether because of women's own efforts, employer response to women's increased work attachment, or a decline in discrimination."[28] Another factor, one not beneficial to blue-collar men, also contributed to the relative advantage of women during the 1980s, the authors determined. Blue-collar, mostly male occupations, experienced a decline in real wages over the decade, thus helping to shrink the male-female wage gap. The authors anticipated that the blue-collar relative decline in wages would be a short-lived phenomenon, swamped in the long-run by the changes that they had noted in female human-capital investment. This appears to have been another accurate prediction, since the figures for 1996 indicate a further improvement in the female-to-male earnings ratio, having reached over the 74 percent mark in that year.[29] The wage gap as of 1996 had shrunk to an all-time low of 26 percent, uncorrected for the various factors that differentiate male from female workers.

Other critics of comparable worth were equally skeptical of the conclusion of market discrimination that the supporters derived from the wage gap. Jennifer Roback pointed to the fact that in 1950 there were only 17.8 million women working, but that the figure had risen dramatically by 1982 to 47 million. This increase in supply, naturally, would be associated with a decrease in price, just as the baby boomers' entry into the workforce depressed the market for entry-level positions, with those positions commanding 63 percent of the wages of older workers in 1968 and only 54 percent in 1974 when many of the boomers came of age. She was particularly skeptical of cross-section studies conducted by the supporters, in which they tried to weigh the attributes of male and female jobs, reducing the earning gap by half, and then characterizing the residual gap as discrimination. If the same were done for a cross-section of jobs dominated by white males, she argued, only 40 to 50 percent of the wage gap between comparable positions could be accounted for. She concludes:

> [I]t seems quite likely that residual earnings disparities are not really an index of discrimination; in fact, the possibility that there is no discrimination whatsoever cannot be ruled out. . . . So it is possible that men and women have widely different amounts of unmeasured characteristics, at least enough so that if they could be measured, there might be no significant wage differential at all. . . . Comparable worth asks policymakers to make precise wage adjustments to correct for a problem of unknown size.[30]

Roback, like O'Neill, found the similarity in the wages of single males and single females quite revealing. Absence from the labor force to bear children has economic consequences and these have nothing to do with discrimination. In the past women who expected to have children chose occupations with relatively easy movement of skills and skills that did not quickly become obsolete or atrophy. As women's expectations have changed, as households have become more dependent on women's wages—70 percent of households depended solely on male earnings in 1950, but by 1984 this figure had plunged to 15 percent—more women have entered male occupations. These women have placed more emphasis upon financial rewards and less on flexibility.[31]

Remarkably by the late 1990s, in two-earner families in which both spouses worked full-time, 22.7 percent of these households included wives who earned more than their husbands. In 1981 the figure was 15.9 percent—significantly lower.[32] Between 1951 and 1997, the rate at which married women participated in the labor force nearly tripled, from 22.9 to 62 percent.[33]

Roback's emphasis on the different roles of men and women in the

family and the effect these differences have on the earnings and occupations of women is a frequently voiced refrain among comparable worth's
detractors. Sociologist Brigitte Berger pointed out that women are engaged
in a "heroic balancing act" as they try to juggle work and family. Without
women's entry into the workplace to supplement family income, U.S. families would have experienced a substantial decline in real incomes. The
large number of women who are employed part time indicates the extent
of this supplementary role. While in 1981 62 percent of married women
worked, only 46 percent of these working women were employed in full-
time, year-round jobs. The majority of married women who worked in the
early 1980s did so on a part-time basis, a clear indication that, for these
women, work was of a supplementary nature.[34] Based on figures from the
1996–1997 *Current Population Survey*, 25 percent of the 54 million working
women in the United States work part time, with these women comprising
69 percent of part-time workers.[35]

Berger cited studies that showed that women often chose less-
demanding jobs so that they could have the time free to devote to their
families. Studies on income disparities between male and female doctors
and lawyers indicated that the differences were not due to discrimination,
but rather to women's preferences for working in those subdisciplines that
had fewer time commitments, freeing them to devote time to their families. When women without children were compared with men, the gap decreased. The differences in family roles and the effect these have on
earnings was succinctly captured by Anna Kondratas:

> The pay gap between married men and unmarried men is about
> the same as between men and women overall. Married men earn
> far more than unmarried men and married men with children
> earn even more than married men without children. There is al-
> most no pay gap between single men and single women. Think
> about that. Married women, on the other hand, earn far less
> than single women, and married women with children earn less
> than married women without. Obviously this reflects not labor
> market discrimination, but the different roles of men and
> women in the family.[36]

In the same spirit Solomon William Polachek, an economist, identified
differences in family characteristics as of key importance in explaining the
wage gap. While being married and having children depressed women's
earnings these life events had exactly the opposite effect on men's.[37] The
opponents wondered why the pay gap between married and unmarried
men—which stood at 61 percent in the 1980s and was larger than the male-

female gap—was not also attributed to discrimination by the supporters of comparable worth.

What the comparable worth enthusiasts failed to understand, finally, is that most women choose the occupations they are in; if they become nurses, secretaries, and teachers they do so because these are the jobs they prefer.[38] Where the opponents saw freedom of choice, the advocates of comparable worth saw societal oppression; molding of women into stereotypical roles; and discrimination. To market advocates, the comparable worth supporters did much to undermine the feminist cause by viewing women as helpless pawns of societal oppression.

The arguments of comparable worth's opponents are strengthened by examining some recent trends. Women's work experience from previous decades was not etched in stone. In 1975 23 percent of employed women worked in managerial and professional occupations—the highest income category—but by 1997 their ranks had swelled to 32 percent of women, a very substantial change over such a short period of time.[39] In 1995 women held 43 percent of managerial positions compared to 22 percent in 1975 and 53 percent of professional positions compared to 45 percent. In high-profile occupations, women's progress has been substantial. Between 1975 and 1995 the percentage of women physicians nearly doubled (from 13 percent to 24 percent) while the number of lawyers nearly quadrupled (from 7 percent to 26 percent). Economist Barbara H. Weston writes that "the distribution of men and women in specific occupations in 1995 while still very different from one another were much less so than twenty years ago."[40] Employment in many occupations became less sex-segregated over this period.

Comparable worth supporters had rather strong reactions to the derogation of their wage-gap arguments, since their case for comparable worth relied principally upon the wage-gap contention and its interpretation as resulting from discrimination. By the latter stages of the debate in the late 1980s, many of the advocates conceded that the wage gap was not nearly as large as the rhetoric of the activists suggested. But whatever residue remained, after statistical analysis accounted for differences between men and women, the proponents still attributed to discrimination.

They viewed many of the factors that the opponents used to militate against the wage gap as themselves infected by discrimination—such factors as the level of schooling and duration of workforce experience. The family, and women's responsibilities in it, were typically viewed in a much more malign perspective by the supporters. If women are placed at a competitive disadvantage as a result of marriage, this is not a freely chosen lot, but one foisted upon women by an oppressive society. It is society that forces a woman to take on a disproportionate load of family responsibility, even when she works full time as does her mate. Liberation from family responsibilities, or at least a fairer sharing of them between husband and wife, would go a long way toward allowing women to compete on a more equal footing with men.

Seemingly so far apart on the wage-gap issue, on closer examination, both sides were not that far apart at all on the facts of the wage gap, at least if one considers only the academics and not the activists. They may have differed over percentages, but they concurred that the wage gap was something less than the 40 percent figure popularly quoted in the 1980s. The gap remaining after statistical analysis varied depending on who was (and who is, now) doing the statistical manipulation. But what really divided the two camps was what interpretation ought to be placed on the residual: for the supporters of comparable worth the explanation was discrimination; for their adversaries, it was a combination of factors, of role differences, tastes and preferences, and other intangibles that are difficult to quantify, with discrimination playing a noted but relatively negligible role.

Sex Segregation and Undervaluation

Just as the market advocates viewed the causes of the wage gap much differently than did the supporters of comparable worth, the opponents saw the sex-segregation contention as unpersuasive. Again they pointed to the investments in human capital that women make when they take courses in school and when they prepare for lives that, until recent decades, have been centered on their families.[41] Women's choices—their preferences for jobs with flexibility and easily transferable skills that lend themselves to a balancing of family needs—account for the apparent sex segregation of the workforce; discrimination does not, at least not to a very large or precisely measurable extent. What they found particularly disconcerting about comparable worth was that rather than mitigating the presumed problem of sex segregation, the "remedy" would only have exacerbated the situation. Even if the proponents' analysis of the problem had been correct, which they denied, the solution would have only intensified the segregation.

Why is this so? If comparable worth were mandated (as some revivalists still desire), women would be encouraged to remain in traditionally female occupations and they would feel less pecuniary pressure to enter traditionally male fields. Even worse, women would come to see themselves as weak and dependent upon the state to reward them when they could not succeed on the open market. With the high level of divorce in the country, women need to prepare themselves for new challenges and more lucrative careers. Comparable worth would do nothing to encourage this.

Opponents found equally unpersuasive the supporters' argument that women's work is undervalued because women do it. Frequently cited by the comparable worth forces was the example of secretaries: as the vocation turned from male to female, so the claim went, the job lost prestige and wages declined. O'Neill responded that the character of the job changed when women entered the ranks, as it became more routinized and less managerial, thus accounting for the decline. Rather than attributing lower salaries in traditionally female occupations to discrimination, free-market economists viewed it, again, as a result of women's choices. Given her options and her preferences and tastes—her desire to balance family and job—it may very well be rational for a woman to prefer secretarial work to truck driving or garbage collecting, even though she knows her wages will be less. That is simply one factor that must be weighed in her assessment of job options. Even by the close of the 1990s, a substantial number of women, especially married women, still viewed their work and the resulting income as supplementary.

Job Evaluations

Skeptical of the ingredients of the comparable worth proponents' case, the adversaries were equally skeptical of their tool for achieving the remedy: job evaluations. Comparable worth job evaluations proceed by assessing each employment classification in a workplace usually on the basis of four factors: knowledge and skills, mental demands, accountability, and working conditions. Points are assigned for each factor, added together to reach a final number, and that number is then compared to others. Every assumption of the technique fell under scathing critical attack, from the notion of objective value in jobs to the claim that compensation experts can measure the components of jobs and then compare the totals to arrive at a hierarchy. Comparing apples and oranges is an impossibility, they maintained, despite one critic's unusual experience of having a comparable worth enthusiast whip out a chart that compared the various nutritional attributes of the two fruits, while remaining blithely unaware that those comparisons had nothing at all to do with the relative prices of the two.[42]

The search for an objective measure of job worth they found particularly misdirected. Such an effort harkens back to the medieval notion of a "just price," departures from which were punishable by one's vocational guild.[43] Later the classical economists and Marx also mistakenly thought that they could find in the labor-time embodied in a commodity the true value of the good to society.

Economic science, however, progressed beyond these primitive notions to a subjective theory of value, one that viewed all commodities as receiving the equivalent of their marginal utility to the consumer and all labor as receiving its marginal productivity to the firm. This newfound emphasis on utility (at the marginal or final unit purchased) and productivity (at the marginal contribution of the last worker employed) established the importance of consumer evaluations in pricing.

If the quest for objectivity or intrinsic worth is misguided from the outset, then it is not surprising that the critics found all the steps necessary to implement comparable worth defective. Job evaluation, the chosen tool of the proponents for rationalizing the labor market, was seen as riddled with subjectivity and bias. Instead of using job evaluations as large firms traditionally have used them—that is, as one tool toward achieving internal equity for a whole host of jobs that do not have directly correlative jobs in the marketplace—the comparable worth forces wished to use it as the tool.

Where large employers use benchmark jobs to make comparisons directly to prevailing wage rates in their local labor markets, comparable worth involves entirely ignoring the external labor market because it is allegedly contaminated by discrimination.[44] Job evaluations for these large employers are not used in isolation to set wages for non-key jobs; they may be supplemented with different job evaluation techniques and with the need to respond to supply and demand for each type of labor. But comparable worth rids job evaluation of its very narrow, limited function and enshrines an unscientific, nonobjective technique into a replacement for the market.

Without the market as a check on the accuracy of a particular job evaluation scheme, the comparable-worth-type job evaluation would be arbitrary, depending for its outcome upon who performed the study and the way the study was structured. It would only be the merest of coincidences if two studies produced identical or even similar results.

Richard Burr, a research analyst, conducted a study comparing the results of comparable worth evaluations in the states. By examining the rankings of the same jobs from one study to the next, he found that the disparities were substantial. To take one example of a secretary, a data entry operator, and a laundry worker, the secretary would be ranked first in Washington and Iowa, but last in Minnesota and Vermont, while the data entry operator would place first in Minnesota but third in Iowa and second in Vermont and Washington. Table 1 reproduces his results.[45]

Table 1
Variations in Job Rankings Across States

	Iowa	Minnesota	Vermont	Washington
Data Entry Operator	3	1	2	2
Laundry Worker I	2	2	1	3
Secretary	1	3	3	1

In a more extensive comparison of the rankings of jobs in Iowa, Minnesota, and Washington, he discovered "vast discrepancies" in the job scores and rankings in these states:

> In Minnesota, for instance, a registered nurse, a chemist, and a social worker all have equal values and would be paid the same. However, Iowa's study finds the nurse worth 29 percent more than the social worker, who in turn is worth 11 percent more than the chemist. While the chemist also receives the lowest point score of the three positions in the Vermont study, the social worker and nurse reverse rankings. The social worker is valued about 10 percent more than the nurse, who is worth 10 percent more than the chemist.[46]

More curious results emerge, Burr found, when one compares the scores of the same job across states. Vermont values its photographers twice as highly as Iowa, while Minnesota's photographers are worth 25 percent more than Iowa's. Burr also found great disagreement about the factors to be evaluated, the weights given to various factors, and the points assigned to each job. In the New Mexico study, four of the eight evaluators could not agree on the level to be assigned to jobs in 824 of the 896 classifications evaluated.

From his study, Burr concluded that "comparable worth is a concept riddled with bias and arbitrariness." The market—"not whimsical committees of lawyers and aggrieved feminists"—is the proper mechanism for setting wages.[47]

Values cannot be eliminated, and to pretend that they can is to abandon rational discourse and claim scientific accuracy—objectivity—where such is inherently impossible. On such slippery grounds of pseudo-scientific objectivity, the comparable worth forces wished to supplant the marketplace with the opinions—for, indeed, that is all they can be—of "experts." But who chooses these experts will determine the outcome. These experts, many of them smitten by comparable worth's allure, will overrule the decisions of millions of individuals exercising their freedom in the marketplace. So, as the opponents see it, you have on the one hand the decisions of so-called experts and, on the other, the free choices of millions of average people: comparable worth or the marketplace?

Brigitte Berger argued that the comparable worth experts are biased in favor of educational credentials—which are easy to measure—and against the kinds of skills acquired on the job in manual and service vocations. Ironically, while comparable worth professes to benefit women workers, it actually discriminates against the poorest and neediest and in favor of the "white-collar credential jobs." She wrote:

> If this comparable worth vision should take hold and become the accepted definition of the value of work in America, a blatant antiworking-class and antiblue-collar work bias will be introduced under the disguise of justice and equality.[48]

Comparable worth, she concluded, is "one of the more aggressively elitist visions of modern life that has surfaced in recent decades."[49]

Given the intractable problems of subjectivity and arbitrariness in the comparable worth methodology, it would be left to legislators, judges, or bureaucrats to determine which "expert's" view ought to be imposed on all of society.[50] Should legislators decree which technique is to constitute comparable worth, or should judges be left to decide that on a case-by-case basis?

If comparable worth were read into Title VII of the Civil Rights Act as the supporters urged, judges would have to decide between competing expert testimony, using competing methodologies, and arriving at contradictory findings. The complex cases currently litigated under Title VII and the Equal Pay Act of 1963 would look delightfully simple compared with what judges would now be called upon to decide. This sorry state of affairs would create havoc for employers, as no one would know from day to day whether he was violating equal employment law, and the courts would sink under the burden of cases this uncertainty would generate.

To complicate matters even further: Why, the opponents wondered, would men sit back and watch their relative positions in the wage scale erode? Why would they not demand comparable worth, too, once it had been enshrined in law or by judicial interpretation? Why should men not receive their assessed worth on a job evaluation scheme? Why should they not have a cause of action when they do not receive the same pay as another male-dominated job that received the same number of points? By asking these questions, the critics exposed a slippery slope in comparable worth—that once implemented for women it could not be contained and would soon be imposed on the entire workforce. At that stage, the market for wages would be gone; chaos would ensue, followed inexorably by calls for even more government regulation and interference.

Where the comparable worth enthusiasts saw the concept as a cure for the discriminatory animus against women that exists in the marketplace, the opponents saw only a radical, if not revolutionary, half-baked scheme to overturn our market economy. The market can live with an Equal Pay Act and even a Title VII, but the critics feared that comparable worth was not simply an adjustment to the marketplace to make it more equitable toward women. Rather, it was a competing economic system, one more akin to the central planning of the now late but unlamented Soviet Bloc, and one likely to produce as chaotic and inequitable an economy.

Flawed from its inception in the notion that jobs have objective value, comparable worth compounded its initial error by calling for job evaluations freed from market constraints. This set the supporters adrift in a sea of subjectivity. Since values cannot be eliminated, they sought to replace the values of millions of free individuals expressed every day in the marketplace with the values of job-evaluation experts imbued with feminist ideology. And a misguided feminism at that. The women's movement in its early modern period in the late 1960s and 1970s emphasized women's capacity, women's ability to perform jobs traditionally dominated by men. Comparable worth's heyday as a feminist rallying cry in the 1980s set an entirely different agenda, portraying women in an unflattering light that enshrined their incapacity. Instead of encouraging women to engage in new ventures, it conceded that they will be secretaries, nurses, and teachers for a long time to come and only asked that they be paid more.

As David Kirp and his colleagues observed in their book, *Gender Justice*, the "most significant effect [of comparable worth] would be to perpetuate widespread job segregation": certainly an ironic twist.[51] Sex stereotyping, an early subject of attack by feminists, would only be magnified by comparable worth: another irony.

The critics of comparable worth were not unsympathetic to the frustrations and concerns that motivated many women's support of the movement. They saw hope for the improvement of women's position in the marketplace and the eventual erosion of the wage gap in the increased educational attainment of women, their pursuit of more technical, job-oriented courses, their more long-range commitment to market participation, and their entrance into traditionally male occupations. As for legislation, they saw no need for anything beyond what was already in place—Title VII and the Equal Pay Act—which aimed to promote equality of opportunity by making jobs open to all irrespective of sex and by guaranteeing equal pay for equal work.

Attempts to resuscitate comparable worth—or a fraternal twin—in the new millennium may be anticipated, since collectivism in its true colors has been discredited by the fall of centrally planned systems. Comparable worth is something of a Trojan horse for statism, or statism with a less-menacing façade. Bad ideas, especially collectivist ones, have a way of recycling themselves in the guise of the hottest new public policy idea. It seldom hurts to reprise the arguments that were so successful by the early 1990s in slaying this particular Trojan horse, arguments that relied on free market economics, individualism, and belief in the adaptability and ingenuity of women. All three were vindicated in the 1990s, as women flooded graduate and technical schools and entered the professions and the new computer-driven economy in record numbers. The shrinking wage gap is symbolic of the success of free-market policies, just as the defeat of comparable worth as an idea is a testament to the cogency of free-market ideas.

Notes

1. "Highlights of Women's Earnings in 1998," U.S. Department of Labor, Bureau of Labor Statistics, Report 928 (April 1999). Figures on the wage gap were first made available by the bureau in 1979 when the gap stood at 39 percent. More recently, in 1998, the gap had shrunk to 24 or 26 percent (depending on the source).

2. George H. Hildebrand, "The Market System," in E. Livernash, ed., *Comparable Worth: Issues and Alternatives* (Washington, D.C., 1984), 85. He views the labor market as divided into two basic types: the quoted market price and the *bourse*. In the former the wage is quoted and is not usually subject to negotiation, while in the latter the price constantly shifts as supply and demand fluctuate.

3. For an argument of this sort see: June O'Neill, "An Argument for the Marketplace," *Society* (1985), 55. O'Neill writes:

> . . . in product markets we do not require that a pound of soybeans be more expensive than a pound of Belgian chocolates because it is more nutritious, or that the price of water be higher than that of diamonds because it is so much more important to our survival. If asked what the proper scale of prices should be for these products, most people—at least those who have taken Economics I—would give the sensible answer that there is no proper scale—it all depends on the tastes and needs of millions of consumers and the various conditions that determine the costs of production and the supplies of these products.

See also June O'Neill and Solomon Polachek, "Why the Gender Gap in Wages Narrowed in the 1980s," *Journal of Labor Economics* vol. 11, no. 1, pt. 1 (1993).

4. *Ibid.*, 56.

5. *Ibid.*, 55.

6. "Comparable Worth: An Interview with June O'Neill," in *Comparable Worth: Will it Close the Pay Gap? Manhattan Report* 4 (1984), 3–4.

7. At least for a time. When international competition flourishes, inflated prices for labor in highly unionized industries spell the need for wage concessions, productivity gains, plant closings, or failing these, bankruptcy.

8. See "Discrimination and the Marketplace: An Interview with Robert Higgs," in *Comparable Worth: Will It Close the Pay Gap?* Higgs argues that discrimination is more prevalent by government officials than by the marketplace because:

> Discrimination in the market often imposes a cost on the discriminator, whereas discrimination by a public official often works just the other way. It may actually provide the public official with a benefit by enhancing his chances of reelection or his popularity with the majority public.(9)

9. Gary S. Becker, *The Economics of Discrimination* (Chicago, 1971). For an example of Becker's influence see June O'Neill, "Role Differentiation and the Gender Gap in Wage Rates," in Laurie Larwood, Ann H. Stromberg, Barbara A. Gutek, eds., *Women and Work* (Beverly Hills, Calif., 1985), 64–66.

10. Becker, *Economics*, 153.

11. One finding of Becker's that might count against the free-market view of the marketplace operating in the long-run to diminish discrimination is that blacks during the period from 1910 to 1950 had improved their average occupational position in the North and the South, but their position relative to whites had been "remarkably stable" (156) He tentatively concluded that the level of discrimination against blacks had remained relatively stable during those four decades.

12. *Ibid.*, 159.

13. *Ibid.*, 19.

14. *Ibid.*, 21.

15. Higgs, "Discrimination and the Marketplace," 9.

16. Jennifer Roback, "A Skeptical Feminist Looks at Comparable Worth," *Cato Policy Report* 8 (1986), 6–7; and *A Matter of Choice* (New York, 1986), 33–38, which Roback wrote for the Twentieth Century Fund. See also George H. Hildebrand, "The Market System," in E. Robert Livernash, ed., *Comparable Worth: Issues and Alternatives*, 84.

17. Roback, *A Matter of Choice*, 38.

18. Michael Levin, "Comparable Worth: The Feminist Road to Socialism," *Commentary* 13 (1984), 18. Levin was a bit more extreme than many of the critics, as he argued that the socialization that the comparable worth supporters deride as oppressive because it fashions little girls for traditional roles is really the result of innate, ineluctable features of the female sex (19). For another prediction of economic chaos, see Michael F. Carter, "Comparable Worth: An Idea Whose Time Has Come?" *Personnel Journal* 60 (1981), 792, 794.

19. Jeremy Rabkin, "Comparable Worth as Civil Rights Policy: Potentials for Disaster," *Comparable Worth: Issue for the 80's*, A Consultation of the U.S. Commission on Civil Rights, vol. 1 (1984), 187–195.

20. See Charles Waldauer, "The Noncomparability of the 'Comparable Worth' Doctrine: An Inappropriate Standard for Determining Sex Discrimination in Pay," *Population Research and Policy Review* 3 (1984), 141. Waldauer attempted to test the com-

parable worth notion of discrimination in the marketplace by examining the pay scales for academics in higher education. The observed differences in pay between different disciplines were not, he concluded, the result of discrimination, but rather were responses to the opportunity costs facing faculty in terms of the employment opportunities available to them outside the academy. Thus engineers and scientists enjoyed higher pay than professors in liberal arts who had few alternatives available to them. In fact the labor market imbalances in academia are testimony to the fact that external market forces have not been allowed to hold full sway. He concluded from this example that the comparable worth doctrine is economically defective "because it ignores supply factors in labor markets" (160).

21. Hildebrand, "The Market System," 103.

22. Thomas Sowell, *Civil Rights: Rhetoric or Reality* (New York, 1984).

23. June O'Neill, "An Argument Against Comparable Worth," *Comparable Worth: Issue for the 80's,* 179 and "The Trend in the Male-Female Wage Gap."

24. See O'Neill, "Role Differentiation and the Gender Gap in Wage Rates." She argues that fertility and other factors give women a comparative advantage in performing household work. Their role in the family is unlikely to be the result principally of discrimination in the labor market.

25. *Ibid.,* 182.

26. June O'Neill, "The Trend in the Male-Female Wage Gap in the United States," *Journal of Labor Economics* 3 (1985), S91, S113–S115.

27. O'Neill and Polachek, "Why the Gender Gap," 205.

28. *Ibid.,* 225.

29. "Household Income at Record High: Poverty Declines in 1998," Census Bureau Reports, September 30, 1999. The Bureau reported that in 1998 the female-to-male ratio had slipped to 73 percent, a figure that it called "not significantly different" from the 1996 high of 74 percent.

30. Jennifer Roback, *A Matter of Choice,* 28–29.

31. *Ibid.,* 30–32.

32. *Wall Street Journal,* January 4, 2000, A1 (based on statistics from the Bureau of the Census). The major part of this gain had actually been achieved by 1992, when the figure stood at 22.4 percent.

33. "Measuring 50 Years of Economic Change," Bureau of the Census, Current Population Reports, September 1998, 27.

34. Brigitte Berger, "Comparable Worth at Odds with American Realities," *Comparable Worth: Issue for the 80's,* 69. Charles Waldauer mentions another factor that ought to be considered in explaining the male-female wage gap: the differences in the supply of labor in response to variations in pay. Married women are much less geographically mobile than men; their hours of availability are less flexible; and women tend to be tied to the geographical location of their mates' jobs. The labor supply of women is less price-sensitive. "The Non-comparability of the 'Comparable Worth' Doctrine: An Inappropriate Standard for Determining Sex Discrimination in Pay," *Population Research and Policy Review* 3 (1984), 141, 143–144.

35. "Highlights of Women's Earnings in 1998." The *Current Population Survey* is produced monthly by the Bureau of the Census for the Bureau of Labor Statistics and is based on a sample of fifty thousand households.

36. "Comparable Worth: Pay Equity or Social Engineering?" *The Heritage Lectures* no. 63 (February 5, 1986), 3.

37. Solomon William Polachek, "Potential Biases in Measuring Male-Female Discrimination," *Journal of Human Resources* 10 (1975), 205.

38. Rachel Flick, "The New Feminism and the World of Work," *Public Interest* 33 (1983), 43.

39. "Explaining Trends in the Gender Wage Gap," A Report by the Council of Economic Advisers, June 1998, 6.

40. Barbara Wooton, "Gender Differences in Occupational Employment," *Monthly Labor Review*, April 1997, 17.

41. On human capital theory as an explanation of apparent sex segregation, see Solomon William Polachek, "Woman in the Economy: Perspectives on Gender Inequality," *Comparable Worth: Issue for the 80's*, 45–51.

42. Anna Kondratas, "Comparable Worth: Pay Equity or Social Engineering," Updating Heritage Lecture no. 63, February 5, 1986, 4.

43. For those who argued in this manner see Daniel Seligman, "'Pay Equity' is a Bad Idea," *Fortune* 109 (1984), 133, 140; Hildebrand, "The Market System," 83; Rita Ricardo-Campbell, *Women and Comparable Worth* (Stanford, Calif., 1985), 2.

44. See Hildebrand, "The Market System," 88–89; Waldauer, "The Non-comparability of the 'Comparable Worth' Doctrine," 142.

45. Richard E. Burr, "Rank Injustice," *Policy Review* 73 (1986), 73. See also Burr, *Are Comparable Worth Systems Truly Comparable?* (St. Louis Mo., 1986).

46. *Ibid*.

47. For other critics of the subjectivity and arbitrariness of job evaluations see Clarence Thomas, "Pay Equity and Comparable Worth," *Labor Law Journal* 34 (1983), 3, 7, taken from his testimony before the House Subcommittees on Civil Service, Human Resources, and Compensation Employee Benefits of the Post Office and Civil Service Committee, September 30, 1982; Geoffrey Cowley, "Comparable Worth: Another Terrible Idea," *Washington Monthly* 52 (1984)55–56; Carter, "Comparable Worth: An Idea Whose Time Has Come," 793; Kondratas, *Comparable Worth: Pay Equity or Social Engineering?* 3–4.

48. Brigitte Berger, "Comparable Worth at Odds with American Realities," in *Comparable Worth: Issue for the 80's*, p. 71.

49. *Ibid*.

50. See for example Phyllis Schlafly, "Shall I Compare Thee to a Plumber's Pay," *Policy Review* 76 (1985), 76:

> Since it is unlikely that people will agree on allocations of specific numerical points for such imprecise factors as "accountability" and "mental demands," the bottom line is that wages would be fixed by judges or bureaucrats. It's hard to conceive of a more radical attack on the private enterprise system.

51. David Kirp, Mark G. Yudof, and Marlene Strong Franks, *Gender Justice* (Chicago, 1986), 171.

WOMEN
and
VIOLENCE

Rita J. Simon

❁

Women and Violent Crime

MUCH OF THE RHETORIC OF THE CURRENT FEMINIST MOVEMENT HAS FOCUSED on women as the major target of violent offenders. It is women, they claim, and especially young women, who are most likely to suffer assault, rape, and homicide at the hands of violent men. Andrea Dworkin writes that in the United States violence against women "is pervasive. It is epidemic. It saturates the society. . . . We have, in the United States, an incredible, continuing epidemic of murders of women. We have huge missing pieces of our populations in cities."[1]

It would be absurd to say that violence against women is unimportant or insubstantial—a position Dworkin ascribes to mainstream society. In fact no one denies that violence, manifestly including violence against women, is far too common. Dworkin writes, however, as if we lived in a nonviolent society with the exception of violence against women. Do the data support this fearful picture? Are women the major targets of violent crime?[2]

Who Are the Major Victims of Violent Crime?
Table 1 provides 1998 data on homicide victims by race, sex, and age, and table 2 does the same for victims of aggravated assault. For both these crimes, three trends are clear: men have higher victimization rates than women, blacks have higher victimization rates than whites, and the young have higher victimization rates than the old. Thus young black males have the highest victimization rates and white older women have the lowest victimization rates. The data for 1998 are not special in this regard. The same pattern has existed for decades.[3]

Table 1

Homicide Victimization by Age, Race, and Gender 1998*

Age	Male White	Male Black	Female White	Female Black
14–17	5.6	32.7	1.8	5.9
18–24	14.5	117.1	3.4	14.3
25+	5.3	40.5	2.2	9.2

* Rate per 100,000 population
(From Bureau of Justice Statistics: Homicide Trends in the United States)

Table 2

Aggravated Assault Rate by Victim Age, Race, and Gender 1998*

Age	Male White	Male Black	Female White	Female Black
12–19	49.5	44.7	14.3	18.7
20–24	19.4	36.7	6.6	24.6
25–34	9.4	18.6	5.5	9.3
35–49	8.1	15.9	5.2	3.7
50+	3.9	12.4	3.1	3.9

* Rate per 1,000 population
(From Bureau of Justice Statistics, Criminal Victimization in the United States)

Homicide and aggravated assault are not unique. Except for rape and sexual assault, every violent crime victimization rate for males is higher than for females. Overall, women are about two-thirds as likely as men to be victims of violence.[4] And blacks experience higher overall rates of violent crime than whites and persons of other races. Teenagers and young adults are more likely to become victims of violent crime than are older persons.

More than any other group, young black males are subject to extraordinarily high rates of violent crime. The data are especially shocking with respect to homicide. Black males ages 18–24 currently have homicide rates more than eighteen times as high as those in the general population (117.1 to 6.3 in 1998). The relative rate rapidly increased in the late 1980s as violence in the inner city among young black men skyrocketed. As late as the mid-1980s the homicide rate among young black males was "only" ten times as high as among the general population. Although crime, including the homicide rate among young black males, has declined markedly since it peaked in the 1991–1993 period the relative homicide rate has remained at or near an all-time high.

In comparison white females of all ages have homicide rates which are typically half or less than half the rate in the general population and are thus thirty to sixty times lower than among young black males.

Rape

Excluding the male prison population, women are more than ten times more likely to be victims of rape or attempted rape than men.

Table 3

Rape and Attempted Rape Rate by Sex of Victim, 1995*

| | Male | | Female | |
	Number	Rate	Number	Rate
Rape/Attempted Rape	19,390	0.2	214,780	1.9
Rape	1,940	0.0	138,880	1.2

*Rate per 1,000 persons age 12 and over
(From Bureau of Justice Statistics, Criminal Victimization in the United States)

In 1992 the Crime Victimization Survey was revised and, according to BJS, one of the goals of the redesign was to produce more accurate reporting of the incidents of rape and sexual assaults and of any kind of crimes committed by intimates or family members. In their August 1995 Special Report, BJS wrote:

> The new NCVS questionnaire encourages reporting of incidents in several ways. Questions were added to let respondents know that the interviewer is interested in a broad spectrum of incidents, not just those involving weapons, severe violence, or violence perpetrated by strangers. New methods of cuing respondents about potential experiences with victimizations increased the range of incident types that are being reported to interviewers. And behavior-specific wording has replaced criminal justice terminology to make the questions more understandable.

Despite the reworking of the survey many experts believe that rape is still underestimated in the United States and male rape particularly so.

Male rape is also shockingly common in the prisons where unlike the typical nonprison rape it is repeated and systematic. Only a few studies have
been done on prison rape but most indicate that if prison rape were to be
included in the above statistics that male rape would exceed female rape.[5]

More on Female Rape

A review of the literature on rape quickly shows that some groups report
vastly different figures on the number of rapes than does the FBI or Bureau of Justice Statistics. In 1992 the Crime Victims Research and Treatment Center released the results of its National Women's Study. They
estimated that between the fall of 1989 and 1990, 683,000 women were
raped in this country, and that one in every eight adult women in this
country has been a rape victim. This figure is more than twice the number
reported by the Bureau of Justice Statistics from their survey and nine
times the number of rapes reported to police as tallied by the FBI.

In 1988 the Ms. Report, based on a national survey of 3,000 college
women conducted by psychologist Mary Koss, reported that 15.4 percent
of the respondents claimed that they had been raped—a rate of 154 rapes
per 1,000 college women. According to this report another 12.1 percent said
they had been victims of attempted rape. These figures are approximately
1,000 times greater than the FBI statistics for rape and attempted rape on
university campuses. In 1993 the FBI statistics showed that there were 408
cases of rape or attempted rape reported to the police on 500 major college
and university campuses with an overall population of 5 million students.
That is less than one incident of rape or attempted rape per campus, and
an annual rate of .16 for 1,000 women students.

Some of the variation between the government's rape statistics and
those reported by the National Women's Study and Mary Koss can be explained by the fact that each group defines "rape" in different terms. Both
the FBI's Uniform Crime Reports and the National Crime Victims Survey
(NCVS) define rape as "carnal knowledge of a female forcibly and against
her will"; and both break down their reports into completed and attempted
rapes. But in the National Women's Study rape was defined as "an event
that occurred without the women's consent, involved the use of force or
threat of force, and involved sexual penetration of vagina, mouth, or rec-
tum." This is a broader definition than the one used by FBI and NCVS,
but this alternate definition alone cannot account for the differences between the reported numbers.

The best explanation for the difference lies in the fact that the National Women's Study and Koss's study depended on "outside" researchers
to make decisions as to when a woman had been a victim, rather than leav-

ing that decision to the woman herself. UCR and NCVS data depend upon women who believe they have been the victims of rape or attempted rape and either report it to the police, or reveal it in the victimization survey. But in the Koss study researchers often counted as rape victims women who would not classify themselves as such. Incidents that were labeled as rape by the researchers were also labeled as rape by only 55 percent of the victims for situations in which the perpetrator was a stranger; by 27.7 for situations involving a nonromantic acquaintance; and by 18.3 percent for situations involving a steady dating partner. For the large majority of "acquaintance and date-rape victims, it was the researchers who defined the act as rape, and not the victims themselves." As an indication of the importance of these considerations, note that 42 percent of the "victims" had sex again with the man who supposedly raped them.

Rape is a violent, dehumanizing, horrendous experience. Every rape is a tragic event and it is not necessary to inflate the statistics on rape to recognize this fact. Rape does occur less often than other violent crimes. In 1995 the BJS data estimated the number of attempted and completed rapes at 1.1 per 1,000 people or 1.9 per 1,000 women, compared to 8.7 per 1,000 people for aggravated assaults, and 5.3 per 1,000 people for robberies. Certainly most women would regard rape as more serious than even aggravated assault but it remains true that rape is less common than other violent crimes.

Violence Among Intimates

If we break the data on violent acts into categories of victims and the relationship of offenders to victims a distinct pattern across gender emerges. Most male victims of violent crime are victimized by strangers (58.3 percent) but most female victims of violent crime are victimized by someone they know (65.4 percent).[6] If we restrict further to violence by intimates (spouses, boyfriends, girlfriends, and former spouses, boyfriends or girlfriends) the distinction is even more stark. Victimization by an intimate accounts for 21 percent of the violence experienced by females but only 2 percent of the violence experienced by males. Although females are less likely than males to experience violent crime overall, they are more likely to experience violent crime from an intimate.

The September 1995 BJS Special Report "Spouse Murder Defendants in Large Urban Counties," indicates that the criminal justice system treats violence by male intimates seriously. Men who kill their wives are treated more harshly than wives who kill their husbands; this is true at every step of the process. Wife-killers, for example, are more often prosecuted and less often acquitted than are husband-killers. Overall, 81 percent of the wife-killers are sent to prison but only 57 percent of the husband-killers. Prison sentences for wife-killers are almost three times longer than those for husband-killers (16.5 versus 6 years on average). The criminal justice system does not ignore or make light of crimes against females, contrary to what some feminists may have suggested.

The most recent data show that there has been a decline in the homicide of intimates, especially male victims.[7] The number of husbands, wives, boyfriends, and girlfriends killed in each race and gender group has fallen over the last two decades: among black female victims by 46 percent, black males by 77 percent, white males by 55 percent, and white females by 14 percent.

For both fatal and nonfatal violence, however, women are at a higher risk than men to be victimized by an intimate. Female homicide victims are more than twice as likely to have been killed by husbands or boyfriends than male victims are to have been killed by wives or girlfriends. For those cases in which the victim-offender relationship is known, husbands or boyfriends killed 26 percent of female murder victims and wives or girlfriends killed 3 percent of the male victims.

Careful examination of the BJS and the NCVS data provides a clear answer to the question: "Who are the major victims of violent crime in American society?" The answer is young black males. More generally crime is typically higher among the young than the old, blacks than whites, males than females. Since young black males who are on the negative end of these categories are also often poor (another category in which crime increases), crime among this group is staggering. Women are the predominant victims of violence commited by intimates but such crimes account for only about 13 percent of all criminal violence, and 9 percent of all homicides. Crime is a concern for everyone and nothing here should be interpreted to imply that a crime against a female is less important than one against a male. On the contrary, every innocent victim is to be regarded equally which is why it is important to remember that the major victims of all violent acts are men by a ratio of about ten to one. And among these men, blacks outnumber whites by one-and-a-half times.

Notes

1. Andrea Dworkin, "Terror, Torture and Resistance," *Canadian Woman Studies/Les Cahiers de la Femme* 12:1 (1991). See also Dworkin, *Life and Death: Unapologetic Writings on the Continuing War Against Women* (New York, 1997).

2. The Bureau of Justice Statistics (BJS), the FBI, and the National Crime Victims Survey (NCVS) are the major sources of data for this essay. The Bureau of Criminal Justice Statistics website contains extensive data on all aspects of crime for many years. Available at www.ojp.usdoj.gov/bjs/welcome.html. Reports used in this study include Criminal Victimization in the United States, 1995 (May 1995, NCJ 171129) and Violence by Intimates (March 1998, NCJ-167237) as well as other general information.

3. Extensive data on all aspects of crime and crime victims going back decades is available from the Bureau of Justice Statistics at www.ojp.usdoj.gov/bjs/welcome.html. The FBI's Uniform Crime Reports are also available online at www.fbi.gov/ucr/ucr.htm.

4. Males are also more often the perpetrators in homicides and other violent crimes: males are more than nine times more likely than females to commit murder. Interestingly offenders, whether male or female, are more likely to target male than female victims.

5. On male prison rape see Lee H. Bowker, *Prison Victimization* (New York, 1980); Daniel Lockwood, *Prison Sexual Violence* (New York, 1980); and Richie J. McMullen, *Male Rape: Breaking the Silence on the Last Taboo* (London, 1990). The Stop Prison Rape website also contains useful information. See www.spr.org/.

6. Both figures from BJS data (1998).

7. *Ibid.*

*Richard W. Stevens, Hugo Teufel III,
and Matthew Y. Biscan*

❦

Disarming Women
Comparing "Gun Control" to Self-Defense

INDIVIDUALIST FEMINISM AFFIRMS THE POLITICAL AND SOCIAL EQUALITY OF the sexes.[1] Under this feminist view the government and laws must serve the individual rights to life, liberty, and property of all persons equally. The laws must empower individuals to exercise these rights, and must not promote the exploitation of one sex by the other.[2]

In American society today, women suffer much criminal violence and domestic abuse because they are typically smaller and physically weaker than men, and because women do not typically prepare themselves to protect and defend themselves with force. Given the biological differences between the sexes, the individualist feminist might ask why many women apparently accept social and legal restrictions on their personal right to self-defense.

When facing a risk or actuality of violent attack, the victim has two main choices. She can defend herself, using deadly force if necessary, or she can rely upon a government-based protection system that might use deadly force on her behalf. Which is the better choice for women? On a policy level should "gun control" laws be enacted to discourage or prohibit citizens from exercising the right to use deadly force for self-defense?

Violent Crime in America
Despite large decreases in most violent crimes since the early 1990s, U.S. violent crime rates are much greater today than they were thirty to thirty-five years ago. Consider these facts:[3]

- Total violent crime in 1995 was 76 percent higher than in 1976, and was 240 percent higher than in 1965.[4]

- The 1995 murder rate was over 60 percent higher and the 1998 rate over 20 percent higher than in 1965.

- The rate of homicide committed against females has declined only slightly in the 1976–1998 period.[5]

- FBI statistics show that 1,634,773 serious violent crimes were committed in 1997, including:[6] 1,022,492 assaults (63 percent); 497,950 robberies (30 percent); 96,122 rapes (6 percent); and 18,209 murders (1 percent).

The figures from the FBI are based on crimes reported to police. The United States Department of Justice has estimated that victims overall report crimes only 38 percent of the time and about half of all rape, robbery, and burglary victims report those crimes.[7] Some authorities suggest that these rape statistics are low because women report rape victimizations only 7–10 percent of the time.[8]

Women experience much less violent crime from strangers than do men, in part perhaps because they restrict their freedoms to avoid such violence. Women, however, are the major victims of crime from intimates. Although the total rate rose from 1997 to 1998, domestic violence (violence between intimate partners) has trended slightly downward in recent years.[9] As with other crimes, exact figures are hard to establish, given that about half of domestic violence victims do not report crimes against their persons for a variety of reasons including fear of the abuser.[10] In May 2000 the Department of Justice, through the Bureau of Justice Statistics, issued its report entitled *Intimate Partner Violence*.[11] That report updated the statistics for 1998 domestic violence incidents:

- Victims of domestic violence numbered 876,340 women and 157,330 men.

- Rate of violent victimizations by an intimate partner was 7.7 per 1,000 women and 1.4 per 1,000 men.

- Intimate partner homicides were approximately 1,800 (a decrease from 1976 when there were more than 3,000 such homicides).

- Homicides were most often committed with firearms though that rate has been decreasing, while the number of non-firearm homicides has remained fairly constant over time.

- From 1976 through 1996 male intimate partners were responsible for 29 percent of female murder victims. Female intimate partners were responsible for only 5.9 percent of male murder victims during that time.

In the typical domestic abuse case the women know their attackers well, while in other situations the attacker is a stranger. What can women do to protect themselves in either scenario?

When facing the risk of violence, a person can physically resist, flee, or seek help from others to stop the attacker. In practical situations, when a criminal threatens a woman, she can try to escape, obtain government assistance with a protective order or restraining order, call police for help, or resist the threat with force. The escape option is largely situational, but the other three options can be analyzed generally.

Relying On Police Protection, Emergency "911" Systems, and Protective Orders

Since 1968 Americans who face a criminal attack have been advised to "dial 911" and rely upon emergency police response for protection.[12] Indeed, "the public has built up extraordinary levels of expectation and reliance on the [911] system's effectiveness. We have taken for granted that 911 always will work perfectly."[13] Meanwhile "in recent years, many law enforcement executives have questioned the entire foundation on which 911 is built—the idea that police can stop crimes by responding rapidly to citizens' 'emergency' calls."[14]

In practice, does dialing 911 actually protect crime victims? Less than 5 percent of all calls dispatched to police are made soon enough for officers to stop a crime or arrest a suspect.[15] Frequently it can take ten minutes or more for police to respond to calls for help, and some writers have called the average police response to domestic violence calls "grossly inadequate."[16] The 911 bottom line: "cases in which 911 technology makes a substantial difference in the outcome of criminal events are extraordinarily rare."[17]

Even when it functions at its best, the 911 system cannot adequately protect crime victims. When citizens rely solely upon 911 and police protection from imminent criminal attacks, their risks of harm increase due to slowed police response times, clogged emergency telephone lines, and occasional partial or total 911 system outages.[18] More striking is the position of the law in nearly every state: the police have no legal obligation to protect individual citizens from violent crime.[19] In fact the police in most states do not even have to respond to 911 calls adequately or at all.

Can a woman facing danger of "separation assault" by a former partner depend upon police protection?[20] In one landmark California case, a woman separated from her husband and he retaliated with threats and violence.[21] Over a period of a year, Ruth Bunnell had called the San Jose police at least twenty times to report that her estranged husband Mack had violently assaulted her and her two daughters. Mack had even been arrested once for an assault.

One day Mack called Ruth to say that he was coming to her house to kill her. Ruth called the police for immediate help. The police department "refused to come to her aid at that time, and asked that she call the department again when Mack Bunnell had arrived."[22] Forty-five minutes later Mack arrived and stabbed Ruth to death. Responding to a neighbor's call, the police eventually came to Ruth's house . . . after she was dead.

Ruth's estate sued the city police for negligently failing to protect her. The California appeals court held that the City of San Jose was shielded from the negligence suit because of a state statute and because there was no "special relationship" between the police and Ruth—the police had not started to help her, and she had not relied on any promise that the police would help.[23] Case dismissed.

In a particularly brutal Washington, D.C., case three women discovered that the law promises them no protection against brutal attack by strangers.[24] All three women were sleeping in their rooms during the early morning hours when two men broke down the back door of their three-floor house in northwest Washington. The men first entered the second floor room and violently assaulted one woman there.

From the third floor room they shared, the other two women heard the screams and commotion so they called the police. The call was dispatched at "Code 2" priority which was a lower priority than the "Code 1" given to crimes in progress. Four police cruisers responded to the dispatch within a few minutes. One of the police cars drove through the alley without stopping to check the back door and then went around to the front of the house. A second police officer knocked on the front door but left when he got no answer. All the officers left the scene just five minutes after they had arrived.

The two women, who had escaped to an adjoining roof, then climbed back into their room, and still hearing screams they called the police again. The duty officer assured them that help was on the way. That second call was logged as "investigate the trouble" but was never dispatched to any officers.

A few minutes later the two women thought the police were in the home and called down for them. There were no policemen there, but the attackers heard the calls and came upstairs. All three women were kidnapped, taken to one of the attacker's homes, and raped, robbed, beaten, and sexually abused.

The three women victims sued the District of Columbia and the officers for negligently failing to provide adequate police protection, but their complaint was dismissed. Under D.C. law, "official police personnel and the government employing them are not generally liable to victims of criminal acts for failure to provide adequate police protection."[25] This rule "rests upon the fundamental principle that a government and its agents are under no general duty to provide public services, such as police protection, to any particular individual citizen."[26] Many other state courts follow and apply the same rule.[27]

The Supreme Court has held that neither the U.S. Constitution nor the federal civil rights laws require states to protect citizens from crime.[28] As one federal appeals court observed, ordinary citizens have:

> no constitutional right to be protected by the state against being murdered by criminals or madmen. It is monstrous if the state fails to protect its residents against such predators but it does not violate the due process clause of the Fourteenth Amendment or, we suppose, any other provision of the Constitution. The Constitution . . . does not require the federal government or the state to provide services, even so elementary a service as maintaining law and order.[29]

When a woman relies solely upon a telephone and the expectation of immediate police help, she is placing her trust in a system that legally owes her nothing.[30] That understood, it only makes sense for women and other potential victims to prepare to protect and defend themselves and their families from violent criminals.

Victims of threatened or real domestic violence can seek a court-issued "protective" (or "restraining" or "civil protection") order. Such orders typically direct the alleged abuser, stalker, or other known person to move out of a shared residence, and stay away from and not make any contact with the victim.[31] To obtain a protective order in a domestic violence situation, the complaining party must show by a preponderance of the evidence that there is "good cause to believe" the alleged perpetrator "has committed or is threatening an intrafamily offense."[32] The alleged perpetrator has the opportunity in such cases to testify and challenge the claim.[33]

The main pitfall with protective orders is that they will not deter, forcing the victim to rely once again on the 911 system that rarely stops a crime in progress. Ideally only a true victim of domestic violence moves for and receives a protective order. In the real world, however, there is a real danger that a protective order will be used against the victim and will prevent the victim from defending herself against attack.

Courts often issue protective orders essentially upon request and without investigating the facts or adhering closely to the law. Many times the batterer obtains a restraining order against the battered intimate partner.[34] Courts sometimes order "mutual" restraining orders against both partners.[35] Some judges routinely issue mutual orders to appear to be fair and neutral. It has been estimated that upwards of 40 to 50 percent of all protective orders are obtained under false pretenses.[36]

Victims should not seek or quietly accept a mutual protection order. A mutual protection order suggests that the victim was at least partially at fault and validates the abuser's tendency to blame the victim for the violence. As a practical matter, when police come to the scene of further domestic violence, they might arrest both parties—or neither party—for violating the order. An inappropriate mutual protection order can thus allow the abuser to enlist police help in harassing the victim with "mutual" arrests, or it can leave the victim unprotected when police leave both parties alone.[37]

Protective orders also do not equalize the physical power of abuser and victim. When a man violates a protective order and attacks a woman, the woman suffers much more than would a man attacked by a woman. Intimate violence study data from the National Family Violence Survey indicated that the frequency of wife-on-husband assault (124 incidents per 1,000 couples) is about equal to the frequency of husband-on-wife assault (116 per 1,000). Although a great deal of domestic violence might be mutual, researchers point out that "the greater average size and strength of men and their greater aggressiveness mean that the same act (for example, a punch) is likely to very different in the amount of pain or injury inflicted."[38] Recent data suggest that 50 percent of female victims of domestic abuse suffer physical injuries, while only 32 percent of male victims are physically injured.[39]

When the victim is a woman and her male batterer decides to violate the protective order, she faces a significant disadvantage. Most likely his physical strength will be superior to hers. More importantly, she will not be able to predict the time he will attempt to attack her; the attacker will determine the time and the location of the confrontation. Often the police will arrive too late to prevent his abusive and possibly murderous assault.[40]

A local judge's protective order arising out of a domestic violence problem triggers a federal "gun control" statute that prohibits the person subject to that order from possessing a firearm. That federal statute, United States Code Title 18 Section 922(g)(8), makes it a felony for any person to possess a firearm if that person is subject to a court order:

1. That was issued after a full hearing;
2. That restrains the person "from harassing, stalking, or threatening an intimate partner" or from "conduct that would place an intimate partner in reasonable fear of bodily injury to the partner"; and
3. That includes a court's finding that the "person represents a credible threat to the physical safety of such intimate partner," or a court's order expressly prohibiting the person from using, attempting or threatening to use "physical force against such intimate partner" that "would reasonably be expected to cause bodily injury."[41]

Section 922(g)(8) seemingly addresses the problem of death or serious bodily injury of battered persons, often wives, ex-wives, and girlfriends, by decreeing that intimate partners subject to a domestic protective order are liable for a federal felony if they possess a firearm.[42] That law is fundamentally flawed for two reasons: it ignores the true nature of the abuser, and it deprives the battered woman of an effective means of defending herself.

There is little reason to believe that a confirmed, repeat abuser would be deterred significantly by a protective order or by the consequences of violating Section 922(g)(8). The odds are high that the abuser is already a criminal and has already ignored other state laws or court orders. If such an abuser ignores the protective order, then the victim will have little recourse but to rely on self-defense.[43]

Once a domestic violence protective order is issued, if the person subject to the order possesses a firearm he instantly becomes a federal felon under Section 922(g)(8). If the abuser succeeds in obtaining a protective order against his accuser, then the abuse victim also falls under the statute. If the woman complies and does not obtain a firearm for protection, then she is deprived of the ability to defend herself against assault or murder. But if she does obtain a firearm, she becomes a felon. The added federal penalty likely will not faze the typical domestic abuser. He has already shown his willingness to risk a lengthy prison term for his violent conduct.

Women's Exercise of the Right to Armed Self-Defense

The inadequacy of 911 and protective-orders as methods of protecting against violence suggests that self-defense may be a better option for many women and other potential victims of crime.

Women who face criminal violence, whether domestic or otherwise, have the moral right to self-defense. The right to self-defense comes from a nearly universal recognition of the sanctity of human life.

Under Judeo-Christian law and tradition, self-defense is a right and duty. The Bible at Exodus 20:13 and 22:2 declares that murder is wrong, but injuring or killing in defense is justified. Jewish law set forth in the Talmud states, "If someone comes to kill you, arise quickly and kill him."[44]

Christian doctrine has long asserted the right and duty of self-defense.[45] "Someone who defends his life is not guilty of murder even if he is forced to deal his aggressor a lethal blow."[46]

Thinkers in the Western tradition also have considered the right to self-defense using arms to be an essential right of humankind.[47] Modern nonreligious thinkers likewise have recognized self-defense as a primary right.[48] Libertarian Murray Rothbard wrote: "If, as libertarians believe, every individual has the right to own his person and property, it then follows that he has the right to employ violence to defend himself against the violence of criminal aggressors."[49] Philosopher and novelist Ayn Rand wrote: "The necessary consequence of man's right to life is his right to self-defense."[50]

With a venerable pedigree and near unanimity to support the right to self-defense, all that remains is for individual men and women to have the tools to exercise that right when they face the risk of violent attack. Firearms directly and powerfully provide those tools.

Women differ from men both physically and in the sex-role stereotypes applied to them. Each of these differences affects a woman's ability and orientation to use force to protect herself against violence.

On the average, men are physically bigger and stronger than women. Male batterers, for example, are on average forty-five pounds heavier and four to five inches taller than their female victims.[51] With serious martial arts training, a woman can fight off an unarmed larger man in many cases, but she likely still faces a disadvantage if attacked by multiple or armed persons.[52]

A woman with a firearm, however, can credibly threaten and deter an attacker of any size, shape, or strength.[53] Even though weaker and unskilled in firearms use, she can protect herself with a sidearm without firing a shot.[54] In over 92 percent of defensive gun uses, the defender succeeds by firing only a warning shot or never firing the gun at all.[55]

A sidearm can "equalize" physical disparity between a woman and her attacker.[56] For a battered woman the equalization can make all the difference, because such a woman is more likely to be prepared for an abuser's attack. Typically the battered woman can sense cues of impending violence from her male partner (in the home) more quickly and accurately than can a person who has not been threatened and abused.[57] Because she can prepare, she can more effectively use the sidearm to deter or prevent a looming violent episode.

A woman can overcome a male attacker's relative advantages in physical size and strength using defensive tools such as the sidearm. Social and psychological factors, however, can weaken a woman's willingness to prepare and actually defend herself using force.

Some writers argue that American women generally have a victim mentality because of sex-role stereotyping. In our society, nonaggressiveness is a characteristic of what is supposed to be "normal" heterosexual femininity. Men are supposed to protect "their women." Male rapists look for the weak and fearful "damsel in distress." The more stereotypically feminine and passive a woman is, the more likely that she will be a victim of aggression. The same nonaggressive woman is unlikely to learn self-defense techniques and obtain defense tools.[58]

Owing to the underlying sex-role stereotyping, some writers observe that the legal system actually punishes the assertive woman more than the assertive man and takes a dim view of female self-defense.[59] One researcher found that when women behaved inconsistently with the female stereotype by vigorously resisting a stranger rape or a "date rape," the women "were perceived as having been *more* guilty of precipitating the attack."[60]

Similarly, women who competently shot a burglar were considered more guilty than women who were incompetent with the sidearm and made a lucky hit. For men, the prejudice ran the opposite direction: men who knew firearms and competently shot a burglar were viewed with less suspicion than incompetent male shooters.[61]

Self-defense instructors have reported seeing "physically strong women who at first are so frightened of violence and of fighting that they cower and cry uncontrollably even in a simulated self-defense situation."[62] Even female police officers sometimes need extra training to be willing to fight back against aggressors.[63] This apparently widespread fear of conflict makes women targets of rape and violence.

"Crime prevention" programs that teach only nonviolent resistance actually reinforce the weak/passive female stereotype. The Maryland Community Crime Prevention Institute, for example, reportedly has told women that martial arts training would not decrease the chances of injuries in an attack. Instead the institute has advised women to struggle, cry hysterically, and pretend to faint, be sick, pregnant, or insane.[64] Combining the social indoctrination, prejudices, and sex-role stereotyping that all counsel passivity and nonviolent responses to rape and attack, it is no wonder than many women avoid or actively oppose firearms ownership even for personal defense.

Sexual stereotyping which discourages women from defending themselves can be and is deadly. Studies have shown that women who resist and fight back are less likely to be raped and harmed than those women who submit passively.[65]

Firearms and Public Policy

Some opponents of gun control might admit that firearm ownership could have prevented some of the tragic deaths discussed above yet they may nevertheless oppose the ownership of firearms in general because of their belief that firearm ownership increases the total level of violence in society. We must ask, therefore, whether self-defense through firearms is beneficial not only for battered women or women under imminent threat of violence but also for society as a whole.

Private firearm ownership in the United States is common and has been increasing over the last few decades. In 1973 Americans owned an approximate total of 122 million firearms, of which sidearms totaled 36.9 million. Twenty years later, in 1992, there were over 220 million firearms, 77.1 million of which were sidearms.[66] From 1973 to 1997 the number of civilian-owned sidearms increased by 160 percent.[67]

Who owns firearms? A 1988 CBS News General Election Exit Poll indicated just over 27 percent of voters stated they were firearm owners.[68] The 1996 Voter News Service National General Election Exit Poll obtained poll responses indicating that 37 percent of voters stated they were firearm owners. Firearm ownership in the United States is estimated at 39 percent of the population.[69] Others have estimated that 48 percent of American households admitted to firearm ownership.[70] Undoubtedly a large segment of the general population has access to firearms.

Figures on men and women owning firearms reveal some interesting trends:

- 1988: 40 percent of men and a bit more than 15 percent of women owned a firearm.
- 1996: more than 50 percent of men and nearly 30 percent of women owned a firearm.[71]

Firearm ownership rates among women doubled in less than a decade. Mary Zeiss Stange explains that self-defense is a major reason for the dramatic increase:

> Millions of women are purchasing and using firearms in huge numbers, for recreational shooting and hunting, as well as for self-defense. Women also comprise "one half of purely precautionary gun owners," i.e., those who own firearms solely for the purpose of self-protection.[72]

Stange estimates that of "the approximately sixty-five to eighty million gun owners in America today, by conservative estimate seventeen million are female." She suggests that "a far greater number than that have access to firearms owned by other members of the households."

Because so many women have rejected traditional roles and taken self-defense seriously and personally, "guns and gun control are, indeed, women's issues of ever-increasing importance." These facts, Stange says, divide the feminist movement because they run counter to "conventional" feminist ideology of victim disarmament:

> The above facts are liable to be unsettling to the majority of feminists who have tended to adhere to the conventional wisdom that to be feminist is to be antiviolence, and to be antiviolence is ipso facto to be antigun. Their argument surely has some merit; in the best of all possible worlds, women would not feel the need for lethal force to protect themselves or their children from abusers, known or unknown. However, in our violence-ridden society, most women have a legitimate reason to fear for their safety and the well-being of their loved ones.[73]

Opponents of the private possession and use of firearms for defense assert that greater numbers of firearms equate to more unlawful killings. Put another way, they claim any increase in firearms ownership results in an increase in murders.[74] The facts show otherwise: the overwhelming majority of firearm owners never hurt anyone with a firearm. Increasing the number of firearms available to peaceable, nonviolent citizens—the vast majority of citizens—will not convert those citizens into criminals.[75]

Homicide studies dating back to the nineteenth century show that murderers far from being normal people who "lost control" are extreme aberrants whose life histories feature prior felonies, irrational violence against those around them, substance abuse, and/or psychopathology. "The vast majority of persons involved in life-threatening violence have a long criminal record and many prior contacts with the justice system."[76] These facts appear in homicide studies so numerous and consistent that their findings "have now become criminological axioms" about the "basic characteristics of homicide."[77] In short, everyday people don't commit homicide—violent criminals do.[78]

A simple analysis of the rates of firearm ownership and murder rates in the United States also shows the fallacy of the "more guns, more murders" position. In the United States in 1973:

- Civilians owned approximately 122 million firearms total.
- Civilians owned 36.9 million sidearms.
- Homicide rate was 9.4 per 100,000 population.[79]

In the United States in 1992 (nearly twenty years later):

- Civilians owned over 220 million firearms total.
- Civilians owned 77.1 million sidearms.
- Homicide rate was 8.5 per 100,000.[80]

While firearms ownership rates increased substantially and the number of privately owned firearms nearly doubled, the homicide rate in 1992 was 10 percent lower than the 1973 rate. It is even lower today despite the fact that since 1992 the number of guns has probably increased. The homicide rate over this period rose and fell with no correlation with firearm ownership rates. Despite the increase in the number of firearms in this period, there was no correlation with homicide rates in general nor an increase in the percentage of murders committed specifically with firearms. In 1973 68.5 percent of all murders were committed with firearms. In 1992 the figure was 68.2 percent. Contrary to the "gun control" rhetoric, more guns do not equal more murders.

Simple comparisons between numbers of privately owned firearms and murders do not take into account all other factors that may affect the crime rate. Socio-economic status, rates of prosecution and incarceration, and even the state of the economy might all have some effect, whether positive or negative. When these other factors are taken into account, one finds that far from increasing levels of violent crime, increases in firearms ownership reduces crime.

Professor Hans Toch, of the School of Criminology at the State University of New York (Albany), was a key consultant to the 1968 Eisenhower Commission whose report called for reducing the availability of sidearms to private citizens. Hans Toch and Alan Lizotte, however, expressly disclaimed support for that report's "gun control" recommendation and explained why.

Toch observed that "where firearms [ownership rates] are most dense, violent crime rates are lowest, and where guns are least dense violent crime rates are highest." Research results had convinced him that *"when used for protection firearms can seriously inhibit aggression* and can provide a psychological buffer against the fear of crime."[81] Because national data patterns showed lower violent crime where guns ownership was most dense, Toch concluded that "guns do not elicit aggression in any meaningful way." In fact, Toch wrote, "these findings suggest that *high saturations of guns in places, or something correlated with that condition, inhibit illegal aggression.*"[82]

The Eisenhower Commission's staff report coordinator, Ted Robert Gurr, in 1989 updated the research findings bearing on the commission's recommendations. Gurr all but destroyed the "gun control equals crime control" argument when he wrote:

> Americans looking for simple solutions to high crime rates and to political assassinations have repeatedly proposed and sometimes imposed restrictions on gun ownership. Since about two-thirds of murders and all recent assassinations have been committed with guns, the argument goes, dry up the guns and violence will decline. [Research] . . . demonstrates the implausibility of the argument.
>
> . . . widespread gun ownership deters crime. Surveys sponsored by both pro- and anti-gun groups show that roughly three-quarters of a million private gun owning citizens report using weapons in self-defense [annually], while convicted robbers and burglars report that they are deterred when they think their potential targets are armed.[83]

Even when not a shot is fired, firearms powerfully deter criminal attackers. Gary Kleck has studied the defensive use of firearms, using crime data and analyzing other criminological studies.[84] His resulting 1991 book on firearm policy, *Point Blank: Guns and Violence in America*, received the American Society of Criminology's Hindelang Prize for the most significant contribution to criminology in a three-year period. Kleck found that victims who used firearms to defend against violent crime did not need to fire their guns to successfully defend themselves, avoid injury, and prevent crime. Kleck estimated that there are two to three million incidents each year of citizens using firearms in self-defense, basing that statistic on fifteen different surveys dating back as far as the late 1970s.[85]

Kleck's conclusions stimulated vigorous debate within the academic community. Even so, Marvin Wolfgang, who loudly proclaimed "I hate guns" and has strongly opposed private firearms ownership, had to admit Kleck's results on defensive firearm use were sound:

> I am as strong a gun control advocate as can be found among the criminologists in this country. . . . Nonetheless the methodological soundness of the current Kleck and Gertz study is clear. I cannot further debate it. . . . The Kleck and Gertz study impresses me for the caution the authors exercise and the elaborate nuances they examine methodologically. I do not like their conclusions that having a gun can be useful, but I cannot fault their methodology. They have tried earnestly to meet all objections in advance and have done exceedingly well.[86]

If Kleck's work were not enough to show the self-defense effectiveness of private firearms ownership, then John R. Lott's research finished the job. Lott reported an exhaustive study of effects of the laws enacted in over half of the states since 1976 that make it relatively easy for law-abiding adults to obtain a license to carry concealed sidearms.[87]

Lott expanded on his earlier work in which he and fellow researcher David Mustard correlated the year-by-year enactment of these laws with violence data for the years 1977–1994 from all 3,054 American counties.[88] Lott concluded that the issuance of millions of handgun concealed-carry licenses under these "shall-issue" laws has caused a reduction in violent crime.[89] This reduction has two components: halting crime in progress and deterring crime from happening. Lott demonstrated both. Lott estimated on average that the states which enacted the "shall-issue" concealed-carry laws:

- Reduced murder rates by 8.5 percent
- Reduced rape rates by 5 percent
- Reduced aggravated assault rates by 7 percent
- Reduced robbery rates by 3 percent[90]

Lott's finding that criminals are deterred by the risk that their victims might be armed found support in two independent studies conducted under the auspices of the National Institute of Justice. By surveying two thousand felons incarcerated in several state prisons across the United States, one study reported:

- 34 percent of the felons responded that they personally had been "scared off, shot at, wounded, or captured by an armed victim";
- 69 percent knew at least one other felon who had the same experience;
- 34 percent said that when thinking about committing a crime they either "often" or "regularly" worried that they "might get shot at by the victim";
- 74 percent agreed that one reason "burglars avoid houses when people are home is that they fear being shot"; and
- 57 percent agreed that "most criminals are more worried about meeting an armed victim than they are about running into the police."[91]

A second National Institute of Justice study surveyed juveniles in correctional facilities in California, Illinois, Louisiana, and New Jersey. From the respondents that study found:

- 36 percent had decided at least "a few times" not to commit a crime because they believed the potential victim was armed.
- 70 percent had been "scared off, shot at, wounded, or captured by an armed crime victim."[92]

What the research shows, and what incarcerated criminals know, is that the firearm is an effective means of self-defense. Accordingly there is good reason to believe that potential victims of domestic violence, most of whom are women, could use firearms defensively to stop or prevent such violence.

Solid research shows that private ownership of firearms can effectively deter violent criminals, including domestic abusers. Yet gun prohibition advocates, such as the Educational Fund to End Handgun Violence and the National Network to End Domestic Violence, steadfastly claim that domestic violence victims and other crime victims should not use firearms for protection. These advocates have claimed, for example, that "domestic homicides are 7.8 times more likely to occur in homes with guns than homes without," basing their claim on a paper by Arthur Kellermann.[93] Kellerman never makes that statement. The "7.8" number comes from a statistical "odds ratio" that by no means describes or predicts reality anywhere outside of the study data.

Kellermann's paper offered only the general conclusion that "rather than confer protection, guns kept in the home are associated with an increase in the risk of homicide by a family member or intimate acquaintance."[94] Even that conclusion is flawed for several reasons, including:

- Kellermann's study did not report even a single case of the homicide victim being killed by the firearm that was actually kept in the residence.
- The study did not evaluate how often firearms were used to deter a crime without firing a shot.
- The study expressly excluded all cases where the resident shot an intruder.
- The study offered no information about whether the homicide victims tried to obtain their defensive firearms or even knew where those firearms were in the house.
- The study misused epidemiological methods to conclude that just being in a home where a firearm exists means the occupant is "exposed" to a death-causing agent, akin to being exposed to malaria-carrying mosquitoes or atomic radiation.[95]

Kellermann also failed to consider the women's issues. When a woman is murdered it is usually by a man she knows, generally an intimate partner. The man who kills a woman is generally a person with a life history of violence, particularly against the murdered woman, and of prior felonies, substance abuse, or psychopathology. But when a woman kills a man, she is usually not a habitual criminal. Usually she is acting in self-defense:

> Thus, the fifty percent of interspousal homicides in which husbands kill wives are real murders, but in the overwhelming majority of cases where wives kill husbands, they are defending themselves or their children. In Detroit, for instance, husbands are killed by wives more often than wives are by husbands, yet the men are convicted far more often. In fact, three-quarters of wives who killed their husbands were not even charged, prosecutors having found their acts lawful and necessary to preserve their lives or their children's.[96]

Larish observes that "unlike men, women use guns primarily for defensive purposes—most often as a last resort."[97] Firearms used to stop or prevent domestic abuse crime do not impose costs but actually confer benefits upon society:

> It is . . . tragic when . . . an abused woman has to shoot to stop a current or former boyfriend or husband from beating her to death. Still, it is highly misleading to count such incidents as costs of gun ownership by misclassifying them with the very

thing they prevent: murder between "family and friends" . . . [Such deaths] are not costs. Rather they are palpable benefits of defensive gun ownership from society's and the victims' point of view.[98]

Kellermann does not account for women's use of firearms in the home for self-defense in abuse situations. Kellermann's study implicitly adopts the idea that defending women's lives counts as a cost of firearms owner-ship rather than as a benefit—a view that devalues women. Women at risk reap sizeable benefits from defensive firearms use: over 550 times per day, women use guns to protect themselves against sexual assault.[99] That figure is nearly twice the number of rapes per day.

Arguments for "Gun Control" Play On Sex-role Stereotypes

Some arguments for "gun control" and against armed self-defense play di-rectly on sex-role stereotypes of women. One argument suggests that using a sidearm requires a lot of training, so that the sidearm is more dangerous to the average citizen than it is a deterrent to the criminal. Private citizens generally lack the ability to make the split-second decisions necessary in a stressful situation. Therefore, the argument goes, only the police and mili-tary should have sidearms.[100]

This argument emphasizes incompetence and lack of training as rea-sons not to be armed. Between the two sexes, women are more likely to be considered incompetent and untrained with firearms. Some women also may tend to view themselves as incompetent and physically weak. This ar-gument works most powerfully to discourage women from learning about and using defensive firearms. The argument suggests leaving the job of protecting women to the men (typically) in uniform who are experts. Yet Lee J. Hicks found that civilian women with two hours of instruction could learn to shoot a sidearm as accurately as police academy cadets in simulated real-life situations.[101]

Another argument raises fears of gun "take-away." That argument as-serts that a criminal can wrest a gun out of the hands of the physically weaker woman. The armed woman can too easily be converted into an un-armed woman at the mercy of a now-armed attacker. The statistics that back this argument come from the cases where police officers in the line of duty had lost their guns to criminals. Because of the risk of a "take-away," the argument goes, woman should not carry sidearms for de-fense.[102]

This argument succeeds with women and men who accept the stereo-type of women as the weaker and incompetent sex. Because the argument is based on police "take-away" statistics it makes a faulty analogy. Police officers must approach, subdue, and take suspects into custody. The officers must therefore come close enough for the suspects to be able to grab the firearm. Personal- and home-defense situations are much different; they do not require the defender to get close to the attacker. Quite the opposite is true: the defender wants to keep the attacker at a distance and that requires no special physical strength except to operate the firearm. A woman strong enough to shoot her sidearm is strong enough to keep an attacker out of reach of her gun.[103]

Women can profit by learning martial arts for protection and to develop self-confidence but unarmed defense techniques have a limited usefulness. In unarmed combat the woman must physically hurt her assailant which means coming close enough to get hurt herself. Against multiple or armed assailants, even the unarmed martial arts expert faces serious disadvantages.[104]

To gain the equal or superior force necessary to deter or stop an attacker, a woman must have a suitable weapon such as a sidearm. "Gun control" laws, however, work directly against firearms ownership, possession, and use, even for defense.

Gun control laws discourage private self-defense by causing firearms ownership and use to be:

- More costly (via higher prices, fees, taxes, travel expenses)
- More inconvenient (via waiting periods, bureaucratic forms and delays, mandatory certifications, "safety devices" that hobble the user from carrying or quickly deploying a defensive sidearm, fewer practice facilities placed in more remote areas)
- More embarrassing or humiliating (via social stigma, fingerprinting and registration, being subject to inspections, being treated like a criminal)
- More legally risky (via potential criminal, civil, and administrative liability for paperwork violations, criminals stealing and misusing guns, accidents caused by others)[105]

The greater the cost, inconvenience, embarrassment, or risk in any activity, the less will people want to do it.[106] When "gun controls" impede firearms ownership, they decrease the number of women who will go to the trouble of getting a firearm for defense. "Waiting periods," for example, ostensibly designed to allow angry people to "cool off" before buying a firearm, can place domestic abuse victims in greater danger.

Sayoko Blodgett-Ford recounts the story of a California woman whose husband shattered her jaw while she held their baby. After she had her jaw rebuilt in a hospital, she tried to press charges against the man but police and county mental health workers persuaded her not to do so because the husband had promised to get counseling. After two sessions even the counselor refused to meet with the husband because of death threats.

The woman obtained a protective order but it did not prevent the estranged husband from prowling around her house, sleeping in her yard, and calling her constantly by phone. When the police refused to arrest the man for violating the restraining order, the woman tried to buy a sidearm. While she was waiting the fifteen days required by California law before picking up the gun, the husband repeatedly assaulted her at home and at work.

The waiting period harmed the woman by requiring that she remain unarmed while she suffered repeated abuse. Once she obtained the sidearm and the abuser knew she was armed, the assaults stopped. The abuser did continue lesser insults against her, such as stealing her mail and harassing her by telephone, but the physical attacks were deterred.

Permit and license requirements, like waiting periods, impose legal delays on a potential victim's obtaining a defensive sidearm.[107] In states where government agencies have discretion to deny permits or licenses, the delay can be indefinite. Even if a permit is granted, the delays can be substantial, ranging into the weeks and months. During that time the victim may have to endure continued stalking, harassment, threats, and violence from an abuser.[108]

Noting that using sidearms for self-defense results in fewer injuries to the defender than using other techniques, one feminist criticized gun prohibition by identifying women as the "losers":

> If the state banned all guns, women would lose because they could not physically fight off men and the viability of alternate methods of self-defense is questionable. . . . Men would lose only to the extent that a complete gun ban is virtually impossible; and criminals would still have access to guns.[109]

Meanwhile, violent men are the "winners" under gun prohibition:

> But men who perpetuate violent crime against women—rape and assault, especially—would greatly benefit from civilian gun bans. Women who previously had the option of legally possessing guns would have to choose between committing the crime of possessing a gun and self-defense. . . . Even with high degrees of self-defense combat training, women have a definite disadvan-

tage [against men] in street fights. More insidiously, society would send women the message that they should not use force to defend themselves. . . . [110]

To decide whether to support or oppose the private ownership of firearms, individualist feminists should consider the options for self-defense, particularly in the case of domestic violence. The data, logic, and human experience all show that potential crime victims in imminent danger of violence are better protected by individual self-defense options than by government laws and centralized police response. Individual women in peril quite frequently fare better when they develop skill and confidence in the carrying and use of defensive firearms. Victim disarmament ("gun control") laws that discourage women from developing the skills and using defensive firearms actually heighten the risks of criminal violence that women face. Such laws place women at a disadvantage against violent men and run against the feminist goal of equal treatment of the sexes under law.[111]

Notes

1. Anita K. Blair, former president of the Independent Women's Forum (www.iwf.org), and Timothy Wheeler, director of Doctors for Responsible Gun Ownership (www.claremont.org), also contributed to this chapter. Material for this chapter was drawn in part from the Brief Amici Curiae of the Independent Women's Forum and the Doctors for Responsible Gun Ownership in Support of Defendant Appellee Timothy Joe Emerson, filed in the United States Court of Appeals for the Fifth Circuit, *United States v. Emerson*, Case No. 99-10331 ("The Emerson Brief Amici Curiae") (December 20, 1999). The authors gratefully acknowledge and thank C. B. Kates and Dr. Alexander Tabarrok, research director at the Independent Institute, for commenting on the text and for providing many research suggestions and materials. The views expressed in this chapter are those of the authors and do not necessarily represent the views of any affiliated organizations.

2. Wendy McElroy, Introduction to *Individualist Feminism* (2000). Available at www.zetetics.com/mac/indfem1.htm.

3. Data in this section were extracted from John R. Lott, *More Guns, Less Crime* 2nd ed. (Chicago, 2000), 40, 43–45, 47 (citing the Federal Bureau of Investigation's Uniform Crime Reports), from Bureau of Justice Statistics, *Criminal Victimization in the United States—1998 Statistical Tables*, May 2000, and from Bureau of Justice Statistics, *Homicide Trends in the United States*, February 2000.

4. Bureau of Justice Statistics, *Criminal Victimization*, showed a recent decline in these statistics, reporting 31 million criminal victimizations of all types in 1998, a decrease from about 44 million in 1973. Crime rates had been steadily increasing from the mid-1960s through the 1970s.

5. Data for 1998 from Bureau of Justice Statistics, *Homicide Trends*, shows the homicide rate of females dropped from 4.2 per 100,000 to 3.0 per 100,000.

6. Data extracted from Federal Bureau of Investigation, Uniform Crime Reports for the United States 1997, 1998, 9, 12, 19, 22.

7. Bureau of Justice Statistics, 1993, 102 and Bureau of Justice Statistics, *Criminal Victimization*.

8. Inge Anna Larish, "Why Annie Can't Get Her Gun: A Feminist Perspective on the Second Amendment," *University of Illinois Law Review* no. 2 (1996), 468–470.

9. We take the term "domestic violence" to connote physical abuse although some feminists use the term to include verbal abuse as well, including arguing, raising one's voice, or not speaking to an intimate partner. See R. Burri Flowers, "The Problem of Domestic Violence is Widespread," in Karin L. Swisher, ed., *Domestic Violence* (San Diego, 1996), 10, 15. The statistics use the term "intimate partner" to include a current or former spouse, boyfriend, or girlfriend (Bureau of Justice Statistics *Intimate Partner Violence* 2000, 2, 8).

10. Bureau of Justice Statistics, *National Crime Victimization Survey*, 1994 and *Intimate Partner Violence*, 7.

11. Data presented here are taken from Bureau of Justice Statistics *Intimate Partner Violence*, *Violence by Intimates*, 1998, and *Homicide Trends* (Intimate Homicides). These data may understate domestic violence against men, however. See National Family Violence Survey, 1985 and Murray A. Straus and Richard J. Gelles, *Physical Violence in American Families: Risk Factors and Adaptations to Violence in 8,145 American Families* (New Brunswick, N.J., 1990), 97–98.

12. Robert Cobb, "Nine-one-one: Three Little Words, Three Big Issues," *American City and County* 111 (June 1996), 48.

13. Tom Gray and Verdette Hall, "FCC Docket 94-102: Its Implications for 911 Calls and Public Safety," *Public Management* 81 (June 1999), 6–12.

14. Gordon Witkin, Monika Guttman, and Tracy Lenzy, "This is 911 . . . please hold," *U.S. News & World Report* 120, (June 17, 1996), 30.

15. *Ibid*.

16. Bureau of Justice Statistics, *Violence by Intimates*, 20 and Larish, "Why Annie," 473, 488.

17. Witkin, "This is 911," 30, quoting the conclusions of the researchers, Northeastern University Professor George Kelling and lawyer Catherine Coles.

18. Michael Cooper, "Police Are Criticized for Responding More Slowly to 911 Calls," *New York Times* late edition, September 24, 1999—Average police response time increased from 9.8 minutes in 1998 to 10.3 minutes in 1999; Tom Zoellner, "911 System Fails Second Time in 2 Days," *San Francisco Chronicle* final edition, May 2, 2000—System "completely dead" for an hour, repaired in 4 hours; Paula Chin, "Calls For Help," *People Weekly* 53 (April 10, 2000), 181–184—Bottleneck in 911 system, police took 40 minutes to respond to 15 frantic calls about gang attack resulting in death.

19. Richard W. Stevens, *Dial 911 and Die: The Shocking Truth About The Police Protection Myth* (Hartford, Wisc., 1999).

20. Sayoko Blodgett-Ford, "Do Battered Women Have A Right to Bear Arms?" *Yale Law & Policy Review* 11 (1993), 509–560. Blodgett-Ford explains that domestic abusers typically try to control and dominate the woman in the relationship. Often the abuser will try to prevent the woman from leaving him by force, and if she leaves, he will retaliate against her or force her to return. This behavior is called "separation assault." Researchers found that "killings of wives by husbands most often were triggered by a walkout, a demand, a threat of separation" which the men take as "intolerable deser-

tion, rejection and abandonment." Over 50 percent of the women who leave their abusive spouses are stalked, harassed, or attacked by those spouses. Battered women "often face a dramatically increased risk of being killed or seriously injured by their abusers after they attempt to escape" (Blodgett-Ford, "Battered Women," 529–530, n. 118).

21. *Hartzler v. City of San Jose,* 120 Cal. Rptr. 5 (Cal. App. 1975).

22. *Ibid.,* 6.

23. California Government Code § 845 states that "neither a public entity nor a public employee is liable for failure to establish a police department or otherwise provide police protection service or . . . for failure to provide sufficient police protection service."

24. *Warren v. District of Columbia,* 444 A.2d 1 (D.C. 1981).

25. *Ibid.,* 4.

26. *Ibid.*

27. Stevens, *Dial 911,* collects statutes and case law from fifty-three American jurisdictions and Canada, nearly all of which follow this rule. See *Ford v. Town of Grafton,* 693 N.E.2d 1047 (Mass. App. 1998), 1054 and *Barillari v. City of Milwaukee,* 533 N.W.2d 759 (Wisc. 1995), 763.

28. *DeShaney v. Winnebago County Department of Social Services,* 489 U.S. 189 (1989).

29. *Bowers v. DeVito,* 686 F.2d 616 (7th Cir. 1982).

30. Larish, "Why Annie," 473 n. 37, observes that although there have been improvements, "police response to domestic violence calls is still for the most part inadequate."

31. Frerica L. Lehrman, *Domestic Violence Practice and Procedure* (St. Paul, Minn., 1997), 4-3, 4-20, 4-21.

32. See District of Columbia Code title 16, § 1005.

33. In many localities a court can issue a temporary restraining order immediately if a complaining party shows that he or she faces immediate danger from the alleged perpetrator—based on the testimony of the complaining party alone (Lehrman, *Domestic Violence,* 4-4, 4-19). See District of Columbia Code title 16, § 1004(d) and Code of Virginia vol. 4A, § 19.2–152.10. Under the law of some states, the alleged perpetrator can lose the legal right to possess a firearm for the duration of the temporary restraining order. See Code of Virginia vol 4, § 18.2–308.1:4, 1999 supplement.

34. Elizabeth Topliffe, "Why Civil Protection Orders Are Effective Remedies for Domestic Violence But Mutual Protective Orders Are Not," *Indiana Law Journal* 67 (Fall 1992), 1054–1056. The Massachusetts Attorney General has expressly recognized the problem with mutual restraining orders. Massachusetts Attorney General's Office, "Report On Domestic Violence: A Commitment To Action," *New England Law Review* 28 (Winter 1993), 334.

35. Topliffe, "Civil Protection," 1055–1056.

36. Cathy Young, "Hitting Below the Belt," *Salon* (1999). Available at www.salon.com/mwt/feature/1999/10/25/restraining_orders/print.html. Ed Lederman, "A Tangled Web: Restraining Orders, Domestic Violence and Hard Wired Therapy," Issue Paper No. 9-99 (Denver, 1999).

37. Lehrman, *Domestic Violence,* 4-36, 4-37.

38. Straus, *Physical Violence,* 97–98.

39. In 1998 there were 937,490 female victims of domestic abuse (actual, attempted, or threatened violence) and 144,620 male victims of abuse. While 471,110 female victims of domestic abuse suffered injuries, only 47,000 male victims of

such abuse were actually injured (Bureau of Justice Statistics, *Intimate Partner Violence*, 6).

40. Witkin, "This is 911," 30.

41. Section 922(g)(8) was declared unconstitutional by a federal district court judge in *United States v. Emerson*, 610–611. That decision was recently (2001) reversed by the United States Court of Appeals for the Fifth Circuit.

42. Additional discussion of Section 922(g)(8) and its impact on domestic abuse victims is found in Nelson Lund, "The Ends of Second Amendment Jurisprudence: Firearms Disabilities and Domestic Violence Restraining Orders," *Texas Review of Law and Policy* 4 (1999), 157–191. Available at www.2ndlawlib.org.

43. Nancy Nordell, "When Restraining Orders Don't Work," *Women and Guns* (Nov./Dec. 1998).

44. *The Talmud, Tractate Sanhedrin* Schottenstein ed. (New York, 1994), 2, 72a and *Babylonian Talmud: Tractate Berakoth* (London, 1990), 58a, 62b.

45. *Catechism of the Catholic Church* (1994), §§ 2263–2265—citing and quoting Thomas Aquinas; Samuel Rutherford, *Lex, Rex, or The Law and The Prince* (Harrisonburg, Va., 1982), 159–166, 183–185—stating the similar Protestant view; Brendan F. Furnish and Dwight H. Small, *The Mounting Threat of Home Intruders: Weighing the Moral Option of Armed Self-Defense* (Springfield, Ill., 1993)—Christianity-based survey of the morality of armed self-defense, including women's self-defense.

46. *Catechism of the Catholic Church*, § 2264.

47. William Meyerhofer, "Statutory Restrictions on Weapons Possession: Must the Right to Self-Defense Fall Victim?" *1996 Annual Survey of American Law*, 1996, 219, 226. Meyerhofer states that the right to self-defense has been recognized in law since at least the sixteenth century. Don B. Kates, "Handgun Prohibition and the Original Meaning of the Second Amendment," *Michigan Law Review* 82 (1983), 231–233, lists and cites Aristotle, Cicero, Machiavelli, Sir Thomas More, Thomas Hobbes, Algernon Sidney, Rousseau, Blackstone, Montesquieu, and Cesare Beccaria. Stephen P. Halbrook, *That Every Man Be Armed: The Evolution of a Constitutional Right* (Oakland, 1984), 7–54, quotes and cites classical, English, and other authorities affirming the right to defense with arms. Don. B. Kates, "The Second Amendment and the Ideology of Self-Protection," *Constitutional Commentary* 9 (1992), 87–104, concisely shows the legal and moral basis of self-defense as understood at the time the Second Amendment was drafted and ratified.

48. See Samuel C. Wheeler, "Self-Defense Rights and Coerced Risk-Acceptance," *Public Affairs Quarterly* 11, no. 4 (October 1997), 431–443. Applying an informal "law and economics" analysis, Wheeler finds that the restrictions on the right of self-defense impose social costs that exceed social benefits.

49. Murray Rothbard, *For A New Liberty* (New York, 1973), 128.

50. Ayn Rand, *The Virtue of Selfishness* (New York, 1964), 108.

51. Blodgett-Ford, "Battered Women," 534.

52. Robert L. Barrow, "Women with Attitude: Self Protection, Policy, and the Law," *Thomas Jefferson Law Review* 21:1 (1999), 59–101.

53. *Ibid.*, 71–72.

54. Blodgett-Ford, "Battered Women," 534, n. 142.

55. Gary Kleck and Marc Gertz, "Armed Resistance to Crime: The Prevalence and Nature of Self-Defense with a Gun," *Journal of Criminal Law & Criminology* 86 (Fall 1995), 173, 185.

56. Larish, "Why Annie," 494.

57. *Ibid.*, 503 and Blodgett-Ford, "Battered Women," 534.

58. Barrow, "Women with Attitude," 67–68.

59. Larish, "Why Annie," 498–506, argues that the common law of self-defense does not fairly and adequately protect women's rights to use force to deter or stop domestic violence.

60. Blodgett-Ford, "Battered Women," 553.

61. Ibid.

62. Barrow, "Women with Attitude," 67.

63. Ibid.

64. Barrow, "Women with Attitude," 66.

65. Ibid., 67 and U.S. Department of Justice, Law Enforcement Assistance Administration, Rape Victimization in 26 American Cities (Washington, D.C., 1979), 131.

66. Gary Kleck, Targeting Guns: Firearms And Their Control (New York, 1997), 96–97.

67. See Don B. Kates and Daniel D. Polsby, "Long-Term Nonrelationship of Widespread and Increasing Firearm Availability to Homicide in the United States," Homicide Studies 4 (May 2000), 190–191. The article describes the constantly increasing supply of civilian-owned firearms in comparison to the increasing population and variations in homicide rates, citing Kleck, Targeting Guns.

68. Lott, More Guns.

69. Ibid., 36–37 and n. 2.

70. David B. Kopel, The Samurai, the Mountie, and the Cowboy (Buffalo, N.Y., 1992), 109 n. 15, citing Martin Killias, "Gun Ownership and Violent Crime: The Swiss Experience in International Perspective," Security Journal 1, no. 4 (1990), 171. Kopel states "Killias's results are consistent with surveys by Gallup, Harris, and others."

71. Lott, More Guns, 37, fig. 3.1. United States Department of Justice, Research in Brief—Guns in America: National Survey on Private Ownership and Use of Firearms (Washington, D.C., 1995), 2–3, states however that only 9 percent of women and 42 percent of men own firearms. The difference between the Justice Department survey and other studies may be due to the reluctance of some survey respondents to tell the federal government about their possession of firearms. Differences in definition of "ownership" will also affect survey rates. One survey may record that a husband and wife both "own" the same gun; another survey may record only the husband as the owner, since he was the purchaser of record.

72. Mary Zeiss Stange, "Arms and the Woman: A Feminist Reappraisal," in David Kopel, ed., Guns—Who Should Have Them (Amherst, N.Y., 1995), 16.

73. Ibid.

74. National Network to End Domestic Violence, et al., Brief for Amici Curiae submitted in United States v. Emerson (1999), 9.

75. In an unpublished manuscript entitled The Myth of the Virgin Killer: Law-abiding Persons Who Kill in a Fit of Rage, authors Don B. Kates and Daniel D. Polsby show that murder is rarely committed by otherwise law-abiding citizens.

76. Delbert S. Elliott, "Life Threatening Violence is Primarily a Crime Problem: A Focus on Prevention," University of Colorado Law Review 69 (Fall 1998), 1093. Elliott states: "For the vast majority of persons who become involved in life-threatening violence, this behavior is embedded in a pattern of criminal behavior, most frequently beginning in early childhood or adolescence" (1097).

77. David Kennedy and Anthony Braga, "Homicide in Minneapolis: Research for Problem Solving," Homicide Studies 2 (1998), 267.

78. See Kates, "Longterm Nonrelationship," 19. The article develops this point with additional citations.

79. Data from 1973 extracted from Bureau of Justice Statistics, Sourcebook Of Criminal Justice Statistics—1989 (Washington, D.C., 1989), 365, table 3.118. See Kates,

"Longterm Nonrelationship," 189–192, showing lack of correlation between firearms availability and homicide rates.

80. Data from 1992 and comparisons from Randy E. Barnett and Don B. Kates, "Under Fire: The New Consensus on the Second Amendment," *Emory Law Journal* 45 (Fall 1996), 1249.

81. Hans Toch and Alan Lizotte, "Research and Policy: The Case of Gun Control," in Peter Suedfeld and Philip E. Tetlock, eds., *Psychology and Social Policy* (New York, 1992).

82. *Ibid.*, 232, 234.

83. Ted Robert Gurr, ed., *Violence In America* 1 (Newbury Park, Calif., 1989), 17–18.

84. Gary Kleck, "Crime Control Through the Private Use of Armed Force," *Social Problems* 35 (February 1988), 1–21.

85. Gary Kleck, *Point Blank: Guns And Violence In America* (New York, 1991) and Kleck, *Targeting Guns*.

86. The study in question: Kleck, "Armed Resistance." Marvin E. Wolfgang, "A Tribute to a View I Have Opposed," *Journal of Criminal Law & Criminology* 86 (Fall 1995), 188–192.

87. Lott, *More Guns*.

88. See John R. Lott and David Mustard, "Crime, Deterrence, and Right-to-Carry Concealed Handguns Laws," *Journal of Legal Studies* 26 (January 1997), 1–68.

89. Lott, *More Guns*, 114–115.

90. John R. Lott, Jr., "More Guns, Less Violent Crime," *Wall Street Journal*, August 28, 1996, summarizing research findings.

91. Data extracted from James D. Wright and Peter Rossi, *Armed and Considered Dangerous: A Survey of Felons and Their Firearms* (New York, 1986), 145, 150, 154, and table 7.1.

92. Data extracted from Joseph Sheley and James D. Wright, *In The Line Of Fire: Youth, Guns And Violence in Urban America* (New York, 1995), 63.

93. Arthur Kellermann, et al., "Gun Ownership as a Risk Factor for Homicide in the Home," *New England Journal of Medicine* 329 (October 7, 1993), 1084–1091.

94. *Ibid.*, 1084.

95. See analysis of these and other flaws in the Kellermann study and other "public health" studies in Richard W. Stevens, "Disarming the Data Doctors: How to Debunk the 'Public Health' Argument for 'Gun Control,'" *Firearms Sentinel*, Winter 1997, 2–6; Don B. Kates, et al., "Guns and Public Health: Epidemic of Violence or Pandemic of Propaganda?" *Tennessee Law Review* 62 (1995), 583–595, and Edgar A. Suter, "Guns in the Medical Literature—A Failure of Peer Review," *Journal of the Medical Association of Georgia* 83 (March 1994), 133–146.

96. Don B. Kates, "The Value of Civilian Arms Possession as Deterrent to Crime or Defense Against Crime," *American Journal of Criminal Law* 18 (Winter 1991), 128–129.

97. Larish, "Why Annie," 473, 494–495.

98. Kates, "Value of Civilian," 128–129.

99. Kleck, "Armed Resistance," 185.

100. Barrow, "Women with Attitude," 90.

101. Lee J. Hicks, "Point Gun, Pull Trigger," *Police Chief* (May 1975), 52–55.

102. Barrow, "Women with Attitude," 93.

103. *Ibid.*

104. *Ibid.*, 70–71.

105. For additional discussion about the disincentives of "gun control" and "gun

safety devices," see articles collected at www.jpfo.org, such as "Dead Batteries Make Dead People: The Truth About Restricted-use Firearms and Trigger Locks," and "There is No Such Thing as a Reasonable 'Gun Control' Law." Don B. Kates, *Guns, Murders and the Constitution: A Realistic Assessment of Gun Control* (San Francisco, 1990), examines nearly every facet of the "gun control" debate, including women's issues and self-defense, and provides extensive footnote citations.

106. Paul Heyne and Thomas Johnson, *Toward Understanding Micro-Economics* (Chicago, 1976), 16–17.

107. Based upon their original research, two "gun control" advocates reluctantly admitted that the 1994 federal law requiring states to institute background checks and waiting periods for all sidearm purchases from licensed dealers ("Brady Handgun Violence Prevention Act," Public Law No. 103-159, 107 Stat. 1536), did not reduce overall homicide or suicide rates in the states where the law applied (Jens Ludig and Philip J. Cook, "Homicide and Suicide Rates Associated with Implementation of the Brady Handgun Violence Prevention Act," *JAMA* 284 (August 2, 2000), 585).

108. Blodgett-Ford, "Battered Women," 546–547.

109. Larish, "Why Annie," 504–505

110. Larish, "Why Annie," 505.

111. For an opposing view, see Alana Bassin, "Why Packing a Pistol Perpetuates Patriarchy," *Hastings Women's Law Journal* 8 (Fall 1997), 363, which concludes: "Regardless of the means, as a matter of public policy, women need to take a stand in preventing gun use in society. Contrary to patriarchal rhetoric, packing a pistol is not powerful—it is lethal. For both women and society, a better society is an unarmed society."

WOMEN
and
TECHNOLOGY

Wendy McElroy

❦

Breeder Reactionaries

The "Feminist" War on
New Reproductive Technologies

"59-Year-Old Woman Gives Birth to Twins on Christmas Day!"
Although it reads like one, that is not a headline from the *National Enquirer*. In early 1994 reputable newspapers around the globe rushed to report that a fifty-nine-year-old British businesswoman had produced two healthy children from donated eggs which had been implanted in her uterus. She was soon overshadowed by a pregnant sixty-two-year-old Italian woman who wanted a baby to replace her only child, a son who had died in an accident.

Then a black woman gave birth to a white baby and the world confronted a host of new questions: Should parents be allowed to choose the race of their children? Or the sex? Should "designer" babies be encouraged? Or should the new reproductive technologies that allow such possibilities be banned, as several European nations are now attempting to do?

The controversial procedures causing such a flap encompass a number of fully achieved technologies as well as some still in the development stages. They include: sperm donation, by which a woman is impregnated with sperm from someone other than her partner; egg donation, by which one woman conceives with an egg donated by another; sperm and egg freezing; embryo adoption, by which a donated egg and sperm are cultured into an embryo; embryo freezing; and embryo screening. The world has certainly come a long way since 1978 when Louise Brown became the first test-tube baby.

The main appeal of reproductive technologies is that they give people more choices and more flexibility in a domain previously ruled by biological chance and limits. And, sensational headlines notwithstanding, the typical beneficiaries of reproductive technologies are individuals in their child-bearing years. Still, the proliferation of new options means that the social implications of the new reproductive technologies are staggering. Essentially women can reset their biological clocks at will. Instead of having children during their peak career years, women can wait until retirement to raise a family. A single infant can now have more than two parents, all of whom might die of old age before he or she begins to teethe. If recent experiments on mice are an indication of things to come, a woman could abort a female fetus and, using its ovaries and eggs, later give birth to her own grandchild.

The prospect of such a reproduction revolution raises important and vexing ethical questions. For example, with two possible sets of "parents," how should the courts adjudicate custody claims? What will prevent governments from commandeering this science to produce "better" citizens? Will women be pressured to abort "defective" fetuses? Who will define a defect?

Because they often utilize donors and surrogates, the new reproductive technologies also raise many serious questions about individual rights and contract law. Does a donor or a surrogate have any rights beyond sharply delimited contractual obligations? Is it possible to contract out motherhood—or fatherhood—itself? Congress and the courts have begun to address these questions and, if 1987's "Baby M" case is any indication, the final answers are certain to be long and hard in coming.

These are the types of questions that will alter the reproduction debate in the next decade. They promise to alter reproduction itself. Women can now choose to have children when, where, and with whomever they want.

Such fundamental change inevitably inspires champions and detractors and, in the cacophony surrounding the new reproductive technologies, one would think feminists would be among the staunchest advocates for freeing a woman's body from the restrictions of nature. This, after all, has been one of the main goals of the feminist movement since its inception. As Shulamith Firestone wrote in the 1970 feminist classic, *The Dialectic of Sex: The Case For Feminist Revolution*, "The first demand for any alternative system must be. . . . The freeing of women from the tyranny of their reproductive biology by every means available."

The new reproductive technologies, like effective contraception and access to legal abortion, seem to provide women with the "choice" central to virtually all brands of feminism. So are they not part and parcel of the "reproductive freedom" that was so hotly contested at the United Nations'

International Conference on Population and Development held in Cairo? One would think only the pope and other reproductive traditionalists could be critical of such technologies. And one would think feminists would shout with joy now that their long-time rallying cry—"a woman's body, a woman's right"—is on the verge of fulfillment.

When high-profile feminists have commented on the topic at all, they have been outspoken in their attacks on new reproductive technologies ranging from innovations in birth-control methods to refinements of in vitro techniques. Consider the words of Janice Raymond, professor of women's studies at the University of Massachusetts and author of *Women as Wombs*. Raymond disparages the technologies as "reproductive abuse," a product of the "spermatic economy of sex and breeding" or "spermocracy," and "medicalized pornography."

This rejection has nothing to do with the ethical questions posed above. Critics such as Raymond are radical feminists who consider men and women to be separate political classes, with interests that dramatically—and necessarily—conflict. Within the radical feminist ideological belief system, anything developed within the "patriarchy"—the "seamless web of male oppression" that radical feminists say characterizes our world— must be condemned, regardless of the apparent benefits for women.

The radical feminists sometimes call themselves "post-Marxists," but it is not clear just how far they have moved past Marx—or Engels, for that matter. Like Marx, they tend to single out capitalism as a particularly exploitive system and, like Engels, they see it as the root of all gender injustice. More important, radical feminists rely on a Marxist "base/ superstructure model" of analysis. In traditional Marxist analysis, a particular economic base (i.e., capitalism) creates a particular superstructure or culture which simultaneously camouflages and perpetuates the economic base. The process is subtle enough that people within the system do not even understand they are part of it, much less being exploited by it. That is why workers need to be organized; "class consciousness" is suppressed by the superstructure. And because the superstructure is determined by the base, any attempt to alter the superstructure without fundamentally changing the base is meaningless. Hence, raises in wages and benefits may seem progressive but, because they placate workers, actually help to shore up an evil system.

Radical feminists have taken this basic argument and substituted gender relations for economic ones. In place of capitalism, there is patriarchy (of which, it should be noted, capitalism is a manifestation); in place of class exploitation, there is gender exploitation. Developments apparently benefiting women—such as longer lifespans, birth-control pills, increased access to property, wealth, and education—actually maintain the patriarchal status quo.

Patriarchy, say the radical feminists, is a cancer rooted so deeply in our culture that even the language with which we speak and think reinforces male dominance: The word *history* rather than *herstory* is merely one obvious example among many. For radical feminists, then, the new reproductive technologies are particularly abhorrent for two reasons. First, they are a creation of a "male science" which seeks to dominate nature rather than remain open to it. Already convinced that the medical establishment is out to control women, radical feminists insist that the new, ostensibly liberating procedures are actually another attempt to exploit female reproductive functions and turn women into baby factories under male management. Second, the legal grounds on which the new reproductive technologies will be implemented stand on notions of individual rights, enlightened self-interest, and contract law—all of which radical feminists see as extensions of an inherently exploitive capitalist system.

The above arguments may sound absurd and contradictory. But because radical feminists are almost the only women in the feminist movement currently discussing the implications of the new reproductive technologies, they enjoy tremendous influence over the terms of debate. At the university level, they often chair women's studies programs and occupy administrative positions. Radical feminists are also defining the terms of the reproductive debate outside the academy. The shelves of libraries and bookstores are stocked with radical feminist works from major publishers, all of which argue against new reproductive technologies. These include: *Living Laboratories* by Robyn Rowland; *The Mother Machine* by Gena Corea; *The Politics of Reproduction* by Mary O'Brien; and such anthologies as *Made to Order: The Myth of Reproductive and Genetic Progress*; *Man-Made Women: How the New Reproductive Technologies Affect Women*; and *Test Tube Women*.

Radical feminists are even shaping the political process that will monitor and regulate access to and information about the new reproductive technologies. Janice Raymond, for instance, testified in 1987 against surrogacy contracts before the House Judiciary Committee of Michigan. The Sixth International Women's Health Congress, held in 1990, drafted a resolution opposing, among other things, the development of anti-pregnancy vaccines. In Canada, groups such as the National Action Committee on the Status of Women have been preparing studies and statistics in hope of restricting fertility clinics.

The critics opposing the radical feminist position tend to be far removed from the world of "gender studies"; as a result, they are often dismissed as uninformed or irrelevant by radical feminists. For instance, John Robertson, professor of law at the University of Texas, has argued that, because the right to reproduce follows from the constitutional guarantees to privacy that underwrite *Roe v. Wade* and *Griswold v. Connecticut*, access to the new reproductive technologies should be similarly protected. But since radical feminists dismiss the U.S. Constitution as a document written by and for white slave-owning males, they reject any appeal to privacy because it places reproductive rights beyond considerations of the "female" values of social justice and social ethics. "Privacy rights," say the radical feminists, are just another attempt to tie reproduction to the male-dominated tradition of property rights.

It is worthwhile, then, to examine and refute the radical feminist rejection of the new reproductive technologies on its own terms. By looking at the misinformation and the illogic of their attacks on science and individual—as opposed to group—rights, the implications of the radical feminist mindset become clear. It calls for nothing short of a "gender revolution" that will overturn individual rights, private property, and any other institution tainted by "patriarchy." "In order to stop . . . systematic abuses against [women]," writes Andrea Dworkin in her 1976 book *Our Blood*, "We must destroy the very structure of culture as we know it, its art, its churches, its laws."

And, of course, its science. The radical feminist objections to the technological aspects of the new reproductive technologies are actually a specific application of a larger anti-scientific argument. "Science" seeks "objective" knowledge; it is the opposite of radical feminism, which seeks to articulate "subjective" voices. Where the scientific method stresses evidence and replicable results, feminists "privilege" personal experience. In a paper delivered at the Second Annual Women's Studies Association Conference in 1980, researcher Judith Dilorio described feminist methodology thusly: "Researchers will utilize first-hand, immediate and intimate contact with their subjects through direct observation and reflective analysis, drawing upon her or his own experiential observations of what others say and do in order to relate subjective and objective dimensions." This form of research, which has been called "experiential analysis," can be seen in feminism's approach to sexual harassment. A woman's feelings about the alleged harassment are taken as proof it occurred.

For radical feminists "scientific truth," like any other kind of truth, is nothing more than what scientists declare it to be. Science is just one more "discourse" among competing alternatives; its claim to rationality, disinterested inquiry, and predictive value are merely "male" rhetorical conceits designed to make it seem more authoritative. Contrary to the way science is usually discussed, say the radical feminists, science is not value-free. By seeking to analyze and control nature, it embodies the very ethos of patriarchy.

Since technology is an outgrowth—a handmaiden—of science it is by definition anti-woman, even when apparently providing women more options. In "How the New Reproductive Technologies Will Affect All Women," Gena Corea writes, "[T]he technologies will be used by physicians for seemingly benevolent purposes. These kindly looking physicians may even speak with a feminist or a liberal rhetoric, passionately defending a woman's right to choose these technologies and 'control' her own body."

Elsewhere Corea has stated, "The new reproductive technologies represent an escalation of violence against women, a violence camouflaged behind medical terms." Her derisive attitude is summed up by her comments on embryo flushing, a key procedure in artificial insemination by which an embryo is separated from the womb: "That's done in cows," she writes. The implication is clear—men view women and cows alike as domesticated animals.

Corea is hardly alone in linking technology to patriarchy. The ironically titled anthology *Healing Technologies: Feminist Perspectives*, for instance, dismisses electronic fetal monitors—which have been heralded as a lifesaver for mother and child alike—as the result of "males and male values" and of the merger of "business and health care systems . . . another male alliance."

Even birth control, once sacrosanct to feminists, is being redefined as oppression. In "In His Image: Science and Technology," in the 1992 anthology *Twist and Shout*, Heather Menzies explains how female contraceptives are actually tools of patriarchy: "I didn't immediately see the pill or the IUD as sinister in themselves; I began to see them, though, in context, as part of a larger system . . . they are a part of a particular phrasing of the role of reproduction in society geared to production and consumption, and a particular phrasing of the problem of women's bondage to their own bodies."

As long as the "context" is patriarchy (and for radical feminists, the context is always patriarchy), reproductive technologies of any sort are inherently oppressive. Additionally they "marginalize" the role of women in the birth process. Through the "medicalization" of childbirth, women are said to be losing the monopoly of power they once enjoyed over giving life. History, it should be noted, does not smile upon this interpretation. In seventeenth- and eighteenth-century Europe, for instance, when technological intervention in childbirth was virtually unknown, children had only a 50 percent chance of living until their first birthday. Women had a 10 percent chance of dying in labor and a 20 percent chance of being permanently injured by midwives, who commonly punctured the amniotic sac with dirty fingernails.

But the radical feminist dismissal of science has seriously flawed foundations. Radical feminists invalidate science on the grounds that it, like all other forms of human knowledge, is necessarily selective and provisional. Which is to say, in order to process the vast amount of data bombarding us at every turn, individuals select out what they consider to be important. This is not evidence of bias (patriarchal or otherwise) but merely a description of how the human brain functions. Actual bias occurs only when human beings refuse to reconsider or alter their conclusions in the light of reasonable doubt.

If anything, scientific research methods consciously acknowledge the limits of human knowledge: That is why theories are continually revised, updated, and changed to better account for countervailing phenomena. The search for truth is the process of selecting and integrating data and experience. Precisely what is distinctive about scientific discourse is its willingness to test its hypotheses in such a way that impartial observers can verify or refute results.

To invalidate an area of study because it selects and revises its knowledge—because it decides what data are relevant to its concerns—is to preclude the possibility of human beings ever achieving knowledge in any area, including feminism. It is curious to note that despite their rejection of objectivity and the possibility of truth, radical feminists seem able to claim absolute knowledge when it comes to condemning patriarchy and technology. If they are not being consciously mendacious, the radical feminists are at least ensnared in a major contradiction: Their own position refutes their claim.

Radical feminists fall into a similar contradiction when it comes to discussing their second major objection to the new reproductive technologies: the legal context in which they will be selected. They must deal with the moral question wrapped up in the feminist ethos of "a woman's body, a woman's right." Specifically, they must deal with the issue of choice, the right of every woman to decide for herself what medical procedures she wishes to undergo.

What do radical feminists tell women who choose to "medicalize" the birth process by using such devices as electronic fetal monitors? Or the many women who seek out new technologies in order to have a child? Or the women who choose to be surrogate mothers? Would radical feminists deny these women the right to exercise medical choice over their own bodies?

In a word: Yes.

In *Women as Wombs*, Janice Raymond writes, "Feminists must go beyond choice and consent as a standard for women's freedom. Before consent, there must be self-determination so that consent does not simply amount to acquiescing to the available options." Here, radical feminists are trying to establish a conflict between choice and self-determination. They concede that some women appear to choose procedures such as in vitro fertilization. But they deny that these women are actually choosing, or even capable of doing so, because their options are all delimited by the twin male evils of technology and the free market. Only when women are freed from oppression, say the radical feminists, will true choice be possible for them.

The grounds of debate are shifted from choice to self-determination, from sexual or reproductive freedom to gender liberation. This shift must be ideologically uncomfortable for many radical feminists who once championed "choice" in unfettered terms, but it offers a distinct advantage. They can dismiss women who choose the new reproductive technologies as lacking self-determination. They can also cancel out the possibility of such embarrassing choices cropping up in the future by simply banning them. This ideological two-step allows them to gloss over the incredible tension inherent in their competing claims that women must control their reproductive functions and certain reproductive choices are unacceptable. The radical feminist position is not simply a rejection of bad choices. It amounts to a denial of women's ability to choose anything at all.

Just as the specific rejection of technology stems from a general anti-science argument, the denial of female choice is part of a larger case against patriarchy. Every choice is made under the influence of a culture (or cultures) and the very notion of choice—of selecting one thing instead of another—implies limited options. This is true of women today and would be true of women in some future feminist utopia. To claim that such influences somehow negate a woman's free will—and the right to control her own body—is to deny that anyone, male or female, ever truly chooses anything. It strips women of the only defense they really have against destructive influences: the ability to act freely in their own self-interest.

To this, radical feminists reply that patriarchal technology and the free market are not mere influences; they are forms of violent coercion, like guns pressed against the temples of women. Indeed, technology and capitalism exert such compelling pressure that direct force is unnecessary to confuse obviously weak-minded, weak-willed women. Gena Corea illustrates how this works in "How the New Reproductive Technologies Will Affect Women." Weak-willed women will find themselves overwhelmed by the cultural pressures to use reproductive technologies.

The irony is staggering. For centuries men have declared that women do not know their own minds, that they can not be trusted with important decisions. Now radical feminists mouth the same old patriarchal line. Since they define women as an oppressed "class" that is denied choice, they must attack the very concept of individual choice because it threatens class solidarity.

The most dramatic expression of radical feminists' contempt for individual choice is their passionate rejection of surrogate motherhood, by which one woman agrees to bear a child for another. In essence, they call for the prohibition of surrogacy contracts, because such an arrangement is said to convert women into breeding stock against their will.

In testifying before the House Judiciary Committee of Michigan in October 1987, Janice Raymond railed against surrogacy contracts: "[They] should be made unenforceable as a matter of public policy . . . they reinforce the subordination of women by making women into reproductive objects and reproductive commodities." Notice that Raymond characterizes women as passive objects and contracts as active agents. Although the woman in fact makes the contract, Raymond speaks as if the situation were the reverse.

The radical feminist case against surrogacy contracts has been spelled out in detail by Phyllis Chesler in her 1990 essay "Mothers on Trial: Custody and the 'Baby M' Case," published in the collection *The Sexual Liberals and the Attack on Feminism*. This was the custody battle which took place in 1987 before the New Jersey Superior Court. The surrogate mother sought custody of the child conceived with sperm provided by a couple who had contracted her services.

Chesler writes:

> Some feminists said, "We must have a right to make contracts. It is very important. If a woman can change her mind about this contract—if it isn't enforced—we'll lose that right!". . . . They didn't consider that a contract that is both immoral and illegal isn't and should not be enforceable. They didn't consider that businessmen make and break contracts every second. . . . Only a woman who, like all women, is seen as nothing but a surrogate uterus, is supposed to live up to—or be held down for—the most

punitive, most dehumanizing of contracts. No one else. Certainly no man.

The radical feminist objections against surrogacy contracts rest on two basic points, which are commonly raised against all forms of reproductive technology. First, the woman is selling herself into a form of slavery; and second, the woman cannot possibly give informed consent because she does not know how she will feel later toward the child she is bearing.

As to the first objection, it can be easily argued that there is nothing different, in kind, from a surrogate renting out her womb and other women who routinely rent out other aspects of their bodies in employment contracts: doctors, computer programmers, secretaries. The real question at issue is what constitutes slavery.

The essence of slavery is what has been called "alienation of the will"—that is, a person transfers over to another person not merely the limited use of her body, but all moral and legal jurisdiction over it. In effect, she transfers title to herself as a human being. But if she signed such a contract, she would instantly lose all responsibility for living up to its terms, because she would no longer be a legal entity capable of being bound by contracts. In this way a "slavery contract" is a contradiction in terms. All that can be contracted out are services.

The second objection to surrogacy contracts—that a woman cannot give informed consent—similarly raises general questions of contract law. And on this point, the legal system at times seems to agree with the feminists. Although in the Baby M case, Judge Sorkow found in favor of the biological father and against the surrogate mother, his ruling implicitly criticized surrogacy contracts:

> [The surrogate mother] never makes a totally voluntary, informed decision, for quite clearly any decision prior to the baby's birth is, in the most important sense, uninformed, and any decision after that, compelled by a pre-existing contractual commitment, the threat of a lawsuit, and the inducement of a $10,000 payment is less than totally voluntary. Her interests are of little concern to those who controlled this transaction.

But this ruling does not so much invalidate surrogacy contracts as it invalidates the possibility of any contract whatsoever between human beings. The court wrongly identifies contractual obligations, voluntarily entered into, as somehow coercive. Consider what the court views as a lack of informed consent.

First, the surrogate does not know how she will feel about the baby she is carrying until it is born. A similar statement could be made about almost any contract. If I sell my family home, for example, I do not know how much I will miss the memories and associations it contains until the house is gone. If I am commissioned to paint a landscape, I do not know how emotionally attached I might become to the painting until it has been executed. To claim that a woman can change her mind about a contract, with impunity, simply because she has second thoughts, is to say no contract exists at all.

Second, the surrogate is said to be "compelled by a pre-existing agreement" and "the threat of a lawsuit." These two factors are almost the definition of what constitutes a contract: an agreement that binds parties to certain actions and leaves them vulnerable to damages if they fail to follow through. If these factors are inherently coercive, then contracts themselves are coercion.

Third, the interests of the surrogate "are of little concern to those who controlled the transaction." Again, this is true of all contracts, which are binding agreements between people who are pursuing their own perceived best interests. If the surrogate is of age and in her right mind, it is assumed that she is looking out for herself. If the surrogate later discovers that keeping the baby is in her actual self-interest, she can breach the contract and pay the damages involved.

The feminist rejection of surrogacy, then, is just another assault both on women's right to make "wrong" choices and on the free market, which is the arena of her choices.

This becomes clear whenever radical feminists waffle on what they call "limited individual situations"—such as one sister carrying a baby for an infertile sibling. This, some maintain, should be tolerated for compassionate reasons, on the same level as a bone marrow transplant between relatives.

In the anthology *New Approaches to Human Reproduction*, editor Linda M. Whiteford makes a distinction between commercial surrogacy and the altruistic kind. "Commercial surrogacy exploits socioeconomic class differences," argues Whiteford, "using financial need and emotional need as currency. The exchange of money transforms surrogacy from an altruistic gift between sisters or friends into baby selling or womb renting."

But "humanitarian" surrogacy is still the medicalization of childbirth. Here the object of radical feminist condemnation becomes clear: It is not reproductive technology but the free market that is the true evil. Women may compassionately lend their wombs, but they should never be allowed to materially profit by the process.

Such profiteering would exploit the wombs of underprivileged women.

In other words, if a surrogate truly needs money, her contracts are invalid on the grounds of socio-economic coercion. But it is precisely those who need money who most need the right to contract for it. To deny a poor woman the right to sell her services—whether as a waitress or a surrogate—deals a death blow to her economic chances. Her services and labor may be the only things she has to leverage herself out of poverty. If anything, she needs the right to contract far more than rich and powerful women do.

The true issue surrounding the new reproductive technologies remains "a woman's body, a woman's right." In essence, radical feminists wish to alter feminism's most famous slogan to read: "a woman's body . . . sometimes a woman's right."

But however fuzzy radical feminists may be in arguing against the new reproductive technologies, they are crystal clear about their end goal. Radical feminism is a call for revolution, not for reform. As Gloria Bowles and Renate Duelli Klein put it in their introduction to the anthology *Theories of Women's Studies*, "The present structure of education (and the nature of societal institutions at large) can [n]ever accommodate feminist claims because its very existence depends on the perpetuation of patriarchal assumptions and values. . . . What we are at is nothing less than an intellectual revolution: we challenge the dominant culture at its source."

Similarly radical feminists do not seek to regulate reproductive contracts and procedures. Instead they demand their abolition. They seek to outlaw increasingly widespread practices such as surrogacy, in vitro fertilization, and the implantation of contraceptives. They call for legal sanctions against anyone who sells or provides such services—e.g., doctors and hospitals—and a cessation of research in this area.

While such demands for "technological justice" may indeed be radical, it is difficult to see them as particularly "feminist."

Lois Copeland

❦

I Am in Mourning

A Doctor Writes to Her Senators and Representatives

AT FIRST READING ONE MIGHT WONDER WHAT THE ISSUE ADDRESSED IN "I AM *in Mourning" has to do with individualist feminism—is this a feminist issue?*

On several levels it is. Individualist feminism stresses economic self-sufficiency, psychological independence, and "realistic attitudes toward female competence, achievement, and potential." Lois Copeland, the author of the letter reproduced under the title "I Am in Mourning," is a woman who did all that in her long difficult apprenticeship in the medical profession. And look what Medicare is now doing to her:

The members of Congress to whom the letter was addressed would know that the elderly have no alternative to Medicare Part B—the payment of doctors—except doing without insurance altogether. In her efforts to do something about the situation, Copeland has written to—and been turned down by—all the large insurance companies and the American Association of Retired Persons (a major senior citizens' lobby). She has even been trying to get physicians to establish a private group insurance policy (perhaps a self-insurance scheme), for physician fee reimbursement, not hospitalization, for patients now covered by Medicare Part B. Unfortunately she has been informed that physicians who offered their own policy in competition with Medicare and refused to deal with Medicare at the same time would be subject to anti-trust prosecution.

But the impact of government bureaucracy on a woman who took the American Dream seriously is not the primary reason that this is a feminist issue. Mainstream feminists have made it a feminist issue. They have been saying that issues of poverty, welfare, and care of the elderly are feminist issues, because women are so disproportionately represented in the ranks of the poor, the recipients of welfare, and the elderly. Women have longer lifespans than men, they are more apt to be poor than men are, those who believe that society needs to have some sort of government "safety net" can easily be persuaded that deficiencies in services are deficiencies in the treatment of women.

But Lois Copeland's senior citizen patients are not against what she hopes to do. Every one of them with whom she has discussed the problem say they would welcome the opportunity to have alternatives to Medicare and say they would subscribe to any affordable plan. As she wrote to the AARP, if she can not foster the establishment of an alternate insurance plan: "I have an alternate plan: that the senior citizens rise up against government tyranny with their physicians and force the recognition of our Constitutional rights by the government, thereby returning dignity to my profession and our relationship."

All feminists who are concerned about women who are poor and elderly should look carefully at this account of government policy. Lois Copeland did not start out as either a feminist or a libertarian. It is a sad commentary on the "safety net" in the United States today that it is government policy toward her profession—and her patients—that is rapidly turning her into both.
—Joan Kennedy Taylor

I would like to introduce myself to you: I am an internist in solo private practice, and I am in mourning.

Training to Be the Best
Let me review my past with you briefly. I graduated first in my High School class of 1960, going on to Cornell University where I majored in Zoology and was elected to Phi Beta Kappa and Phi Kappa Phi, graduating in 1964 in the top 1 percent of my class, Magna Cum Laude with Distinction in All Subjects. I went on to Cornell University Medical College with full scholarship aid, and in 1968 graduated to become an intern in Internal Medicine at New York Hospital.

I am sure you have heard of the hardships involved in internships and residencies. I was on call two of three nights during internship, leaving on the third night at 7 P.M. only to return at 6 A.M. to draw blood from patients. I lost twenty pounds during that year from an already slim frame, but despite my exhaustion I learned a great deal and was molded into a caring physician of ability.

After a year of residency at New York Hospital, I transferred to additional residency and a hematology fellowship at New York University. Following this I performed six months of a chemotherapy fellowship at Sloan Kettering Institute, which fellowship was interrupted when my husband, a fellow Cornellian, was drafted and went to serve a hardship post in Exmouth, Australia, with our Navy. (We had married in June of 1970 when he was a surgical intern at Roosevelt Hospital, and I was permitted only a weekend honeymoon, as no further personal time could be fit into the medical training "schedule" of New York Hospital.) I returned from Australia because I could not work there as a physician and continued my training, working seven days as well as two nights a week, in clinics for the poor in the South Bronx, at a diagnostic center in Manhattan, and nights for an emergency service screening emergency telephone calls.

Establishing a Practice

When my husband returned from Australia we decided to begin a family, bought a home in New Jersey, and when seven months pregnant I answered an advertisement in the *New York Times* to buy the practice of a disabled physician in Hillsdale, New Jersey. My husband was still training as a surgeon in New York City, but I gulped hard and took the plunge, assuming the practice and succeeding with hard work, availability, and ability. Working full time until labor began while I was making my rounds at the hospital, I gave birth to my son in October of 1974 and returned to work three days later, as soon as I was released from the hospital. I had three additional children, in 1976, 1981, and 1985, returning to work only a few days after each delivery.

I have been devoted to my work and have practiced full time ever since.

During these years I have become close to many of my patients, a large number of whom are senior citizens. I have always looked upon my patients as friends, and as individuals with unique experiences of life. Despite the great difficulties involved in having a large growing family and in having so little time to spend with them (often returning home at 9 to 10 P.M., only to be called out again for an emergency), I had never in the past considered leaving the practice of medicine. I am thinking of it now.

Government Demands

The heavy hand of government bureaucracy has now come down upon my practice and has turned my patient friends into potential enemies and potential seeds of my destruction. Now my elderly patients carry with them the burdensome need to waste my already limited time looking up codes in heavy volumes, to replace the written word which would flow easily from my brain to my pen. If I fail to do so, I shall be fined two thousand dollars per occurrence.

My wealthy elderly, despite their ability to repeatedly travel the world, are forbidden to share in my ever-rising practice costs. (My garbage disposal fee rose from $25 per quarter 3 years ago to $333 per quarter now, with the cost of disposing of medical waste additional; the salaries of my employees have doubled in a short 5 years; and malpractice insurance cost continues its upward climb financially as well as emotionally.)

I must increase my charges to my working patients, who have children to educate and mortgages to pay, in order to pay my bills. When I return to my home late at night to the boisterous greetings of my children, I must turn them aside in order to reply to the Medicare carrier's letters of accusation, which are false and based upon their own errors in coding or interpretation of my patients' submitted insurance forms (errors for which they are not subjected to fines).

Each senior citizen's visit brings with it the fear of coding mistakes or misunderstandings which threaten to take my hard-earned possessions and savings from me, because of fines of five thousand dollars per error.

And now my government further enslaves me by forcing me to submit all my Medicare patients' insurance forms without compensation. My employees have already given me notice that they have no time to do so, and I will have to hire another employee to do this work at great cost to me.

Who Would Be a Slave?

Yes, I find myself thinking very seriously of leaving the profession I have until now loved and willingly worked so hard to attain, at great personal cost to my youth, family time, and personal freedom. Already many of our brightest young people have deleted medicine as a career choice. Many of my colleagues have all but forbidden their children to follow in their footsteps. Ask any medical school admissions officer about the recent numbers and general quality of his applicants and you will be told they have declined in both quality and quantity.

Young people of talent, intelligence, and ambition have rightly decided that they see no future for themselves in this system. I have heard of a course at New York University called Alternate Careers for Physicians, which I understand is fully subscribed and which I am considering taking. Instead of sleeping I spend nights trying to decide what the future should be for me.

The Losses Are Great

I am in mourning for the nobility and dignity of a profession that has been destroyed by the rules and regulations of a government bent upon solving the deficit by enslaving and destroying the American physician and the practice of medicine as we have known it. A Russian emigré physician at my hospital has told us that the field of medicine in his former homeland was never so viciously attacked.

I am in mourning for that special relationship I had with my senior citizens before the forced introduction of codes and threats and fines.

Before it is irrevocably lost, please return freedom and dignity to my profession.

Faith Gibson

❀

The Official Plan to Eliminate the Midwife 1899–1999

The practice of midwifery is as old as the human race. Its history runs parallel with the history of the people and its functions antedate any record we have of medicine as an applied science. Midwives, as a class, were recognized in history from early Egyptian times. The practice of midwifery is closely bound by many ties to social customs.
　　　　　　　　　—Dr. E. R. Hardin,[1] 1925

. . . increasing mortality in this country associated with childbirth and the newborn is not the result of midwifery practice . . . therefore, their elimination will not reduce these mortality rates.
　　　　　　　　　—Dr. Julius Levy,[2] 1924

Gender—Ground Zero in the One Hundred Years' War Against Independent Midwifery

For women, few areas of life are so central to gender as is our relationship to childbearing.[3] Whether our preference is to do it, not do it, do it our way, do it later, or we did it already and are living with the consequences (i.e., children), sexual reproduction is a central fact of women's lives. And few things are so central to childbearing as the maternity care we receive (or do not receive). Whether we are cared for by a doctor or midwife may profoundly shape our experience and relationship to our biology, our gender, and our sense of self. The quality of the childbirth experience as defined by the mother extends beyond the moment or manner of delivery and can affect the mother physically and psychologically for months or years, perhaps even becoming a pivotal point in her life. It must always be remembered that pregnancy produces a mother as well as a baby.[4]

The disciplines of midwifery and bio-medicine represent two dramatically different philosophies and relationships with women and the biological foundation for pregnancy, birth, and early parenting. Childbearing in a healthy population is not itself fundamentally dangerous and does not routinely benefit from surgical skills. Midwifery is not a practice of medicine. It is a separate discipline that serves the physical, psychological, and social needs of childbearing women and their newborn babies. Obstetricians play a crucial role as consultants and specialists, called in when a potential problem or complication arises or a mother requests anesthesia.

Midwifery is noninterventive, high touch, low-tech, and designed to support the normal spontaneous biology of birth. By contrast, obstetrics is a high-tech surgical specialty that treats the diseases and dysfunctions of reproduction and fertility. Midwifery and obstetrics are at opposite ends of a continuum, spanning the most simple to the extremely complex. Their respective expertise overlaps in the middle of the spectrum but is not identical. Both benefit from the abilities of the other. The midwifery model has been repeatedly proven to provide the most appropriate caregivers for healthy women experiencing normal pregnancies.[5] In many European jurisdictions the law actually requires a midwife to be involved in all vaginal births.

Nineteenth- and twentieth-century science has contributed to the safety of childbearing women and their babies. But most people are surprised to learn that the most important contributions to maternal-infant health did not come about as a result of advances in medical science. Maternal-infant health improved because of the more mundane sciences of public health, sanitation, and nutrition combined with higher incomes and improved living arrangements. The great contributions to safer pregnancies were better housing, indoor plumbing, ample food, and understanding of nutrition. Thankfully it is rare today for mothers or babies to die or be permanently damaged by childbirth.

The United States today spends more money per capita on childbirth services than any other country in the world. One out of every seven dollars spent in the United States goes toward health care. Maternity care accounts for 20 percent of those U.S. health care dollars. Forty percent of all hospital births are paid for by Medicaid out of public funds. Although 70 percent of childbearing women are healthy throughout their pregnancy and their childbirth is normal, physicians are still attendants for 95 percent of all births.[6] Yet for all this spending and physician attention, the United

States ranks third from the bottom in perinatal mortality—twenty-second out of twenty-five industrialized countries. Countries that spend less and do better do it very differently.

In the five countries with the best mother-infant outcomes the midwifery model of care is the standard for normal birth. Midwives attend 70 percent of all births as independent practitioners in Japan and most of the countries of Europe. In some European countries, including England and Germany, the midwife is designated as the primary caregiver. Her presence is required for every mother even when obstetrician care is also needed. Within the midwifery model of care, midwives are recognized as guardians of normal birth and an advocate for the mother and baby. Their role is to protect both of them from impersonalized care and overzealous application of technology. These countries have far less medical intervention, fewer operative deliveries, better maternal-infant outcomes. They spend less money and achieve superior results. Worldwide 60 percent of mothers are attended by midwives, delivering their babies at home or at maternity clinics at a cost of a few hundred to a few thousand dollars. In the world at large, the midwifery model of care is the gold standard for normal maternity services.

By contrast childbirth is the single most frequent reason for hospitalization in the United States. The impact of such a mother-unfriendly system is not merely economic. According to the CDC, approximately eighty thousand Americans die each year from hospital-acquired infections and complications of medical or surgical treatments. When healthy mothers are routinely hospitalized it needlessly exposes them and their babies to a host of antibiotic resistant bacteria. It increases the rate of cesarean sections (CS) with all the potential complications of major surgery.[7] For low-risk women having a hospital birth, the rate of cesarean delivery is three times that of mothers planning to give birth at home or in a free-standing birth center and costs up to six times as much.[8]

For the last thirty years about 1 percent of the childbearing women in the United States have preferred to give birth out-of-hospital. This type of community-based midwifery care does not mean being locked out of the conventional healthcare system as mothers are electively transferred to the hospital and their care taken over by a physician whenever deemed necessary. Community midwives have a transfer rate between 5 and 10 percent.[9] A study comparing home and hospital births in the United States found home-based birth care to have the very lowest level of neonatal mortality—one per one thousand and the lowest CS rate—less than 3 percent, and costs 76 percent less than hospital-based services. Hospitals' CS rate for these same mothers ranged from 8 percent to 27 percent.[10]

Midwifery and home-based maternity care are controversial in the United States. Both are the subject of strong political forces. A major reason is that doctors object to the economic competition. Historically physicians have had a gender-based prejudice against midwife-attended births that traces back to the early twentieth century. Male doctors at that time complained about the "midwife problem," which was the problem doctors were having as they tried to take the profession of midwifery away from midwives. Some physicians genuinely believed that doctors were safer and more scientific and that midwives were old-fashioned and inferior. Other physicians had baser motives. Both schools of thought agreed that the midwife problem could easily be solved by making the practice of midwives illegal. In conjunction with that strategy was another aimed at reducing the demand for midwives by denigrating their abilities and record of safety.[11]

In the early 1900s there were approximately 2.5 million births per year in the United States, more than half of which were attended by midwives. The campaign to eliminate the midwife, however, was largely successful in a single decade. By 1920 only 13 percent of births were attended by midwives and by 1972 only 1 percent. An effective propaganda campaign, combined with the power of organized medicine to ban and control the midwife through legislation, had effectively suppressed the independent practice of midwifery. The effect of this campaign was profoundly negative. For women and infants the initial, tragic effect was an increase in maternal mortality. Replacing the skilled midwife's style of "patience with nature" with the routine use of drugs and surgery by marginally trained doctors raised maternal mortality by 50 percent and the birth injury rate by 61 percent over the next two decades. Even today, maternal mortality is lower in Europe where midwifery remains more common than in the United States. The elimination of the midwife has also changed our understanding of the nature of childbirth.

In the United States our relationship to childbirth has been defined by an obstetrical narrative for the entire twentieth century. This man-made story heavily influenced what people think, as well as defining public policies in regard to maternity care and how the health-care dollar is spent. The medical profession justified the elimination of midwives by opining that all childbirth, even for healthy women, was an impending medical emergency. Dr. Joseph De Lee made this clear by writing in 1915 that:

> If the profession would realize that parturition, viewed with modern eyes, is no longer a normal function, but that it has imposing pathologic dignity, the midwife would be impossible of mention.[12]

Instead of treating childbirth as a normal bodily process physicians related to the care of healthy childbearing women as an opportunity to develop their skills in interventive obstetrics by routinely using chloroform, episiotomy, forceps, and manual removal of the placenta at every normal birth. It is no wonder that anesthetic deaths, hemorrhage, infection, brain injury to newborns, and long-term gynecological complications for mothers followed in the wake of these ill-conceived ideas. Unfortunately it was equally easy to conclude that these bad outcomes indicated that childbirth itself was intrinsically pathological when in fact it was the application of emergency interventions to normal circumstances that was so predictably dangerous. Nonetheless, this false association between normal birth and medical emergencies fueled the propaganda campaign to further medicalize childbirth, cause having been confused for effect.

From 1920 to 1970 it was routine to use narcotics and the drug scopolamine on women during labor and to give general anesthesia for birth. This treatment produced amnesia in the mother and respiratory depression in the baby. Drug safety is a special problem in obstetrics. The 7-pound baby gets the same dose (i.e., ratio) of medication and anesthetic as its 140-pound mother. The routine use of drugs and anesthesia also had deleterious effects on the social fabric as it obliterated the oral tradition and left mothers unable to describe their birth experience to their daughters. Society was left to conclude that labor was so awful that the mother had to be drugged into semi-consciousness and birth so unimaginably dreadful that she had to be knocked out completely. As recently as 1960 death from anesthesia was the fourth leading cause of maternal mortality.

These extreme complications are not frequent, but they are devastating to the families involved. More to the point, it is to the advantage of childbearing parents and society for us to find more practical and less expensive ways to address the natural stress and pain of childbirth. Midwifery care does not take the pain of labor away, but even in hospital births the epidural rate is reduced by 40 percent when mothers are cared for by nurse midwives.[13] In the media today we are bombarded with fearful images about childbirth that cannot be justified by the actual facts. Improved social and economic conditions and medical advances have reduced maternal mortality relative to normal childbirth from 0.5 to 0.0001. Cesarean surgery is three times riskier than vaginal birth.[14] In spite of laudable improvement in maternal health and safety, our culture seems to be controlled by an exaggerated and debilitating fear combined with a dearth of accurate information about normal birth. For healthy women who are well fed, well housed, well educated, and well cared for during pregnancy, the greatest realistic danger today is overtreatment and its complications.

When drugs and anesthesia are seen as the solution to all difficulties it is because we assume that there is no redeeming purpose in the hard work and sometimes painful nature of childbearing. This can be viewed as a subtle form of sexism, which perceives childbearing women as biologically defective or psychologically unable to cope. In so many other areas of a woman's life—sports, schooling, professional, political, or artistic achievements—we honor her hard work, respect the determination it takes, we provide support for the painful aspects of it, and celebrate it as a victory when she succeeds. For childbirth, we do just the opposite—we tell women they are crazy to even try a natural birth and sabotage the mother's best efforts by asking every twenty minutes if she does not want a "little something to take the edge off the pain." We do not value or respect the hard work of labor or provide the circumstances for its success.

The elements of that success include a recognition of the quasi-sexual nature of childbirth. This means that the mother has an absolute need for privacy and the right to control the participation of persons and medical procedures that transgress the boundaries of her body or her sexual psyche. Likewise she needs to be free from performance pressure and arbitrary time constraints. The spontaneous biology of birth is heavily influenced by psychological factors—both negative and positive. This is a well-known aspect of normal sexuality. The childbearing woman has a right to the kind of care from her companions and her caregivers that does not disturb or interfere with the spontaneous progress of labor and birth.

By creating an environment in which she feels unobserved yet secure, with emotional support by familiar people, midwifery care addresses the mother's pain, her fears, and her privacy needs. This includes an environment in which the mother feels free to make sounds of all sorts and to be unclothed if she chooses. Many women find that their labor cannot progress naturally without a supportive environment and encouraging companions. It is also necessary to take into account the positive influence of gravity. Right use of gravity stimulates labor, dilates the cervix, and helps the baby descend through the bony pelvis. Encouraging the mother to be upright and mobile not only helps labor process normally but also diminishes the mother's perception of pain, perhaps by stimulating endorphins. To ignore the well-known relationship of gravity to spontaneous progress is to do so at the peril of mother and baby.

The complex interplay of the physical and the psychological are a biological verity of childbearing. Women have an undeniable right to have their maternity care providers make right use of gravity and take into account the emotional needs of the mother-to-be and the sexual nature of spontaneous labor and normal birth. This is the historical core of the midwifery model of care. In the absence of this kind of support, the mother will frequently need narcotic medication for pain and additional drugs to overcome the labor-retarding effects of the narcotics. The need for episiotomy, forceps, vacuum extraction, or cesarean section often represent the failure of the maternity care system, or individuals within it, to account for the influence of the mother's psychological status in regard to the events of labor and birth. As a culture, this is our failure and not hers.

The current configuration of obstetrician care for normal pregnancies (approximately 70 percent of all births) is illogical, unnecessarily expensive, and not used anywhere else in the world. It does not routinely address the psychological and emotional needs of the women it serves, nor does it deal directly with her developmental needs in taking on the complicated and demanding role of motherhood. The core of our problem in the United States is the uncritical acceptance of unscientific principles as the foundation for our national maternal-infant health policies. The 1966 edition of a well-respected obstetrical textbook puts it quite succinctly "There can be no alibi for not knowing what is known."

The campaign to suppress or abolish the independent practice of midwives unintentionally put the medical establishment in the position of also denigrating the universal principles and practices which make up the distinct discipline of midwifery. Medical education in the United States has historically failed to recognize that the body of knowledge and philosophy of practice for midwifery (care of healthy mothers experiencing normal pregnancies) was distinct from obstetrics (treatment of pathological states and complications of pregnancy and childbirth).

As a result doctors did not and still do not respect the noninterventive practices of midwifery, such as patience with nature. Nor are they knowledgeable about the technical skills which are the common knowledge of midwives such as nonpharmaceutical pain-relief measures, vaginal breech delivery, methods to avoid routine episiotomy, and perineal lacerations. Quite the contrary. Nowhere in the world and no place in history has obstetrical management proved better or safer than the midwifery model of care for providing maternity services to a healthy population. The deficiency of the obstetrical approach can be documented today in the United States by our high CS rate—second highest in the developed world—combined with our low ranking in perinatal mortality. Approximately 20.6 percent of U.S. births are by Cesareans; second only to Brazil.

For the last ninety years medical education has faithfully reiterated its irrational and self-serving bias, as it continues to give both doctors and the lay public the erroneous impression that normal birth is intrinsically pathological, that physicians and hospitals make normal birth safer, and that midwifery care remains inherently substandard, even dangerous, and should be actively suppressed. Doctors think that they are fully informed about midwifery when in fact they are mainly misinformed. The real story of midwifery and its active suppression by organized medicine might help reverse these irrational prejudices and help move us a little closer to a shared maternity care system as is enjoyed by the rest of the world.

The Story of the One Hundred Years' War Against Midwives
The plan to abolish midwives was not based on any categorical deficiency of midwives or a new medical "discovery" that made the principles and skills of traditional midwifery obsolete. Instead it was based on physician self-interest and supported by propaganda and political power. The most crucial years were 1910 to 1915—a time when women did not have the right to vote and many practicing midwives were immigrants who had been formally trained in Europe but were not literate in the English language. The records of this campaign to eliminate the influence and economic competition of midwives were published in medical journals and especially in transcriptions of the yearly meetings of the American Society for the Study and Prevention of Infant Mortality. These documents are full of vitriolic language that was obviously never meant to see the light of day. They read like the interoffice memos of the tobacco companies and prescribe a strategy for manipulating information and events to the professional advantage of organized medicine and the detriment of midwives.

Medical propaganda against midwives centered on the false idea that physician-attended deliveries were safer than giving birth with a skilled midwife. This has never been true, but the statistical information to refute it was not generally available to the lay public. The propaganda campaign thus misrepresented the dangers of childbirth and inflated the abilities of medically based care to eliminate them, while denigrating and dismissing midwives.

The doctors were correct in one respect—mortality due to childbirth at the time was very high. However, the reason for poor maternal health and bad outcomes was poverty, not midwives. Poverty magnifies mortality and morbidity in specific ways. In particular it greatly increases the likelihood of becoming sick as malnutrition compromises the immune system. Cramped and crowded living conditions bring the childbearing woman into frequent and intimate contact with contagious people and substances. Jobs and living arrangements are more likely to expose women to toxic substances or the physical damage from dangerous work. Lack of money, transportation, cultural bias, and medical prejudice keep the poor from identifying problems early while they can still be easily treated. Poverty, combined with poor access to medical care, resulted in large numbers of child-bearing women with deformed pelvises from rickets, or suffering from untreated or untreatable diseases such as tuberculosis, kidney disease, and high blood pressure.

Ill health and malnutrition not only made pregnancy and childbirth dangerous to the mother but greatly increased the risk to the baby. At the turn of the century one fifth of all babies born in the tenements of New York City died before reaching the age of five. The detrimental effects of poverty were magnified by the inability of medical science, which was still in its infancy at that point, to intervene in the resulting medical emergencies. Without antibiotics, blood typing, and safer anesthesia—life-saving measures that would not be developed for another forty years—medical science could not effectively fight infectious diseases, safely give blood transfusions, or perform safe surgery.

Fact versus Prejudice

For both mothers and newborns in the United States, the care of midwives has always been statistically safer than that of physicians. Neither the professions of midwifery nor medicine, however, were equipped to mitigate the mortality triggered by social factors beyond the reach of any individual caregiver or system. Of the two professions, only midwives were blamed for this situation; it was doctors doing the blaming. Data on the superiority of care by midwives was available at the time and known to physicians and a few experts in the field but not to the lay public. The most extensive studies were conducted by Julius Levy, director of the Board of Health for Newark, New Jersey. Levy first compared infant and maternal mortality in various cities around the United States and found that cities like Newark, where a large proportion of births were attended by midwives, had lower rates of both infant and maternal mortality.[15] He then examined Newark in particular and traced the attendant at birth of 1,247 infants who died during 1915 and 1916. His results were as follows:

Table 1

Rate of Infant Mortality in Newark, N.J., 1915–1916

Birth Attendant	NNMR/1,000
Midwives	70.7 per 1,000 births
Physicians	74.3 per 1,000 births
Hospitals	97.4 per 1,000 births

(From Levy, "Maternal and Infant Mortality")

Levy also found that maternal mortality rates were lower in midwife-attended births in Newark. Similar data was discovered by Josephine Baker as noted by Neal DeVitt.

> Baker [1913] reported that for New York City as a whole, mid-wives attend 40 percent of all births but had only 22 percent of the maternal deaths from puerperal sepsis while physicians, with 60 percent of the births, had 69 percent of the deaths from sepsis in their practice.[16]

One explanation for the above data is that on average physicians handled the more difficult cases, thus explaining their higher rates of complications and neonatal mortality. Several lines of argument suggest, however, that such an explanation is implausible. First, midwives served more women of low income than did physicians both for reasons of class and ethnicity and because midwives charged considerably less than doctors. As noted above, low income is correlated with other privations such as lack of indoor plumbing and poor nutrition which reduced the health of both mother and baby thus increasing the rate of complications and death. If anything it was often midwives not physicians who served the more difficult cases. Also one of the major sources of maternal mortality—death from "childbed fever" or puerperal sepsis—was most frequently caused or spread by caregivers. Consistently physicians had much greater ratio of mortality from sepsis than did midwives.

Williams tried to explain "the discrepancy," by the fact that, "with a few exceptions, midwives recognize their inability to cope with obstetrical emergencies and therefore limit their activities to the care of apparently normal cases of labor."[17] Yet in the figures from Baker given above "death was attributed to midwife practice if she was ever present at the labor even if she turned the case over to a physician or hospital."[18] Certainly it is not difficult to imagine physicians refusing to accept blame for any complication of delivery if a midwife provided a convenient scapegoat—thus we must suspect that if anything the statistics are biased against midwives.

Moreover, Levy was plainly surprised at his results and he performed several tests designed to highlight physician superiority.[19] First he suggested that rather than looking at infant mortality (deaths under one year) a better measure of birth attendant care would be deaths under one month of age, neonatal mortality. He recomputed his results and found:

Table 2

Rate of Mortality for Infants Under One Month in Age in Newark, N.J., 1915–1916

Birth Attendant	NNMR/1,000
Midwives	25.1 per 1,000 births
Physicians	38.2 per 1,000 births
Hospitals	57.3 per 1,000 births

(From Levy, "Maternal and Infant Mortality")

Second, Levy noted that primiparous (first births) more often lead to complications than multiparous (subsequent) births.[20] If doctors served a proportionately greater percentage of primiparous births this could explain their higher infant and maternal mortality rates. Separating primiparous from multiparous births Levy found that indeed doctors served a larger percentage of the more difficult primiparous births and that this explained part of their poor performance. Overall, however, "even among primipara the rates were lower among midwives."

As a result of his studies, Levy concluded:

> These figures certainly refute the charge of high mortality among the infants whose mothers are attended by midwives and instead present the unexpected problem of explaining the fact that the maternal and infant mortality for the cases attended by midwives is lower than those attended by physicians and hospitals.[21]

In another study, Levy looked at Newark in 1921 and again found that infant, neonatal, and maternal mortality were all lower among midwives. Nor was Levy alone in his findings; other doctors reported similar results from their observations. In a survey of professors of obstetrics, Dr. J. Whitridge Williams, whose textbook *Williams Obstetrics* is and was canonical (it is in its twentieth edition), found that twenty-six of thirty-five professors with an opinion thought that incompetent doctors killed more women than the care of midwives, three thought the rates were equal, only six thought that midwives performed worse than the typical general practitioner.[22] Thus Williams argued:

> Why bother the relatively innocuous midwife, when the ignorant doctor causes many more absolutely unnecessary deaths.[23]

Similarly, Dr. Ira Wile noted:

> In NYC, the reported cases of death from puerperal sepsis occur more frequently in the practice of physicians than from the work of the midwives.[24]

Dr. Van Blarcom agreed, writing:

> The diagnostic ability of midwives is generally good and in the case of many, remarkably excellent. In this respect, the average midwife is fully the equal of the average physician.[25]

In 1923 Dr. Baily compared the record of student midwives at the Bellevue Hospital School of Midwifery to that of physicians:

> Their handling of normal cases of labor has been conducted with fewer deaths of the mothers from sepsis and with as low a number of stillbirths and eye infections of the babies as the cases handled by the medical profession.

In 1937 the noted obstetrician Dr. Alan Frank Guttmacher wrote about one of the last experiments with midwifery, the Frontier Nursing Service of Kentucky:

> We have had a small but convincing demonstration by the Frontier Nursing Service of Kentucky of what the well-trained midwife can do in America. . . . The midwives travel from case to case on horseback through the isolated mountainous regions of the State. There is a hospital at a central point, with a well-trained obstetrician in charge, and the very complicated cases are transferred to it for delivery. . . . In their first report they stated that they have delivered over 1000 women with only two deaths—one from heart disease, the other from kidney disease. During 1931 there were 400 deliveries with no deaths. Dr. Louis Dublin, President of the American Public Health Association and the Third Vice-president and Statistician of the Metropolitan Life Insurance Company, after analyzing the work of the Frontier Nurses' midwifery service in rural Kentucky, made the following statement on May 9, 1932: "The study shows conclusively that the type of service rendered by the Frontier Nurse (midwife) safeguards the life of the mother and babe. If such service were available to the women of the country generally, there would be a savings of 10,000 mothers' lives a year in the US, there would be 30,000 less stillbirths and 30,000 more chil-

dren alive at the end of the first month of life." . . . What are the advantages of such a system? It makes it economically possible for each woman to obtain expert delivery care, because an expert midwife is less expensive than an expert obstetrician. Midwives have small practices and time to wait; they are expected to wait; this is what they are paid for and there they are in no hurry to terminate labor by ill-advised operative haste.[26]

The international data, then and now, also suggested that midwives had lower rates of mortality, primarily because midwife-attended births led less often to the operating room than physician-attended births. Guttmacher again comments on the international differences:

Though we cannot make an exact comparison between the maternal mortality in the United States and that in European countries, we can at least make a rough comparison. All who have studied the problem agree that the rate for Holland, Norway, Sweden, Denmark is far superior to our own. Why? It cannot be because of our ignorance, for in the scientific phases of obstetrics, America is one of the world's leaders; it must be due to a difference in the patients themselves and differences in the way that pregnancy and labor are conducted in the two regions. . . . What about the conduct of labor in the two regions? Here is where the major differences lie. In the first place . . . at least 10 percent of labors in this country are terminated by operation. In the New York Report 20 percent of the deliveries were operative, with a death rate of more than 1 in each 100 of the operated, and 1 in 500 of those who delivered spontaneously. Fifty-one percent of all the maternal death in Scotland occurred in the 24 percent in which the labor was operative. Let us compare the operative rates of these relatively dangerous countries (USA, Scotland) with those of the countries which are safer. . . . In Sweden the interference rate is 3.2 percent, in Denmark it is 4.5, while in Holland . . . it is under 1 percent. . . . What is responsible for this vast difference in operative rates? . . . Analgesics and anesthetics, which unquestionably retard labor and increase the necessity for operative interference, are almost never used by them in normal cases; and more than 90 percent of their deliveries are done by midwives unassisted. And midwives are trained to look upon birth as a natural function which rarely requires artificial aid from steel or brawn.[27]

Testimony by Louis Reed on the efficacy of midwifery care before the 1931 White House Conference on Child Health and Protection by the Committee on Prenatal and Maternal Care concluded:

> ... [the fact] that untrained midwives approach and trained midwives surpass the record of physicians in normal deliveries has been ascribed to several factors. Chief among these is the fact that the circumstances of modern practice induce many physicians to employ procedures which are calculated to hasten delivery, but which sometimes result in harm to mother and child. On her part, the midwife is not permitted to and does not employ such procedures. She waits patiently and lets nature take its course.[28]

The most important and stunning evidence in favor of the midwife, however, is the disturbing fact that as midwives were eliminated maternal-infant mortality in the United States rose dramatically, in many places in direct proportion to the increase in physician-attended births and corresponding drop in midwife-attended births. When the Massachusetts Supreme Court (*Hanna Porn v. Commonwealth*) declared midwifery to be an illegal practice of medicine in 1907, the state's maternal mortality was 4.7 per 1,000 live births. By 1913 it had risen to 5.6 and by 1920 it was up to 7.4.[29]

Dr. Neal DeVitt proposed "that the slow decline in infant mortality would have been greatly accelerated had not the campaign to eliminate midwives been undertaken."[30] The Committee on Maternal Welfare of the Philadelphia County Medical Society expressed concern that from 1920 to 1929 the rate of deaths of infants from birth injuries increased 62 percent. This was simultaneous with the decline of midwife-attended births and the increase in routine obstetrical interventions.

> Whether because midwives provided more skilled care or because obstetricians were too eager to interfere in labor and birth, obstetric mortality rates often rose as ... midwife practice declined.[31]

Medical Education, 1900–1920

To understand why physician care was relatively poor it is important to remember the depressing state of medicine in general in the decades around the turn of the last century and the miserable state of obstetrics in particular. It is only with the knowledge of the status of obstetrical science in the United States in the early 1900s that one can reasonably evaluate the obstetricians' campaign to eliminate the midwife. Obstetrical education in the early 1900s in the United States was not based on clinical training— that is actual hands-on practice, but textbook learning, lectures by professors and "observation" of care rendered by others. No one knew the state of obstetrical knowledge and training better than obstetrician J. Whitridge Williams:

> In 1850, Dr. James P. White, introduced into this country clinical methods of instruction in obstetrics. Yet, during the following 62 years . . . our medical schools have not succeeded in training their graduates to be safe practitioners of obstetrics. . . . After 18 years of experience in teaching what is probably the best body of medical students ever collected in the country—the student body at the Johns Hopkins Medical School for the years 1911–1912. . . . I would unhesitatingly state that my own students are absolutely unfit upon graduation to practice obstetrics in its broad sense, and are scarcely prepared to handle the ordinary cases. . . . In general . . . the medical schools in this country and the facilities for teaching obstetrics are far less than those afforded in medicine and surgery; while the teachers as a rule are not comparable to those in the German Universities . . . yet young graduates who have seen only 5 or 6 normal deliveries, and often less, do not hesitate to practice obstetrics, and when the occasion arises to attempt the most serious operations.[32]

Referring to Williams's 1911 survey of the obstetric profession Devitt writes:

> Williams found that more than one-third of the professors of obstetrics were general practitioners. "Several accepted the professorship merely because it was offered to them but had no special training or liking for it." 13 had seen less than 500 cases of labor, 5 had seen less than 100 cases and one professor had never seen a woman deliver before assuming his professorship. Several professors of obstetrics were not able to perform a Cesarean section.[33]

The Flexner Report, published in 1910, severely criticized the lack of clinical training in U.S. medical schools, especially as contrasted with the highly prized medical training available in Europe. The same criticisms were found in the obstetrics community:

> The story of medical education in the country is not the story of complete success. We have made ourselves the jest of scientists through out the world by our lack of a uniform standard. Until

> we have solved the problem of how NOT to produce incompe-
> tent physicians, let us not complicate the problem by attempting
> to properly train a new class of practitioners. The opportunities
> for clinical (i.e. "bedside") instruction in our large cities are
> all too few to properly train our nurses and our doctors; how
> can we for an instant consider the training of the midwife as
> well?[34]

In comparison with physicians, a significant number of midwives
(40–60 percent in cities on the eastern seaboard) had been formally educated in highly respected European schools of midwifery. These professional training programs required midwifery students to manage a
minimum of twenty deliveries under the watchful supervision of their instructors. There was also a school of midwifery started in 1911 at Bellevue
Hospital in New York City.

> New York City is entitled to the honor of having established the
> first School for Midwives in the United States under municipal
> control.[35]

In 1915, Dr. Edgar described the rigorous program:

> Each midwife must witness or assist in at least 80 deliveries and
> in addition, deliver a minimum of 20 cases. When this course is
> completed, a practical and oral examination is given by a visiting
> obstetrician and if the candidate successfully passes these a
> diploma is granted.[36]

As noted by Williams, even some professors of obstetrics were poorly
trained and had little experience—a situation far more common among
typical general practitioners. A common complaint by public health officials was that newly graduated physicians offered maternity care without
sufficient clinical training, routinely attempted to hasten birth through the
injudicious use of drugs and surgical instruments, and frequently did not
follow public health regulations. By contrast, health officials and other
physicians observed that midwives as a group were more cooperative in up-
grading their skills, following the directives of public health officials, and
complying with laws requiring treatment of newborn eyes and filing of
birth certificates than were physicians. While it was true that a minority of
midwives were untrained and or unskilled, especially in the South, whatever real or imagined deficiency in midwifery education and practice that
may have existed during this era, the ethical response would have been to
support the establishment of midwifery certification and training programs. This was not the response of the obstetrical community.

The greatest obstetrician of the day, J. Whitridge Williams, knew that skilled midwives were safer than doctors

> The generally accepted motto for the guidance of the physician is "primum non nocere" (first, do no harm), and yet more than 3/4 of the professors of obstetrics in all parts of the country, in reply to my questionnaire, stated that incompetent doctors kill more women each year by improperly performed operations than the . . . midwife.[37]

Nevertheless, in an amazing example of cognitive blindness, he rejected these facts, most likely because of where they might lead.

> A priori, the replies seem to indicate that women in labor are safer in the hands of admittedly ignorant midwives than in those of poorly trained medical men. Such conclusion however, is contrary to reason, as it would postulate the restriction of obstetrical practice to the former (midwives) and the abolition of medical practitioners, which would be a manifest absurdity.[38]

Virtually no attention was paid to the midwife controversy by the popular press during this era (1890–1930) and as a result, the fate of midwives was argued about almost exclusively in the professional journals of physicians, nurses, and public health associations. The midwife herself was not privy to those sources which described her as being unwashed, uncouth, ignorant, and inept; nor was she an active participant in the forces that would shape her life and diminish her vocation. All the major acts of this drama were played out before women had any direct political power. As Dr. Devitt put it,

> Despite what seemed to be early and convincing proof that midwives could provide (maternity) care at least equal to that given by doctors, in addition to the household and public health benefits of the routine (postpartum) care, opposition to the midwife did not abate. Perhaps the facts of the matter were not that important.[39]

Motives of the Medical Establishment for the Suppression of Independent Midwifery

The underlying motive for the elimination of the midwife was threefold, to raise the incomes of obstetricians, to raise their status both among other physicians and the public, and to provide more "material" for obstetrics students to observe and practice their techniques. These motives were intertwined:

the basis of the campaign to eliminate the "un-American mid-wife" was the self-interest of obstetricians. The primary issue of self-interest was the desire of the obstetricians to expand the in-fluence and increase the status of their specialty. During this pe-riod obstetricians worried constantly about the status of their profession.[40]

The Heart of the Matter—Money and Power Politics

A number of public health officers were aware of the superiority of mid-wife care to that of physicians and advocated enhanced training of mid-wives, along the lines of the European system.[41] As part of this reform effort midwives would be legally recognized as an independent profession and would not be subject to prosecution for "practicing medicine without a license." Obstetricians, however, were vehemently opposed to such plans, as these comments from 1912–1915 illustrate:

> Legalizing the midwife will . . . work a definite hardship to those physicians who have become well-trained in obstetrics for it will have a definite tendency to decrease their sphere of influence.[42]

> No attempt should be made to establish schools for midwives, since, in my opinion, they are to be endured in ever-decreasing numbers while substitutes are being created to displace them.[43]

> I am opposed to educating and licensing midwives . . . I do not believe it possible to train women of the type of even the best of the midwives to practice satisfactorily.[44]

> . . . the great danger lies in the possibility of attempting to edu-cate the midwife and in licensing her to practice midwifery, giv-ing her . . . a legal status which cannot . . . be altered.[45]

As was often the case, Dr. Joseph De Lee, one of the giants of the pro-fession alongside that of Williams, was most blunt and revealing.

> Do ophthalmologists favor a school for the instruction of op-tometrists . . . ? Why not train the chiropractor and Christian Scientists also?[46]

Many "medical men" of the day complained that licensure "would give the midwife too much dignity and importance."[47] Preventing licensure of midwives also meant that there was no danger of doctors having to become formally educated in the principles of midwifery. If midwives acquired the legal protection of an independent profession (that is "exclusive title" to a legally defined scope of midwifery practice as providers of normal maternity care of healthy women), it would prevent physicians from practicing within the scope of midwifery unless the legal scope of medical practice was expanded to encompass the principles and techniques of midwifery. Were that to occur, physicians would either have to be trained in midwifery as a part of their medical education or they would need to refer all healthy women to the care of midwives.

Obviously physicians did not want to do either. This further fueled the resistance to midwifery training schools. As Dr. Chaplin put it the medical profession prevented midwives from having access to the "discipline of rigorous institutional training which led to the prestige of professionalism." "They consequently," he continued, "kept from the midwife the ability to assume the aura of medical progress."[48]

Status

Obstetricians desperately wanted to distinguish themselves from midwives because the status of women in general at this time was very low and the common perception was that the practice of midwives reflected negatively on obstetrics. The theory was that if a mere woman, not formally educated in medicine, could deliver babies, then childbirth managed by doctors was not a "respectable" practice of medicine nor worthy of a higher fee than the customary pittance paid to the midwife. Consider the following revealing comments from De Lee:

> The midwife has been a drag on the progress of the science and art of obstetrics. Her existence stunts the one and degrades the other. For many centuries she perverted obstetrics from obtaining any standing at all among the science of medicine. . . . Obstetrics is held in disdain by the profession and the public. The public reason correctly. If an uneducated women of the lowest class may practice obstetrics, is instructed by doctors and licensed by the State, then (attendance at a birth) certainly must require very little knowledge and skill—surely it cannot belong to the science and art of medicine.[49]

And Williams:

> . . . the ideal obstetrician is not a man-midwife, but a broad scientific man, with a surgical training, who is prepared to cope with most serious clinical responsibilities, and at the same time is interested in extending our field of knowledge. No longer would we hear physicians say that they cannot understand how an intelligent man can take up obstetrics, which they regard as

> about as serious an occupation as a terrier dog sitting before a
> rathole waiting for the rat to escape.[50]

Devitt notes that the issue of status was fortified by bias against women:

> A final underlying issue which contributed to the opposition to
> the midwife was the remaining 19th century bias of the medical
> profession, particularly obstetrics and gynecology, against
> women. The nature of this bias, a contempt for women's intelli-
> gence and physical stamina has been well-documented by
> Ehrenreich and English (1973) in *Complaints and Disorders*. The
> vicious tone of the physicians' articles on "the midwife problem"
> surely reflect this general contempt for women. This distortion
> of facts, exemplified in previous quotations, demonstrates that
> at least the most vocal opponents of the midwife were unable to
> evaluate her practice objectively. As long as obstetricians sought
> to gain the esteem of the "medical men," they could not tolerate
> competition by the midwife.[51]

The campaign against midwives included the notion that chloroform
and the routine use of forceps were an important "improvement" in maternity care and that it was unethical to deny such "advantages" to the "disadvantaged" clients of midwives.[52] Obstetricians were especially eager to
promote these techniques because they wanted obstetrics to be perceived
as a branch of surgery, with all the respect and admiration that position
warranted:

> For the sake of the lay members who may not be familiar with
> modern obstetric procedures, it may be informing to say that
> care furnished during childbirth is now considered, in intelli-
> gent communities, a surgical procedure.[53]

> Engelman says "The parturient suffers under the old prejudice
> that labor is a physiologic act," and the profession entertains the
> same prejudice, while as a matter of fact, obstetrics has great
> pathologic dignity—it is a major science, of the same rank as
> surgery.[54]

In the following quote De Lee answers the question of how the campaign to "elevate the public conscience" was to be carried out and what exactly the goal of it was to be:

> Let us begin with the Women's Clubs in the United States. Let
> us tell them of the facts we have learned here today. The

> Women's Clubs in the US are an enormous power, and they are
> growing more powerful in the civil and social betterment of this
> country. If we can disseminate among the women of our land
> the facts regarding obstetrics, there will rise an undeniable
> clamor for good obstetrics. The public will be forced to furnish
> the materials, and the patients, for the proper instruction of the
> doctors. They will build maternity hospitals the equal, if not the
> superior of any surgical hospital.[55]

The above quote is worth reading twice for with characteristic clarity
Dr. De Lee indicates the goals of the (dis-)information campaign against
the independent midwife. "The public will be forced to furnish the materials and the patients for proper instruction of doctors" (the clinical material
issues discussed below), the public "will build maternity hospitals,"
thereby raising the income of obstetricians, and the public will build maternity hospitals "the equal, if not the superior of any surgical hospital"
thus raising the status of obstetricians. As De Lee indicates:

> When public opinion has thus been raised and educated regard-
> ing obstetrics, the midwife question will solve itself. With an en-
> lightened knowledge of the importance of obstetrical art, its
> high ideals, the midwife will disappear, she will have become in-
> tolerable and impossible.[56]

The Demand for Clinical Material
Closely tied in with the issues of income and prestige was that obstetrical
hospitals lacked enough patients for student teaching and observation.
Since only poor or immigrant women were considered to be appropriate
for student doctors to "practice" the surgical arts of obstetrics upon, the
lower-class clientele of midwives was greatly coveted by medical educators
as valuable "clinical material":

> It is generally recognized that obstetrical training in this country
> is woefully deficient. There has been a dearth of great obstetri-
> cal teachers with proper ideals and motives but the deficiency in
> obstetrical institutions and in obstetrical material for teaching
> purposes has been even greater. It is today absolutely impossible
> to provide [teaching] material.[57]

When a mother or infant died at a midwife-attended birth, physicians
blamed this on the midwife. But amazingly when a mother or infant died
at a physician-attended birth this was also blamed on midwives. The excuse being that if midwives had not "wasted" all the teaching material

physicians would have been much better trained. Obstetricians of the time spoke plainly about this "problem":

> I should like to emphasize what may be called the negative side of the midwife. Dr. Edgar states that the teaching material in NY is taxed to the utmost. The 50,000 cases delivered by midwives are not available for this purpose. Might not this wealth of material, 50,000 cases in NY, be gradually utilized to train physicians?[58]

> Another very pertinent objection to the midwife is that she has charge of 50 percent of all the obstetrical material [teaching cases] of the country, without contributing anything to our knowledge of the subject. As we shall point out, a large percentage of the cases are indispensable to the proper training of physicians and nurses in this important branch of medicine. . . . In all but a few medical schools, the students deliver no cases in a hospital under supervision, receive but little even in the way of demonstrations on women in labor and are sent into out-patient departments to deliver, at most, but a half dozen cases. When we recall that abroad the midwives are required to deliver in a hospital at least 20 cases under the most careful supervision and instruction before being allowed to practice, it is evident that the training of medical students in obstetrics in this country is a farce and a disgrace. It is then perfectly plain that the midwife cases, in large part at least, are necessary for the proper training of medical students. If for no other reason, this one alone is sufficient to justify the elimination of a large number of midwives, since the standard of obstetrical teaching and practice can never be raised without giving better training to physicians.[59]

> No one can read these figures without admitting that the situation is deplorable, and that the vast majority of our schools are not prepared to give the proper clinical instruction to anything like the present number of students. . . . The paucity of material (i.e. teaching cases) renders it probable that years may elapse before certain complications of pregnancy and labor will be observed . . . to the great detriment of the student. Moreover, such restriction in [teaching] material greatly hampers the development of the professor and his assistants by the absence of suggestive problems and his inability to subject his own ideas to the test of experience.[60]

Midwives and midwifery training were both considered to be expendable in exchange for the "greater good" as defined by Dr. De Lee's paper on "Ideal Obstetrics":

> It is, therefore, worth while to sacrifice everything, including human life to accomplish the (obstetric) ideal.[61]

> If such conclusions are correct, I feel that . . . [we must] insist upon the institution of radical reforms in the teaching of obstetrics in our medical schools and upon improvement of medical practice, rather than attempting to train efficient and trustworthy midwives.[62]

> We can get along very nicely without the midwife, whereas all are agreed that the physician is indispensable.[63]

Methods of the Medical Establishment for the Suppression of Independent Midwifery

In addition to distorting the facts of midwifery and the quality of care provided, many physicians were vitriolic in their denunciation of their competitors. The physicians of the day insisted that midwives were ignorant, dirty, and dangerous. For example Gerwin referred to "the typical, old, gin-fingering, guzzling midwife . . . her mouth full of snuff, her fingers full of dirt and her brain full of arrogance and superstition."[64] Midwives were especially common among blacks in the South and bias against midwives was overlaid with racism. F. Underwood called midwives "filthy and ignorant and not far removed from the jungles of Africa."[65] Mabbott called midwives "un-American" a peculiar insult but perhaps a reference to the fact that many of the best midwives were European born and trained.[66] Emmons and Huntington said the midwife was "unprincipled and callous of the feelings and welfare of her patients and anxious only for her fee."[67] Furthermore:

> The midwife is a relic of barbarism. In civilized countries the midwife is wrong, has always been wrong. The greatest bar to human progress has been compromise, and the midwife demands a compromise between right and wrong. All admit that the midwife is wrong.[68]

> Any scheme for improvement in obstetric teaching and practice which does not contemplate the ultimate elimination of the midwife will not succeed. This is not alone because midwives can never be taught to practice obstetrics successfully, but most

especially because of the moral effect upon obstetric standards.[69]

Defining Midwifery as the Illegal Practice of Medicine

Instead of training and acceptance, the campaign to abolish the midwife
included a strategy to make the practice of midwives illegal wherever possible.

> In states where the midwife is practically unknown, it should be
> seen to that the Medical Practice Law excludes the possibility of
> midwives practicing within the limits of the state. In states
> where the midwives are not forbidden by law and are numerous,
> a well organized license and regulation system should control
> those in practice. Outline for them the minimum standard for
> their cases and enforce at least this standard by taking away the
> licenses of those who violate the law. Renew the old licenses
> every year and issue NO NEW ONES. Thus the midwives will
> gradually be excluded from practice by their own incompetence
> and by the lapse of time.[70]
>
> . . . the best argument for a state law, namely, because a midwife
> once convicted of a crime would afterwards be disqualified to
> practice by reason of said conviction. First catch your rabbit.[71]

The physicians reported that it was difficult to convict a midwife for
breaking the law because public opinion strongly supported midwives and
their practice, thus the necessity for the propaganda campaign in addition
to doctor-friendly legislative changes:

> But more important than all is the fact that public sentiment is
> not sufficiently aroused to make convictions popular. In many
> localities officers of the law are unwilling to prosecute cases
> even when the law and its violations are directly brought to their
> attention. In one city in Massachusetts when the city marshal
> was informed of the law and the fact that a midwife was openly
> violating it, and that the Supreme Court [of Massachusetts]
> found the midwife liable, he replied that in his opinion the judge
> who would make such a decision merely gave evidence of intoxi-
> cation. When such is the popular feeling, we cannot expect
> much result from the laws as they now exist. What we must first
> do is arouse public sentiment and first of all we must have the
> enthusiastic support and united action of the medical frater-
> nity.[72]

Low-cost Substitutes Financed by the Rockefeller and Carnegie Foundations

Obstetricians had a problem, however, even when midwives were made illegal or heavily regulated. Even given large efforts at "educating" the public as to the danger of midwives there would still be a large demand for midwives since they were considerably less expensive than physicians. The midwife, in addition to helping with the delivery of the baby, would typically counsel the new mother in child care, and she would often remain in the home for several days helping to maintain the home, cook, and clean. Physicians would never perform these duties and certainly not for the fees midwives did. A solution was hit upon—third party reimbursement for doctors and hospitals for providing care to poor women. According to the *New York Journal of Medicine*:

> The development of substitute agencies is the most essential factor in the elimination of the midwife, and the element of competition [free services] will do more to eliminate their practice than anything else.[73]

And from the 1915 transcript of meetings of the American Journal of Public Health Association:

> (H)owever, to entirely eliminate the midwife, it will be necessary for the government to substitute some cheap service at the time of birth. A woman will employ a midwife who will render such services as she can at the time of birth and attend to the women for a certain period after birth, giving many ministrations to the mother and child that no doctor will undertake to furnish. The only way to eliminate the midwife is to furnish some proficient and at least equally cheap service.[74]

Low-cost substitutes were indeed organized by physicians and financed at first largely by the Rockefeller and Carnegie foundations. These obstetrical charities provided free antepartal clinics during pregnancy, free hospitalization in charity wards for birth, and free obstetrical care by medical students (thereby easing the "clinical material" problem). Many doctors of the era insisted that this system of free care in exchange for becoming a "teaching case" should be paid for by government out of tax revenues, in recognition of the "great benefit" derived from medical education to the public. By the 1960s this historical marriage of the medically indigent with medical education had been transformed into the federal Medicaid program.

For many physicians, especially some noted obstetricians, there is no midwife problem; they have long since settled the question by vehement condemnation of the midwife and the recommendation that all who engage midwives from tradition or economic necessity should be delivered in finely appointed hospitals at public expense.[75]

Protection for Physicians to Keep Them from Being Legally Required to Assist Midwives in Case of Complications

Midwifery licensure would also have required physicians to respond to requests from midwives for medical assistance in complicated cases and would have established legal penalties for those doctors who did not comply.

> ... concerning management of complicated midwifery cases by German midwives—the midwife ... must notify a physician in writing ... or communicate personally over the telephone. And the physician must in such case respond at once, unless actually engaged on a case that requires his immediate attention, when he must so communicate to the midwife or messenger. Should the midwife or the physician fail to follow these laws, (they both) are subject to punishment.[76]

This was one aspect that particularly irked the medical community—the very idea of "medical men" (as doctors of the day preferred to be called) being "bossed" around by a midwife at a time when their own wives did not have the authority to demand their cooperation. Physicians of the era expressed distress at the idea of being forced to provide supervision of midwifery cases and to respond to their requests for help. One must remember the state of gender relationships in the late 1800s and early 1900s. The social foundation of male sovereignty was used to configure an equally sovereign practice of medicine which remains unchallenged and unchanged today.

An added complexity in the physician-midwife relationship was the recognition by the medical community that many doctors did not effectively treat a patient referred to them by midwives because it was so easy to explain a bad outcome by simply saying that the midwife should have called him sooner:

> Then too the physician when called to such a case he is far from being as careful as if it had been his case from the beginning, for

it is so easy to say that had he been called earlier "all would have been well."[77]

A Strategy of Ever-escalating Educational Requirements and Regulatory Control

In areas where midwives had already achieved legal status, the tactic was to suppress and eventually abolish them by ever-escalating educational requirements and regulatory controls:

> I believe that the midwife should be eliminated as rapidly as possible. She should, however, not be given a license but should be given a certificate, to be renewed from time to time or canceled as deemed advisable under the circumstances. Licensing her will not add to her knowledge, and will not make her more efficient but will place upon the state permanent responsibility for her work.[78]

> It is quite possible by strict educational requirements, by imposing certain qualification as to the experience and training and in other ways, to restrict the practice of midwifery to such a degree as to amount to practical abolition. Such a method is necessarily more slow than direct abolition. It can be carried out . . . according to the forms of law.[79]

> Have the license to practice be an annual affair based on the record for the previous years. Then by gradually raising the standard and providing dispensary care (free clinics and home delivery by medical students) . . . the problem in a few years would simply (solve) itself.[80]

> Where midwifery was outlawed, its practice was gradually eliminated by enforcement of the law. In other jurisdictions midwives were gradually eliminated from practice by ever stricter examinations. Such a policy was followed in Washington, DC, where the proportion of births attended by midwives decreased from 50 percent in 1896 to 5.5 percent in 1918.[81]

Dividing Up the Profession of Midwifery Between Physicians and Nurses

Another important historical strategy was to eliminate independent (or non-nurse) midwives from the profession of midwifery by dividing up midwifery practice between physicians and nurses. The big piece went to doctors (the independent and high-paying end) and the smaller (subservient and low paying) one went to nurses. In contrast to doctors, midwives had always worked closely with expectant mothers, answering their questions about birth and child-rearing, and reassuring them. As part of their service, midwives would often remain in the home for up to a week helping out new families with cooking, cleaning, and looking after the new baby. Physicians were not against these services, they just did not want to perform them. Neither, however, did they want midwives competing on their turf. To overcome this dilemma they substituted the nurse, who was subservient to the doctor, in place of the independent midwife.

> Of the 3 professions—namely, the physician, the trained nurse and the midwife, there should be no attempt to perpetuate the last named (midwife), as a separate profession. The midwife should never be regarded as a practitioner, since her only legitimate functions are those of a nurse, plus the attendance on normal deliveries when necessary.[82]

The bottom line was the "necessity" (as seen from the physicians' perspective) to maximize their per unit/patient profit by minimizing their per unit/patient time. This was to be achieved by having nurses do most everything but catch the baby (and collect a representational share of the fee).

> The doctor must be enabled to get his money from small fees received from a much larger number of patients cared for under time-saving and strength-conserving conditions; he must do his work at the minimum expense to himself, and he must not be asked to do any work for which he is not paid the stipulated fee. This means . . . the doctors must be relieved of all work that can be done by others . . . nurses, social workers, and midwives. . . . The nurses should be trained to do all the antepartum and postpartum work, from both the doctors' and nurses' standpoint, with the doctors always available as consultants when things go wrong; and the midwives should be trained to do the work of the so called "practical nurses," acting as assistants to the regular nurses and under their immediate direction and supervision, and to act as assistant-attendants upon women in labor—conducting the labor during the waiting period or until the doctor arrives, and assisting him during the delivery. . . . In this plan the work of the doctors would be limited to the delivery of patients, to consultants with the nurses, and to the making of complete physical and obstetrical examinations. . . . Under this arrangement the doctors would have to work together in a coop-

erative association with an equitable distribution of the work and earnings.[83]

Removing the Word "Midwife" from the Birth Certificate Law

Originally midwives were required to file birth certificates and faced legal sanctions if they failed to do so, as the collection of the vital statistics was said to be essential to the development of state health policy. The 1915 California Health and Safety statutes, regarding the mandatory registration of birth reads:

> In case no physician was in attendance [at the birth] it shall be the duty of the midwife or person acting as midwife to file such certificate.[84]

Last but certainly not least in the legislative weapons of the medical establishment was a strategy to remove the word "midwife" from the birth registration statutes. Henceforth only physicians could register the birth. This was a statistical advantage for the medical community, as there was no longer any category of "midwife-attended" birth to contrast unfavorably with physician outcomes, to establish the safety of midwife-attended birth or reveal the high level of complications associated with physician care when applied to healthy low-risk women. Conveniently, it also gave the medical board "proof," in the form of a signed birth certificate, to use in disciplinary actions against doctors who "cooperated" with the "enemy"— midwives.

> What we must first do is arouse public sentiment and first of all we must have the enthusiastic support and united action of the medical fraternity. . . . We feel that the most important change should be in the laws governing the registration of births. The word "midwife" as it occurs, should be at once erased from the statute books. . . . We believe it to be the duty and privilege of the medical profession of America to safeguard the health of the people; we believe it to be the duty and privilege of the obstetricians of our country to safeguard the mother and child in the dangers of childbirth. The obstetricians are the final authority to set the standard and lead the way to safety. They alone can properly educate the medical profession, the legislators and the public.[85]

Until September 2000 this strategy was alive and well in California. The 1957 California birth registration statute, in which the word "midwife" was conspicuously absent (conspicuous because state-certified midwives were practicing at the time) read:

> For live births that occur outside of a hospital, the physician in attendance at the birth, or in the absence of a physician, either one of the parents shall be responsible for entering the information on the certificate, securing the required signatures, and for registering the certificate with the local registrar.[86]

As a result all domiciliary births attended by nurse and direct-entry midwives have been statistically classified as "unattended" home births.

Until recently the California Office of Vital Records declined to acknowledge the category of "midwife-attended" birth (citing the absence of the word "midwife" in the law). One explanation given by the office was that the "The California Medical Association doesn't want the midwives to sign birth certificates as it would give them too much authority"—a 1999 comment that is almost a verbatim quote from Dr. Mabbott's 1907 comment that allowing a midwife to sign a birth certificate "would give the midwife too much dignity and importance." Leaving midwives out of the birth registration process means that the vital statistics for professionally-attended home births were statistically lumped together with unattended births. These inaccurate statistics affect the setting of maternity policies within each state. Computerized records, which reiterate the inaccuracies, are then sent into the national data bank to further muddy the waters at a national level. (See the below section entitled "A New Paradigm" for recent changes in California.)

Historical Consequences of "Pathologic Dignity"

Sadly the result of the successful strategy to suppress and eventually abolish the independent practice of midwives was to inadvertently eliminate the safer and noninterventionist principles of midwifery. The statistics indicate that the suppression of midwifery caused tens of thousands of unnecessary deaths per year, deaths that were preventable by the application of a well-known, globally-respected principle—that of skilled midwifery care. The campaign to eliminate the midwife changed our conception of birth from that of natural process to a medical emergency, unnecessarily pushing millions of women into hospitals and from there into surgical operating rooms. And true to form, surgical births have more complications and higher rates of mortality and morbidity, especially for mothers:

> The quality of obstetrics was hampered not only by the past failing of medical education but perhaps more so by the nature of

the campaign to eliminate the midwife. To discredit the competence of the midwife as a birth attendant, obstetricians had argued that pregnancy, labor and delivery were not normal physiological processes but so fraught with danger that only an obstetrician could safely attend birth.[87]

A 1988 report from the World Health Organization indicated:

> ... there is evidence that a strong independent midwifery profession is an important counterbalance to the obstetrical profession in preventing excessive interventions in the normal birth process.[88]

Similarly, a British director of midwifery argued that:

> Midwifery provides a balance between family and (the) medical perspective on birth. To negotiate and balance the different meanings and perspectives of birth within the health care system, it is essential for midwives to have a legitimate and powerful role within the system. Midwifery should be powerful enough to influence both the nature and the delivery of services. This, I believe, would greatly enhance maternity care, which ultimately is the crux of the matter.[89]

The bizarre and self-serving philosophy of "pathologic dignity" of obstetrics has not only impinged on midwives and midwifery historically but the ability of family practice doctors to provide maternity care. By the 1970s obstetricians, successful as they had been in abolishing independent midwifery, turned this same argument against the provision of maternity care by general practitioners and family-practice physicians. Through the influence of obstetricians on hospital policy-setting committees, not only midwives but family practice doctors have, by and large, been prevented from attending normal births in the hospital.

> The philosophy underlying the campaign to eliminate the midwife created a self-justifying bias towards medical interference in birth. Every time the physician applied forceps or performed a Cesarean delivery, he proved to himself that birth was pathologic and therefore he, the obstetrician, was necessary.[90]

Fact versus Prejudice Revisited—Modern Developments
Having closely examined the classical "midwife problem" and the organized campaign to eliminate traditional forms of independent midwifery, we are called upon to face disturbing facts—the elimination of midwives

was never justified on the grounds of maternal-infant safety or the public good. The independent midwife was eliminated by the coercive acts of a government acting on the behalf of a powerful special interest lobby. Perhaps even more importantly the current suppression of the independent midwife is also not justified on the grounds of maternal-infant safety or the public good. The reverse is true. The contemporary problem is to eliminate prejudices—not midwives—and to rehabilitate medical and midwifery practice laws and ultimately, restore midwifery to its traditional place. The midwifery model of care should be normative in providing care for healthy women, both in and out of hospitals.

The statistics on midwifery are not just from the past. Since the early 1940s, our maternal mortality statistics have improved dramatically, due primarily to an improved standard of living and also to the development during the Second World War of antibiotics, cross-matching for blood transfusions and safer anesthetics and surgical techniques. But our perinatal death rate (up to twenty-eight days after birth) in the United States is only twenty-second out of twenty-five surveyed nations. Our operative delivery rate, especially our sky-rocketing cesarean sections rate, is the second highest in the world. Again, this leaves the United States at the bottom of the pile—twenty-third out of twenty-five countries. On average, one of every five mothers giving birth in hospitals and cared for by obstetrical services finds herself having major abdominal surgery. The maternal mortality rate for cesarean section is two to six times what it is for spontaneous vaginal birth.

Table 3
Deaths per 100,000

Cesarean Section	31
Breast cancer	26
Most dangerous occupation (taxi driver)	22
Auto accidents	20
Vaginal birth	6

(From Liliford, et al., *British Journal of Obstetrics and Gynaecology*)

When given a equal chance the midwife has always produced superior results. A modern-day example of this occurred as a result of a pilot nurse-midwife program established from July 1960 to June 1963 at Madera County Hospital, California.[91] The program served mainly poor agricultural workers. During the 3-year program, prenatal care increased, and prematurity and neonatal mortality rate decreased at the county hospital. After it was discontinued at the insistence of the California Medical Association, the neonatal mortality rate increased even among those women who had received no prenatal care, which suggests that the intrapartum care delivered by nurse-midwives may have been more skillful than by physicians. After the program was ended the overall neonatal mortality rose from 10.3 to 32.1 per 1,000 live births. The researchers concluded that the discontinuation of the nurse-midwives' services was the major factor in these changes.[92]

In 1999 Dr. Peter Schlenzka examined one million California birth certificates matched with the discharge summaries for both mother and baby.[93] Dr. Schlenzka's work calls into question the use of obstetrical methodology for normal pregnancy and identifies as without scientific foundation the idea that only hospital-based obstetrical care is safe. Schlenzka concludes ". . . the already apparent disadvantages of the obstetric approach have such large order of magnitude, that in any clinical trial it would be considered unethical to continue with the obstetrical 'treatment.'" A popular book entitled *The Thinking Woman's Guide to a Better Birth* by Hence Goer articulates these same issues for the lay public and journalists and provides numerous scientific citations to support its conclusions.

Although past and contemporary studies both in the United States and abroad support the efficacy and safety of independent midwifery it remains true that the independent midwife is vilified, denounced, and most important, prevented by law from practicing in twenty of the fifty states. In arguing against a bill to license and regulate non-nurse midwives in 1977, the chief of obstetrics of a major teaching hospital on the West Coast stated:

> If we want an increase in cerebral palsy, mental retardation, extended hospitalizations for mothers undergoing infections, fistulas, hemorrhages, and other severe and disabling results of neglected childbirth, only then could one endorse bill AB 1896.[94]

Twenty years later almost identical sentiments were voiced by an obstetrician practicing in a state with licensed direct-entry (non-nurse) midwives in his response to a question about midwifery:

> In my opinion issuing a license to a (non-nurse) midwife is giving away a license to kill. . . . I think licensing this activity in the name of competition is wrong. In the name of quality of care it is wrong. In fact, it is just plain wrong.[95]

In contrast to this categorical condemnation of independent midwives was the admission by a representative of the American College of Obstetricians and Gynecologists in 2000 that their opposition was without any logical foundation. During a recent hearing in the Virginia state legislature an obstetrician from ACOG testified in opposition to midwifery licensing. At the conclusion he was asked by a senator if he had any evidence that home birth is unsafe or that nationally certified professional (non-nurse) midwives are not performing well in other states. His answer was "No. No evidence."

Feminism and Independent Midwifery

The suppression of independent midwifery by organized medicine from the early 1900s to the 1960s eventually succeeded in erasing the collective memory of midwifery care and the desire of women to be cared for by midwives. In the late sixties several factors converged to bring about a resurgency in independent midwifery. The age of "flower power," anti-war demonstrations, feminism, the expanding woman's movement, and the general propensity of modern people to embrace change and want to do things differently than their mother's generation—all these forces coalesced to bring about an evolving relationship between women and childbirth that put it more and more on a collision course with the standard conventions of obstetrical care. Oddly, it also started us down a path of mounting tension between mainstream feminism and the supporters of community-based midwifery.

Books such as *Childbirth without Fear* by Dr. Grantly Dick Read, *Thank You Dr. Lamaze* by Marjorie Karmel, and *Husband Coached Childbirth* by Dr. Robert Bradley were widely read and their message embraced by many women. Excited by this new perspective many women began to question the prevailing "knock 'em out, drag 'em out" style of obstetrics which considered childbirth to be a surgical procedure requiring general anesthesia. In addition to objections to routine use of amnesic drugs and anesthetics, women also began to question other so-called normal procedures such as the admission shave and enema and drugs given routinely after birth to suppress breast milk production. An interest in birth preparation classes, the active participation of fathers and the "awake and aware" childbirth movement as promoted by birth educators led consumers of maternity services to demand changes in hospital policies. This was the first time that recipients of such care had any input into the manner and circumstances of their care (previously most mothers were unconscious and could not complain). The new and improved version included the formally shocking idea of husbands staying with their wives throughout labor and even accompanying them into the delivery room. Each step of the way physicians resisted while predicting dire consequences due to liberalized policies, such as the fear that fathers would faint or contaminate a sterile field. However there never was any compelling scientific foundation for these interventions and restrictive policies so these fears proved groundless.

As long as policies were somewhat "modernized" most child-bearing women were content with a physician-controlled hospital birth. But a significant number of people became truly radical and questioned the whole idea of medically-controlled and institutionalized child bearing. Beginning in the late 1960s and early 1970s a spontaneous resurgence of community-based midwifery occurred in many places across the United States. Women who aspired to become "independent" midwives revived the tradition of a woman-centered, woman-controlled form of care, defined by women and for women which depended on a mentor-based apprenticeship training process and home-based midwifery care. Truly this was a bold political statement. The legality of non-nurse or "lay" midwifery practice varied from state to state. About a third had midwifery laws on the books that permitted the legal practice of independent midwifery. In another third of the states the 1910 propaganda campaign by organized medicine left its mark through laws expressly forbidding and criminalizing independent midwifery. The rest of the states were either neutral or had a hodgepodge of conflicting laws and statutory "gray" areas open to various interpretations. However certified nurse midwifery, which is more closely aligned with medicine, is legally recognized in all fifty states.

In states with a hostile legal climate a thriving underground homebirth movement arose. Other states with mother- and midwife-friendly laws were successful in establishing formal direct-entry midwifery training programs (Washington State, New Mexico, Texas, and Florida). State and national midwifery organizations arose and led to a national certification of community midwives by the North American Registry of Midwives, a sister organization to the Midwives Alliance of North America (MANA). MANA was originally founded in 1981 by Sister Angela, a Catholic nun and a nurse midwife, who was trying to bring about a cooperative alliance between midwives of all educational backgrounds. MANA represents both direct-entry and nurse midwives as professional caregivers. Over the last three decades there has been a "mainstreaming" of independent midwifery care with professional licensing for direct-entry midwives in sixteen states, midwifery neutral laws in another fourteen and attempts to pass midwifery legislation in many of the remaining twenty states.

However the issue of feminism and independent midwifery has, until very recently, been a source of frustration for midwives. The controversy over the nature of childbirth (pathological vs. normal) sharply divides many people—especially women—and has been a central factor in the rocky relationship that feminism has had with independent midwifery and natural childbirth. In regard to childbearing there seem to be four major categories. Feminist thought and the women's movement gave rise to a fairly large number of vocal and politically active women who do not plan to have children anytime in the foreseeable future, if ever. Historically this group has not been particularly interested in the politics of either midwifery or obstetrics. At the opposite end of the spectrum are women who plan to have children and are perfectly comfortable with conventional obstetrical care. For them there is no question or problem as they like to have a doctor manage their pregnancies and want to give birth in the hospital. More toward the middle there are women who are planning to have children but prefer a liberalized form of hospital care, perhaps in an "alternative" birth room with curtains and a Jacuzzi but staffed by hospital nurses and providing on-site access to medical care.

Finally there are those who also want to have children but who do not want "business as usual" obstetrical care. They studied the issues themselves, reading such books as Suzanne Arms's *Immaculate Deception*, Henci Goer's *Thinking Woman's Guide to a Better Birth*, and Dr. Marsden Wagner's (former WHO director of maternal child heath) book *Pursuing the Birth Machine*. It is only this latter category of personally opinionated women—under 1 percent total—who are attracted to community-based midwifery. A small number of community midwives rose to serve these mothers and despite their diminutive size, have become a very politically vocal group. To be practicing midwifery independently is recognized by midwives to be an intensely political act.

For the most part midwives considered themselves to be living out the feminists' perspective and naturally expected to be welcomed into the women's movement. Midwives were shocked to realize that most feminist groups had an anti-childbirth bias or blindspot which left midwifery out of the spectrum of their concerns. Some midwifery supporters observed wryly that the women's movement was more interested in freedom from childbirth than freedom in childbirth. The ideological split between the so-called pro-life and pro-choice camps in regard to abortion and the right of women to determine when, if, and under what circumstances they will bear children blocked interest in how they might bear those children. As a result of this controversy in the women's movement, a major area of political support has been unavailable to independent midwives for the last two decades.

Roe v. Wade—A Collision Course for Abortion, Childbirth, and Midwives

A particularly ironic twist of fate has legally intertwined the U.S. Supreme Court's 1973 abortion decision (*Roe v. Wade*) and childbirth services in an unexpected and negative way. Initially this only influenced the situation in California but over the last five years this legal theory was used to declare midwifery illegal in other states, making the estrangement between feminism and midwifery all the more troubling. In the mainstream women's movement, *Roe v. Wade* is central to the feminist theory which champions the autonomy of the woman to make reproductive decisions via the exercise of her constitutionally protected privacy rights. In a 1976 ruling by the California Supreme Court, known as the Bowland decision, independent midwifery was declared to be illegal in California depending in part on a perverted interpretation of *Roe v. Wade* for its rationale. These legal contortions were made necessary because midwifery laws in California were at that time statutorily neutral to the practice of midwifery, meaning there was no other legal or legislative underpinning for the court's decision to criminalize direct-entry midwifery. Without *Roe v. Wade* uncredentialed midwifery could not be considered a "crime" in California.

Based on an interpretation of *Roe v. Wade* granting to state governments the authority to prevent the abortion of a viable fetus for nonmedical reasons, the 1976 Bowland court ruled that a woman's constitutional right of privacy did not extend to the manner and circumstances of childbirth. The state's protective "interest" in the baby is to take precedence over the civil liberties of the mother once the fetus reaches the stage of viability. This uses the basic theory embodied in *Roe v. Wade* against itself. It asserts that once a woman declines to abort a pregnancy before the stage of viability, she has, according to this theory, not only surrendered the right to terminate the pregnancy after it reaches the stage of viability but also loses her autonomy as a matter of course to choose the "manner and circumstances" of her birth, not because she has been proven incompetent or because it has been established that her behavior directly threatens the fetus. Interestingly enough this overreaching decision simultaneously protects and upholds the woman's right to have an unattended birth or to be assisted by friends, family members, or any other layperson. According to the Bowland decision only midwives are prevented from assisting a woman during normal birth.

The Bowland decision assumed the government was better able to act in the interest of the baby than the mother herself. The issue in regard to midwifery care is not the performing of abortions but the right of a competent and fully informed mother to make maternity-care choices that are lawful around the world and in thirty out of fifty states, that do not have as their goal the purposeful termination of human life, and that are in fact protective to both mothers and babies.

Over the last twenty years, other states used this dubious legal theory to criminalize non-nurse midwifery. With a slightly different twist, this same perverse principle of *Roe v Wade* is also being used by some states as their authority to prohibit so-called alternative forms of health care, in particular those considered by organized medicine to be "unproven," which generally means nonallopathic treatments. The theory is that unproven treatment may harm the patient by virtue of displacing standard allopathic therapies. The same theory that authorizes state governments to take on the role of protector of the state-defined "interest" of the unborn fetus or newly born baby has now been extended to include adults who have given fully informed consent to nonconventional treatment. Most people agree that sometimes babies (born or otherwise) need to be protected from their mothers. I doubt that as many people would likewise agree that we as adults need to be protected from making informed treatment decisions, including the decision to utilize nonallopathic care.

A New Paradigm
The Bowland decision has aroused opposition and in the fall of 2000, following much lobbying and diligent work by Frank Cuny, CEO of California Citizens for Health Freedom, and legislature consultant Jay DeFuria, state Senator Liz Figueroa introduced a bill amending California's Licensed Midwifery Practice Act of 1993. Senator Figueroa's expert "midwifing" of this legislation was extraordinary and Senate Bill 1479 passed both houses on a unanimous vote and was signed into law on September 5, 2000 by Governor Gray Davis.

Although SB 1479 made only minor (but useful) changes in the laws affecting the practice of midwifery it introduced a very important protection for the rights of child-bearing women. The "intent" language of the bill effectively negates that part of the Bowland decision which stated that the legislature has never recognized the right of child-bearing women to have control over "the manner and circumstances" of childbirth. The amended midwifery licensing law now acknowledges that pregnancy and birth are a normal process and not a medical condition and defines the midwifery model of care, recognizing for the first time in law the emotional, social, and spiritual aspects of childbirth. SB 1479 acknowledges the child-bearing woman's right to choose among all the "safe" options available, including community-based midwifery care. Senator Figueroa is to be commended for her profound contribution to reproductive freedom in the state of California.

SB 1479 also corrects the "fatal flaw" in the California Health and Safety code that has, for the last quarter of a century, prevented community midwives (both LMs and CNMs) from filing birth certificates. For the first time since it was removed in 1957, the word "midwife" has now been returned to the statute that regulates registration of home births. Over the course of the next few years this should permit a body of statistics to develop documenting the effectiveness of community-based midwifery.

There has also been an important recent shift, if not a transformation, in the historical relationship between feminism and independent midwifery. The National Women's Organization for the first time passed a resolution in 1999 supporting the right of child-bearing women to choose the manner and circumstance of their pregnancy care and childbirth, including access to midwifery care and home-based birth services. The Maternity Center Association, a woman's organization with eighty years of political activism in the field, has recently published a "Statement on the Rights of Childbearing Women" which acknowledges women's right to midwifery care and to give birth in the location of their choice, including at home with a professional midwife.

Modern Day Solutions—Midwifery Practice Acts

One of the ongoing criticisms of non-nurse midwifery has been the "lack of formal education" and the absence of uniform licensing for direct-entry midwives similar to the national certification used by certified nurse midwives. Fourteen states, including California, addressed this through legislation. In 1993 the Licensed Midwifery Practice Act was signed into law which professionally licenses direct-entry midwives using a psychometrically validated national exam developed by the North American Registry of Midwives. However in other jurisdictions the lack of professional licensing or the criminalization of community-based midwifery continues.

It is important to remember that a central strategy to eliminate midwives was to block both the training and licensing of midwives. The result is that formal training in traditional (non-nurse) midwifery has not been available for sixty years. Instead of a modest number of formally educated and certified midwives, we have a larger number of "lay" midwives which, unfortunately, includes a small number who are inadequately trained and who occasionally bring harm to the mothers or babies they serve. However physicians are not blameless. Not only can obstetrical care occasionally bring harm to child-bearing women but the stiff-armed response of the obstetrical community continues to exacerbate the problem by preventing the establishment of training programs for student midwives, licensing for new midwives, and interactive collaborative relationships between practicing midwives and physicians.

A Vision for the Future

A maternity-care system should be judged on its results—the number of mothers and babies who graduate from its ministration as healthy (or healthier) than when they started. We cannot let our prejudices get in the way of the plain facts—nations that look to midwifery care as the standard for normal births have statistically improved outcomes. This cost-effective and efficacious form of maternity care serves the social and emotional needs of healthy child-bearing families far better than our expensive and inflexible high-tech model. Coupled with the opportunity to better serve the social and emotional needs of child-bearing families are the restraints of modern-day economic realities, making reform all the more imperative. When more than 50 percent of all hospital admission for persons under sixty-five years of age (including both men and children patients) are for childbirth, we must come to terms with the economic impact of the "child-birth business."

The question is how do we go about reconciling these divergent positions between midwifery and medicine? The overall purpose is a shared maternity-care system such as is enjoyed in most of the world. This can only come about by sharing authority and control over the provision of maternity care, with lines of demarcation naturally following the inherent differences between the noninterventive scope of practice of midwifery and the specialized scope of obstetrical and perinatal medicine. The real question is how to bring about such a shared maternity-care system.

The missing link is respect by the medical community for what it might learn from midwives. In the rush to "sanitize" professional midwifery with hospital-based, medicalized training programs and dependent licensure under physician supervision, obstetricians and others are acting out the same prejudice used during the early 1900s against midwives. It seems that rehabilitation of our maternity-care system is unlikely unless we can reconcile the long and honorable history of midwifery and reintegrate it with its younger sibling—modern medicine.

The traditions of midwifery precede the practice of medicine as an applied science by more than two thousand years. The knowledge base and skills of midwives in regard to normal parturition and complications of childbearing became the foundation of obstetrics as practiced by physicians from the time of the Egyptian physician-priests in 1300 B.C. to the

Greek physician and writer Soranus in the first century A.D. Socrates' mother and Pericles' wife were both midwives. Aristotle spoke of the wisdom and intelligence of the midwives of early Greece.

Historically speaking beginning in the early 1600s the body of knowledge which reflected the discipline of midwifery was taken over by the medical profession. Textbooks written by midwives in the fifteenth, sixteenth, and seventeenth centuries were used as a foundation for the first obstetrical texts. King Louis XV's official midwife, Madame Du Coudray, invented the obstetrical teaching manikin. At the king's bidding she taught the science of midwifery and classical obstetrics for thirty years to hundreds of surgeons throughout France. These midwifery resources were built upon by professors of medicine and combined with knowledge gained in anatomy, through dissection, and other scientific studies. The modern art and science of obstetrics is the aggregate of both traditions. Recognition of these shared historical origins does not diminish the contemporary science of obstetrics in any way.

In modern times midwifery has incorporated the contributions of science and technological assistance from medical devices such as blood pressure cuffs, fetascopes, information available through laboratory analysis of blood and body tissues, ultrasound imaging of body organs, and services of fully equipped hospitals. The historical background commonly know as the "oral tradition" and a contemporary scientific knowledge base together form the foundation of the midwifery model of care as an evidence-based phenomenon that results in a well-rounded and robust modern discipline. The midwifery model of care in the twentieth century is not specific to the type of caregiver—it can be provided by both physicians and midwives, either in hospital or out. Within that context, professional midwives are capable of contributing to the care of all pregnant women in some measure and are particularly well suited to be the primary caregiver for the 50 percent of child-bearing women who complete pregnancy in a state of health and who experience a normally progressive labor. The basic information about midwifery needs to be as widely known as the bias that preceded it.

Midwives are suggesting, in the strongest of terms, that an exchange of expertise is in order. It is as much the responsibility of physicians to be familiar with the time-honored philosophy, principles, and skills of midwifery as it is the duty of midwives to know the principles of anatomy and asepsis. Midwives are in agreement that modern obstetrics has much to teach and much to contribute to the well-being of the families it serves. As midwives we have already availed ourselves of both formal and informal study of obstetrical science. Likewise, the honorable but unassuming traditions of midwifery—the art of being "with women"—the quietness of spirit, the patience with nature, the intimacy skills which serve child-bearing families so well are also of great value to the bio-medical sciences. Physicians cannot begin to examine their prejudices without specific information on the nature of these principles and the opportunity to build personal and professional relationships with practicing midwives:

> Historically, obstetrics has been the standard to which mid-wifery is compared. Perhaps the time has come for obstetrics to be held to a midwifery standard for normal childbirth.[96]

The late Dr. Galba Araujo, in an article urging an "articulated model of midwifery" into contemporary obstetrics stated:

> We have learned much from the traditional (midwife) and re-spect is mutual between our parallel groups. We have learned to teach our (obstetrical) students less invasive delivery and above all, to use the vertical position for the mother. Perhaps this is the most valuable lesson among the many we have learned.[97]

In spite of the many fears within the obstetrical community, midwives do not represent a feminist conspiracy to eliminate the obstetrician. Quite the opposite—midwives seek to augment, supplement, and complement the contemporary medical model of care. Independent midwifery is not intrinsically in conflict with the true purpose and glory of obstetrical care—the compassionate correction of dysfunctional states and the treatment of pathological ones.

A philosophy of reconciliation is perhaps best described in a little-known story told about Eleanor Roosevelt during the years that she was the mother of young children as well as First Lady. When asked what she put first in her life, her husband (then president of the United States) or their children, she replied that "together with my husband, we put the children first." I have always appreciated that story as portraying the ideal relationship between physicians and midwives—that together we put the practical well-being of mothers and babies first.

Notes

1. E. R. Hardin, "The Midwife Problem," *Southern Medical Journal* vol. XVIII (January 1925), 347.

2. M. Pierce Rucker, "The Relationship of Midwife to Obstetric Mortality, with Especial Reference to New Jersey," *American Journal of Public Health*, 1924, 816–822. Rebuttal by Dr. Julius Levy, 822.

3. I began this paper with an overview to provide background and the "bigger picture" so the reader can examine this historical material in the context of our past and future. The main body of the work is the historical story, told for the most part in direct quotes, with citations from professional journals of the era. The final section brings the reader up to date on the current legal, legislative, and political situation.

I wish to thank the staff at Stanford University Medical Library for their assistance in helping me access these important but "dusty" resources so that on the eve of the twenty-first century they could, after almost one hundred years of obscurity, be made publicly available for the first time. This historical account comes primarily from documents published between 1900 and 1930 in professional journals. The majority of the material was published in the "Transactions for the Study and Prevention of Infant Mortality," (TAASPIM) (1910–1915). This archival material records the historical blueprint of an official campaign to do away with the independent practice of midwives.

I would also like to thank Alex Tabarrok, research director for the Independent Institute, for extensive comments and editorial assistance and for believing in the importance of the material. I could not have presented this material without his encouragement.

4. Albers, et al., "Midwifery Care: The 'Gold Standard' for Normal Childbirth?" *Birth* 261 (March 1999).

5. WHO Report on Health Promotion and Birth Prepared by the North American and European Consulting Group (1986), reprinted in Marsden Wagner, *Pursuing the Birth Machine* (Australia, 1994).

6. Peter Schlenzka, "Safety of Alternative Approaches to Childbirth," Ph.D. thesis submitted to Stanford University, March 1999.

7. Rondi E. Anderson and David Anderson, "The Cost Effectiveness of Home Birth," *Journal of Nurse Midwifery*.

8. *Ibid.*

9. Patricia Aikins Murphy, "Outcomes of Intended Home Birth in Nurse-Midwifery Practice: A Prospective Descriptive Study," *Journal of Nurse Midwifery*.

10. Anderson and Anderson, "Cost Effectiveness."

11. Neal DeVitt, "The Elimination of the Midwifery in the United States 1900–1935," doctoral thesis, Cambridge University Press 1975.

12. Joseph De Lee, "Progress Towards Ideal Obstetrics," Transactions of the American Association for the Study and Prevention of Infant Mortality (TAASPIM) (1915), 114. The full text of papers by Dr. J. Whitridge Williams and Dr. De Lee and extensive excerpts from TAASPIM are available at www.goodnewsnet.org/.

13. Roger Rosenblat, et al., "Interspeciality Differences in the Obstetric Care of Low-risk Women," *Journal of Public Health* 87:3 (1997), 344–351.

14. R. J. Liliford, et al., "The Relative Risk Cesarean Section (Intrapartum and Elective) and Vaginal Delivery," *British Journal of Obstetrics and Gynaecology* (1990), 97883–97892

15. Julius Levy, "The Maternal and Infant Mortality in Midwifery Practice in Newark, NJ," *American Journal of Obstetricians and Gynecologists* v. 77 (1918).

16. DeVitt, "Elimination."

17. J. Whitridge Williams, "The Midwife Problem and Medical Education in the US," TAASPIM (1911).

18. DeVitt, "Elimination."

19. Levy, "Maternal and Infant Mortality."

20. *Ibid*.

21. Levy, "Maternal and Infant Mortality," 44.

22. Williams (1912).

23. Williams, "Midwife Problem," 180.

24. Ira Wile, in Josephine Baker, "School for Midwives" TAASPIM (1911), 246.

25. Van Blarcom (1913).

26. Alan Frank Guttmacher, "Into This Universe: The Story of Human Birth" (New York, 1937), 136.

27. *Ibid*., 133–135.

28. L. Reed, *The Costs of Medicine: Midwives, Chiropodists, and Optometrists* (Chicago, 1932).

29. R. Woodbury, *Maternal Mortality*, Children's Bureau Publication #158 (1928).

30. DeVitt, "Elimination."

31. *Ibid*.

32. Williams, "Midwife Problem," 178.

33. DeVitt, "Elimination."

34. Arthur Brewster Emmons and James Lincoln Huntington, "Has the Trained and Supervised Midwife Made Good?" TAASPIM (1911), 207.

35. Baker, "School."

36. J. Clifton Edgar, "The Education, Licensing and Supervision of the Midwife," TAASPIM (1915), 98.

37. Williams, "Midwife Problem," 180.

38. Williams, "Midwife Problem."

39. DeVitt, "Elimination."

40. *Ibid*.

41. Baker, "School"; Josephine Baker, "The Function of the Midwife," *Women's Medical Journal* 23 (1913), 196–197; Wile, "School"; Bacon (1911); Levy (1918).

42. James Lincoln Huntington (1913).

43. Charles Edward Ziegler, "The Elimination of the Midwife," TAASPIM (1912), 227.

44. *Ibid*., 223.

45. *Ibid*., 222.

46. De Lee, "Progress," 115.

47. J. Milton Mabbott, "The Regulation of Midwives in New York," *Am J of Obstetrics* 55 (1907), 516–527.

48. C. Chaplin, "The Control of Midwifery," in *Standards of Child Welfare* no. 60 (Washington, D.C., 1919).

49. De Lee, "Progress," 114.

50. Williams, "Midwife Problem."

51. DeVitt, "Elimination."

52. De Lee, "Progress."

53. Arthur Brewster Emmons, "Obstetrics Care in the Congested Districts of Our Large American Cities" TAASPIM (1911), 214.

54. De Lee, "Progress," 116.

55. De Lee, "Progress."

56. *Ibid*.

57. Ziegler, "Elimination," 226.

58. Emmons, "Obstetrics," 216.

59. Ziegler, "Elimination," 224, 226.

60. Williams, "Midwife Problem," 171.

61. De Lee, "Progress."

62. Williams, "Midwife Problem," 166.

63. Ziegler, "Elmination," 222.

64. W. Gerwin, "Careless and Unscientific Midwifery with Special Reference to Some Features of the Work of Midwives," *Alabama Medical Journal* 18 (1906), 629–635.

65. Flex J. Underwood, "The Development of Midwifery in Mississippi," *Southern Medical Journal* (1926).

66. Mabbott, "Regulation."

67. Arthur Brewster Emmons and James Lincoln Huntington, *American Journal of Obstetrics* (1912).

68. De Lee, "Progress," 114.

69. "The Teaching of Obstetrics," American Association of Obstetrics and Gynecologists.

70. Emmons and Huntington, "Trained Midwife," 209.

71. Mabbott, "Regulation."

72. Arthur Brewster Emmons and James Lincoln Huntington, "A Review of the Midwife Situation," *Boston Medical and Surgical Journal* vol. CLXIV, no. 8 (1911), 260–261.

73. John Van Doren Young, "The Midwife Problem in the State of New York," *New York State Journal of Medicine* vol. XV (1915), 300.

74. Discussion from transcript of meeting held December 1914, Jacksonville, Fla., *American Journal of Public Health Association* vol. 5 (Boston, 1915), 700.

75. Julius Levy, "The Maternal and Infant Mortality in Midwifery Practice in Newark, NJ," Thirteenth Annual Meeting of the American Association of Obstetrics and Gynecologists (Newark, N.J., 1917).

76. Emmons and Huntington, "Trained Midwife," 203.

77. *Ibid.*, 205.

78. Ziegler, "Elmination," 227.

79. Marshall Langton Price, "The Problem of Midwifery from the Standpoint of Administration" TAASPIM (1911), 225.

80. Emmons and Huntington, "Trained Midwife," 210.

81. Chaplin, "The Control of Midwifery."

82. Edgar, "Education, Licensing and Supervision," 104.

83. Charles Edward Ziegler, "How Can We Best Solve the Midwifery Problem?" *American Journal of Public Health* 1922, 412–413.

84. 1915 California Health and Safety Statutes, chapter 548, 723.

85. Emmons and Huntington, "Review," 261.

86. "Registration of Births Not Occuring in a Licensed Medical Facility," California Health and Safety Code, section 10102.

87. DeVitt, "Elimination."

88. WHO Report in Wagner, *Pursuing*.

89. Page, Director of Midwifery, Oxfordshire, England, 1988.

90. DeVitt, "Elimination."

91. B. S. Levy, et al., "Reducing Neonatal Mortality Rate with Nurse Midwives," *American Journal of Obstetrics and Gynecology* 109 (1971), 50–58.

92. *Ibid.*

93. Peter Schlenzka, "The Safety of Alternative Childbirth Approaches," Ph.D. dissertation, Stanford University, 1999.

94. Heinrichs, 1977.

95. Email correspondence 0838 1/17/97 ob-gyn-1@obgyn.net.

96. Albers, "Midwifery Care."

97. Galba Araujo, "The Ethnomedical System Can Be Used in Primary Health Care," *World Health Forum*, vol. 4 (1983).

Janis Cortese

❀

The Third WWWAVE
Who We Are, What We See

IT NEVER OCCURRED TO ME THAT I WOULD EVER HAVE TO DEFEND MYSELF AS A feminist. But that's apparently what's going on lately. I hate the most common versions of sex entertainment, but I am against any form of censorship. I think Catharine MacKinnon is a fool if she honestly believes what she is saying is the truth. I am pro Second Amendment, and my educational website on women and handguns is so well known that some refer to me as the Internet Gun Lady. And the women working at *Ms.* magazine would not call me a feminist.

What I am hearing is a lot of complaints that young women my age (late twenties, early thirties) will not call themselves feminist. "I'm not a feminist but—" drives them up a wall—and me, too. To be fair, I am hearing an awful lot of second-wave feminists saying that "Young women nowadays aren't feminists!" because we do not participate in activism the way they did. No, we do not.

But we do put up websites that the entire universe can read, run for office in huge numbers and win, and get good paying professional jobs and promptly develop an "old girls' network" of handing consulting jobs to friends, just like the men have always done. (I have helped male friends of mine get positions, so it is not all one-sided, but I am completely unashamed about handing off employment and consulting opportunities to other women friends.) And what do we hear in return?

"Well, that's all well and good, but it is not feminism."

So we do not call ourselves feminists enough for you, the second-wave feminists, but when we are proud of what we have accomplished and call it feminism, you tell us we are not feminist! After a while we don't know what you want from us anymore. Do you want us to be just like you? Because we're not—we're different. You won a lot of the old battles, and as a result, we must move on to new ones. (And if we were still fighting those old battles twenty years later, that would mean that you were not terribly successful.) We are moving forward quickly, narrowing the pay gap between men and women and filling the coffers of organizations such as EMILY's List, and as a result, the field looks different to us. Not to mention that the only other person to tell me, "Oh, I'm sure that's all well and good, dear, but it doesn't really matter," upon hearing of the websites I have helped put up is one of the most sexist men I have ever met. When you say things like this, do you really know who you sound like?

Why Are We Different From You?

We grew up watching most of the adults around us voting for someone who was flat-out losing his mind, hearing that "feminism was dead," while at the same time being the first generation to grow up taking reproductive choice as a given. You think that will not make us a little loopy or at least different from you?

You accepted men (a lot more than history admits) as partners in the great struggle, while we inherited a generation of potential husbands who seemed to have stuck their fingers in their ears and hummed, hoping that feminism would all blow over, that they would not have to pry themselves out of their La-Z-Boys, and thinking that marriage still meant free groping rights and never having to clean another dish.

You could afford to accept other hippie guys as partners in the struggle for justice. Our male contemporaries are a little different. We both heard the statistics about "women making sixty cents for every male dollar," but we rolled our sleeves up and set about improving things. Men sat back grinning and figured it was gravy time, that they owned the world because they had a penis ("We make more money than you, nyah nyah!"). After all, that's what they learned in the Reagan years: that we were all "post-feminist," and they breathed a sigh of relief, delighted that it had all blown over before they had to actually change. Then Reagan got voted out. Mr. Post-feminist graduated from college and discovered that he was not going to be J. R. Ewing and he was not going to make a million dollars before he was thirty. Moreover one of those women that he thought he would out-earn without trying may be his boss. And guess who he resents for it.

You fought hard to recover women geniuses from the dusty racks of ignored history—but do any of you really know how few girls in school are taught any of that? What would you think if you knew that in my own high school, a girls' high school, the women's movement and how we won the vote was completely ignored because "we do not have time for it?" I am hardly alone. Every woman I know my age has heard that in school. Even the battles you think you have won look very different to those of us who turn thirty before finding out that women were not "given" the vote and that birth control did not fall out of the sky. Carrie Chapman Catt? Margaret Sanger? Who are they?

You worked to get women's studies departments and women's centers on university campuses, but speaking as someone with a graduate degree in physics, I can say pretty firmly that the "mentoring" programs and the work-study programs that the Women's Resource Center had at Cal Irvine were approximately useless to me. Useless to damned near anyone in the sciences, as a matter of fact. Women's studies was supposed to be some grand training ground for activists—not for the majority of women who came to college to learn a discipline and get a degree. For most women in college, the Women's Resource Center is a sort of Planned Parenthood that they can call in the event that they need counseling—a valuable resource, to be sure, but nowhere near an academic one. After sitting in a circle of women who introduced themselves as activists and performance artists, or young women who were getting humanities and social science degrees, I remember all too well those sidelong looks that were exchanged when I introduced myself as a grad student in high-energy physics and made all those deconstructionists pop a mental clutch. "I'm sorry, but we do not know what to do with you," those looks seemed to say—given by women who were artistes at complaining about the underrepresentation of women in the sciences. They bemoaned the lack of women in the sciences at the same time as they stared at me like a Martian.

You say you wanted to make a world where women could be what we wanted to be, yet women such as Hedda Nussbaum are enshrined as "inspirational" whereas women like us—women who fought our asses off to get to where we are and who won't ever let anyone lay a hand on us again—hear that what we are doing simply by achieving to the best of our ability is not feminism. I see women who let their husbands beat the shit out of them taken to your bosom and fondled lovingly in the pages of *Ms.* (to which I once subscribed until I got too frustrated with it), while women who shot abusive husbands in self-defense are lambasted for falling prey to patriarchal thinking by buying a gun. You were all over Nicole Brown for your PR purposes, but if she had bought a handgun and defended herself, she would have been used as a poisonous example of violence in the home. It is either "Look at the poor abused dead woman, what a lovely martyr for the cause," or "Look at the woman who bought into the patriarchy."

The woman who dies is a good woman. The one who does what she needs to survive is a sign of the coming apocalypse. You say you fought hard to enable us to succeed, but it appears that we can get more lauds from you, or at least more positive attention, by failing than by succeeding.

This is not exactly unusual. It has always been that way for women—the only way we can get attention is by suffering. Look at the typical history books—Joan of Arc, Amelia Earhart, Marie Curie. Dead by murder, dead by getting lost, dead by cancer from studying the very subject she got her Nobel Prizes for. I have no doubt that Shannon Lucid would also have been turned into some sort of sick inspiration had she died in space. But alas, no. She merely succeeded brilliantly, came back home to her family and lots of applause, and set her sights on Mars. And in twenty years, nobody will know who the hell she was. We remember Earhart, though—who screwed up. Society only forgives a woman who challenges gender roles if she fucks up in the end.

Women are only grudgingly accepted into the annals of history if they have died violent deaths and atoned for the sin of having outperformed men. Certainly they accomplished a great deal—but they died in the process. History loves a dead woman. And history loves examples that illustrate to young girls that, yes—success is all well and good, but if you try to fly too high, you will pay for it in the end.

Feminism should not be teaching the same lesson.

What Is Wrong With This Picture?

We say that we are in a more comfortable position now, and we want to start using the power that previous generations of women have worked for. You tell us we are "overconfident" and that the rights and privileges we enjoy now can still be lost—at any time. The truth is that they cannot be—not unless women roll over and play dead. Men cannot do any damned thing to us that they want anymore. Women are victimized—but it is no longer eternal, and it is no longer taken as a matter of course. They will get reproductive choice away from me when they pry it out of my cold, dead hands. Twelve years' worth of stacking on the Supreme Court by the Reagan/Bush nightmare was not enough to overturn *Roe v. Wade*. Stop casting us in roles in which we no longer fit. Stop trying so hard to convince us, after raising us to believe that we can "be anything we want to be," that the world is hostile, dangerous, and can turn on us at any minute. You tell us on one hand that we should go out and do everything previous generations were not able to do—and then you make us schizoid with stories about how we'll get flattened by the Karma Truck of Life by trying. Moreover stop acting like the sixties and the seventies are the only decades we inherited, as if the eighties never happened. Not only did we inherit the second wave of feminism—we inherited all the macho, posturing, lying, hypocritical bullshit that came after it, too. We saw all of your fellow sixties' radicals who thought that dropping acid and screwing anything that moved in Max Yasger's alfalfa field had some sort of "social relevance" turn into the most money-grubbing, acquisitive, lying bastards ever to come down the pike for ten long, painful years. No, we do not trust you. Would you trust you, if that was what you had seen?

There is a distinct possibility that the third-WWWave exasperation with second-wave feminists is one more facet of the way our entire generation is tired of hearing about how yours invented social justice, and that we "aren't doing it right." Not only are we slamming on feminism, we're slamming on all of the sixties political entities, from NOW to the Democratic and Republican parties, both of whose current political beliefs were set in stone during the same decade. Our annoyance is not just directed at you—this is not particular to feminism. We are angry with the whole sixties-informed political landscape.

Make no mistake—this is a generation gap.

What Annoys Us About the Second Wave

Most of you will read this while jumping up and down and wanting to yell, "That's not what it was!" No, it is not. But in many ways it is what it has become—for us. When you were doing far more sane politics twenty years ago, we were not even part of it. We were running around skinning our knees or drooling, if we were even alive at the time. Your experience with the second wave is different from ours. You hear "second-wave feminism" and think of your activism and the feeling of togetherness that you got, the feeling that one always gets when one is doing something important and vital with people one cares about. That is your memory of second-wave feminism. But by the time it got to us, filtered through the Reagan era, it had become something else—

- Catharine MacKinnon attacks the First Amendment and calls women who work in the sex industry "house niggers" (I'm sure the black women I know who write erotica would have a few choice words for her), and the dittoheads uncap another Pabst and laugh at the catfight;
- "Feminist" and "gun-grabber" are almost synonymous (we have the brains to use a uterus, but not to use a gun), until it is gotten to the point where I can vote for someone who will protect my right to an abortion and rip my Second Amendment rights away from me or vote for someone who will pro-

tect my right to own a firearm and try to chain me to a
bassinet;

- Science and engineering are attacked as not having enough
  women, but those women in the fields are seen as freaks or as
  people participating in the "rape of Mother Earth";
- Bisexual women are often shunned, attacked, and generally
  regarded with sneering contempt;
- Bondage sex is officially designated as undesirable by NOW.

Could it be that I am familiar with these aspects of feminism because I
am an erotica-writing, handgun-owning, bisexual dominant woman with
an MS in physics? Naah.

This is not the second wave that you remember, and I know that it was
much, much more than that. But this is what it has become in some ways.
Maybe it is not what you were doing in 1971—but I was five in 1971. Ask me
instead what Andrea Dworkin was doing in the same political corner as
Jerry Falwell when I was in my twenties. To us, that's a lot more relevant.

I know that is not what you fought and worked for. I know that the
largest part of the problem lies with the media for painting you as anti-sex
man-haters. I know that anything you did would have been seen as castra-
tion by a male-controlled media that seems anxious to be castrated in the
first place. I know that whatever you were talking about in the sixties was
not about calling bisexual women traitors and erotica writers "house niggers." But by the time it got to us, that's what it became.

You can no longer say, "But, that isn't what we meant!" because that is
what it has become, regardless of what you meant. You can no longer demand that we telepathically divine what you meant to happen and ignore
dealing with the problems of what has happened to feminism and the culture in general.

It is not your fault. No cataclysmic social change ever goes where the
founders thought it would. If you brought Thomas Jefferson back from the
grave and showed him the modern United States, he'd probably collapse in
horror. The feminism you remember is not the one we inherited. You remember the feminism of grown women getting together to rap and realizing things for the first time, the feminism of lobbying so we could get
credit, get access to birth control, and other things that the world had no
right to keep from us. We remember the feminism of the college campus
that tried to convince us that Beethoven was sublimating rape fantasies in
his music, that said things to us as gunowners that Randall Terry has said
to women who have had abortions, and that sneered at us if we did not
come out in the approved politically correct way. You fought for equality

and fairness (and made incredible, world-changing strides), but today when we cast an eye toward feminism, we see women demanding that pornography be banned as hate speech on one side, and the pro-sex camp on the other saying that if you do not feel sexually liberated by dancing naked on a tabletop while a bunch of paunchy creepy forty-something men gape at you, you are obviously a repressed anti-sex bluenose.

What you did has become, in the intervening twenty or so years, distorted. We have to shove it back on course. And add in some deviations of our own, because our job as feminists is not simply to make feminism into what you wanted it to be. It is to make feminism into what we think it should be, for ourselves and our daughters and sons to come.

What Do We Want to Say? or, "Gen-X vs. Boomer, Yet Again"

We are grateful—believe me. When I think about what it must have been like not to be able to go to school, not to have the job I have now, or the independence it has brought me, not to be able to get access to birth control or abortion if I should need it, my skin blanches. (And in too many places in this world, women are no better off, or considerably worse.) I read some sections of *The Feminine Mystique* and I am thankful that I was not born even one generation ago, or else I would have been one of those valium-sucking housewives screwing vacuum-cleaner salesmen or hanging herself in the basement of her split-level ranch. I am not a fool; I know what my Silent Generation mother sacrificed to raise me and my brothers—Rosalie Costanzi was one of the best violinists of her age group in the entire city of Philadelphia before marrying, and I know how it bothers her. I know the battles that still need to be fought, and their enormity stuns me. Trust me—I'm grateful.

But I'm not you.

I know that the feminism that you remember is not about making women into men—I am well aware that that nonsense is a by-product of the "post-feminist" eighties and that you had nothing to do with it. I am a career woman who loves her job, and I am going to achieve my way—I do not want the heart attacks and ulcers and I know that that was not what you fought for. But a lot of the other things that I fight for are things you want nothing to do with, and you act betrayed when I do fight for them.

I feel that by being born after you, I have somehow signed a contract that says that I have to do everything you say, live up to your expectations, achieve what you wanted to achieve, or else I have betrayed you. It seems that your generation believes it's entitled to measure every crusade for social justice for the rest of time against what you did.

And I'm angry that you do not understand that the sixties and seventies of feminism are not the only decades that influenced us. We are not capable of magically absorbing what you were talking about in 1971. Pour the second wave of feminism through the filter of the Reagan administration, and that's what we got dumped on us. That's what we're trying like hell to reconstruct.

We are adding things that are unique to us, because like it or not, you made mistakes. Your all-out opposition to such things as private firearms ownership, BDSM, and sex entertainment is a huge mistake.[1] We need to recover what you did, fix your mistakes, and add the things that are uniquely us.

Am I unaware that gun ownership comes with a large number of issues attached, many of which are problematic? Of course not. Am I unaware that some practitioners of BDSM, particularly dominant males, are smug and clueless as to the arbitrary nature of their power? God, no. Am I ignorant of how the constant crushing, nauseating tidal wave of naked women while men remain safely clothed screws up the ways that men and women relate to one another? Hell, no.

I do not hate guns—but I do hate the way that a lot of sexist men view them. I do not hate BDSM, but any dominant male who assumes that I will submit to him just because I am female is grossly mistaken. I do not hate sex entertainment, but I do hate the current incarnation of it, where the bimbos are naked and cute and the men are paunchy, unattractive, and clothed. A picture of a naked strong women does not say nearly as much about powerful, autonomous female sexuality as a picture of a naked, pliant man, and someone should inform the pro-sex groupies of this fact. Forget the Spice Girls' version of "Girl Power." When I see five fabulous-looking effeminate boytoys prancing around in latex and spandex, dressed like my sexual fantasy, that is when we'll have "Girl Power."

I am promoting gun education—and I am fighting against the drunken Billy-Bob attitude about guns. I am raising awareness of BDSM sexuality—at the same time that I am knocking down the hoary old belief that male equals dominant and female equals submissive without exception. I am publishing and writing erotica—and simultaneously demolishing the hideous belief in this country that porn is only and ever composed of nekkid chicks.

I am not a sell out—I am a revolutionary.

And this is the very sort of confidence and tenacity that you always wanted women to develop. Why can you not celebrate this—the fact that you worked so hard, fought against tremendous odds, and created a world where we can feel comfortable and confident enough to fight for what matters to us? I could not have any of the things I have now—the education, the lucrative job, the confidence to get together with a bunch of friends and toss up a website, or even maintain my own. I would not have the motivation to help other women achieve the same. I want to present these accomplishments to you as a gift. And you do not want them.

I celebrate the realizations that I am worth defending, that sex and sex entertainment need some serious overhaul, and that I need to spread this to other women—feminist revelations—and you wring your hands and talk about how terribly misguided we poor dears are. I do not want to blame all of you for the puritanical extremism evinced by Catharine MacKinnon and Andrea Dworkin. But I do not want you to point to my every deviation from accepted seventies rhetoric as an example of how we are failing, either.

This generation of feminist women wants to reach outward, to raise awareness and educate other women and men about the things that matter to us. This generation of feminist women wants to show you how proud we are of what we have done—and so often, the second wave of feminism looks at it and says, "This isn't really feminism," and turns away, rushing to enfold the woman who lets her husband beat her kids to death while ignoring those of us who are self-sufficient and accomplished. Do you have any idea how frustrating that is? To offer our accomplishments to the women who made them possible, only to be brushed off? It hurts.

We are not you, and we will not try to be. But we are feminist. Never doubt that.

Notes

1. Bondage/Domination or Discipline/Sadism or Submission/Masochism.

A NOTE ON CONTRIBUTORS

NORMA JEAN ALMODOVAR is a prostitutes' rights activist who speaks from her years of experience as a call girl. Author of *From Cop to Call Girl*, Almodovar was past president of the national sex workers' rights group COYOTE in Los Angeles. She is founder and head of the international, nonprofit organization, the International Sex Worker Foundation for Art, Culture and Education, or ISWFACE. She has appeared in more than five hundred radio, television, and print media interviews all over the world and has lectured at colleges and universities across the country.

MATTHEW Y. BISCAN is a member of the Denver law firm Hall & Evans, LLC, where he practices health care law and general civil and commercial litigation. He is the author of numerous articles and chapters, and is a contributing author of a chapter on the law of Colorado in *Fifty State Compendium of Significant Case and Statutory Law Related to Workplace Violence*, American Law Firm Association, 1997. Listed in the Heritage Foundation's *Guide to Public Policy Experts*, 5th ed., Mr. Biscan is a prolific public speaker.

LOIS COPELAND is a board member and former president of the American Association of Physicians and Surgeons, and was a teaching doctor at New York University before she entered private practice. When her patients wanted and were willing to pay for more house calls than Medicare would pay for, Dr. Copeland began to privately contract with her patients for supplementary care. The Health Care Financing Administration (HCFA) claimed, however, that such contracts were illegal. Dr. Copeland and her patients brought suit (in *Stewart v. Sullivan*, 1992) but the issue was not resolved until, at the insistence of the Clinton administration, private contracting was effectively prohibited by Section 4507 of the 1997 Balanced Budget Act.

JANIS CORTESE is a writer and founding member of the 3rd WWWave: Feminism for the New Millennium website: www.io.com/~wwwave/. She is also well known as the creator and author of the *Handgun Info for Women and Southpaws* website: www.io.com/~cortese/resources/guns.html. She holds a masters degree in physics and currently works as a freelance webmaster and graphics design artist.

RICHARD A. EPSTEIN is the James Parker Hall Distinguished Service Professor of Law at the University of Chicago. A member of the American Academy of Arts and Sciences and the California Bar, he is an editor of the *Journal of Law and Economics* and a member of the Board of Advisors of the *Independent Institute*. A graduate of Oxford and Columbia universities, in 1968 Mr. Epstein received his LL.B. *cum laude* from Yale Law School. His many books include *Principles for a Free Society: Reconciling Individual Liberty with the Common Good, Mortal Peril, Simple Rules for a Complex World, Takings, Forbidden Grounds, The Bill of Rights in the Modern State, Modern Products Liability Law,* and *Torts,* among others. He is the author of more than 160 articles and reviews in journals such as the *University of Chicago Law Review, Harvard Law Review,* the *Yale Law Journal, Stanford Law Review,* and the *New England Journal of Medicine.*

FAITH GIBSON is a community midwife who since 1981 has provided non-medical, home-based care. She is a nationally certified professional midwife under the auspices of the North American Registry of Midwives. She is also a licensed midwife in the state of California where she provides domiciliary maternity care under the religious exemptions clause of the California Medical Practices Act. In 1991, in an attempt to nullify the religious exemptions clause, she was arrested by agents of the California Medical Board and held in jail on a fifty-thousand-dollar bond. After nearly two years of hearings, the charges against her were dropped and the religious exemptions clause effectively upheld. Prior to her current practice she was employed for eighteen years as a vocational nurse in the labor and delivery room and preemie nursery and emergency room of acute-care hospitals. Ms. Gibson is a member of the Midwives Alliance of North America, the American College of Domiciliary Midwives, and the California Association of Midwives. Currently she is the director of the California College of Midwives and is an active participant in state politics on questions of midwifery.

MIMI GLADSTEIN is a professor of English and theatre arts at the University of Texas at El Paso, where she is currently Associate Dean of Liberal Arts. She was the first director of the women's studies program at her university. Ms. Gladstein is the author of *The Ayn Rand Companion; The Indestructible Woman in Faulkner, Hemingway, and Steinbeck;* and co-editor of *Feminist Interpretations of Ayn Rand.*

WENDY KAMINER is a senior correspondent for the *American Prospect.* A lawyer and social critic, she writes about law, liberty, feminism, religion, and popular culture. She is the autor of six books, including *Sleeping with Extra-Terrestrials: The Rise of Irrationalism and Perils of Piety; True Love Waits: Essays and Criticism; It's All the Rage: Crime and Culture; I'm Dysfunctional, You're Dysfunctional: The Recovery Movement and Other Self-Help Fashions;* and *A Fearful Freedom: Women's Flight from Equality.* Her articles and reviews have appeared in numerous publications including the *New York Times,* the *Atlantic Monthly,* the *Wall Street Journal, Dissent,* the *Nation,* and *Newsweek.* Her commentaries have aired on NPR's *Morning Edition.*

WENDY MCELROY is a research fellow at the Independent Institute and is the author of XXX: A Woman's Right to Pornography, Sexual Correctness: The Gender-Feminist Attack on Women, The Reasonable Woman: A Guide to Intellectual Survival, Queen Silver: the Godless Girl, and Individualist Feminism of the Nineteenth Century: Collected Writings and Biographical Profiles. She is the editor of the Independent Institute book Freedom, Feminism, and the State and of the ifeminism site www.ifeminists.com. A contributing editor to several periodicals and the author of many opinion-editorial pieces in magazines and newspapers throughout North America, Ms. McElroy's work can currently be found at www.zetetics.com/mac, www.ifeminists.com, and at www.foxnews.com, where she is a regular columnist.

MARTHA C. NUSSBAUM is Ernst Freund Professor of Law and Ethics at the University of Chicago, with appointments in law, philosophy, divinity, and classics. In addition to numerous journal articles, she is the co-editor of the books Quality of Life (with Amartya Sen), Women, Culture, and Development (with Jonathan Glover), Sex, Preference, and Family (with David Estlund), and Sexual Orientation and Human Rights in American Religious Discourse (with Saul Olyan). She is also the author of The Fragility of Goodness, Love's Knowledge, The Therapy of Desire, Poetic Justice, and Cultivating Humanity. Ms. Nussbaum's most recent book is Upheavals of Thought.

CAMILLE PAGLIA is University Professor and Professor of Humanities and Media Studies at the University of the Arts in Philadelphia. Ms. Paglia's books include Sexual Personae: Art and Decadence from Nefertiti to Emily Dickinson; Sex, Art, and American Culture; Vamps and Tramps: New Essays; and Alfred Hitchcock's 'The Birds'.

ELLEN FRANKEL PAUL is research director and professor of political science at the Social Philosophy and Policy Center at Bowling Green State University and an adjunct scholar of the Cato Institute. A prolific writer, Ms. Paul's previous books include Equity and Gender: The Comparable Worth Debate, Moral Revolution and Economic Science, Property Rights and Eminent Domain, and the edited volumes Human Rights and Liberty and Equality.

RITA J. SIMON is founder and president of the Women's Freedom Network. Since 1988 she has been University Professor in the School of Public Affairs and the Washington College of Law at American University. From 1983 to 1988 Ms. Simon served as dean of the School of Justice at American University. She holds a Ph.D. in sociology from the University of Chicago. A prolific writer and editor, Ms. Simon has edited twelve books and authored more than seventeen monographs and books, including The Jury System in America: A Critical Overview, Women's Movements in America (with Gloria Danzinger), and The Case for Transracial Adoption.

RICHARD W. STEVENS graduated from the University of California at San Diego with a computer science degree, worked for nearly ten years as a computer systems analyst, then began a new career after graduating with high honors in 1988 from the University of San Diego Law School. He practiced civil litigation in California, then moved to the Washington, D.C., area where he taught legal research and writing at the George Washington University Law School and the George Mason University School of Law for several years. Mr. Stevens currently specializes in preparing legal briefs for trial and appellate court cases. His articles on a variety of subjects have appeared in legal and other publications, and he is editor of the *Bill of Rights Sentinel*, a publication of Jews for the Preservation of Firearms Ownership. He also completely revised, expanded, and annotated the *Standardized Civil Jury Instructions for the District of Columbia*, the standard reference book used by litigators and judges in most civil trials there. Mr. Stevens has appeared on television programs and radio talk shows across the country, discussing his book *Dial 911 and Die*, the right to keep and bear arms, and the Bill of Rights.

NADINE STROSSEN is president of the American Civil Liberties Union and a professor of law at New York Law School. Ms. Strossen's previous publications include *Defending Pornography: Free Speech, Sex, and the Fight for Women's Rights*. Ms. Strossen lectures widely and is a featured speaker for Feminists for Free Expression.

ALEXANDER TABARROK is the director of research and vice president of the Independent Institute, a nonpartisan, public-policy think tank, located in Oakland, California. Dr. Tabarrok is the author of many papers in academic journals on a wide range of topics in political economy. He is the editor of several books including *Entrepreneurial Economics* and *The Voluntary City* (with David Beito and Peter Gordon). Dr. Tabarrok's articles have appeared in newspapers throughout North America.

JOAN KENNEDY TAYLOR is the author of *Reclaiming the Mainstream: Individualist Feminism Rediscovered, What to Do When You Don't Want to Call the Cops: A Non-Adversarial Approach to Sexual Harassment* and the editor of *Free Trade: The Necessary Foundation for World Peace*. She has written for newspapers and magazines throughout the world and directed book programs for the Manhattan Institute and the Foundation for Economic Education. She is the vice president of Feminists for Free Expression and the national coordinator for the Association of Libertarian Feminists.

HUGO TEUFEL III is presently an attorney in public service. Previously, he had been in private practice where he focused on government contracts, public entities, and public policy issues. He also served with the Colorado Attorney General's staff as Deputy Solicitor General. He has broad experience in public speaking and writing on firearms rights, government contracting, and litigation against the United States. He has also had significant involvement with firearms rights litigation.

CATHY YOUNG is a research associate with the Cato Institute and the co-founder and vice president of Women's Freedom Network (www.womens freedom.org). She is the author of *Growing Up in Moscow: Memories of a Soviet Girlhood* and *Ceasefire! Why Women and Men Must Join Forces to Achieve True Equality*. Ms. Young is a frequent contributor to the *Washington Post*, the *Philadelphia Inquirer*, the *Wall Street Journal*, and other major newspapers.

SOURCES

Grateful acknowledgment is made to the contributors and the following for permission to reprint copyrighted materials:

"Libertarian Feminism in the Twenty-first Century" by Camille Paglia from *Women: A Cultural Review*, Summer 1999 (London).

"Liberty and Feminism" by Richard A. Epstein from *The Independent Review*, IV, 1 (1999), 5–17.

"On Pornography: Lessons from Enforcement" by Nadine Strossen from *Defending Pornography* (New York, 1995), 217–246, by permission of the Carol Mann Agency.

"Whether from Reason or Prejudice: Taking Money for Bodily Services" by Martha C. Nussbaum from *Journal of Legal Studies*, vol. 27 (1998), 693–724.

Parts of "Chairing the Department: A Matriarchal Paradigm" by Mimi Gladstein were originally published in the "Proceedings of the Women in Higher Education Conference" (Orlando, Fla., 1994).

"Fetal Protection and Freedom of Contract" by Ellen Frankel Paul from *Public Affairs Quarterly*, vol. 6, no. 3 (July 1992), 305–326.

"What Does Affirmative Action Affirm?" by Wendy McElroy, by permission of the author.

"Groping Toward Sanity: Why the Clinton Sex Scandals Are Changing the Way We Talk About Sexual Harassment" by Cathy Young from *Reason*, August/September 1998.

"The Case Against Comparable Worth" by Ellen Frankel Paul from *Equity and Gender* (Piscataway, N.J., 1989).

"Breeder Reactionaries: The 'Feminist' War on New Reproductive Technologies" by Wendy McElroy from *Reason*, December 1994.

"I Am in Mourning: A Doctor Writes to Her Senators and Representatives" by Lois Copeland (with an Introduction by Joan Kennedy Taylor), by permission of the author.

"The Third WWWave: Who We Are, What We See" by Janis Cortese from the 3rd WWWave: Feminism for the New Millennium website (www.io.com/~wwwave/addresses/janisaddress.html).

INDEX

INDEPENDENT STUDIES IN POLITICAL ECONOMY

For further information and a catalog of publications, please contact:
THE INDEPENDENT INSTITUTE
100 Swan Way, Oakland, California 94621-1428, U.S.A.
Telephone: 510-632-1366 • Facsimile: 510-568-6040
E-mail: info@independent.org • Website: http://www.independent.org